A National Health Service?

Also by John Mohan

The Political Geography of Contemporary Britain (editor)

A National Health Service?

The Restructuring of Health Care in Britain since 1979

John Mohan

St. Martin's Press

First published in Great Britain 1995 by
MACMILLAN PRESS LTD
Houndmills, Basingstoke, Hampshire RG21 2XS
and London
Companies and representatives
throughout the world

A catalogue record for this book is available
from the British Library.

ISBN 0–333–57831–7 hardcover
ISBN 0–333–57832–5 paperback

10   9   8   7   6   5   4   3   2   1
04   03   02   01   00   99   98   97   96   95

Printed in Malaysia   १०००४४४३९६

First published in the United States of America 1995 by
Scholarly and Reference Division,
ST. MARTIN'S PRESS, INC.,
175 Fifth Avenue,
New York, N.Y. 10010

ISBN 0–312–12410–4 (cloth)

Library of Congress Cataloging-in-Publication Data
Mohan, John, 1958–
A National Health Service? : the restructuring of health care in
Britain since 1979 / John Mohan.
p.   cm.
Includes bibliographical references and index.
ISBN 0–312–12410–4 (cloth)
1. National Health Service (Great Britain)   2. Medical policy–
–Great Britain.   I. Title.
RA395.G6M64   1995
362.1'0941—dc20   94–22962
                                                     CIP

Contents

List of Tables and Figures   viii

Preface   x

List of Abbreviations   xix

1 From the Royal Commission to the NHS Reforms: A Review of Policies and Statistics   1

Key policy developments and changes   3
Inputs: trends in health care finance   9
Provision: beds, staffing and activity   17
Outcomes?   22
Concluding comments   23

2 Explaining Change in the Welfare State and in Health Care Policy   25

Developmentalism and determinism   26
Political theory: pluralism, Marxism and the New Right   29
Political economy: crises, restructuring, disorganised capitalism and post-Fordism   33
Concluding comments   41

3 Conservatism, Health Policy and Health Care Policy   44

Thatcherism, conservatism and health care policy   46
Redefining the scope of health policy   48
Setting a new agenda for health care   54
A change of pace, not of direction?   65
Concluding comments   70

4 Spatial Resource Allocation: Local Difficulties, Technical Adjustments and Political Solutions   73

RAWP under austerity: from differential growth to equality of misery?   75
A national crisis or a little local difficulty?   84

Technical solutions: from RAWP to weighted
    capitation   91
Planning versus the market: Tomlinson and beyond   94
Concluding comments   98

**5 Imagined and Imaginary Communities: Rhetoric and
Reality in Community Care Policy**   **101**
The ideological appropriation of community   103
Needs, expenditure and services   106
The development of community care policies: themes
    and assumptions   112
Implementing community care: incompetence or
    malice?   115
Caring for People: delays and unresolved questions   123
Concluding comments   126

**6 Producing Health Care: Management, Labour and the
State in the NHS**   **129**
Aggregate trends in the NHS workforce   132
The 'core': medical staff and the recasting of
    administrators as managers   136
The 'periphery': Whitley Council staff   142
Recruitment difficulties and 'geographical pay'   145
The White Paper and beyond   148
Concluding comments   151

7 Blurring the Boundaries: Health Care Outside the NHS **154**
Historical background: state policies and private sector
    growth   155
Dynamics of change in the commercial sector   158
Government–industry relations and the effects of the
    NHS reforms   168
Wider implications   171

**8 The Entrepreneurial State: Commercial and Charitable
Activities by Health Authorities**   **174**
Back to the future? Charitable fundraising and
    charitable trusts   176
The entrepreneurial welfare state: commercialisation of
    health authority activity   180

Self-governing trusts, GP fundholding and the post-
   White Paper organisation of the NHS   185
Concluding comments   191

**9 Powers, Responsibilities and Accountability:
Organisational Reform and Local Autonomy   196**
Organisational reforms   198
Centre versus periphery   204
Beyond the reforms?   210
Concluding comments   214

~10 Conclusions: In What Sense a *National* Health Service?   219
Explanatory pitfalls   219
Geography, locality and welfare   222
Markets, planning and ethics   225
Boundary disputes   228
Alternatives   230

*Appendix: Chronology of Major Developments in Health and
Health Care Policy since 1979*   234

Notes and References   241

Bibliography   258

Index   277

List of Tables and Figures

Tables

1.1 Trends in actual and planned expenditure on the HCHS
in England, 1982–3 to 1993–4   14
1.2 Sources of savings from cost improvement programmes,
1985–6 to 1990–1   18
4.1 RHAs' distance from revenue targets, long-term revenue
growth assumptions and financial increments, 1983–91   79
4.2 Trends in actual current expenditure on the HCHS,
English RHAs, 1983–7   80
6.1 Change in NHS staffing by main staff groups, 1981–91   134
6.2 Vacancy rates for qualified nursing staff by region,
1989–92   147
7.1 Private medical insurance coverage, 1982 and 1987   160
7.2 Contribution of the private sector to elective surgery,
1981 and 1986   166

Figures

4.1 RHAs in England, 1974–94   76
4.2 Regions' distance from RAWP revenue targets, 1979–80
to 1988–9   77
4.3 Percentage change in DHA acute beds, England,
1979–89   83
4.4 Surveys of the financial position of health authorities in
England, 1987–8 and 1988–9   87
4.5 English DHAs: percentage change in budgets if white
paper system in operation   96
5.1 Per capita net expenditure on personal social services,
England, 1990–1   108
5.2 Balance of residential care for the elderly,
England,1980–1 to 1990–1   109
5.3 Provision for persons with mental illness, England,
1983–92   109

5.4   Residential provision for persons with learning
      difficulties, England, 1974–92   111
7.1   Distribution of acute hospitals in the private sector,
      1992   165
9.1   Areas to be covered by proposed regional units of the
      NHS Management Executive   215

Preface

This book grew out of a project that attempted to document some of the regional and local consequences of changes in the NHS under successive Conservative governments since Margaret Thatcher was first elected Prime Minister in 1979. In the course of that project, and certainly once the NHS reforms were enacted, it became clear that a significant question was whether the reforms represented a radical departure for the NHS, or whether they were a natural outgrowth of existing trends. Kenneth Clarke put this succinctly when introducing *Working for Patients* (Secretary of State for Health, 1989a) in parliament: he suggested that the reforms represented a 'change of pace, not of direction'. Certainly it is possible to identify many antecedents of the reforms in the policies pursued since 1979, but this is not to suggest that the Conservatives had in mind a blueprint that has been implemented in an unproblematic fashion. It therefore seemed important to investigate the road the Conservatives had taken (as well as the roads not taken), the pace at which they had travelled along that road and the causes of changes in pace. To continue the navigational metaphor, the government's course was not always straight through a succession of green lights. It involved a certain amount of stargazing and trusting to the compass, it required decisions to be taken at junctions, and very occasionally a potential route was blocked. The journey was not trouble free nor was it an inevitable progression (though some have represented it as such – see Chapter 2).

One could spend a substantial time tracing the roots of present policies, but I argue – following in some respects Davies (1987) – that various consistent strands of policy can be traced at least to 1979. Among these are the following:

- The stress on the *finite public purse*, evoked consistently as justification for both limiting the resources available to the NHS and for introducing new methods of work organisation and management reforms.
- The importance placed on *management* – in the Thatcher and Major years considerable emphasis has been placed on the need for firm and efficient management in the public sector, and this legacy, even

more than specific policy changes, will far outlive their respective administrations.

- The importance attached to the *private health sector* as a potential competitor to the NHS, as a model for innovation that the NHS should strive to emulate, as a desirable supplement to the state's limited resources, and as a useful resource for local managers. While no post war government has attempted to eliminate private health care or private practice, with the exception of Labour's limited attack on paybeds from 1976, no government has attached such importance to the private sector.

- The encouragement of *individual and community initiative* and the placing of more of the burden of health care provision and financing on individuals, families and 'communities'. Much of this has been in the form of ideological statements rather than direct legislative measures, but there have been measures aimed at deregulating the commercial sector and at expanding state support for private health care. In addition, prevention of ill-health has been defined largely as a matter of individual choice and lifestyle.

- An apparent stress on *localism and autonomy*. The government has emphasised its wish to decentralise decision making to the lowest possible level, but in its desire to pursue certain national policies it has regularly contradicted this: in practice there has often been greater central control over local tiers of administration.

Based around these five points, changes in the British health sector are seen not in terms of a technological determinism (an interpretation that would stress the increased capacity, complexity and sophistication of the health care system); nor in terms of assumed parallels between the NHS and other complex organisations (and thus assuming that the kind of organisational reforms that have taken place were natural trends, common to any complex public or private body confronted with growing demands on and expectations of its services), nor even in terms of a supposed 'convergence' in the welfare systems of advanced capitalist states (that is to say, advocating greater spending on private health care because all similar states are going in the same direction). There is more than a grain of truth in all these arguments, but the fact remains that the responses to these economic and technical changes involved particular *political* choices at particular times. This raises the question of whether such responses were really necessary or whether alternatives could have been pursued.

The primary explanatory focus in this book is on the political economy of conservatism: the responses to the trends concerned were and are essentially political decisions. Their satisfactory understanding therefore requires analysis of the political circumstances and constraints under which they came about, their relationship to notions of 'Thatcherism' (and, to the extent that it can be distinguished from Thatcherism, 'Majorism') as a political force, and the particular strategies pursued by successive Conservative administrations. In this context I would argue, contra Klein (1984a; 1989), that it is not the case that the 'reality of politics' has forced a 'retreat from ideology' as far as Conservative health care policies are concerned; nor was there anything 'inevitable' about the 1989 NHS White Paper. Whereas the government's case for the White Paper was based on the persistence of local variability in the costs of NHS activities and throughput, and not on the absence of resources, in practice the problems of the NHS were rather more than local difficulties (Chapter 4). The White Paper was also characterised by many of the hallmarks of the policy-making style of the Thatcher administrations, a style that strongly reflected the populist instincts of the party and the then Prime Minister. Partly as a result, it did not address the real causes of inequalities in health; it merely proposed limited internal reforms within the NHS itself, as opposed to radical alterations to the nature of health care delivery. To link the White Paper to a well-known theme in political science, it was arguably about the symbolic use of politics to address – or rather to present the appearance of addressing – intractable problems (cf. Edelman, 1971) and advance a particular agenda. It was a partial and selective approach to the problems of health care delivery.

Geography, politics and health care

One theme running through this book, then, is changes in health care delivery in relation to perspectives on contemporary conservatism and the political economy of the welfare state. A second theme (without resorting to disciplinary imperialism) is the important effect that space and spatial relationships, and their interrelations with political change, have had on developments in the NHS. In a simple sense this is a matter of uneven development: the differential impact of the changes described had consequences not just for the availability of services at the time, but for their future development as communities become more dependent on resources generated or available locally. These matters are especially important given the growing significance of private sources of health care (Chapters 5 and 7): there may be, to paraphrase Titmuss, an emerging spatial division of welfare.

Secondly, matters of spatial distribution become questions of territorially-based conflict. Even in an ostensibly 'national' health care system there exist spatial coalitions that have greater or lesser degrees of cohesion and homogeneity, and that articulate claims on behalf of particular places. Thus many of the debates around the RAWP formula can be linked to the contentions of backbench MPs from the Home Counties about the relative pace with which services were being developed in London and the South East (Chapter 4). The London lobby, campaigning for the preservation or development of the capital's health care services, is also a key spatial coalition.

Thirdly, some interpretations of Conservative political strategies suggest that since 1979 we have seen the departure of the 'one-nation' politics of the postwar settlement and its replacement by a 'two-nation' politics of inequality (Chapter 3). This spatial metaphor sees the 'first nation' having priority over the 'second nation', with strategies being developed to maximise the electoral support given to the Conservatives from their geographical and social heartlands. The value of this interpretation is explored in Chapters 4, 7 and 8.

Fourthly, the question arises as to whether problems with health care delivery are merely 'local' difficulties, as government ministers have often suggested, or more generalised problems affecting the whole of the service. This has been the subject of considerable debate and it influences the defining of problems and their political solution. Thus the 'crisis' in the NHS in the winter of 1987–8 was initially dismissed as the problem of a few DHAs only, while staff shortages in the mid-1980s were likewise claimed to reflect labour market problems in a few high-cost locations (Chapter 6). This has had political ramifications in terms of potential solutions.

Fifthly, in the light of current debates about citizenship and the rights and responsibilities thereof, one effect of post-1979 policies, perhaps as never before in the postwar period, has been that the services available have come to depend increasingly on the balance between public and private, statutory and community services in any one locality. But was it ever the intention that such capricious influences as the relative cost of nursing-home care in different regions of the country should determine access to long-stay care within the benefit limits imposed by the government? And was it intended that the internal market would deprive residents of certain localities of access to non-urgent procedures, depending on the resources available to and/or the whims of their health authority? The rights of citizenship appear to be geographically differentiated.

Finally, a consistent theme running through debates on the service since 1979 has been the appropriate balance of power between centre and locality (Chapter 9). The changing territorial organisation of the service is one obvious consequence of these debates, as is the extent of local autonomy accorded to health authorities and management units. This raises the question of the extent or otherwise of local control over health services.

Outline of the book

This book is organised as follows. Chapter 1 presents an outline of key policy changes and a statistical review of trends in finance, provision and activity. In Chapter 2 I consider some of the interpretations that might be advanced to explain changes in the character of public service delivery in recent years. The chapter first criticises, as oversimplistic, analyses of developments in welfare states that merely postulate evolutionary trends or rely on narrowly determinist arguments for their explanations. It then considers analyses of the political economy of welfare that relate developments in the welfare state to the apparently contradictory position of state-provided welfare systems: rather than being determined by the so-called crisis of the welfare state, the responses to changed economic circumstances are a contingent matter. Hence analyses need to be pitched at a lower level of abstraction, focusing on the specifics of political developments within individual nation-states. In this context a focus on the political economy of contemporary conservatism is crucial. Consequently Chapter 3 is devoted to an analysis of the various interpretations of Thatcherism and the implications of Thatcherite political strategies for health care policy-making and implementation.

Some of the most dramatic effects of health care policies since 1979 can be seen through an analysis of the political geography of resource allocation within the NHS (Chapter 4). There is, first of all, debate over the pace of resource redistribution between regional health authority areas. Secondly, the regional and subregional consequences of resource redistribution are described, using not only statistics on hospital bed provision and finance, but also survey data produced by the National Association of Health Authorities on the financial situation of district health authorities, and the comments of numerous backbench MPs about the impacts of health care policies on their constituencies. The geographical impacts of the reforms, and of the Tomlinson Report, are also given attention.

As well as the spatial distribution of resources, the sectoral distribution of resources must also be analysed. Community care for the mentally ill and the elderly is an area where policy has persistently failed to match rhetoric. Chapter 5 examines the changes introduced since 1979 to determine how far they represented a break with previous practice and how far they reflected the ideological predilections of the government. It concentrates particularly on community care for the mentally ill and those with learning difficulties, and on care for the elderly, and asks how far there is a commitment to *national* standards and to a *national* service.

In an essentially labour-intensive service such as the NHS, continued attention to labour costs is essential if greater levels of productivity are to be achieved within existing resources. Precisely what measures are taken with this in mind is a matter for political decision, as will be shown in chapter 6 with respect to certain key measures taken since 1979. Equally, for policy innovations to work, the support of certain key workers within the NHS needs to be guaranteed. There has been an element of selectivity about the policies pursued: on the one hand they have prioritised the interests of key workers such as NHS 'managers' and, on the other hand, have marginalised other groups, notably ancillary workers. Consideration is given to the value of the distinction advanced by some commentators between 'core' and 'peripheral' workers.

Chapter 7 explores the development of the private, or more accurately the commercial health sector since 1979, focusing on the internationalisation and commercialisation of health care. The continued growth of commercial health care can only partly be explained by consumerist forces, because state policies have had the intended and unintended effect of expanding commercial health care. Related to this latter point, a number of measures have been deliberately taken to expand the actual and potential role of non-state sources of funds and health care provision, and the actual and likely impacts of these are reviewed in Chapter 8. These two chapters provide an opportunity to consider the various meanings of and explanations attached to notions of 'privatisation'. They also raise the question of whether developments in the 1980s have marked a decisive shift away from a health care service in which the producing and financing of services were de facto monopolies of the state, and whether a 'mixed economy' of services will henceforward be the norm.

No analysis of the political economy of the British health sector would be complete without consideration of the changing balance between central and local tiers of administration in the political process (Chapter 9). The NHS has always been caught between centre and locality, a situation that is hardly surprising given that service providers are accountable both to their local communities, who experience the consequences of their decisions, and to the secretary of state for health, who is ultimately responsible for financial control. Balancing these two accountabilities is a task that will continue to tax politicians, health professionals and authority members. Chapter 9 considers not only the changing spatial organisation of the NHS, but also the apparent decentralisation of authority and the extent to which this is contradicted by the government's determination to impose its authority on local tiers. Finally the effects of the white paper on the territorial organisation of services are examined.

In the concluding chapter some wider issues that will affect the future of health care provision are discussed. These include questions of ethics, in terms of appropriate management of public services, rights, in terms of access to care, and the entitlements and responsibilities of citizenship. In addition, the question of the boundaries between state, market and community provision is discussed, and the question is raised of whether there still exists a truly *national* health service.

This book is not a complete chronology of events since 1979; instead it concentrates on key issues that illuminate areas where the Conservatives have introduced substantial and radical changes that clearly distinguish their policies from those of their predecessors. The focus is also on the macropolitical environment rather than on the technical details of specific initiatives. Other texts are available that cover in more detail the administrative changes in the NHS (for example Ham, 1992; Harrison *et al.*, 1990). Because of its national focus this book does not present the kind of local detail evident in, for instance, the work of Davidson (1987) or Widgery (1988). There remain to be written accounts of the ways in which the NHS reforms have worked out in specific places, and of their impacts on specific groups in the population, and these will necessarily be more qualitative and ethnographic in character. Nor does the book purport to be a formal evaluation of post-1979 changes – see Le Grand *et al.* (1990) or Bloor and Maynard (1993) for an assessment of funding issues, and Le Grand and Robinson (1994) for preliminary assessments of the reforms.

A note on sources

In general this book draws heavily on sources such as Hansard and on the deliberations of government select committees, the areas in which government policy receives its most sustained examination. On occasion these sources also reveal governmental attempts to test the limits of certain strategies (the debates on the Health and Medicines Bill – Chapter 3 – and on the financing of private residential care – Chapter 5 – are good examples of this). Elsewhere, as in Chapters 6 and 8, professional journals are used extensively as the best possible source of up-to-date information on innovations within the service and on the attitude of professional groups. Where possible national statistical sources are used, but comparable data for the beginning and end of the period in question are difficult to obtain, as are subregional data due to various reorganisations of the service. For a number of technical reasons the manner in which certain statistics were collated and presented changed during this period, and the government was regularly criticised for appearing to misrepresent or suppress information in order to make its policies appear in the most favourable light (Smith, 1987; Marmot and McDowell, 1986; Radical Statistics Health Group, 1985, 1987, 1992). The book has relied largely on data published through official sources, with all the limitations that might imply. Given the pace of change in the NHS, I should also point out that the text of the book was finalised in May 1994

Given these caveats, I hope that the book will provoke debate not just about the transformations the NHS has experienced since 1979, but its possible development for the future.

London   JOHN MOHAN

Acknowledgements

First of all I am grateful to the ESRC for financial support through a postdoctoral research fellowship (grant no. A23320036). Although the focus of that project was somewhat narrower than the present one, it nevertheless stimulated the lines of inquiry pursued here. I am also grateful to colleagues in the Geography Department, Queen Mary and Westfield College, for providing a supportive environment for my work. It would be impossible to list those who commented on earlier drafts of several chapters without running the risk of leaving some out, and simultaneously depriving the book of sympathetic reviewers, but I must mention David Smith, who first encouraged me to work at QMW and has supported my work ever since. Both David Smith and Geof Rayner commented, from rather different perspectives, on a draft of this book and I am enormously grateful to them for doing so. As ever, Steven Kennedy has been a patient and constructive commissioning editor.

I would also like to acknowledge the assistance of staff in various libraries, notably the King's Fund Centre, the LSE, the University of London, and Queen Mary and Westfield College, and the help of the technical and secretarial staff in the Geography Department, QMW, especially in the later stages of preparing the typescript. Finally, Ellie, Jennifer and Clare provided – in their different ways – constant support, diversion and disruption throughout the writing of this book.

JOHN MOHAN

List of Abbreviations

ACHCEW	Association of Community Health Councils in England and Wales
AHA	Area Health Authority
AIDS	Acquired immune deficiency syndrome
AIH	Association of Independent Hospitals
AMI	American Medical International
BMA	British Medical Association
BMJ	*British Medical Journal*
BUPA	British United Provident Association
CCMA	Contract Cleaning and Maintenance Association
CHC	Community Health Council
CIPs	Cost improvement programmes
COHSE	Confederation of Health Service Employees
CPRS	Central Policy Review Staff
CRESs	Cash-releasing efficiency savings
DoE	Department of the Environment
DoH	Department of Health
DHA	District Health Authority
DHSS	Department of Health and Social Security
DMUs	Directly Managed Units
DSS	Department of Social Security
EC	European Community
FCE	Finished Consultant Episode
FHSA	Family Health Service Authority
FPC	Family Practitioner Committee
GDP	Gross domestic product
GHS	*General Household Survey*
GLC	Greater London Council
GP	General practitioner
GOS	Great Ormond Street
HCA	Hospital Corporation of America
HCHS	Hospital and community health service
HEA	Health Education Authority
HMOs	Health maintenance organisations
HPSS	Health and Personal Social Services
HSB	Health Services Board

HSJ	*Health Services Journal*
IHA	Independent Healthcare Association
IHG	Independent Hospitals Group
NAHA	National Association of Health Authorities
NAHAT	National Association of Health Authorities and Trusts
NALGO	National and Local Government Officers
NAO	National Audit Office
NHS	National Health Service
NHSME	National Health Service Management Executive
NHSTF	National Health Service Trust Federation
NUPE	National Union of Public Employees
OPCS	Office of Population Censuses and Surveys
PPP	Private Patients Plan
PRB	Pay Review Body
PRP	Performance-related pay
RAWP	Resource Allocation Working Party
RCN	Royal College of Nursing
RHA	Regional Health Authority
RHA	Regional Hospital Board
RMI	Resource management initiative
RPI	Retail price index
SHAs	Special Health Authorities
SMR	Standardised mortality ratio
SWS	Schumpeterian workfare state
WHO	World Health Organisation
WTE	Whole-time equivalent

1

From the Royal Commission to the NHS Reforms: A Review of Policies and Statistics

The report of the Royal Commission on the NHS (1979) arguably represented not only an overwhelming endorsement of the service, but also the high-water mark of a particular style of policy making. The searching inquiry of the Royal Commission, backed up by substantial academic research, aimed to reach a degree of consensus from which the Conservative government elected in 1979 and its successors have subsequently departed quite dramatically. The contrast between the slow and extensive deliberations of the Royal Commission, appointed by the then Labour government in 1976 and reporting in mid-1979, and the extremely rapid production of the 1989 White Paper, described by its progenitors as the most fundamental innovation in the NHS in 40 years, is instructive. The Royal Commission received 2460 submissions of written evidence and held 58 sessions at which oral evidence was given; 2800 individuals were also spoken to in the course of its deliberations, the subcommittees of the Commission held 83 meetings, and six major pieces of academic research were commissioned and their results published. The sheer volume of evidence submitted and considered contrasts sharply with the peremptory production of the NHS review, announced via the novel medium of a television interview and assembled via the secretive deliberations of a team heavily dominated by Treasury ministers. Hugo Young comments on this shift in social policy making:

> The Royal Commission and the departmental committee were traditional power bases for middle-ground intellectuals. But no

1

longer . . . the idea passed into the museum of intellectual dinosaurs. In a climate in which everything was political, detachment was held to be a chimera and objectivity a fraud, and the classes who claimed these virtues lost their foothold in public life (Young, 1989, p. 413, quoted in Jones, 1990, p. 204).

The range of the two inquiries shows a contrast between the comprehensive approach of the Royal Commission and the narrow focus of the NHS White Paper (Secretary of State for Health, 1989a) on the problems of internal resource allocation within the service. The circumstances in which the two documents came to be produced also differed substantially. Both inquiries were announced at a time of considerable unrest in the NHS. In the 1970s the NHS was dominated by two major industrial disputes: that involving ancillary workers and that involving hospital doctors over the paybeds issue. Essentially, then, the unrest was on the part of *producer* groups, concerned on the one hand with the protection of privilege and professional autonomy, and on the other with the continued failure of Labour governments to eliminate low pay in the public sector. What was not at issue was the fundamental structure of the service: there was no question of anything more than organisational reforms being introduced. In contrast the 1989 White Paper was born out of enormous *consumer* dissatisfaction, and of a perception that the public no longer believed that the NHS was safe in Conservative hands. Although it is true that producers had drawn attention to difficulties within the NHS, these were often dismissed as the politics of shroud waving by doctors seeking additional resources. In the post-Griffiths NHS, producer power was no longer the issue it had once been, as pejorative references by government spokespersons during 1988 and 1989 to the British Medical Association's (BMA) role as a 'trade union' made clear. In both cases the government of the day had to be seen to respond: in the 1970s, setting up a Royal Commission was perhaps a time-honoured way to proceed, but by the late 1980s the government was able to use its substantial decisional autonomy (Krieger, 1987) to steer the NHS in its preferred direction. Radical steps were not only desirable but essential for a government that prided itself on its decisiveness and firmness of purpose.

The contrast between 1979 and 1989 (or, more accurately, 1991, when the reforms were implemented) is not just one of style of policy-making; the two documents were separated by a period in which there were significant transformations in the way the NHS was organised and administered. The NHS has been shifted some distance from the top-down, bureaucratic model of the late 1980s to become less statist and centralised and more entrepreneurial. Documentation of this shift, and an attempt to understand it, is the rationale for this book. This first chapter provides the context for what follows by summarising the major policy changes since 1979 and by presenting a selection of key statistics against which to assess some of the developments described herein.

Key policy developments and changes

Appendix I provides a chronology of key dates, documents, bills and organisational and other changes in the NHS, together with a brief description of each. In this chapter I summarise these changes around five themes: health policy versus health care policy; funding sources; organisational structures; managerial innovations; and priorities.

Health policy versus health care policy

The Royal Commission's view was that while individuals ought to take responsibility for their own health, there was a clear case for government action where this could produce identifiable results, for example in areas such as smoking and road accidents. However it did not go as far as the Black Report (DHSS, 1980a), which recommended a greater degree of public intervention in limiting the social causes of ill health. That view was rejected by the government in terms that set the tone for health debates during the 1980s. Collective action to prevent ill health was a low priority for the government, which viewed prevention as the responsibility of the individual in terms of lifestyle choices. Overt statements about prevention were few and far between during the 1980s and the controversial pronouncements of ministers such as Edwina Currie about unhealthy diets and lifestyles attracted much attention (and criticism). Instead of collective action, legislative measures to promote better health emphasised that prevention was a matter for the health service and for individuals; the wider social causes of ill health were conspicuously neglected. The government's reforms of primary health care (Secretary of State for Social Services, 1987) provided GPs with a number of incentives to offer more in the way of preventive services while requiring them to provide basic screening services for their patients. However the subsequent imposition of charges for eyesight tests and dental examinations contradicted the apparently good intentions of those reforms. Nor was there much recognition of possible interventions that might promote health more widely. This was despite numerous reports which showed that inequalities in health status had far from disappeared (Davey-Smith *et al.*, 1990; Smith and Jacobson, 1991).

The government's subsequent white paper, the *Health of the Nation* (Secretary of State for Health, 1992), was notable for the conspicuous lack of reference to social structure and social inequality as causes of ill health and health differentials, emphasising that lifestyles are largely a matter of individual choice. Though the white paper set targets for the improvement of health status (and these would largely have been reached anyway, regardless of government action) this progressive step was contradicted by the government's persistent refusal to contemplate a total ban on cigarette advertising. There were, then, limits to the government's commitment to prevention.

Funding sources and the role of the private sector

The Royal Commission reviewed numerous possible options for raising finance for the NHS from non-Exchequer sources, but rejected them all, even expressing the hope that charges for NHS services would eventually wither on the vine. Despite the Conservatives' 1979 election pledge not to increase prescription charges, this was extremely unlikely. Within a few months of the election health authorities were being encouraged, through the Health Services Act, to expand their charitable activities, and some minor concessions were made to private care. Most controversially, however, the prime minister's Central Policy Review Staff (CPRS) had been charged with examining, during the first Thatcher administration, the alternative options open to the government for financing the NHS. Their report to the cabinet in September 1982 was widely leaked (it included a review of possibilities such as an insurance-based system) and this prompted the prime minister to make her famous pledge that the 'NHS is safe with us' (though there are conflicting accounts of her own reaction to the report; see Chapter 3).

Following the controversy over the CPRS report, proposals for alternative methods of funding were unlikely to receive a favourable airing. Instead there were proposals that gradually extended charges (for example the ending of free dental and eyesight tests via the 1988 Health and Medicines Act), or expanded the scope for health authorities to raise income through the entrepreneurial use of their own assets. Symbolically, the launching in 1987 of a national appeal for funds to rebuild Great Ormond Street Children's Hospital was also important; for some it denoted the government's lack of commitment to a state-funded NHS. Kites were repeatedly flown by backbenchers and Conservative thinktanks, but the prime minister's pledge prevented further moves in the direction of alternative sources of funding. The only changes in the NHS reforms were the introduction of tax relief on private health insurance for the elderly, something for which the private sector had lobbied, unsuccessfully, for many years.

As far as the private sector is concerned, concessions have been limited and indirect. In the absence of a root-and-branch reform on insurance principles, there has instead been limited deregulation of acute care, notably via the Health Services Act of 1980, which abolished the Health Services Board and reserved powers of regulation of private acute hospitals to the secretary of state. In 1979 consultants were given leave to undertake more private work, and from 1981 health authorities were permitted for the first time to contract with profit-making hospitals for NHS treatment. In addition there were minor concessions in the 1981 budget to demands for tax relief on insurance premiums, and in the NHS white paper tax relief was granted on insurance premiums for those above retirement age. In expenditure terms the largest single boost to private care was provided in 1980 when the social security regulations were changed to permit the cost of nursing or residential home care to be met from the social security budget, inadvertently stimulating a major boom in such forms of accommodation (Chapter 6).

Finally, market disciplines have been introduced to the NHS via measures such as competitive tendering (in 1983) and capital charging for NHS assets (introduced via the NHS reforms). The intervention of the latter, in particular, was to help ensure that the private sector competed for patient care on the same basis as the NHS. The reforms themselves have had the effect of bringing the private sector more into the ambit of the public sector since NHS purchasers are now free to contract with both public and private institutions for patient care.

Organisational structures

In the absence of major changes in the funding of the service, organisational reforms have assumed greater importance. The Royal Commission recommended the abolition of one tier of administration below the level of the fourteen Regional Health Authorities (RHAs); this was duly enacted in the 1982 reorganisation of the NHS, though one consequence of the abolition of Area Health Authorities (AHAs) was the loss of coterminosity between health and local authorities. The

1982 reorganisation did not follow up another recommendation of the Royal Commission, which was to reconstitute family practitioner committees (FPCs); these were eventually reorganised in 1985. Both the 1982 reorganisation and the NHS reforms reduced local influence on health authorities by limiting or eventually removing the right of local authorities to nominate authority members. The reforms also introduced executive membership of health authorities for several senior managers, who are therefore more closely involved in decision-making than previously.

The NHS reforms also signalled major changes in the responsibilities of health authorities. The principal innovation was the attempt to produce an internal market by separating out the purchaser and provider roles of the authorities. In the past health authorities' budgets had been set at the beginning of the financial year to reflect historic patterns of activity and patient flow. This guaranteed their income but was criticised for producing inertia and inefficiency, as well as controversy towards the end of the financial year when some health authorities ran out of funds and fell into the 'efficiency trap', having treated a larger number of patients than their budgets would permit. By establishing the purchaser–provider split it was hoped that efficiency would be stimulated: purchasers would seek the most economical contracts for treating their patients while producers would have an incentive to minimise costs and thus price their activities competitively. The intention was that, rather than being under the direct control of health authorities, the preferred form of organisation of services would be through NHS trusts, controlled by separate boards. Purchasing responsibilities were also offered to larger general practices, which could apply for fundholding status, empowering them to draw up their own contracts with providers of elective surgery.

The autonomy to be given to trusts rapidly became controversial, and as a consequence regional 'outposts' of the Department of Health were established to oversee the operations of the trusts. But the decentralist logic of the reforms ultimately cast doubt on the future of the RHAs: with purchasing controlled through local health authorities, and the outposts existing to monitor the activities of trusts, the role of RHAs was attenuated. The compromise reached was the replacement of the fourteen RHAs by eight regional divisions of the Department of Health, which no longer had the regional representation of the former RHAs. This led to criticism of the lack of accountability of such units.

There have also been changes in the NHS's relationships with other agencies. The Community Care legislation, introduced in 1993, makes local authorities the lead agencies in community care, though they are expected to draw up plans with other relevant agencies for delivering services (Chapter 5). Despite this there would appear to be little prospect of the integration of local government and the NHS (Chapter 9).

Managerial innovation

A government committed to reducing public expenditure while constrained by election promises to support the NHS was likely to seek to improve the efficiency of the service from within. Criticism of the uneven performance of the NHS had been voiced by several organisations inside and outside the service. The NHS was therefore an early candidate for the Rayner scrutinies of public expenditure. These led to the adoption of such forms of financial management as cost improvement programmes (CIPs) and cash-releasing efficiency savings (CRES) – all indicating that resource growth in the NHS came to depend on the service's success in making continued improvements in efficiency. Initially health authorities had some of their budgets held back as an incentive to do so, though a less centralist approach was subsequently adopted.[1] Criticism of the lack of outcome measures led to the development and refinement of systems of performance indicators from 1983. However these were largely concerned with comparative financial statistics and indicators of resource use, rather than with the outcome of the treatments offered by the service.

The key managerial innovation was the introduction of general management into the NHS following the Griffiths Report (DHSS, 1983a). Drawing on criticisms of the previous system of consensus management, notably the inflexibility of the service and the impossibility of holding individual managers to account, the Griffiths Report recommended the appointment of a general manager at regional, district and unit level, greater emphasis on delegation, a stress on consumerism, and firmer financial control through management budgeting and the increased involvement of clinicians in management. Through performance-related pay and short-term contracts for managers, general management was designed to enhance the efficiency of the service by enabling management to manage, giving them incentives to do so and rewarding them for success. The emphasis placed on management has been a notable feature of the post-1979 period: from being reviled as supernumerary bureaucrats, managers are now celebrated as the key to efficiency in the post-reform NHS (Chapter 6).

Improving the management of resources has also been strongly emphasised. Techniques for clinical budgeting and the resource-management initiative (introduced in 1986 at six sites and subsequently extended) were both designed to enhance financial control by identifying the costs of health care more accurately. Budgetary responsibilities were devolved to clinical directorates within hospitals, and managers negotiated workload agreements within these directorates. Doctors and nurses were given enhanced responsibilities for the management of resources. It was the intention that doctors would consider carefully the consequences of their actions for expenditure and resource allocation.

There have also been measures that add up to a transformation in the role of health authorities. Whereas previously the role of health authorities was to deliver services within the constraints of a defined budget, there has been a growing emphasis on an enabling, entrepreneurial role. Health authorities have been seen in government statements and policy documents as having a coordinative role, drawing on all possible sources of care in a given locality; this was notable in the planning guidance issued to the post-1982 District Health Authorities (DHAs) (DHSS, 1981a). This role was perhaps first enunciated by Norman Fowler in speeches in the early 1980s concerning welfare pluralism (Chapter 3), and it is implicit in the purchaser–provider split: purchasers can seek to obtain care from any appropriate source rather than just from NHS providers.

Priority services

Whereas the Labour government had specified targets for the priority services (services for the elderly, the mentally ill and people with learning disabilities: DHSS, 1977a), these targets were abandoned by the Conservatives and left to local discretion. The priority services remained a low national priority. Statements in the early years of the Conservative administration indicated a rather less state-centred vision of policy, emphasising care *by* the community (DHSS, 1981c). Ministerial references stressed the importance of the informal sector, and private nursing homes experienced rapid growth due to the changes (from 1980) in supplementary benefit regulations. But criticism of the failures of deinstitutionalisation (Social Services Committee, 1985a) and of the lack of control of social security payments (Audit Commission, 1986) forced community care up the political agenda. This prompted the appointment of Sir Roy Griffiths to review community care policies (Griffiths, 1988). Significantly, however, there were subsequent delays in responding to his report – community care proposals were eventually brought forward, but were then delayed again because of the impact local authority involvement would have on the size of the poll tax. Consequently the reforms were not implemented until 1993.

The community care reforms attempt to distinguish more clearly between the responsibilities of the health and local-government services, the former being concerned with health care, the latter with 'social' care, although there is some confusion over the precise boundary between the two forms of care (Chapter 5). Local authorities are the lead agency as far as social care is concerned and the community care reforms are potentially crucial in ensuring both that patients are not discharged when inadequate facilities are available to them in the community and that patients do not impede the efficient operation of hospitals by blocking beds for want of adequate domiciliary support.

In the limited space available it is clearly impossible to describe in detail all the policy changes since 1979, though the Appendix should provide at least the skeleton of a chronology of events; other accounts (for example Ham, 1992) give more detail on specific points. The aim here, instead, has been to pick out the major dimensions of change in this period in a way that presents individual issues chronologically; individual chapters take up these issues in more depth. However, as well as describing the policy innovations that have been introduced, it is also relevant to present a summary of major statistical trends in the NHS as a context for the later chapters.

Inputs: trends in health care finance

Public debate and media coverage of the NHS has been polarised between government claims of record inputs (principally financial resources) and outputs (numbers of patients treated) and dramatic and alarmist reports of bed closures, lengthening waiting lists and occasionally patients dying for lack of treatment. In part following and updating Le Grand *et al.* (1990), this chapter analyses trends in several key indicators of the state of the nation's health care system. First among these is the resource input into the service, which allows comparison with the performance of other nation states. Secondly, this section reviews the 'services versus resources' debates and considers how far the NHS has succeeded in keeping pace with increasing demands. Finally, the efforts of health authorities to generate resources internally, by various measures designed to improve efficiency, are reviewed.

Health care expenditures in comparative context

There are three ways in which meaningful analyses can be made of trends in health care expenditure: by investigating the extent to which expenditure has increased in terms of volume; by comparing health care expenditure and spending on other public programmes; and by international comparisons.

By any standards vast sums are now being spent on health care, totalling some £37 bn. in the 1993–4 financial year. In 'real' terms (that is, after deflating by the GDP price deflator) NHS expenditure in 1991–2 was estimated to be approximately 47 per cent higher than in 1978–9, which was substantially ahead of the overall growth in public expenditure of 23.6 per cent over the same period (Le Grand *et al.*, 1990). However in 'volume' terms (that is, after using a deflator reflecting input costs in the NHS) there was just one year of rapid growth, followed by six years of limited growth and in two cases (1983–4 and 1986–7) decline (Table 1.1). Because of the range of possible deflators that could be used for the cost of NHS inputs, it is 'difficult to make very definite statements about whether the volume of NHS expenditure rose or fell in a particular year in the 1980s' (Le Grand *et al.*, 1990, p. 97). In addition, because of the funds injected into the NHS for the implementation of the White Paper, figures for the financial years around 1991 are inflated. The Department of Health (DoH) suggested that in real terms expenditure on the NHS would grow by 4.4 per cent, 6.6 per cent and 5.9 per cent in the 1990–1 and the two subsequent financial years, respectively, before allowing for new cash-releasing efficiency savings (Health Committee, 1993a). These figures also include the costs of implementing the reforms and of recruiting additional managerial staff for the service, which together are estimated to have increased spending by some £700 mn. (Primarolo, 1993), or some 2 per cent of the gross cost of the service. However, they do suggest that, allowing for the difficulties experienced during the 1980s, there has been substantial growth in finance over the period in question, though this has not always been smooth and unproblematic.

Secondly, examining its share of total public expenditure, the NHS accounted for 12 per cent of public spending in 1978–79; however by 1992 health care expenditure was estimated at around 14.2 per cent of total public spending and was projected to increase to 14.4 per cent for 1992–3 (OHE, 1992, table 2.17). This would indicate some degree of priority, although law and order increased its share of public spending from 3.9 per cent to 5.9 per cent over the same period. However in the Conservatives' first term of office, although NHS expenditure rose in real terms, it increased by far less than expenditure on defence and law and order (Lee *et al.*, 1983), indicating, perhaps, the Conservatives' greater sensitivity, in the late 1980s, to criticism of their record on the core programmes of the welfare state.

Thirdly, considered as a proportion of GDP, health care expenditure in Britain compares unfavourably with states at similar levels of economic development (OECD, 1993). The USA, for instance, spends 5.2 per cent of GDP on *public* health care, slightly less than Britain, but *in total* spends 12.4 per cent of GDP on health care; conversely, Sweden spends 7.8 per cent on public health care and 8.7 per cent in total. In Britain, health care spending's share of GDP fell slightly from 5.1 per cent in 1981–2 and 1982–3 to 4.8 per cent in 1986–7, though it rose again to 5.2 per cent in 1990. One government response has been that this comparatively poor showing reflects the relatively low spending on private health care, leading to wistful speculation that one way to resolve the problems of the health service would be to encourage private sector expansion (Chapters 3 and 7). The public sector accounts for 83.3 per cent of spending on health care in Britain, which is a higher proportion than all but five West European states (OECD, 1993, table 7.1.1). As an indication of the growing significance of private care in Britain, public sector spending accounted for 85.2 per cent of health care spending in 1960 and 91.1 per cent in 1975, but fell back to 83.3 per cent in 1990. However OECD statistics show that, as proportions of GDP, both private *and* public spending are higher in comparable West European states than in Britain (see also Moran, 1992).

To summarise the above: health care expenditure undoubtedly has grown in Britain, quite substantially so, although the recent rapid growth may be partly illusory in view of the costs of implementing the White Paper. Compared with states at similar levels of economic development, Britain's spending remains low, and as a proportion of GDP is approximately the same as in 1978–9. The fact that this clearly reflects political priorities is encapsulated in the relative amounts devoted to increases in health care expenditure compared with that given away in tax cuts since 1979; the vast revenues available from North Sea oil and from privatisation proceeds offered a unique opportunity to invest in the public services, which was instead passed up in favour of regressive tax cuts.

Finally, in terms of sources of funds, we should note several measures designed to transfer some of the burden of financing the service onto the individual and the 'community' as well as onto the commercial sector. The most important of these, at least symbolically, have been the increase in prescription charges by approximately 2300 per cent between 1979 and 1994, although in real terms the increase is much less; the introduction of charges for eye tests and dental examinations following the passing of the Health and Medicines Bill in 1987; and the encouragement given to health authorities to raise income for themselves either through increased private treatment or via income generation schemes.[2]

A large number of people are exempt from NHS charges, but income derived from charges now accounts for approximately 4 per cent of NHS expenditure compared with 2.2 per cent in 1978–9.[3] The proportion of NHS finance derived from direct taxation is now (at 79.5 per cent) at its lowest point for many years, indicating the ways in which the costs of services have been passed to users. Nowhere is this more noticeable than in dental care: patient contributions accounted for only 20.5 per cent of the cost of the service in 1979–80 but by 1989 that proportion had increased to 38.7 per cent, though it had fallen again to 33.5 per cent by 1991.[4]

Related to this, there has been a succession of measures that implicitly suggest that health care expenditure has increasingly come to depend not solely on direct taxation but upon the capacities and resources of individuals, health authority managers and local communities. Thus health authorities have been exhorted to develop their entrepreneurial and charitable activities (Chapter 8). There has been encouragement of individual and community responsibility, which legitimates the calls for the expansion of private care (Chapter 7) and community care policies. Although state finance still provides the great bulk of funds, these policies suggest a divergence between localities in terms of their ability to draw upon other resources to care for patients.

Services versus resources: debates about 'underfunding'

One of the most persistent foci for debate on the NHS during the 1980s has been the question of whether the service is in some sense underfunded. Because it is cash-limited, such debates relate mainly to the hospital and community health service (HCHS). Critics have usually charged that funds have lagged behind rising demands generated by demographic and technical change, rising expectations and medical innovation. In defence, government spokespersons have argued that what matters is not so much aggregate growth, but the way resources are used. Arguments have concentrated on the allowances to be made for various cost pressures and for growing demands and needs.

Demographic change has had the greatest impact on demand for health care and it is widely agreed that the increase in the proportion of the elderly in the population is placing ever-increasing pressure on the NHS. Although its impact varies slightly from year to year, it is estimated that demographic change has required expenditure growth averaging 0.8 per cent per annum since 1981–2, ranging from 0.6 per cent to 1.4 per cent (Health Committee, 1993a, p. vii). Rising demands also follow from increased public expectations and from the increased capacity afforded by medical technology, not just in terms of encompassing a broader range of conditions, but also in terms of keeping people alive longer so that they survive to make additional claims on services in old age. Use of the retail price index (RPI) underestimates inflation in the health sector, and finally the health sector is very labour-intensive and the scope for increased productivity is consequently limited. For all these reasons, simply adjusting NHS expenditure in line with inflation, or (even more simplistically) asserting unprecedented growth in resources since a carefully chosen starting date, is inadequate: figures must be presented that show how growth compares with needs.

In this context successive Social Services Committee reports have concluded that, for instance, 'expenditure on the NHS has barely succeeded in keeping pace with increased demand' (Social Services Committee, 1984, p. ix). Estimates vary: the Social Services Committee's 1986 estimate was £1.325 bn (1986, para 12); their estimate for the end of the 1987–88 financial year was £1.9 bn (1988a, para 22); Ham *et al.* (1990) cite £1.8 bn for 1981–2 to 1988–9; and OHE (1992), extrapolating NHS expenditure assuming 2 per cent growth per annum, claim that the cumulative deficit in net revenue expenditure was £1.7bn to 1990–91, reducing to £1 bn by the end of 1992–93.

At times the government appeared to agree with some of the arguments on this point: for instance Barney Hayhoe (minister of state, DHSS) argued in 1986 that 'health authorities need to grow by about 2 per cent a year in order to meet the pressures they face'.[5] While disputed (John Major, then chief secretary to the Treasury, claimed in 1988 that it was difficult 'to get accurate figures for the growth that is required in real terms')[6] the Social Services Committee regarded 2 per cent per annum as the 'best available estimate' of the scale of growth required. However the NHS chief executive declared in 1991 that the government had never accepted that figure.[7]

Table 1.1 summarises estimates of the effects of increases in cash allocations for the HCHS from 1982–3 to 1991–2. Although in cash terms expenditure rose by at least 5 per cent per annum, in real terms (net of the GDP deflator) the increases were marginal in 1982–3 and 1983–4 and a real-terms reduction was experienced in 1985–6; only from 1986–9 and in 1990–1 were substantial real-terms increases experienced. If one adds the effects of new, cash-releasing CIPs, consistent increases greater than 1 per cent were achieved in all but 1982–3 and 1983–4; but overall, real growth in the service was

Table 1.1   Trends in actual and planned expenditure on the HCHS in England, 1982–3 to 1993–4

	Current net spending (£m)	Cash increase over previous year (%)	Change in real terms (%)[1]	Change in purchasing power (%)	Estimated margin for service development[2] (%)
1982–3	8185	7.3	0.1	0.8	0.8
1983–4	8600	5.1	0.6	0.0	0.0
1984–5	9090	5.7	1.3	−1.0	0.1
1985–6	9835	5.4	−0.8	0.2	1.4
1986–7	10573	7.5	3.9	0.6	2.0
1987–8	11690	10.5	4.9	1.8	3.1
1988–9	12965	10.9	3.2	0.4	1.7
1989–90	13812	7.2	0.6	0.1	1.2
1990–1	15556	12.7	4.4	4.8	6.1
1991–2	17699	13.7	6.6	N.A.	N.A.
1992–3 (forecast outturn)	19434	9.6	5.9	N.A.	N.A.
1993–4 (plan)	20088	3.5	0.7	N.A.	N.A.

NOTES:
1. Cash increase minus GDP deflator.
2. Combines a measure of increased purchasing power (cash increase, net of increased unit costs) plus cash-releasing cost improvements.
SOURCES: Social Services Committee, 1987a, table 1.1; Health Committee, 1991a, table 1.1; Health Committee, 1993d, table 1.1.

sustained, in the mid-1980s, only with the aid of quite substantial CIPs. This is significant in relation to developments in the mid-1980s, when it proved impossible to redistribute funds geographically without large-scale reductions in the resources available to certain regions and districts (Chapter 4).

Furthermore, the growth in the NHS of central initiatives and national specification of targets for health authorities has reduced authorities' scope for manoeuvre, and the absence of any relationship between specification of such targets and exhortations about priorities was a matter of concern, since managers had been required to cope with an 'ever-increasing number of central, isolated initiatives within increasingly tight cash limits'.[8] Aggregate expenditure figures also include spending on special programmes (such as those for AIDS treatment) and such additional sums as the government has occasionally granted in the form of 'transitional allocations' to health authorities suffering from rapid net transfers of funds. These were conceded somewhat grudgingly, under political pressure, and it seems rather disingenuous to represent them as genuine increases. For critics these sums represented:

> drip feeding . . . small amounts just topping up local problems are not the right way to go about it . . . the policy seems to be one of applying elastoplast as soon as a sore appears. So the whole body has become covered with patches of elastoplast and new sores are erupting.[9]

Nor has the growth in funding been smooth and unproblematic, since government decisions have created management difficulties for health authorities. The increase in VAT from 8 per cent to 15 per cent in 1980, for instance, was not accompanied by compensation for or exemptions to public authorities (costing English health authorities approximately 0.64 per cent of their budget – Social Services Committee, 1980a). Likewise the 1 per cent cut in the NHS's revenue budget in July 1983 was imposed nearly one third of the way through a financial year, and so had a disproportionate impact on health authority finances. Even the transitional allocations to DHAs in the late 1980s had to be spent in the financial year in which they were announced. Persistent under-funding of pay awards, justified by the government as a stimulus to efficiency, imposed severe pressure on many health authorities.

There are numerous points of dispute between the government and its critics on the question of underfunding. These include whether the NHS should be judged on the resources committed to it (a measure of the political priority attached to it by government) or by the results of spending those resources (a measure of the efficiency with which those funds are used). They also include debates on how best to assess the NHS's performance: for instance the measures employed to assess changing need for health care, the measure of inflation employed, and whether one should be measuring purchasing power alone or the effectiveness of resource utilisation (the DoH routinely disputed the Health Select Committee's stress on purchasing power, preferring measures of efficiency such as cost improvements). Any estimate of underfunding is complicated by two further issues. Firstly there is no objective way of knowing whether and to what extent the service has been underfunded in the past (arguably it always has been – see Webster, 1988). Secondly, patterns of service are always changing – for example, most would agree on the desirability of community-based care for chronic conditions – and using past trends in expenditure as a basis for future extrapolations ignores this.

Whatever the government's view, it is difficult to explain the perceived 'crisis' of the NHS in the winter of 1987–8 (perhaps the decisive event producing the NHS Review) as anything other than one of underfunding. Widespread media and professional concern, focused partly on particular cases of postponed operations but also on the wider question of the lack of resources available to the service, culminated in an almost unprecedented joint statement on 7 December 1987 from the presidents of the Royal Colleges of Physicians, Surgeons and Obstetricians who called on the government 'to do something now to save our Health Service, once the envy of the world'. Whatever statistics the government could produce ('barely relevant multiples of past expenditure, staff employed or numbers going in and out of hospital doors' as Sir George Godber put it)[10] could no longer hide the visible deficiencies in the service in terms of services not provided or lengthening waiting lists; the 'blood is seeping through the bandages', to quote Neil Kinnock[11]. And this was no 'local difficulty' but a generalised crisis (chapter 4).

Generating resources internally: efficiency savings, cost improvement programmes and the NHS

Successive Conservative governments have placed substantial emphasis on the need for health authorities to achieve greater levels of efficiency with the resources allocated to them. This has been pursued in two ways: through direct injunctions to health authorities to achieve efficiency savings by withdrawing a certain proportion of funds (around 0.5 per cent) from them at the start of the financial year; and through national policy initiatives such as competitive tendering. The principal methods by which resources have been generated internally include rationalisation of services, competitive tendering and other reductions in labour costs; added impetus was given to these by the introduction of general management (see Chapter 3). In total savings through CIPs (or CRES) have amounted to a maximum of 1 per cent of the HCHS budget (Table 1.2). The primary sources of savings were initially through measures directly or indirectly affecting wage costs (Table 1.2, line 2, plus competitive tendering). Rationalisation of patient services is clearly playing a more important role in these overall savings. In 1985–6 such savings accounted for 21.5 per cent of the total from CIPs, but in 1990–91 this proportion had risen to 34.3 per cent (though this partly reflects reduced savings from competitive tendering). This rationalisation includes reductions in beds, concentration into fewer sites and the more intensive use of facilities. Arguably this imposes additional (travel and time) costs on users (Pearson, 1992), though there are medical arguments for centralisation. Competitive tendering likewise achieves savings at the expense of labour costs and service quality (PSPRU, 1992). So perhaps cost *improvements* could better be referred to as cost *displacement* programmes since they inevitably entail a negative impact on some patients and workers. Whether such programmes could genuinely be sustained, producing recurring revenue savings, was also a crucial question. The Health Committee (1991b) expressed its 'concern about reliance on CIPs as the NHS enters a period when the internal market is being implemented . . . market pressures coupled with pressures to achieve CIPs can affect quality', and recommended that the DoH should plan to reduce its reliance on CIPs. Despite such warnings, ministers have continued to insist, on numerous occasions over several years, that sustainable savings can be made through greater efficiency, and departmental plans include, if anything, a still greater reliance on these measures.[12]

Provision: beds, staffing and activity

Beds

One of the commonest reasons for a state of 'crisis' being proclaimed in the NHS has been that large numbers of hospital beds have been closed and/or that closures are taking place in an *ad hoc*, unplanned fashion, and in particular that replacement facilities have not been provided.

Table 1.2 Sources of savings from cost improvement programmes, 1985–6 to 1990–1

	1985–6 (£m)	(%)	1986–7 (£m)	(%)	1987–8 (£m)	(%)	1988–9 (£m)	(%)	1989–90 (£m)	(%)	1990–1 (£m)	(%)
Rationalisation of patient services	29.8	21.5	37.3	23.5	35.4	23.2	51.5	30.1	55.5	35.0	68.6	34.3
Other reductions in labour costs	38.3	27.7	23.6	14.9	35.4	23.2	44.1	25.8	35.5	22.4	55.2	27.6
Rayner scrutiny savings	7.5	5.3	7.6	4.8	3.6	2.4	4.3	2.5	2.6	1.6	2.8	1.4
Supply cost savings	9.5	6.9	7.8	4.9	10.2	6.7	11.1	6.5	9.5	6.0	9.3	4.7
Energy savings	6.8	4.9	8.7	5.5	8.5	5.6	10.6	6.2	9.7	6.1	7.5	3.8
Other savings	30.2	21.8	25.0	15.8	29.1	19.0	38.1	22.2	37.4	23.6	48.1	24.1
Competitive tendering[1]	16.3	11.8	48.4	30.5	30.6	20.0	11.5	6.7	5.9	3.7	5.3	2.6
Competitive tendering[2]	N.A.	N.A.	N.A.	N.A.	N.A.	N.A.	N.A.	N.A.	2.4	1.5	3.1	1.5
Total	138.4	100.0	158.4	100.0	152.8	100.0	171.1	100.0	158.5	100.0	199.9	100.0

NOTES:
1. Primarily catering, domestic services, and laundry.
2. Greater range of services included from 1989.

SOURCES: Health Committee, 1991a, table 1.6; Health Committee, 1993a, table 1.5.

There have been dramatic reductions in acute bed provision, from 148 000 in 1979 to 115 000 in 1992, or an average of 22.3 per cent;[13] in individual DHAs reductions have been as high as 50 per cent (Chapter 4) and there has also been a large number of temporary closures, accurate documentation of which is difficult to obtain.[14] However bed numbers in themselves do not necessarily mean very much, as government spokespersons and civil servants have repeatedly asserted:

> beds close, open and re-open for a number of different reasons . . . some closures, especially temporary closures, are effected in the face of financial problems. However, temporary closures 'for financial reasons' do not necessarily provide evidence of 'underfunding' . . . They may become necessary as a result of over-optimistic expansion of other services. Or they could indicate problems in financial planning and control . . . some closures may be attributed to a mixture of reasons'.[15]

The Social Services Committee's (1988b, p. vii) acerbic response to this was that on such reasoning 'one could never conclude that underfunding by the Government was the cause of any closure'. The type of beds being closed and the type of hospital being affected must be taken into account; changes in bed numbers may reflect changing medical philosophy and practice, especially in the case of single-specialty and long-stay hospitals.[16] In the latter case, though there have been welcome reductions in the number and scale of such facilities,[17] the crucial issue is how far community-based provision has compensated for the reduction in beds (Chapter 5). In geriatric provision there have also been rapid reductions in hospital capacity, partly associated with the transfer, by some health authorities, of responsibility for long-stay care into the private sector (see Chapter 5).

Activity

Activity in the NHS has unquestionably increased, though the precise extent of this is not clear due to changes in the ways in which patient activity is recorded. In the mid-1980s the basis for recording information changed from discharges and deaths to the finished consultant episode (FCE). The effect has been to inflate statistics about hospital activity, because it is possible that an inpatient stay can include several FCEs, such as attention in a casualty department, various tests, and perhaps more than one form of treatment; all of these may be under different consultants. For general and acute services in

England, total cases treated as inpatients rose from 4.18 million in 1978–9 to 5.92 million in 1989–90, an increase of 41 per cent.[18] Simultaneously, available acute hospital beds declined from 147 000 to 119 000, so throughput rose dramatically, from 28.4 cases per bed to 48.7.[19] At the same time the average length of stay in hospital was reduced, falling in the acute sector from 9.4 days to 6.1 between 1979 and 1990–1, a reduction of 35 per cent.[20] Day cases treated in NHS hospitals in England rose from 592 000 in 1979 to 1 548 000 in 1991–2, an increase of 161 per cent.[21] These accounted for 16.6 per cent of all non-psychiatric patients treated in hospital in 1991–2. Thus there has been a rapid increase in the use made of existing facilities, with growth in patient throughput being the main source of the apparent improved efficiency of the service. One of the results of less invasive forms of surgery, is that patients are discharged at an earlier stage of their recovery, and a higher proportion may therefore require readmission. It has been suggested, using data from the Oxford Record Linkage Study, that for the ten-year period 1975–84 about 20 per cent of the total increase in admissions represented readmissions (Goldacre *et al.*, 1988). A related point is that earlier discharge places a greater burden on community services and relatives, whose assistance during convalescence is assumed. Yet the availability of primary and community care services varies considerably. Indeed a constraint on the implementation of the NHS reforms may well prove to be the inadequacies of community care, which may prevent the speedy discharge of patients (Chapter 5).

The government has seen the rise in activity as an index of its success, but critics have argued that waiting lists are a key indicator of the extent to which the NHS is meeting needs. Waiting list statistics are controversial: recording practices vary, there are arguments over whether the numbers on the list or the length of waiting time are the most appropriate indicators, and any analysis of trends is complicated by the effects of industrial action in 1978–9 and 1982, both of which added substantially to the numbers waiting. Waiting lists have also been the subject of action through specific initiatives, for example to reduce the number of people waiting for urgent treatment or those waiting for more than one year, so changes in lists do not necessarily say much about the overall impact of government policies. It is not surprising that Frankel and West (1993, p. 116) suggest that waiting lists say far more about the management practices of consultants than about need for treatment, and they may indeed 'proteet patients and practitioners from being forced to acknowledge the triviality or intractability of particular conditions'. Bearing these remarks in mind, however, the recent rise in the number of those waiting surely demonstrates that, despite government rhetoric, there remains a substantial gap between the resources available and the need for health care. Looking simply at figures for inpatient waiting in England from 1979, for all the government's efforts and despite exercises in better validation of lists, they have remained at or slightly under 700 000, with peaks in 1979 (752 000) and 1982 (726 000). More recently, figures aggregated from returns to RHAs, and incorporating day-case waiting lists, suggested that in March 1994 1.07 mn people were waiting for NHS hospital treatment, representing an increase of 7.2 per cent from the March 1993 figure of 993 000,[22] which included an increase of some 80 000 between 1991 and 1992. At the same time the government can claim some success in reducing quite substantially the numbers waiting for more than one year (by some 33 per cent from 1991–2) due largely to its own waiting list initiatives. The government's emphasis is firmly on waiting times, of course, but there have been criticisms that in targeting long waiting times, cases of greater need have been neglected.

People

Given the labour-intensive nature of health care, any policy of cost containment must concentrate on the wage bill, which amounts to around 75 per cent of NHS costs. Policy was explicitly directed towards achieving ever-greater levels of 'productivity' from all grades of staff. In addition, while the numbers of staff employed directly by the NHS fell by 23 900 (2.9 per cent) between 1981 and 1991 (see Table 6.1),[23] this hides the sharply different experiences of specific staff groups. Growth was achieved, in line with declared policy, in medical and nursing staff numbers. Successive public expenditure white papers advertised the government's intention of maximising the proportion of 'frontline' staff delivering services directly to patients, that is, doctors, nurses and professional and technical staff.[24] In 1991 these three groups accounted for 66.4 per cent of all directly employed staff compared with 60.4 per cent in 1981. The most dramatic reduction was in ancillary personnel, where the number of directly employed staff fell by 50.1 per cent. The number of administrative and clerical staff rose by 17.9 per cent over this ten-year period, apparently contradicting the government's declared policy of reducing the proportion of staff not directly involved in patient care, and leading to controversy about the extent and cost of this growth (Chapter 6). These aggregate figures hide the growing extent to which the NHS came to rely on part-time staff and agency personnel. Government statistics cover whole-time equivalents so it is difficult to assess how far part-time employment grew within the NHS, but trends from the early 1980s suggest that it was significant (Mohan, 1988b). Agency staff expenditure peaked at £297 mn in 1990,[25] or 2.9 per cent of the wages bill in the service, while in some localities it assumed even greater significance (Mohan and Lee, 1989; see also Chapter 6).

Outcomes?

The relationship between health care provision and health status is unclear; there are no obvious direct links between health care expenditure and agreed comparative measures of health status such as infant mortality rates or life expectancy. Much is beyond the scope of health services: heart disease mortality is falling, for example, in Britain and elsewhere, but the respective contributions of government intervention, healthier lifestyles and diets, and economic and environmental changes is a matter for speculation. This means that assessment of the impact on health of recent changes in the health care system is virtually impossible. However the effect of policies outside the health system seem undeniable: recently commentators have drawn attention to the widening gap in living standards and health status between the richest and poorest citizens in Britain, attributing these unequivocally to government policies (Davey-Smith and Egger, 1993).

What, therefore, of the impact of changes within the service? In attempting to evaluate the impact of the changes described here, the influence of a number of factors must be separated out and numerous caveats entered. Firstly, if patient throughput measures are a key performance indicator, technical innovation has permitted a growing proportion of operations to be treated as day cases, greatly increasing patient throughput. This may lead to a reconceptualisation of the role of the hospital: assuming the availability of adequate support services, there will be less need for acute hospital beds (and so another key statistic, bed closures, will assume less significance). If increased throughput is crucial, what of increases in readmissions, for which data are unreliable? If waiting lists or times are a key indicator, these have been subject to severe manipulation, most notably in the period prior to the 1992 general election, in which health authorities unashamedly concentrated on those patients who were otherwise likely to wait more than two years for treatment (as John Yates, formerly leader of the government's waiting list task force, commented, if the government was so convinced of the merits of the internal market, why did it need waiting list task forces, blitzes and so on if not for political reasons?).[26] If the NHS reforms are to be properly evaluated in terms of their effect on the quality of health care, then since increases in funding were much more rapid in the financial years preceding the reforms and the 1992 election, it is impossible to separate the effects of the reforms from the effects of increased funding.[27] However a welcome recent development has been the greater attention being given to the effectiveness of treatment and to questions about the best way to purchase better health care. Arguably the new emphasis on 'health gain' will be potentially the most progressive element – or effect – of the reforms: if authorities are to make decisions about priorities for purchasing decisions, they will have to take account of data on the effectiveness of different forms of intervention, though such evaluative techniques are in the early stages of development.

Concluding comments

Perhaps the key question raised by this brief statistical and policy overview is the best way in which to judge the 'performance' of the NHS. Government spokespersons are obviously unhappy with simplistic analyses of the resources committed to the service, yet these are the only way in which direct international comparisons of the priority attached to 'public' health care can be made. Britain does spend less on health care than comparable states and growth in the public sector has been limited; indeed without the contributions of both additional charges and sales and the resources released by CIPs, hardly any growth in resources would have taken place in some years, notably in the mid-1980s.

It is not surprising, then, that government spokespersons have sought to avoid such terrain in favour of pronouncements about record levels of activity. Resources are unquestionably being used more 'effectively' if one accepts a narrowly economic view of this question: increased numbers of patients are being treated and they are spending less time in hospital than previously, due in part to less interventionist techniques. However, what is not available is evidence of what is happening to the quality of treatment and care under the NHS: rationalisation of services means greater travel costs and inconvenience; more rapid throughput, other things being equal, means a greater impact on informal carers and primary care services, and probably increased repeat admissions; and waiting times and lists have increased. All of these suggest at least a qualitative change in the nature of the service offered by the NHS.

The situation, then, is one in which health care expenditure remained largely static in real terms until the implementation of the reforms and the imminence of the 1992 election forced the government rapidly to increase spending. There have been rapid increases in health service activity and patient throughput, but these reflect a combination of increased funding and greater efficiency, the impact of technical changes (minimising the time people stay in hospital), and policy decisions to speed up hospital discharge and rely to a greater degree on informal care. But in many respects the most important aspects of restructuring and change in the health sector relate less to aggregate expenditure figures, important though they are, than to the nature of service delivery – to the character of the health service and the way it is run: it is a long way from the Royal Commission to the White Paper. The argument in the rest of this book is that while superficially little has changed – after all, the NHS is still substantially financed by direct taxation and is run largely by public servants under public organisations – the character of the service and its operational rationality are being steadily transformed. This may have the potential to change the service away from something concerned largely with equity-oriented goals to one governed, to a much greater degree than when it was conceived, by market criteria. As Chapter 2 now makes clear, there are several ways in which the changes in health care delivery may be interpreted.

2

Explaining Change in the Welfare State and in Health Care Policy

The central concern of this chapter is how one attempts to interpret changes in health care policy. At one end of the spectrum some commentators appear to suggest that developments in the NHS merely reflect changes elsewhere in the economy; thus, changing patterns of labour organisation (Chapter 6) or subcontracting of work (Chapter 8) represent a translation to the NHS of more widespread economic changes. Likewise technological developments (the enhanced capacities of contemporary medicine and information technology) are said to require and facilitate the implementation of market-based reforms. Conversely, at the opposite end of the political spectrum, events in the welfare state are interpreted in terms of a 'crisis' in state welfare, or the 'restructuring' of welfare in the interests of capital, or are even linked to a covert agenda to privatise the service.

Both types of explanation are somewhat one dimensional; neither, on their own, seem satisfactory. Between the pitfalls of the two (neglecting wider structural determinations on the one hand and ignoring the specifics of the health policy arena and events within one nation-state on the other) there seemed to be scope for an account that emphasised the ways in which change in the British health sector were not simply technical responses or conflict-free refinements of the existing system, nor were they Pavlovian reactions to international economic crises. Instead the ways in which such wider economic difficulties were mediated by state policies were what required analysis.

This chapter first considers arguments that can be classed either as developmentalist (because they presume that all states follow similar patterns of economic development and welfare provision) or deterministic (because they explain change in welfare provision in relation to technical change). I then examine variants of political theory that account for state intervention in welfare policy in very different ways (pluralist, Marxist, the New Right). Finally I consider contributions from a broader-based political economy, which link changes in welfare provision to the changing character of capitalism and the economic crises that have beset capitalist states in recent decades, concentrating on the relevance, to analyses of welfare provision, of the notion of a transition from Fordism to post-Fordism.

Developmentalism and determinism

I borrow the term 'developmentalism' from Taylor (1989), who argues that much theorisation about economic development has presumed that all countries will follow substantially the same paths to growth and social progress. In discussion of the welfare state this is most notable in what became known as 'logic of industrialism' accounts, which stressed the convergence between states in terms of levels of industrialisation, welfare provision and so on. Whatever their superficial attractions, such accounts can be somewhat misleading if uncritically applied to individual states.

R. Taylor (1984) contrasts some general models of the 'structural roots of variation in the development of welfare states in capitalist societies'. One model explains health policy in terms of a convergence of ideas, attitudes and values across different states (p. 91). A second relies on statistical associations between welfare expenditure and rates and levels of economic development, concentrating on the processes of 'modernisation' and the logic of industrialism (Flora and Alber, 1981; Ringen, 1987). Such accounts rely heavily on evolutionary, developmentalist theories of how societies work. For instance Flora and Heidenheimer (1981, p. 23) claim that because non-democratic and non-capitalist societies have established very similar institutions, the welfare state 'seems to be a far more general version of modernisation, not exclusively tied to its 'democratic-capitalist' version', while Wilensky (1975, p. xiii) rejected 'brittle categories' and dichotomies (socialist/capitalist; collectivist/individualist) as having limited explanatory power. Such analyses can identify important general tendencies, but the interesting features of individual nation states are thus subsumed under broad categories: 'general deductions based on national values' cannot provide a satisfactory explanation of the development of social policy in any one country (Weir *et al.*, 1988; see also Melling, 1991). Such accounts demonstrate association but not causality: they show that 'economic and industrial development has been a necessary background condition for the development of welfare states . . .. [but] given this premise, the *particular form* that the welfare state takes may be crucial' (Pierson, 1991, p. 18 – emphasis in original). Just as those forms vary from state to state in periods of growth (such as in the postwar 'long boom', when developmentalist accounts may have been at least descriptively accurate), so too the forms they take in periods of decline will vary depending on particular conjunctures of political forces. Thus Day and Klein's initial response to the NHS reforms was to see them as reflecting 'less an ideology of privatisation . . . than as part of an international trend towards imposing a managerial rather than a professional definition of efficiency and effectiveness in health care' (Day and Klein 1989, p. 3). But surely this rules out of court the ways in which such international trends are mediated within nation states?

One could make similar points about accounts that see health care policy making merely as a technical process, concerned with determining the most rational way of administering or managing health care, or as something determined largely by technological limitations and capacities. This is evident in the debate between Fox and Webster concerning regionalism in British health policy. Fox (1986) presents the development of hospital policy as the result of broad agreement on the *technical* advantages of 'hierarchical regionalism'. In contrast Webster (1990) suggests that Fox ignores the ways in which policies were *contested* by a whole range of interest groups and political coalitions, and questions the extent to which genuine 'consensus' about the NHS actually existed. Likewise, Klein's accounts of the development of the NHS (for example 1983, 1989) accord primacy to the internal technical difficulties faced by the service. For instance he was persuaded that, in the early years of the Thatcher era, the 'reality of politics', notably public support for the NHS, the difficulties of imposing a market solution on the service, and the ability of powerful vested interests to block change, had prevented fundamental reform; change had been marginal and confined largely to issues on which there was broad agreement such as organisational reform (Klein, 1984). Davies (1987) disputed this, arguing that while *superficially* little had changed, nevertheless various measures had been implemented that had prepared the ground for a determined attempt to break up the NHS's *de facto* monopoly of health care. Similarly Pearson (1992) argues that the successive terms of office of the Conservatives have been marked by a steady encroachment of commercial disciplines and management styles from the periphery of the NHS inwards, culminating in the White Paper's proposals.

In considering the circumstances surrounding the NHS review, it might be possible to construct an explanation based on technological determinism. If we accept that technological developments, notably improved information systems, facilitate clinical audit, and that a primary purpose of the reforms was to gain control over the medical profession's claim to authority in resource allocation, then it could be argued that the reforms were determined by such developments and were largely inevitable (see Stoker, 1990, pp. 247ff, for a similar argument about local government, and Macnicol, 1993, for some speculations about the history of the NHS). An alternative might have been to interpret changes in the NHS by analogy with changes elsewhere in the economy. From this perspective the government's reforms were part of an inevitable process whereby 'the trend is from centralised institutions to networks, from hierarchic, top–down models of organisation to looser constellations' (Day and Klein, 1989, p. 9; see also Klein, 1989, pp. 199ff). But just how do such changes come about? Could one really interpret some of the national initiatives in the 1980s simply as managerial responses to the internal difficulties of the service, or as something born out of 'desperation rather than ideology', designed to 'overcome the rigidities of the NHS and the difficulties of getting change in a highly unionised, segmented organisation' (Klein, 1985, p. 204)? Given that many innovations in the NHS were imposed by fiat from central government, such a voluntaristic interpretation has its limitations. Furthermore, if these were simply technical responses to changed circumstances, does this not present changes in policy as if they were the 'product of more or less rational policy debate within identifiable policy communities' (Cochrane, 1993, p. 81)? Yet one could hardly characterise the NHS review process – open only to a privileged cabal of insiders and dominated by Treasury ministers – as a debate, much less an open one designed to produce consensus. Furthermore, there had been numerous efforts during the 1980s to initiate experiments in service delivery. In some respects these departed from the ways in which the NHS had traditionally been run and anticipated the market disciplines of the NHS reforms (Chapters 3 and 8). And if the need for reform had been such an obvious technical necessity, why was it not anticipated, in any way, in the Conservatives' 1987 election manifesto? (Of course it could be argued that that would have courted electoral disaster, but they were defending an enormous majority). Rather, we might emphasise the extent to which the government used its own 'decisional autonomy' (Krieger, 1986; 1987) to impose its own vision on the service, often by interfering with the decisions of individual health authorities (Chapter 9). Pollert (1988) makes a similar point in criticising the unacknowledged translation of models of the so-called 'flexible firm' to the public sector without considering the very different circumstances that obtain therein; she regards the development of characteristics of the flexible firm in the public sector as an element of political strategies rather than the result of absorbing of private sector lessons (see also Cousins, 1988).

To summarise, however convenient it might be to suggest that the NHS reforms (and other changes in the health sector during the 1980s) were the inevitable product of external trends, this seems too much of a simplification. Technological change might best be viewed as an enabling factor, not a determining one. Whatever the parallels between events in the NHS and elsewhere, and however descriptively accurate such parallels might be, economic and technological changes are always politically mediated, and the focus should therefore be on how best to explain the process of mediation.

Political theory: pluralism, Marxism and the New Right

Conventionally, most accounts of health care policy making oppose pluralist and Marxist accounts while allowing some space for corporatism. They often neglect the distinctive contribution of the New Right's theoretical arguments, but given the acknowledged influence of theorists such as Hayek on the Thatcher governments, such a neglect is indefensible.

Pluralist accounts stress that political power is widely distributed and that no one group is dominant; consequently each can exercise some influence. There is no systematic bias to the exercise of power and therefore what is important to pluralists is the minutiae of negotiating processes. The strength of such an approach is its emphasis on detailed description of the actions of key individuals and interest groups in shaping health care policy (for example Pater, 1981; Rivett, 1986; see also Harrison *et al.*, 1990). However pluralists downplay wider social and political influences and constraints on state intervention, concentrating on details of policy formulation and seeing the state as an independent and benevolent arbitrator. Not all groups can enter the health policy arena on an equal basis, since the medical monopoly of knowledge is itself a source of power. Hence the interests of community and consumer groups are 'repressed' (Alford, 1975). More generally the state can effectively dictate and shape the policy agenda by its own decisions on who shall and shall not be incorporated into the policy process. In such circumstances the pluralist claims of equal access to and participation in the policy process ring rather hollow, and in any case pluralism is of little use in a situation in which the elective dictatorship of a substantial parliamentary majority permits a government considerable latitude in pursuing its own ends, as has been the case in Britain. Finally, however interesting they are in their attention to detail, pluralist accounts can 'degenerate into blow-by-blow story-telling from which it is very difficult to extract any larger patterns of constraints and enabling forces' (Harrison *et al.*, 1990, p. 17).

Marxists have persistently criticised such approaches, arguing that health care policy is primarily determined by the nature and outcomes of class struggles (Navarro, 1978, 1986), eschewing general theories of welfare state evolution, in favour of 'specific historical accounts of state responses to the political articulation of class interests' (R. Taylor, 1984, p. 98), and highlighting the structural constraints on state intervention, albeit sometimes mechanistically and in a somewhat essentialist manner. Thus the fact that the state is capitalist *by definition* limits its capacity to intervene in or solve social problems (for example Renaud, 1975).

The more general problem with Marxist accounts is their functionalist attribution of events to the needs of capital, the demands of the working class, or a combination of both. For Navarro (1978), for instance, events in the British health sector are usually 'determined' on the one hand by working-class demands (indexed by the degree of militancy of organised labour), and on the other hand by capital's requirements, notably for the reproduction of a healthy workforce, but it is not always clear which is dominant or determinant. Navarro fails to show the precise links between the demands formulated by the working class and the articulation of these demands in policy formation. Two problems arise: the functionalism inherent in attributing certain actions to the requirements of capitalism (see Urry, 1981, pp. 116–21; Hindess, 1987); and the teleology of explaining welfare policy developments – indeed all developments in state policy – in relation to the 'balance of class forces' prevailing at any given time (Harris, 1980).

To the extent that accounts of welfare policy stress conscious political struggle and mobilisation, they are preferable to an ahistorical and functionalist attribution of policy change to the needs of capital. This cannot be reduced to class politics: there is no automatic guarantee that the existence of a working class will lead to the articulation of demands for welfare, nor that class struggle will lead to such demands (Wetherly, 1988). Sectionalism within the working class can impede the development of pressure for welfare services, while an emphasis on *political* class struggle would neglect interests not structured along class lines (Weir *et al.*, 1988; Williams, 1992). Neither the working class nor capital can impose its will unambiguously; the policies produced in the NHS do not simply accord with the perceived needs of capital, even in a situation in which the Conservatives have enjoyed the virtually untrammelled pursuit of power. This latter point also hints at the importance of producer and professional interest groups in the health care policy arena. The medical profession is the most obvious example here, and Cawson (1982, p. 91) claims that 'the post-war history of the NHS can be persuasively analysed as an unfolding interplay between professional and managerial elements'. This is because of the conflict between the interests of the medical profession in practising without financial constraint, and the interests of managers and the state in controlling the ways in which resources are spent. The strength of groups such as the medical profession, and their incorporation into the mechanisms of governance, has led some to interpret the role of the state in a corporatist light (for example Schmitter, 1974). In this view the medical profession becomes an elite sanctioned by the state, with an ability not just to control and license medical practitioners, but also to influence government policy. This privileged status allows elite groups effectively to rule off the agenda policies that might challenge their authority. However the relevance of corporatist analyses in contemporary Britain is highly debatable, since the Conservatives have explicitly repudiated corporatism and have challenged professional power in several contexts (see Chapters 3 and 6).

The New Right and public choice theory

The 'New Right' is a catch-all term used to describe an heterogeneous set of views and arguments about state intervention. Rejecting group bargaining and party competition, the New Right's normative model of political decision making relies on market analogies, treating decisions as the resultant of the expressed preferences of individuals seeking to maximise their utility. Drawing on Hayek's methodological individualism, it is argued that government intervention can never work, even on its own terms, and that intervention is ultimately coercive, removing decision making and choice from individuals (see Bosanquet, 1983; Wainwright, 1994).

Hayek's *Road to Serfdom* (1944) encapsulates these core arguments. The state's role ought to be minimalist, concerning itself with a small number of general laws and functions on which there is broad agreement (substantially, the protection of property rights and the defence of the nation state). Any more detailed planning and regulation threatens freedom, especially where intervention begins to impinge on particular sections of society rather than the whole. Implicitly, state intervention threatens a moral order of individual responsibility: individuals ought to be free to choose for themselves, rather than having decisions made for them. In this context the issue of freedom from state control was sharply illustrated by the NHS paybeds conflicts of the mid-1970s, which enabled the Conservative Party to present itself as the party of free choice (Chapter 7). Indeed some New Right commentators go further, arguing (drawing on the evidence for community support of health services prior to the NHS – Green, 1985) that the alleged restriction of choice by the NHS actually led to underprovision (see Chapter 3; for criticisms see NHS Unlimited, 1988; Powell, 1992; Socialist Health Association, 1988).

Hayek lays greater emphasis on the technical inadequacies of state administration. Relying on the invisible hand of the market, the price system is said to reflect changes in demands, technologies and resources more quickly and effectively than institutions such as the state ever could. The state can never possess the intelligence required to coordinate markets effectively. Furthermore state agencies inevitably develop an interest in their own survival and become open to special interest groups and political pleading. This is why centralised state bureaucracies were for so long the target of the New Right, and it helps to account for the arguments against bureaucracy on the part of Conservatives, as well as for some solutions (for example performance indicators, the internal market). Finally the market is claimed to be egalitarian and democratic: egalitarian, because competition will, in theory, whittle away supranormal profits; and democratic, because the market enfranchises individuals rather than bureaucracies, and because the market will tailor the distribution of goods and services to individual needs.

These arguments have received much attention; they have certainly drawn strength from the apparent triumph of capitalism over socialism while they resonate with the experience of the beneficiaries of the rapid economic growth of the 1980s. But there are great difficulties applying them to health care. Most obviously, the asymmetric relationship between doctors and patients vitiates the idea that patients can genuinely exercise choice in the marketplace; even in the private health sector, choice is largely restricted to convenient operation times and the quality of accommodation. The fixed investment in health care institutions renders them highly inflexible, and this goes to the heart of the dilemmas over the rationalisation of hospital services under the reforms (Chapter 4). Markets do not clear at the point at which all demand is met, so they are arguably incompatible with a comprehensive NHS. Finally, is it possible to institute a market within the NHS without a degree of decentralisation that is incompatible with the public control of public money? (see Chapter 9.) Notwithstanding these difficulties, Conservative thinktanks advanced a range of proposals for the reform of the NHS, but they have not gained the ascendancy. This is partly because of the impracticability of some of their ideas, but it is also related to the government's reluctance to advance a more radical agenda. Although the arguments of the New Right helped prepare the ground for reform, their blueprint has not been uncritically adopted.

Political economy: crises, restructuring, disorganised capitalism and post-Fordism

Crises of the welfare state?

The term crisis has become so heavily used in the social sciences that it may have ceased to have analytical value (Hilton, 1987). But by the late 1970s there appeared to be a widely shared view that the expansion of state welfare provision, which had accompanied the capitalist 'long boom' of the postwar years, could no longer be sustained. If the welfare state had 'grown to limits' (Flora, 1986) it was also something that was both an insuperable obstacle to advanced capitalism and something indispensable to continued capital accumulation (for example Offe, 1984). Some in fact suggested that the welfare state was irreversible (Therborn and Roebroek, 1986). Arguably something had to give, and the ways in which the 'crises' became manifest in the health policy arena were in relation to debates about cost containment, the limitations on what national health care systems could be expected to deliver, and the question of access to treatment.

Pierson (1991, p. 144) isolates three principal uses of the term crisis: crisis as turning point, crisis as external shock, and crisis as long-standing contradiction. He also notes how the term 'crisis' has been appropriated by both left and right. The idea that the crisis was simply the product of a one-off external event (that is, the oil price increases of the 1970s) appeared naive in retrospect as the full magnitude of 'changes in the international political economy which collectively shattered the stability of the post-war economic order' (p. 160) became clear. These changes have not just altered the environment in which welfare states have to operate, they may also materially alter individuals' interests and associated political mobilisation (p. 177).

The notion of a crisis as a long-standing contradiction has also been evident in New Right critiques. Marxists had always pointed to the ambiguities and paradoxes of state welfare provision, but in the 1970s they were joined by those New Right commentators who contended that the welfare state was inherently unstable, ungovernable, inefficient and profligate (earlier voices had cried in the wilderness; see Powell's (1966) reflections on his period at the Ministry of Health). The welfare state was deemed incompatible with capitalism and the response was to recommend the returning of as many of its functions as possible to the market place (for example Adam Smith Institute, 1984). But such arguments never attained the ascendancy required to make a major impact.

So it is not really obvious that, to use the medical sense of the term crisis, the welfare state and the NHS have reached a critical condition from which they will either recover or die. However defenders of the welfare state argue that the notion of crisis has been used more insidiously by the government, to advance policies inconsistent with the traditional notion of state-funded and state-provided welfare (Johnson, 1987), and thereby eroding popular support for state intervention. Some accuse the government of manipulating public expenditure statistics to create an atmosphere of crisis (for example Johnson, 1986), thereby serving the valuable political goal of reducing expectations. The ways in which government ministers and MPs have emphasised the limitations of public funds and the necessity for invention in the acquisition of other resources seems entirely conformable with this notion of the political construction and use of the term 'crisis' (Chapter 3). In fact, the Conservatives clearly saw the 'crisis' experienced in the winter of 1987–8 not just as a political challenge, but as something that provided them with an opportunity to effect radical change within the service. But to rely upon such explanatory referents as consensus and crisis leads to rather simplified accounts of complex political changes. It may be more helpful to see crises as being politically constructed in a discursive attempt to win support for particular strategies or policy initiatives.

Restructuring

Gough (1979) identified several options open to a government wishing to limit the rise in state expenditure at a time of economic crisis. He suggested that because of the contradictory nature of the welfare state (both a constraint on capital accumulation and a functional necessity for it) we should find 'not so much cuts or a dismantling of the welfare state, but its restructuring':

> the capitalist state, acting in the interests of its national capital, will seek to alter and adapt social policies to suit the perceived needs of that capital . . . broadly speaking there will be pressure on social policies to aid and abet the accumulation of capital and its reproduction, and pressure to cut back on services designed to meet 'needs' which do not aid the achievement of these objectives (Gough, 1979, p. 138).

Gough identified four possible options: adapting policies to secure more efficient reproduction of the labour force; emphasising the social control of potentially destabilising groups in society; raising productivity within the social services; and reprivatising parts of the welfare state. Gough was of course speaking of tendencies, and his argument was developed before the 1979 election, though some of the measures he noted were evident in the monetarist policies pursued by Labour (Ormerod, 1980). But policy developments since 1979 have not come about purely because of some systemic logic; political contingencies have influenced the character and timing of policies, and at least as much weight has to be placed on pragmatism and opportunism as on the requirements of capital.

What makes analysing restructuring in the health sector more complicated is that there are crucial interdependencies between different elements of the formal and informal health care systems. The balance between state, market and community (Papadakis and Taylor–Gooby, 1988), or between formal and informal care, will vary historically and geographically, and for several reasons: political circumstances, demographic and technical changes, changing ideas about medical practice and challenges to the cultural authority of medical practitioners. Health services can also be produced in a variety of ways: within households (usually through the labour of women), through markets, by voluntary or charitable organisations, and by the central or local state (Pinch, 1989, after Mark–Lawson *et al*, 1985). These are not exclusive categories since services are increasingly provided through some form of partnership arrangement or through contractual arrangements between, for instance, the state and a providing agency (Wolch, 1989). As a consequence of all this there is considerable potential for substitution between agencies.

This potential for substitution is politically mediated and contested. It is not just a matter of administrative responses to technical problems, though of course new forms of care (for example day surgery) become available due to technical change. Even here, however, the provision of public support to those discharged quickly from hospital is a matter of political decision, as community care policies (Chapter 5) make clear. While in the commercial sector competitive conditions dictate the possible responses of private firms, this is not so in the health sector. The key determinant of 'restructuring' in the NHS is not just the funds made available by central government, but also government policies as to how those funds are to be spent. The precise measures adopted, and their timing and strength, will invariably reflect issues such as the broad political strategy of the government, their view on the likely gains and costs of antagonising specific social groupings, and short-term political expediency, rather than being simply responses to external events or to the requirements of capital.

Transition models: disorganised capitalism, post-Fordism, and the welfare state

Gough saw accounts of restructuring as substantially determined by the requirements of capital, which exposed his analysis to the charge of neglecting the processes whereby restructuring in the welfare state is managed politically. Remedying this neglect has occupied a number of commentators. Jessop *et al.*'s analysis of Thatcherism is one attempt to deal with this problem (see Jessop *et al.* 1987, 1988, 1990). The government's policies are interpreted as the pursuit of a 'two-nation' politics of inequality, designed to consolidate the government's core support from specific places and social classes. This interpretation is considered in more depth in Chapter 3, and there are clearly ways in which such an account is applicable to the NHS (see, for example, Chapters 4 and 7). Other accounts draw upon attempts to theorise the broader changes taking place in the world economy. Two prominent examples in this context are the notion of a transition from 'organised' to 'disorganised' capitalism, and (to which rather more attention will be given here) the notion of a transition from a Fordist regime of accumulation to a 'post-Fordist' one. Lash and Urry (1987, p. 231) argued that capitalism is undergoing a transition from an 'organised' to a 'disorganised' phase. In their opinion this has correlates for the welfare state; as capitalism moves through this transition, centralised, bureaucratic modes of service delivery will be replaced with localised, variegated modes of provision – a mixed economy of welfare. Although perhaps descriptively accurate, one might question the ways in which links are established between the macroscale changes considered by those authors and the microlevel changes in institutional structures of, for instance, welfare states. Furthermore, whether capitalism is in fact becoming more disorganised is perhaps debatable.

Another attempt to engage with this issue is to draw upon the regulationist school, which suggests that capitalism is currently in a transitional phase from Fordism to post-Fordism, and that the welfare state is changing in complex ways associated with this. In brief, Fordist economies are based on the mass production of standardised goods and services; production is organised on hierarchical lines; and collective bargaining agreements set wages at levels that maintain high levels of consumption. Post-Fordism, in contrast, is characterised by flexible specialisation, where what is important is the ability to switch product lines or to differentiate basic products according to customer demands. Associated with this are flexibilities in labour markets and (potentially) a more flexible form of state intervention in the economy.

Jessop (1989, 1991a, 1991b, 1993) suggests that there are four principal levels at which the term Fordism has been applied: as a labour process, as a stable mode of economic growth, as a mode of social regulation, and as a mode of what he terms 'societalisation'. As a *labour process*, Fordism implies the mass production of standardised products on assembly lines using semi-skilled labour. As a *mode of economic growth*, Fordism refers classically to a virtuous circle of growth based on mass production, rising productivity based on scale economies, rising incomes linked to productivity, increased mass demand underpinned by rising real wages, increased profits based on full utilisation of capacity, and increased investment in improved mass production equipment and techniques. As a *mode of social and economic regulation* Fordism entails separation of ownership and control in large corporations, union recognition and collective bargaining, wages indexed to productivity growth and retail price inflation, and monetary policies orientated to securing effective aggregate demand. Finally, as a *pattern of societalisation*, Fordism involves the consumption of standardised mass commodities in nuclear family households and provision of standardised, collective goods and services by a bureaucratic state. This is clearly linked to the rise of Keynesianism and to a universalist welfare state, but neither is essential for the growth of Fordism.

Though there is little evidence to date of the application of such analyses to the NHS, some commentaries on local government have identified parallels between the Fordist state and the Fordist era. Thus Hoggett (1987, 1991) suggested that mass production of standardised products was common to both the Fordist local state and Fordist production, as were hierarchical systems of management and formalised, collective systems of wage determination. Likewise Murray (1991, p. 22) argues that the form of twentieth-century administration was that of mass production. Designs were standardised to basic models with common components and standard processes of construction, and provision was on a large scale; one might certainly describe postwar hospital policy in this way. But merely drawing parallels between Fordist production in the private sector and the massification of public services, or parallels between the labour process in each sector, does not tell us very much about why that correspondence exists (Duncan *et al.*, 1993), nor does it help us to interpret present events and predict likely future ones.

Stoker (1989, p. 141) lays greater emphasis on political strategies and tactics. He regards the Conservatives' policies towards the public sector as efforts to transform the 'production process, the pattern of consumption and the arrangements for political management' in ways compatible with the enterprise culture, a two-tier welfare structure and the flexible economic structures associated with the transition towards flexible accumulation. Moves to expand the private sector's role in acute health care (Chapter 7) and to open up opportunities for entrepreneurial activities within the NHS (Chapter 8) certainly accord with this interpretation. However he emphasises terms such as flexible accumulation, social polarisation and information technology – rather than the wider ensemble of social relations held to constitute a mode of social regulation. While describing numerous empirical trends in local governance, he does not really establish the ways in which these are connected to the transition to post-Fordism. By extension, we could say that there are certain parallels between the organisation of the NHS and Fordism, but there are also dissimilarities: the labour process in the NHS, especially the labour of clinicians, was never fully under managerial control along classical Fordist lines.

The most useful elements of the regulationist approach for the analysis of the welfare state seem to be the insistence that – for example – the 'crisis' of the welfare state is an example of the difficulties encountered in a transition from a Fordist to a post-Fordist regime of accumulation (rather then being merely a fiscal difficulty); in other words the Keynesian welfare state of the Fordist era is said to be ultimately *incompatible* with the emerging regime of flexible accumulation. This allows Jessop to distinguish an analysis of conservatism based on regulationist concepts from his earlier work, which sometimes presented Thatcherism purely as a divisive 'two-nation' politics of inequality. He insists that such a one-dimensional approach over-simplifies a strong case. Instead he has recently reinterpreted Thatcherism as a neo-liberal variant of a state strategy designed to secure a stable mode of social regulation consistent with post-Fordism. The value of regulationist concepts, then, and of the distinction between Fordism and Post-Fordism, is that they conceive of state intervention as part of an ensemble of regulatory practices and structures that are integral to securing conditions for a particular regime of accumulation. Other concepts, for example Fordism as a labour process or as a mode of economic growth, however, seem less directly relevant to the welfare state.

Jessop identifies an emerging 'Schumpeterian workfare state' (SWS), which he regards as potentially providing the 'best possible political shell' for post-Fordism (Jessop, 1993, p. 7). The defining feature of the SWS is the promotion of the skill base of a nation as a source of innovation and competitive advantage (hence 'Schumpeterian'), and the linking of social policy – indeed its subordination – to economic criteria, notably to the demands of 'labour market flexibility and structural competitiveness' (hence 'workfare') (Jessop, 1993, p. 18). One 'particularly noteworthy discursive shift' in the transition to a SWS is the 'demotion of concern with "productivity" and "planning" and the emphasis now placed on the need for "flexibility" and "entrepreneurialism"' (1993, p. 19). In a neoliberal variant of the SWS, the consequence is a market-led transition to a new regime, involving the extension of privatisation and the imposition of commercial criteria on the residual public sector of the economy (1993, p. 29). Clearly such a discursive shift is highly relevant to the recent changes in the British health services, when one considers the internal market and the range of changes aimed at stimulating market-led processes of change within the NHS (see Chapters 3 and 8).

Jessop also refers to the 'hollowing out' of the nation state as part of this wider process. Hollowing out refers to a 'complex triple displacement' of the powers of the nation state upward, downward and outward (1993, p. 10). This comes about as state capacities are transferred to supranational organisations, devolved to the regional or local level within nation states, or assumed by emerging local networks of power, thereby bypassing central states. Jessop also refers to a 'stronger role for the local state' (1993, p. 23) under the SWS, as economic development becomes more and more a matter for interlocality competition involving a range of partners from the business and political communities and as the central state proves unable to pursue programmes sensitive to the needs of particular localities (1993, p. 24). While the declining significance of the regional tier of administration may be relevant, the extent to which local autonomy has genuinely been enhanced within the NHS seems debatable (see Chapter 9).

The superiority of an analysis based on the putative transition from a Fordist to a post-Fordist regime of accumulation is that it portrays state strategies towards welfare not as *ad hoc* responses to economic crises, but as efforts by the state to secure the conditions for a successful transition from one regime to another. The disadvantage is potentially that of determinism: it almost seems irrelevant which government is in power during this transition, since they are in the grip of irresistible system shifts (Rustin, 1989). The cost of locating change in the public sector within this wider structural shift is that 'the whole process become a 'necessary' one, however that 'necessity' is qualified' (Cochrane, 1993, p. 91). Analysis is thus reduced to a process of examining change for signs of correspondences between prior grand theories and empirical trends, which is akin to 'cataloguing butterflies' and is methodologically suspect, because 'every piece of evidence for flexibility is accepted at face value' (ibid.). Furthermore, there is a presumption that the state has both the strategic intelligence to identify a successful accumulation strategy and the capacity to pursue it.

Perhaps, then, the Fordist/post-Fordist dichotomy exaggerates the significance of changes introduced by the post-1979 governments. Perhaps these reflect less a systematic strategy than a pragmatic, tactical approach worked out with some awareness of political costs and benefits. Thus the Conservatives' strategies may have more to do with a thinly disguised attack on collectivism than with a carefully thought out accumulation strategy. Krieger (1986, 1987) suggests that Marxist political economy gives insufficient autonomy to the state, representing the state as an automaton, merely responding to external demands or circumstances. This, he argues, fails to capture something emphasised by numerous commentators – that the state does indeed have some autonomy, which permits it to be used in a proactive way to pursue a political agenda (Mann, 1984). Marxist analysts are right to emphasise the external pressures on the state that may force change, but the ground for the implementation of policies that serve capital's needs has to be established politically. In contrast Krieger claims that in certain circumstances the state can obtain a substantial degree of 'decisional autonomy' (Krieger, 1987): within the parameters imposed by economic circumstances, the state has some scope to establish its own vision of how welfare services (for example) shall be run, rather than merely making programmed responses to constraints. In Britain, I shall argue, the Thatcher governments used this autonomy to impose a radically new conception of what a national health service should consist of and, particularly, how it should be delivered. In this vision the top-down, bureaucratic, producer-dominated and centralised models of service delivery were to be replaced by localised, entrepreneurial and ostensibly consumer-driven forms of service delivery. The reforms to health care provision are important not just because of their material and practical consequences but because of their ideological impact as part of a continuing war of position concerning economic management, the role of the state, citizenship rights and so on. From this perspective, what has been happening to the welfare state is part of a wider deintegrative political strategy in which the government has consciously sought to erode services that people experience collectively, attempting instead to persuade the electorate to consider options in terms of their own, immediate self-interest.

Concluding comments

These wider debates are essential preliminaries to a discussion of the specifics of the changes introduced and ways of categorising them. While it is oversimplistic to see changes in the British health services as the result of changing patterns of need or technical imperatives, it is equally oversimplistic to see them as a consequence of the encounter of the welfare state with global economic crises, as the state merely dancing to the tune of capital, or as the result of the impress of 'Thatcherism' on the NHS. Policies are not amenable to such reductionism, as is emphasised by the next chapter, which stresses the motivations for a whole range of Conservative policies. This contrast in explanatory accounts leads to rather different views of key developments such as the White Paper: from one perspective it was simply a technical measure on which there happened to be a measure of agreement; from another it was an explicitly ideological challenge to what had become the status quo of welfare provision and a cornerstone of the welfare state, and was part of a far wider political project.

Although change in health care cannot be explained in terms of the operation of a simple or single explanatory principle, it is easier to say what is to be avoided than precisely what is to be done. Thus Marxists are still pursuing the theoretical Holy Grail of an anti- or non-functionalist version of a theory of the state. This is exceptionally difficult with regard to welfare policy since almost any policy can be interpreted as serving capital's needs in some way or as a victory for working-class pressure. But such a simplistic account barely does justice to the complexity of state power and to what is increasingly seen as the autonomous power of the state (Mann, 1984). The strength of Marxist ideas lies in their emphasis on political economy – on the interconnections between external changes in the global economy, their national impact on political and economic structures, and the ways in which nation-states attempt to deal with those changes. The weakness is that there is no automatic and functional correspondence between the policies produced and the needs of capital (Hindess, 1987).

This raises a second point about the limitations of grand theorising, which is the necessity to specify precisely at what level theoretical statements can be expected to be valid (Jessop, 1982; Sayer, 1984). Much of this book analyses the dynamics of national policy formulation, so it will be concerned with the interplay between central government, various interest groups within the NHS, and electoral and external pressures. The explanatory focus is necessarily on the changing politics of conservatism and the ability of the Conservative government to use parliamentary power to advance its agenda and alter the terms of the health care policy debate. Pluralist approaches are rejected as inappropriate here, as are corporatist accounts of the state, not least because the medical profession – conventionally taken to be a group with a privileged place at the policy table, and therefore classically representative of corporatism – has by and large been squeezed out by the government's determination to reshape the NHS. However the analysis also pays attention to the details and more local impacts of policy, especially when discussing the geographical implications of the various initiatives examined here. It emphasises not only changes internal to the NHS, but also changes that are external to it, notably the expansion of scope for the private sector, as well as the gradual encroachment of commercialism into the NHS. Even if similarities can be observed with comparable states, the way these changes work out is a contingent matter.

It is vital to be aware of the uneven impact of the changes described herein. Despite the welfare state's contribution to the reduction of social divisions and inequalities, in practice the welfare state often stands accused of preserving and exploiting social division (Ginsburg, 1992). Welfare state policies are often predicated on a particular gender division of labour (for example community care programmes –

Chapter 5), while selective personnel and managerial policies have been used, it can be argued, to divide and rule the NHS workforce, thus limiting its capacity to resist change (Chapter 6). It could also be claimed (Chapters 3 and 4) that some of the driving forces behind the NHS reforms were pressures from backbench MPs from the 'core' areas of the Conservative party's support for a system of resource allocation that would, in the guise of rationality, accelerate the process of redistribution of funds towards their constituencies. There are many other examples. The point is that change has both costs and benefits, and the distribution of those costs and benefits requires close examination. Where those benefits accrue, and where those costs fall, is determined by political strategies and tactics. Hence we turn now to an overview of Thatcherism and its impacts on Conservative health care policies since 1979.

3

Conservatism, Health Policy and Health Care Policy: From the Royal Commission to the White Paper

The Conservative party's attitude towards the NHS has always been somewhat ambiguous. For example it voted against the third reading of the NHS bill in 1946, a gesture usually interpreted as indicating opposition to the principle of a bill, rather than to its technical limitations (see Foot, 1975). Conservative chancellors during the 1950s, a similar period of electoral ascendancy, attempted to challenge the concept of a state-funded and publicly provided NHS (Lowe, 1989; see also Pimlott, 1989). On the other hand the Conservatives introduced the Hospital Plan of 1962 (MoH, 1962a), the largest single injection of new capital investment into the service. Given the public attachment to and political support for the NHS, attempts to alter its basic structure – to date – have not proved feasible. While Conservative ideologues have consistently probed the limits to state funding of health care, the government's policies towards the welfare state have focused more sharply on social security and housing than on health; the distinction between parts of the welfare state seen to be 'deserving' of support and those 'undeserving' seems relevant here. Once radical options from the left (such as implementing the preventive programmes proposed by the Black Report – DHSS, 1980a) or right (insurance-based schemes) were ruled out, the government's scope for manoeuvre was going to be greatly circumscribed.

This chapter charts the ways in which the government pursued its agenda within such constraints, outlines principal policy themes and attempts to relate them to interpretations advanced for the nature and changing character of Conservative politics during the 1980s. The chapter shows the roots of present policies and tries to analyse continuities and discontinuities with previous practice. Policies towards health and health care issues can be shown to have a greater or lesser degree of coherence. Some reflect political instinct and opportunism, while others are clearly ideological and even irrational, drawing, as do any ideological frameworks, on reservoirs of popular opinions or prejudices that have some limited grounding in everyday experience.

There are two principal strands to health and health care policy: those that emphasise the limits to what is considered justifiable state intervention, and those that, accepting these limits, determine the ways in which services shall be provided within that framework. Considerable effort has been invested, since 1979, in an ideological strategy to (re)define health policy. This has sought to convey the message that, firstly, health and health care is the responsibility of individuals, families, and 'communities', that these 'informal' sources of care and of the prevention of disease should be promoted, and that the state should not be the first port of call for those in need; and secondly, that some of the problems of the British health care system reflect the inadequate contribution made by the 'private' or 'commercial' health sectors, particularly in comparison with other European states.

Secondly, health care policy discussion has centred on the perceived inefficiencies of state-funded and state-provided services, and so has focused on the importance of internal reforms of the way the health service is run. This has drawn on critiques of bureaucracy, attacks on the apparent lack of managerial direction in the service, criticisms of the power of professional interest groups and evidence of considerable variation in the 'performance' of health authorities. These are not particularly novel criticisms, but the government's responses to them reveal much about continuities and discontinuities between the Thatcher and Major governments and their predecessors.

The chapter therefore commences with an examination of some accounts of Conservative policies and politics since 1979, focusing in particular on debates on the notion of 'Thatcherism', and on how these might affect health policy. It then examines the ways in which the legitimate scope of health policy has been redefined, before looking at the dominant features of the new agenda set for the health service during the 1980s. It proceeds to examine the style and content of the NHS review before presenting an interpretation of the foregoing in the light of various debates about the nature of contemporary Conservative politics. If the character of state intervention in health care *has* been decisively transformed, this transformation is not entirely reducible to the impact of 'Thatcherism' on the health policy arena;

it also results from the complex interplay of technical developments in health care delivery, wider political and economic influences on the organisation of society, and various elements of pragmatism and opportunism.

Thatcherism, Conservatism and health care policy

Thatcherism is used here as shorthand for the political strategies and tactics of the Conservative governments since 1979. The discontinuities between the Thatcher and Major administrations in health care policy are regarded as insignificant. Thatcherism is a complex entity that defies reductionist, one-dimensional explanations. It combines elements of economic liberalism, authoritarianism, and populism.

Drawing inspiration from Hayek and Friedman, a key challenge is to roll back the frontiers of state intervention and promote the free market and the associated virtues of independence, property ownership and entrepreneurship. Where possible and feasible, therefore, state-run services have been privatised; where this has not been politically possible, competition – the 'sanitising discipline of the trusty market' (Pollitt, 1986) – has been relied upon to guarantee the efficiency of the public sector. However a fully neoliberal strategy would have established a connection between the labour-market position of individuals and health insurance, and/or made the financing of health care dependent upon the success of the local economy. Neither of these happened; what Jessop (1993) describes as the Schumpeterian workfare state was in *some* respects still-born. But on a discursive level the need for services to become more businesslike and entrepreneurial are crucial features of the Thatcher years (Chapter 8).

The authoritarian side of Thatcherism is evident in the belief that *only* a strong state can guarantee the freedom, and therefore the efficiency, of the economy (Gamble, 1988). The restoration of market control requires a strong state that can protect the national interest against challenges from abroad while limiting the ability of organised interest groups to interfere with the market order. This has been accompanied by a tendency to see democracy as something that undermines authority and weakens the power of the central state. Consequently, in addition to anti-democratic measures such as the abolition of the metropolitan counties, there has been a profound centralisation of authority: 'the Thatcher government's own diagnosis of the crisis of state authority constantly impelled it towards intervention' (Gamble, 1988, p. 231). Examples of this centralisation are all too evident and seem to conflict with the apparent determination to secure maximum decentralisation and local accountability which has been a feature of policy since 1979. In this sense the free economy is seen to require a strong central authority (Chapter 9).

A third element of Thatcherism has been its strongly populist strand. Drawing on simple nostrums (for example the virtues of competition versus the vices of public provision) and traditional totems (the family, the community, the nation) the government has waged an ideological campaign. This seems to have been designed to convince the electorate that the state should not be the first port of call and that individuals, families and communities must provide for themselves. Rhetorically, public provision is equated, by some Conservatives, with dependence; private provision, in contrast, is equated with independence and self-reliance (Chapter 7). Furthermore, individual responsibility has the moral virtue of removing part of the burden on the state. Even those unable to provide for themselves can still care, and the ideological notion of 'community' has been wielded to a considerable degree by a government seeking low-cost alternatives to state provision (Chapter 5).

These elements of political strategy do not operate uniformly across the nation. For Jessop *et al.* (1988) Thatcherism is seen as a two-nation politics of inequality, in which deliberate attempts are made to promote the interests of those seen as 'core' groups of supporters while marginalising those unlikely to fall within that group. Broadly this means prioritising the interests of the 'productive' members of society (the 'first nation') while at best paying lip service to those groups regarded as being 'unproductive' or 'parasitic' (the 'second nation'). Hence Thatcherism is viewed in terms of a series of oppositions – public/private, employed/unemployed, owner-occupier/tenant, north/south, manufacturing/services (Jessop *et al.*, 1988; Gamble, 1988). Elements of this view are certainly relevant. Arguably those with access to private care are more likely to support the Conservatives, while those without, and dependent on public services, are not. The policies pursued towards staff groups in the NHS could be characterised as a two-nations strategy, with a heavy emphasis on 'front-line' staff and a competitive tendering policy that has had most adverse effects on ancillary workers (Chapter 6). If there is some evidence that post-1979 policies have exacerbated 'divisions of welfare' (Ginsburg, 1992), the extent to which the whole range of health care policies pursued since 1979 could be subsumed under this two-nation rubric is highly debatable. However it is undeniable that Thatcherism relied on electoral support from, and the continued economic success of, South East England (Jessop *et al.*, 1990, p. 92), so it is not surprising that some of their policies seemed deliberately designed to prioritise the interests of Conservative voters in constituencies there. These arguments echo those of Krieger (1986, 1987) who suggests that the overwhelming electoral advantage of the Conservatives gave them a substantial degree of 'decisional autonomy', permitting them to pursue policies unbeholden to anything other than their own electoral self-interest. This view regards Thatcherism as a purely political strategy and not – contra Jessop *et al.* – one designed to advance a particular accumulation strategy.

These arguments about Thatcherism should not be regarded as an interpretative template. The great danger in relying on oversimplified accounts of Thatcherism is that of presenting it as a unified political force, with its own internally consistent logic and externally consistent statecraft. Arguably there is not one 'Thatcherite' health policy or health care policy but several, and pragmatic, tactical considerations may deserve greater weight than they would be accorded by such simplified commentaries. There were also divisions within the government with some MPs encouraging an acceleration of the processes of reform and privatisation while others urged caution and a more tactical approach. Even if propositions about Thatcherism represent an advance on arguments about the capitalist state in general, they have still to be used with caution as interpretative frameworks. Finally, it is not obvious that, in the domestic policy arena at least, there is much difference of substance in the policies pursued by the governments led by John Major. Although NHS resources have certainly grown more rapidly in the early 1990s, some of this reflects the considerable costs of implementing the reforms, of minimising the transitional costs associated with market-led restructuring, and of the inevitable pre-election boost to public spending. Although Major has attempted to distance himself from the cruder two-nation rhetoric of his predecessor, the roots of current policies are firmly grounded in the Thatcher era, and need to be interpreted as such.

Redefining the scope of health policy

Individuals, health inequalities and health promotion

The question of where to draw the line between individual and collective responsibility for health is one on which the divisions between the Conservatives and their predecessors are in some cases very clear but in others rather more blurred. While Labour's white paper (DHSS, 1977b) suggested that prevention and health were 'everybody's business', it did not call for the wider programmes of public expenditure or audit of the health implications of all public policies characteristic of more recent proposals for a revived public health movement. The Royal Commission (1979, Chapter 5) regarded preventive services as being largely those operated by the NHS itself – screening in particular, but also health education; however it was silent on whether a broader programme of collective action might help prevent ill health. The definition of and the explanations adopted for health inequalities very much reflect political ideology (Carr–Hill, 1987), so debate has been polarised between materialist and individualist explanations. The Conservative government sternly rejected the materialist explanations of the Black Report (one health minister dismissed the report's explanations as 'Marxist' – Townsend and Davidson, 1982) in favour of an individualist approach in which people make their own health choices. But such choices are made in a context structured heavily by government decisions (Smith and Jacobson, 1991). Hence remarks from government ministers that suggest that lifestyles and diets are the root cause of health problems, often relying on crude regional stereotypes, are undoubtedly over-simplifying a complicated case, even though there are important variations in the 'healthiness' of diets according to national survey data (Cox *et al.*, 1987). The limited public debate and the suppression, or limited circulation, of data on health inequalities (Marmot and McDowell, 1986; Townsend, Phillimore and Beattie, 1988) amply illustrate the government's sensitivity on these matters. Even where the government did seek to encourage prevention (such as the incentives for GPs to carry out more preventive work, introduced in 1987 – Secretary of State for Social Services, 1987), their initiative was marred by being connected to proposals to introduce charges for dental check-ups and eye examinations.

Even if the government was correct in its apparent rejection of the importance of social class and social inequality as determinants of health status, its preferred approach appears to ignore the influence of political decisions and a range of other public programmes on people's experiences of health. The debates about the social impacts of unemployment are a good example here. Although these ultimately said more about the limitations of particular research strategies than the issues at stake (Bartley, 1992), it hardly seems contentious to suggest that mass, long-term unemployment would have considerable effects on both material well-being and psychological welfare. A hidden cost of the government's economic policies is therefore the impact on health service budgets of the effects of unemployment and resultant poverty on health standards. However the government persistently denied that any such connection existed, a disavowal extending to the lack of reference to poverty and the limited references to social influences on health status in the *Health of the Nation* white paper (Secretary of State for Health, 1992), which was criticised for its lack of reference to social inequality and social structure.[1] It referred coyly to 'variations' rather than inequalities, and suggested that the causes of such 'variations' were complex and not easily analysed. This analytical circumspection was not matched by, for example, the government's dogmatic insistence on the rectitude of its market-based reforms of the entire health service and its refusal to pilot them in any form. Furthermore, the WHO had, at the same time, put attacking health inequalities at the top of its agenda, but the *Health of the Nation* largely ignored the WHO's recommendations. There is also a more general point about the government's refusal to acknowledge the effects on health and the health services of decisions taken in other areas of public policy. Thus Patrick Jenkin, speaking in 1980 after social services budgets had been curtailed, suggested that neither this nor the rapid increase in unemployment at the time would have measurable effects on the health service (Social Services Committee, 1980a, pp. 99–100).

Thus the government's approach to health education and prevention has been a limited and partial one. It has persistently emphasised that healthy lifestyles are largely a matter of choice, rather than discussing constraint. In relation to health education, the reconstitution of the Health Education Council as the Health Education Authority (HEA) was widely seen as an attempt to lead that particular horse to drink from a pool more acceptable to the government – in particular, to neutralise its campaigning voice (Beattie, 1991). There have also been suggestions that the moral stance associated with conservatism and in particular with Margaret Thatcher, led the HEA to soften and arguably obscure the message of its AIDS campaigning, in sharp contrast with states elsewhere in Europe.

Families and communities: back to the future?

The vital question here is how far the government has sought to transfer greater burdens of health care delivery to the family, or what some regard as the mythical 'community'. Here Conservatives have drawn on New Right commentaries, which have asserted that the pre-NHS system actually served everybody well (for example Green, 1985) and that, if left to themselves, communities and families could do equally well today. There are two elements to this: encouraging individuals to provide for themselves through formal health services, for example by taking out private insurance; and encouraging 'families' and 'communities' to take on a greater part of informal caring.

There has been consistent encouragement of individuals taking responsibility for themselves via support for private medical treatment, and the government have asserted that this relieves the NHS of some of its burden and represents a valuable addition to the state's necessarily limited funds. In practice, though, government support for the private sector has rarely gone further than limited deregulation (Chapter 7). The government has defended its support for private health care on the grounds of freedom of choice, though again presumably individuals do not make choices without consideration of whether or not the state can provide for them, so such choices are not independent of government decisions about the scale of funding for the NHS.

The government's policies on community care appear to have been underpinned by a view that informal, unpaid care by relatives should be the first port of call and is a duty – indeed a moral obligation – of families. The assumption that it is primarily women who will be providing that care – unpaid – does not divide the Conservative Party from the opposition (indeed unpaid informal care was central to the Beveridge Report). Thatcher explicitly opposed state intervention in this sphere since:

> we know the immense sacrifices which people will make for the care of their own near and dear . . . and the immense 'part which voluntary effort even outside the confines of the family has played in these fields. Once you give people the idea that all this can be done by the state . . . then you will begin to deprive human beings of one of the essential ingredients of humanity – personal moral responsibility (quoted in McDowell, 1989, p. 180).

This explicit critique of the state as sapping moral fibre stresses the deleterious effects of state intervention. Subsequent policy has clearly affirmed the importance of informal care:

> the primary sources of care for elderly people are informal and voluntary. . . . It is the role of public authorities to sustain and where necessary develop – but never to displace – such support and care. Care *in* the community must increasingly mean care *by* the community (DHSS, 1981c, p. 3).

The problem has been that policies based on care by the community are only cost-effective if they do not put a financial value on the contribution of the carer. The unacknowledged contribution of informal carers requires support if it is to be maximised; it cannot be presumed that it is a resource, waiting to be called upon (Chapter 5).

The notion of active citizenship is also relevant to these debates. It extends the notion of family responsibility: as well as caring for their immediate family, individuals have a wider responsibility for events in their immediate locality or community. But the question is whether the policy of active citizenship is one of 'coherence or convenience' (Kearns, 1992, p. 25). Arguably it is a smokescreen for the anti-greed backlash that the government suffered especially in the late 1980s, a backlash that required a move towards an apparently more 'caring' version of conservatism than the strident Victorian values of Thatcherism. The strategy required a certain degree of moral coercion, with individuals being pressed to put something back into the community as the moral price for their material well-being. This was at odds with the wider neoliberal aims of the Thatcherite project, since active citizenship was not a matter of choice but of necessity. This diagnosis applies strongly to the health sector, where charitable appeals have been predicated on the notion that the state's funds are limited, and that therefore community support is required – indeed is essential if desirable service developments are to proceed. Finally, the capacities of communities either to care or actively to support their local health services is likely to be greatly differentiated (see Chapters 5 and 8). The assumption that women are likely to be available to assume the burden of informal care is contradicted by economic realities that force many into paid employment (McDowell, 1989).

Confronting corporate power

Health care is very big business and so is the production and prevention of ill health. Here, governments since 1979 have refused to pursue policies that might in some ways promote better health and/or reduce costs to the NHS. A range of policies could in principle be regarded as being concerned with health in its widest sense – most obviously housing legislation, pollution controls, and sanitation, but also regulation of the food, alcohol and tobacco industries (P. Taylor, 1984), road safety (Whitelegg, 1987) and town planning. These all affect health in one way or another, and state policies in one sphere can contradict those in another. Yet the government has consistently increased cigarette taxation by less than the rate of inflation, despite the established evidence about the role of smoking in causing ill health. Indeed tobacco advertising was the subject of a dispute between the government and the European Community, with the British government refusing to accept the EC's directives on tobacco advertising. Virginia Bottomley took up the anti-European cudgel in suggesting that such controls represented 'unnecessary interference from Brussels'. She also insisted that voluntary controls were adequate, that a ban on such advertising would infringe commercial freedom of speech, and that the tobacco industry contributed more to the Exchequer than the costs of related illness to the NHS.[2] Yet the Public Accounts Committee (1989) had previously pointed out the limitations of this compartmentalised policy-making, stressing that decisions made by other government departments 'profoundly influence' the underlying causes of (in that particular case) heart disease. Mrs Bottomley's comment highlighted the fact that, welcome as *Health of the Nation* was, the government lacked a comprehensive health strategy.

The government's wider policies of deregulation may also have hidden effects on the need for health care through their impacts on occupational health and on safety at work. Promotion of the growth of small businesses was a crucial element in the Conservatives' political strategies, and efforts were made to limit the extent of regulation of such businesses (DE, 1986). The abolition of nutritional standards for school meals in 1982, while justified by the government in terms of the promotion of competitive tendering, may likewise have long-term consequences for health. More generally still, the Black Report's recommendations, which would have involved concerted action on schemes designed to promote better health in selected localities, were unceremoniously rejected by the government on the ground that the public expenditure commitment involved was 'unrealistic in the present or any foreseeable economic circumstances' (Patrick Jenkin, foreword to DHSS, 1980a; but compare the sums involved – up to £2 bn – with the amounts given away in tax cuts or raised in privatisations during the 1980s). A similar reaction attended the Social Services Committee's report on perinatal and neonatal mortality (Social Services Committee, 1980b).

The point of this section has been to document the extent to which the government regards health care provision as the responsibility of individuals and families, and the extent to which it has been prepared to eschew policies that would bring it into conflict with the interests of private capital. In its refusal to countenance greater public expenditure the government was steering by its monetarist lights. Its refusal to acknowledge the concept of inequality was not surprising from a government for whom the pursuit of egalitarianism was over. By emphasising individual and family responsibility, the government sought to relieve the state of some of its burden, though in doing so it ignored the constraints that inhibited individuals' ability to lead healthy lives. It is difficult to discern anything other than a vague anti-interventionist strategy here, coupled with a strongly individualist philosophy and a desire to limit claims on the state. However, in constructing an alternative, the Conservative governments have clearly been limited in their scope for manoeuvre, as the limited concessions to the private sector show, and as is clear from the inconsistencies of the 'active citizenship' strategy. These points relate to the strength of support for the NHS and therefore the difficulties presented to the government in challenging it. In consequence the government was forced to take a rather less direct line on health *care* policy – and the emphasis is deliberate. If a greater degree of privatisation was to prove impossible, then the way forward had to lie in reforms internal to the service.

Setting a new agenda for the health service

Four themes can be identified in relation to the welfare policies pursued since 1979: the critique of bureaucracy and the belief in the inherent inefficiency of the public sector; the attacks on union power; emphases on value for money; and the attempts to disengage the state from (at least some of) its responsibilities for welfare provision, via emphases on the market, the family and the community as providers of care. By any standards, events in the NHS represent an attempt radically to alter the way the service is produced and delivered to patients. Rather than seeing changes as being determined solely by the increased complexity of the service and the growing sophistication of health care (a kind of technological determinism in social policy), I interpret the reforms in relation to interpretations of Thatcherism and conservatism. I seek, in particular, to trace the antecedents of recent policies, and the ways in which national policies were foreshadowed by individual, *ad hoc* initiatives, and the connections between these and interpretations of Thatcherism.

Disengaging the state: alternative sources of funding

While the Royal Commission (1979, chapter 21) stated firmly that direct taxation was likely to be the principal source of finance for the NHS, within months of taking office the government introduced legislation aimed both at expanding the scope for private health care (allowing consultants to do more private practice; weakening controls on private hospital development) and facilitating the raising of funds by health authorities. These measures were among its first legislation, indexing the importance it attached to strengthening the private sector (see Chapter 7). More symbolically, however, the 1980 Health Services Act permitted health authorities to raise money from voluntary sources. Patrick Jenkin insisted that this power:

> no more undermines the principle of a NHS free at the point of use than does [the acceptance of] free gifts. . . . If a small local hospital is threatened with closure because resources are needed to finance the commissioning of a modern new hospital . . . is it unreasonable that the health authority could indicate that, if voluntary funds were forthcoming to meet the whole or part of the cost of keeping that small hospital open, it would be happy to make an arrangement to do just that?[3]

Interestingly this proposal anticipated the later introduction of income generation schemes in its emphasis on the expansion of non-state sources of finance and provision and on the role of the community in preserving its own services. As other Conservative MPs argued, allowing health authorities to raise money themselves 'stimulated community involvement and interest in the health service', which was ironic given that the 1982 reorganisation and subsequent reforms of the NHS reduced local government nominations to authorities. Similarly Dr Brian Mawhinney suggested that resources might be generated for the NHS by 'introducing private beds at NHS cottage hospitals, so that these establishments can be preserved'.[4] In the event health authorities were indeed permitted to reintroduce paybeds, while the growth of charitable appeals in the health service was dramatic (Chapters 7 and 8).

In practical terms the impact of these statements was limited; the public outcry, in 1982, over the leaked CPRS report warned the government off that particular track. The report had examined various possibilities for saving public expenditure, including replacing the NHS with an insurance-based system. There are contradictory accounts of the discussions of the report in cabinet. Thatcher claimed to have been 'horrified' (1993, pp. 276–7) by the report, but according to Young (1989, pp. 300–1) she 'clung on to it [the report] until . . . the majority of ministers had told her she had made a terrible blunder'. Gilmour (1992, p. 151) notes that the prime minister was 'forced reluctantly to retreat' and dissociate herself from the proposals. This extracted her famous pledge that the NHS was 'safe with us'. However, at least some Conservative MPs felt that the 1983 election 'could, and should . . . have been won without that pledge' (Bow Group, 1983) because of the favourable electoral climate. Thatcher's pledge did not prevent the far right putting forward proposals to introduce or increase charges for NHS services, though this was not unopposed; and prescription charges were steadily increased (Chapter 1).

Other charges were also introduced, notwithstanding (sometimes) considerable opposition. Thus regulations for charging overseas visitors – those 'not normally resident' in Britain – for use of the health service came into effect in 1982 (see Gordon, 1983), despite clear warnings as to the discriminatory potential of the legislation in exposing non-white British citizens to challenges to their entitlements, and despite the evidence that collecting the sums due generated considerable administrative costs.[5] Free NHS spectacles were withdrawn from all but children and those statutorily regarded as poor in the Health and Social Security Act of 1983. A proposal to introduce charges for eye tests, included in the 1980 Health Services Bill, was withdrawn because of the opposition to it, and in debates on the Health and Social Security Bill in January 1984 the government declared that it would retain free eye testing. In short, there was continued 'market testing' of market-oriented proposals for change.

Perhaps the most controversial example of this was the 1988 Health and Medicines Act, which abolished free dental and eye checkups. This was presented as a measure designed to raise additional finance for the NHS, which would enable new developments to take place (not a new argument: the 1962 Hospital Plan – MoH, 1962a – was only launched following a major rise in prescription charges). Thus Tony Newton argued that against a background of increased expenditure on the family practitioner services, and because *Promoting Better Health* (Secretary of State for Social Services, 1987) would require 'sizeable additional resources':

> it was reasonable to secure some of the additional resources going into primary care by asking those who can afford it to meet something more of the overall cost of their health care.[6]

While charges were introduced for examinations, charges for non-routine treatment would be proportionately increased, which would 'set the signals much more clearly in favour of those who attend a dentists regularly' and was therefore an incentive to preventive medicine. The government's view was clearly that competitive pressures would minimise the cost of eye tests, and would therefore not act as a deterrent, while it seemed legitimate to recover charges from those it felt were able to afford them. Thus David Heathcote-Amory suggested that 'people should be able to retain more of their own money but *the other side of the coin is that we should expect those people to provide more* of the health care and security of themselves and their families'.[7] Indeed the prime minister declared that many people would feel that 'it was quite wrong if they were not allowed to pay the small sums [for eye tests] *which they can well afford,* to enable *substantial developments* in the NHS to take place'.[8] The material gains of the 1980s had, it was claimed, begun to create a climate in which more of the burden of financing health care could be passed on to those consuming it, while the government was also suggesting that the sums raised from charges would be substantial. The latter was clearly a matter of political priority, however, because any sums raised in charges paled in comparison with the tax cuts of several individual budgets during the 1980s.

The deterrence effect of charges was criticised by opponents: Labour's spokesman on health, Robin Cook, pointed out that 'it would be a curious market which found its equilibrium at the point at which all demand was met'.[9] He also drew attention to the medical and professional advice that had suggested that these charges would deter frequent consultation and lead to illnesses going undiagnosed. Numerous Conservative backbenchers insisted they would not support the government (a former health minister, Barney Hayhoe, argued that the charges were 'superficial and peripheral' to the NHS's problems)[10] – while others stated they would vote for the bill with reservations about the specific measures. It was reported that aggressive whipping tactics were employed to push this measure through its second reading, and the government also had to overturn a Lords amendment to reject these charges.[11] The discussions on this point show how far the Conservatives were seeking to go in the direction of much greater privatisation of services. While they were undoubtedly keen to transfer more of the cost of testing and treatment onto individuals, legitimating this in terms of rising material standards of prosperity, this was not without substantial backbench opposition; they clearly did not feel confident enough of their parliamentary position after the 1979 election to sustain this issue but once the welfare state was firmly on the agenda post-1987, charging was given some priority.

The search for additional sources of finance did not stop with increasing patient charges. A whole raft of ideas were floated by members whenever the NHS was debated in parliament, including, in addition to hotel charges: a national lottery, a national insurance stamp dedicated to health care, tax relief on private health insurance, joint deals with the private sector, establishing NHS hospitals as charitable trusts, and even privatising one of the London teaching hospitals.[12] Policy changes were presented as natural extensions of existing practice. Thus the national income generation initiative was claimed to be a 'good housekeeping measure intended to encourage health authorities to realise to the full the financial potential of the assets at their disposal. . . . We have never claimed that income generation is any more than that'.[13] In addition, the market for radical options was constantly being tested by Conservative thinktanks and politicians, which actively obtained a hearing for new proposals while allowing the government to distance itself from the more extreme versions of market reform.[14]

To deploy the terminology of debates about citizenship, these changes heralded a move away from rights of entitlement to services and towards rights guaranteed through the market. They are revealing about the government's declared political and social priorities: there are many individuals, on the margins of income support levels, for whom such charges represent a considerable expense. They also indicate a move away from universalism, despite claims to be protecting the NHS as an entity, and in the case of charges for overseas visitors the potential was there for exclusionary policies that discriminated against some British citizens. Furthermore whether such initiatives make sense as health policy is debatable: reductions in numbers taking dental and optical checkups, due to charges, may well store up problems for the future as undetected conditions deteriorate. What they do not indicate is restructuring the NHS along the lines of a 'workfare state' in which access to welfare benefits would depend directly on one's labour market position; for the moment, that still seems to have been ruled off the agenda.

Critiques of bureaucracy and attacks on inefficiencies in the public sector

The Conservatives were elected on a commitment to eliminate bureaucracy and waste in the public sector, and they diagnosed the excessive layers of administration as a burden on the NHS. The Royal Commission had concluded that 'there was general agreement that the structure of the NHS needed slimming' (para 20.33), and proposed that below the RHA level only one management tier should carry operational responsibility for all services and for collaboration with local government (para 20.46). Initially the government proposed the abolition of AHAs in order to decentralise decision taking to the local level. A recommendation of the Royal Commission that was not picked up by the Conservatives was that proposing the integration of health authorities and FPCs. Subsequently, despite a rhetoric of decentralisation, policy has involved a greater degree of central scrutiny and control of health authority decisions.

Patients First (DHSS, 1979a) did not recommend any departure from the then system of consensus management; nor did the Royal Commission. However, an implicit goal of the 1982 reorganisation was an attack on what the government saw as the 'unnecessary proliferation'[15] of administrative posts after the 1974 reorganisation, while the 1982 reorganisation was also accompanied by strict management cost limits for health authorities. It was not until 1983 and publication of the Griffiths Report that the question of management appeared on the political agenda. Commissioned in response to government concern about rising administrative costs, the Griffiths Report soon fastened on management arrangements within the service. The Griffiths Report's emphasis on external scrutiny by appointed individuals was also a departure, in policy-making terms, from the Royal Commission approach. Introducing the report, Norman Fowler stated that the most fundamental problem for the NHS was 'how the health service works, how it gets things done or, sometimes, fails to get things done'.[16] The crucial diagnosis of the report was that, having put in place a system that was to increase the accountability of health authorities, there was no – one below authority level with responsibility for carrying out programmes of action.[17] Fowler insisted that, in contrast with the views of critics, there was no division between general management and consensus management, and that the reservations of doctors about management interference in the allocation of resources could be overcome by the greater involvement of clinicians in management decisions. In short the aim was to institute a more businesslike structure in order both to streamline decision making and to ensure that decisions taken centrally were implemented locally. In opposition, Michael Meacher claimed that, notwithstanding the importance of efficient management, the real issue was the under-funding of the service: 'however good the management, one cannot get a quart out of a pint pot'.[18] The Labour Party was also suspicious of the centralisation of authority presupposed by Griffiths, and of the emphasis in the report on cost-improvement programmes, seen as a euphemism for cuts and a means of promoting privatisation. The idea of a chief executive for the NHS was regarded as a highly problematic concept and the relationships between this person and Parliament proved fraught, at least initially. Furthermore there were fears that the proposals would bypass the decision-making powers of authority members by concentrating power in the hands of chairs and managers. In this sense Griffiths anticipated subsequent changes to authority membership that further limited local representation. It also put in place the cost-improvement programmes that came to take on such importance to resource growth in the NHS from 1983 onwards (Chapter 1). The emphasis of Griffiths on managerial prerogatives – the 'right to manage' was almost a public sector slogan at the time – is probably its most important legacy. If the service could not be privatised, introducing the quasi-commercial disciplines associated with identifiable managers on performance-related pay was the next best thing. Commentators such as Hall (1985; 1988) regard the emphasis on public sector management, performance and efficiency as one of the defining features of the Thatcher years. In various ways, therefore, demands for increased efficiency began to dominate the NHS and general management was identified as a key element of the strategy to achieve savings in this way.

Welfare pluralism and the 'mixed economy'

Welfare has always been plural: the question is, what sort of balance is there between the public and private, collective and individual components of it? Notions of 'welfare pluralism' and a 'mixed economy' of welfare make sense only against the background of particular political and social circumstances. Whatever the merits of the NHS's near-monopoly of health care from 1948, any move towards a mixed economy would not only invite charges of reverting to the 1930s, it would also inevitably involve decisions to prioritise the non-state sector over the state sector. The Conservatives abhorred monopoly – though apparently not in the case of formerly public utilities – and also lack of choice, so a new force had to be given to notions of a plural welfare system.

Although there are approving references to the merits of collaboration with the private sector in various speeches from 1979, *Care in Action*, the planning document setting out the role of the new DHAs post-1982, was probably the first evidence of the ways in which notions of welfare pluralism were to be used. Davies (1987) argues that the role of local health authorities was redefined from being a monopoly provider of care to being essentially coordinative in character. Authorities were explicitly encouraged to take account of existing and likely future private provision of services when developing their plans for the future (DHSS, 1981a). *Care in Action* emphasised the freedoms DHAs had been given by the Conservatives: freedom to raise funds, develop private beds, collaborate with the private and voluntary sectors, and in general to operate in a more flexible manner than hitherto. The introduction of cash planning (as opposed to norms-based planning) put pressure on authorities to maximise the resources available to them by drawing on all available funds in a locality. If government funds did not permit them to provide desired levels of services, additional resources would need to be sought. Davies suggests that this would fundamentally challenge the whole concept of a 'statutorily provided service, administered through health authorities, and accountable through a central health department' (Davies, 1987 p. 303). The ideological significance of this was in the attempt to create an acceptable marketplace and thereby roll back the state.

Ministers therefore spoke approvingly of public-private sector collaboration where this had begun to happen, and began to encourage both the growth of non-state forms of service provision and to exhort public authorities to take account of non-state services in planning the development of their activities. A clear statement of the emerging philosophy of 'welfare pluralism' was a speech by Norman Fowler in 1984:

> that constant pressure [on the NHS] . . . emphasises the importance of a sense of balance and readiness to mobilise all the sources of care in the community. . . . Our job is not simply to develop public sector services. We need to welcome and encourage the kind of family, voluntary and private sector contribution to which I have referred. That is support that the public sector never could, and never should, replace.[19]

However, this eulogy for the informal carer was not accompanied by financial backing for developing more appropriate forms of community care (Chapter 5). Measures taken to expand choice were ill-considered and resulted in uneven growth of services unrelated to needs, the obvious example being the expansion of private residential care for the elderly (Chapters 6 and 7). Furthermore, the financial pressures on health authorities were such that several ran down capacity in geriatric hospitals, preferring to see services developed in the private sector. And although the government eventually accepted the case for much greater priority to be given to community care, this was only after considerable prevarication. Ironically, the government's attempts to expand non-state provision of services have not been entirely welcomed: witness the criticisms from the private sector about the apparently ambiguous attitude of the government (Chapter 7), or about the limits set on payments for patients accommodated in residential-care homes (Chapter 5). Finally, the government's enthusiasm for welfare pluralism has been at the expense of control of public expenditure, as a glance at the almost blank-cheque financing of the nursing-home sector will indicate. Thus the notion of welfare pluralism, somewhat like active citizenship, was a rather incoherent one.

Central–local state relations

The various reforms introduced by the government have all entailed an ostensible decentralisation of power to the lowest appropriate level, but this has been accompanied by two trends that reduced direct local representation and involvement: greater central control over the affairs of local tiers of the NHS, and greater ministerial control over appointments and fewer authority members being appointed as nominees of local authorities.

Initially the government's rhetoric was decentralist. Norms-based, top-down planning was largely abandoned, while Patrick Jenkin spoke of the NHS as a series of local services, responsive to local needs and with a strong involvement from the local community.[20] This localist emphasis has continued in various ways, which is interesting in what is still known as a *national* health service, and the tensions between centralism and localism are explored in various contexts in subsequent chapters. The 1982 reorganisation of the NHS was justified on similar decentralist grounds: *Patients First* (DHSS, 1979a) emphasised the importance of decisions being taken as close as possible to the operational arms of the service. With hindsight the first term of office was the most decentralist of the four terms to date, although legislation was introduced to make cash limits binding on health authorities, while the government appointed commissioners to replace the members of the Lambeth, Southwark and Lewisham AHA, who had refused to implement financial cuts (though Patrick Jenkin subsequently had to apologise to parliament for exceeding his powers in doing so).[21]

In contrast the 1983–7 government introduced what Rhodes (1992, pp. 64–70) has termed a 'command territorial operating code'.

Following the Griffiths Report, more clearly defined lines of performance review, from individual operating units upwards, were established. In addition there was a stress on central specification of targets for achievement in certain areas of activity (Birch and Maynard, 1986). The NHS reforms went even further along decentralist lines by stressing the benefits to be gained from maximising the autonomy of local managers; hence the creation of NHS trusts and the establishment of fundholding practices.

Problems within the NHS are also explained in these decentralist terms. Parliamentary debates are replete with references by ministers to the variations in performance between and the apparent inefficiencies of health authorities. Thus John Redwood claimed that because health authorities:

> have some £20 billion to manage their affairs . . . [service reductions] should not become matters for the national press and the House of Commons but can be dealt with at the local level, as they should be. . . . It is not a matter of money and resource. *It is a matter of management.* [22]

Given the government's declared belief that the level of resources allocated to the NHS has not been a problem, it is only to be expected that health authorities will be told that solutions to their problems are in their hands. The discourse of decentralisation combines with that of managerialism to absolve the government from any possibility of blame for local difficulties. The logic of this would arguably be a more managerial reform, establishing the NHS as some kind of agency, divorced from direct Parliamentary accountability: the recent reforms of the RHAs as regional branches of the Department of Health may represent a move in this direction (Chapter 9).

At the same time subnational government is both agent of and obstacle to central government (Miliband, 1969), while health authorities have to square the circle of ministerial responsibility and local accountability. The balance in this regard has swung towards centralisation. This is evident in the priority attached by the government to obtaining stricter financial control of health authorities. It is also manifest in the government's willingness to intervene in the decisions of individual health authorities when it seems to suit their purpose. For example, competitive tendering and staff reductions were both policy issues where the government reversed decisions of health authorities and, in the case of staff reductions, replaced health authority members who had declined to implement government policy

(Chapter 9). In these cases the veneer of decentralisation was thin. Imposition of the Government's will was made more likely by ministerial willingness to veto appointments to health authorities of individuals not seen as sympathetic to their views, or to impose on authorities known Conservative supporters, and the reservation in the White Paper of ministerial powers of appointment to many health service bodies was a natural extension of all this. The reduction (in 1982) and the subsequent removal (in 1991) of local authority nomination rights to DHAs seemed inconsistent with the greater co-ordination envisaged between the services provided by the two sets of authorities. This was justified on the grounds that the identification of communities is impossible anyway. Managerial skills are deemed more important than local knowledge. Finally, the process of merger of health authorities has taken place not because of the identification of natural communities but according to an economic calculus concerning economies of scale in purchasing, thereby distancing decision-making from local control (Chapter 9).

Events since 1979 betoken not so much a wholesale privatisation of the NHS but a fundamental change in the ways in which it is run. The initiatives designed to secure extra resources are not real innovations in policy but extensions of existing measures. Crucially, electoral considerations have stayed the government's hand to the extent that no attempt has been made to dismantle the service. Instead, policy changes have been introduced that may appear marginal, such as minor, though incremental, increases in charges. It was no surprise that the government stressed the need for authorities to sort out their problems internally, but in its determination to show those authorities how to resolve their difficulties the centre at times exerted considerable, if not excessive, influence over the periphery. It is the internal measures that are of far greater significance, which has led some commentators to describe what has happened as 'privatisation from within' (Haywood and Ranade, 1989). The central state has intervened to establish the conditions in which the private sector can obtain a much firmer foothold in the process of service delivery and, where deemed politically necessary, this has entailed overturning the decisions of local health authorities. As the membership of health authorities has been reshaped in the Conservatives' desired image, it may be no coincidence that conflicts between centre and locality have become far less intense and frequent. In that sense the ground had been laid for the White Paper.

A change of pace, not of direction? The NHS review and the White Paper

Style and content of the NHS review

The review of the NHS, announced in 1988 by the novel constitutional procedure of a television interview with the prime minister, marked the latest stage in a process of shifting the health care policy agenda to the right which began several years ago: many of the central themes of the White Paper had been foreshadowed by previous initiatives or legislation. On the other hand there had been no hint of an imminent review of the NHS in the Conservatives' 1987 election manifesto: if indeed the white paper was merely an incremental adjustment, surely there would have been some indication that the review was about to take place? The crisis in the acute hospital sector, which provoked the review, could hardly have been unanticipated, given the slow pace of resource growth and the difficulty of achieving redistribution of funds.[23] The White Paper bore the classic marks of Thatcherite policy making: minimal consultation, except with a close circle of sympathetic policy analysts; a highly purposeful approach, geared to being *seen to be doing something* about the problem – the symbolic uses of politics, in Edelman's (1971) terms; and a tightly drawn agenda, focused firmly on the problems internal to the NHS and relating to resource management rather than on the broader issues of how best to attack health problems.

The review team consisted of five ministers, chaired by the prime minister, of whom three were Treasury ministers. Evidence was not formally published, nor were the deliberations of the review made public. Notable for their absence were the medical profession, for long beneficiaries of a privileged place at the policy table, but by the late 1980s pejoratively labelled a 'trade union' by the Government and often roundly condemned as a reactionary force (see Chapter 6).

The style of both the review and, latterly, of the White Paper's implementation, were purposeful and direct; this was no Royal Commission. Adverse publicity about the consistent problems in the acute sector in the winter of 1987–8, finally snapped the patience of the prime minister and gave the government an opportunity to introduce far-reaching change, without which no amount of additional funding could 'solve' the NHS's problems. The primary aim was how to achieve better value for money from existing resources, especially within the acute sector, which appeared to offer the greatest possibility for a fuller injection of commercial discipline. Alternative goals to which the NHS might legitimately aspire – notably greater equity in service delivery, or the amelioration of inequalities in health and discussion of the objectives of the service – were conspicuously absent. A further consequence of this peremptory approach was that proposals were endorsed that reflected the prime minister's determination to protect the Conservatives' core support, rather than being the result of considered evaluation, a notable example being granting the elderly tax relief on private health insurance premiums. This proposal was apparently opposed by Kenneth Clarke, the health secretary, right up to the last moment before the publication of the review;[24] its inclusion marked the triumph of ideology over rationality in the review. The urgency with which the review was carried out was matched by what some felt was a refusal fully to evaluate the scheme fully. Requests for pilot schemes relating to the various key proposals in the review were met with the response that the need for change was self-evident: 'change cannot be made conditional on a protracted academic appraisal . . . the crying need for resource management is obvious. The pace at which we must proceed must be more purposeful'.[25]

However, potential reforms were to be limited in scope. Most government spokespersons recognised the technical inadequacy and/or political unacceptability of an insurance-based health-care system. Systems based on vouchers likewise had severe technical difficulties, notably deciding who should receive what voucher value for treatment, and the possibility of adverse selection by doctors (Scheffler, 1989), especially GPs, who could refuse people they thought likely to make excessive demands on their practices. The Health Maintenance Organisation (HMO) system was rejected for similar reasons; while it appears to work well in middle-class, prosperous areas, HMOs have not penetrated inner-city areas to anything like the same extent (Rayner, 1988; Petchey, 1987). Reforms were likely to take place within the existing framework of the service; admitting that at least part of the problem was lack of funds would have been tantamount to conceding the opposition's case, and indeed the review did not consider the levels of funding for the NHS.

It followed that a probable scenario would be some form of internal market. This works on the principle of separating the purchasing function of an organisation from the providing function: purchasers then shop around, investigating the cheapest possible source of care, while providers seek to compete to offer treatment at the lowest possible price; those who fail to compete eventually go out of business. Providers must keep costs constantly under review for fear of failing to attract funds; purchasers must likewise seek to maximise the amount of care they can purchase for the budget they hold. In theory, the net result is greater efficiency (Enthoven, 1985).

The White Paper, then, was born out of a desire to be seen to be doing something about the perceived inefficiencies of the NHS. If the events of the winter of 1987–8 pushed the NHS to the top of the domestic political agenda, international events – the collapse of Communism – presented an ideological justification from an unlikely quarter for what the government proposed. Thus Malcolm Rifkind claimed that at the time the NHS was established, it was believed that:

> *the best way to administer resources was through a form of rigid, centralised planning* . . . the assumption was that there should be nationalisation and many small concerns should be brought together into massive conglomerations and that that would achieve the best use of resources. *That view was shared in Eastern and Western Europe as well* . . . a structure established 40 years ago does not necessarily make sense in the dramatically changed circumstances of the 1980s and 1990s . . . *in this country and elsewhere we have seen a growing disillusionment with central planning and control* as a means of administering resources.[26]

What was presumably required, then, was some form of perestroika in the NHS, though given that this word merely means 'restructuring', it has to be noted that the nature of restructuring and the way it was implemented were clearly matters of political choice, so the precise form of that restructuring remained an open question. Whether there has been an associated glasnost is also questionable, and whether the NHS could really be compared to the elephantine institutions of state socialism is debatable.

Diagnoses and prescriptions of the White Paper

The diagnosis presented laid heavy stress on several themes that have characterised Conservative social policy in recent years: performance and efficiency, consumerism, and managerial autonomy. The prescription involved much more delegation of responsibility to the local tiers of the service. The White Paper itself, and Conservative defenders of it in parliament, made numerous references to the apparently chance variations in performance that existed between different health authorities. But absent was any analysis of precisely why such variations exist; presumably they were regarded as self-evident truths that betokened inefficiency in resource use. Sample studies of specific health authorities, or comparisons with other health care systems, might have given some clue as to whether the variations were systematic (in which case presumably causes could have been identified and dealt with) or random.

The White Paper heavily emphasised localism and local management in the provision of services. Rather than impose centrally determined solutions, it stressed that management should be free to react locally to whatever difficulties arose in their district or hospital. Problems of service delivery were dismissed as being the result of inefficient management or of management being unable to manage. Devolution to the local level would resolve this, for 'experience in both the public service and the private sector has shown that the best-run organisations are those in which local staff are given responsibility for responding to local need'. The vision was one in which local managers were freed to make their own decisions. The innovation of executive membership of health authorities strengthened the hand of managerial interests while the abolition of local authority nomination rights severed direct connections between the NHS and local electoral influence. While ignoring the democratic deficit to which this gave rise, the White Paper also stressed that these freedoms would bring great benefits – local managers would be able to draw on all the resources available in the local community to provide a wider range of services. What would also flow from this devolution was a marked political gain for government: by decentralising responsibilities as far as possible, it was hoped that controversies over unpopular decisions would be avoided.

The central prescriptions of the White Paper were to stimulate competition within the NHS by separating the purchasing role of DHAs from their provider role, and encouraging both purchaser and provider to compete: the former for the best price, the latter for the lowest price in order to attract business. Decentralisation was facilitated by creating several hundred NHS Trusts and by allowing GP practices to go forward to become fundholders. The absence of costings of NHS assets, decried by the private sector for years as offering unfair competitive advantage to the NHS, was rectified by the system of capital charging. Resource allocation formulae were simplified and made essentially population based (Chapter 4). Emphases on welfare pluralism were evident in both the NHS White Paper, where purchasers were encouraged to contract with whomsoever they thought could deliver the best service, and in the Community Care White Paper, which firmly established the enabling role of the local authority in planning appropriate packages of care to those requiring social support rather than health care. The latter was a complement to the NHS White Paper – indeed in order to implement the internal market, with the anticipated increase in efficiency and throughput of NHS hospitals, it was essential to put plans for community care on a firmer footing, not least to avoid bed blocking in acute hospitals by patients unable to return home.

While some aspects of the White Paper subsequently became accepted even by the Labour Party – for example, the purchaser–provider split – nevertheless ideology triumphed over rationality and measures were introduced that simply did not add up, even on a technical level, to sensible health policy. Thus tax relief for the elderly on private insurance premiums would have come some way down a consensus list of priorities for health policies. Fragmentation was highly likely as the numbers of competing provider units increased and as fundholding budgets took away substantial amounts of health authority purchasing power, and therefore potential leverage over health care issues under their jurisdiction. Equity was jettisoned as an explicit objective of policy, being replaced by the goal of market-driven efficiency: the *British Medical Journal* commented that the NHS was to receive a full dose of the enterprise culture of the Thatcher years.[27] From now on, in theory, the internal market would produce an optimum allocation of resources. The problem was that the market was highly unequal: the demographic composition of health authorities, historic disparities in service provision, the condition and age of the capital stock, variations in private health insurance coverage (see Chapter 7), the stress on devolution in personnel policies and competition for scarce staff in areas with relatively low unemployment rates – all these meant that the playing field was anything but even. In short, grafting the notion of an internal market onto a supposedly national health service, while retaining the equity-oriented goals of that service was likely to be problematic, to say the least, and some of the associated implications of this, and the problems of implementing the White Paper, are explored in subsequent chapters.

Finally, because of the government's refusal to pilot its proposals before implementing them nationally, policy was made in an *ad hoc*, reactive fashion. Thus within 18 months of the reforms there emerged regional 'outposts' of the DoH to monitor the activities of NHS Trusts (Chapter 9), the anticipated financial collapse of the high-cost London hospitals (caused by purchasers withdrawing contracts) necessitated a degree of intervention within months of the reforms (Chapter 4), local authorities were directed to spend guaranteed proportions of their community care budgets in the private sector in order to avoid destabilising the market (Chapter 5), and a succession of mergers between various health authorities (and in some cases family health service authorities) took place, altering the whole map of the service, though without any obvious logic or central guidance (Chapter 9). Again, the contrast with the pre-1979 NHS, with its centralist planning, could hardly be clearer.

Concluding comments

Two important questions arising from the foregoing are: how far do the policies introduced since 1979 represent a coherent approach to health policy as opposed to an ideological strategy; and how far do these developments represent the imposition of a particularly 'Thatcherite' or Conservative view of the world as opposed to being merely technical developments that would have happened anyway?

There is little doubt that what we have seen is not a coherent health policy but a strategy for reforming the health service from within. A concern for the 'efficient' delivery of health care has dominated these years, rather than a concern for the social and political measures that would have been required to produce a policy for public health. There is ample evidence to support this view from the nature of the policies introduced by the government and their timing. For instance, after the 1979 election, the immediate priority was seen to be expanding the scope for the private sector and strengthening financial controls on the activities of health authorities, rather than using the Report of the Royal Commission to launch a full-scale debate about the NHS's future. Similarly the post-1983 measures, combining the introduction of general management and competitive tendering with centrally imposed personnel and financial cuts (Chapter 6), seem cynical in their timing, while the response to the 'crisis' of 1987–8 was not an open public debate about the future of the service but a carefully circumscribed review. As a consequence of this we have not seen a carefully crafted strategy, but a pragmatic, opportunistic one. The concept of a state-managed and state-funded NHS has been steadily eroded and, as Johnson (1986) predicted, 'the incrementalism which allowed the welfare system to grow so silently is now being used to effect its contraction . . . enabling legislation . . . will permit the undermining of the existing welfare system'. There seem to be very many respects in which Johnson's remarks apply to the welfare state in general and, to a lesser degree, to the NHS in particular. There has been a gradual process of change since 1979, which has steadily eroded the concept of the NHS as a service divorced from market considerations and mechanisms and steadily changed people's expectations.

Having emphasised the ways in which what has happened clearly reflected political choices first and foremost, to what extent is this strategy coherent by the lights of Thatcherism or contemporary conservatism? Since the problem is defined in terms not of the limited funds available to the service but in terms of the problems arising from the lack of market criteria within the service, the key index of the success of the government's strategies is how far the efficiency of the NHS has been increased, and, related to this, how far services are now being provided by private organisations; to what extent, in other words, the state's monopoly has been broken. On the former count there is little doubt that 'efficiency' has improved but there is little evidence as yet about service quality, while it must be remembered that resource growth is at least partially due to imposing some additional costs on service users, which the government has actively welcomed and supported. The (Thatcher) governments' emphases on cost cutting sit uneasily with the (Major) government's stress on service quality, suggesting some limits to the market strategy within the service. On the latter count there is clearly a long way to go: the success of competitive tendering has been partial and uneven while private health care has still achieved relatively little penetration. Only where vast subsidies have been made available (residential care for the elderly) has the balance been shifted, perhaps irreversibly, from the public to the private sector. One effect of the growth of private care has been the expansion of a constituency with a substantial vested interest in private provision, largely concentrated in the Conservatives' electoral heartlands, and this may be a major stumbling block, in electoral terms, to the prospects of opposition parties, especially Labour (Chapters 7 and 10).

Where the post-1979 changes will probably be judged more successful is in terms of their impacts within the service. The emphasis on the entrepreneurial culture is possibly the most far-reaching change affecting health care delivery (Chapter 8) and this has clear implications for the character of state intervention. For while the NHS has always been short on direct electoral accountability, the steady move away from local authority involvement in the service and the creation of *ad hoc* task forces for particular issues have greatly reduced local influence. This reflects the government's well-known antipathy towards subnational government and their emphasis on the national political arena (Chapter 9). In parallel, the creation of the new cadre of executive members of health authorities gives a further twist to the entrepreneurial strategy for the service: managers will be judged on performance indicators such as how far they maximise revenue and how far they stretch their resources, goals that may not be consistent with local community interests. The state has been reshaped in such a way that it is relatively autonomous and insulated from such pressures. In those circumstances the problem is how far the social goals of the NHS will continue to be maintained. At the national level, similar changes have occurred: Krieger (1986) comments on how the increased decisional autonomy of the Thatcher government allowed it to reshape the social policy agenda in its desired image: the state was no longer the tool of capital, it was a decisive, proactive state. Even in the teeth of considerable opposition from interest groups, these governments have pursued policies consistent with reorganising the NHS along more commercial lines from within. Moreover these developments have not, despite the assertions of Conservative ministers, been the result of inevitable tendencies operating across society in general: what has happened since 1979 reflects specific political choices and strategies, not the working-out of some grand social or economic logic.

   This raises, finally, the question of how far the White Paper marked a radical departure from previous policies, and it should be clear that to all intents and purposes it does not: the antecedents of it were well established before 1989, the ideas incorporated in it were being floated from the early 1980s and Conservative backbenchers – and in some cases frontbenchers and ministers – had missed few opportunities to call for the kind of steps taken in the White Paper. The groundwork, then, had been laid well in advance, whether in terms of creating a climate of resource scarcity or in terms of encouraging experiment with alternative forms of service delivery. The aim of the principal empirical chapters of this book is to demonstrate how this was so with respect to key areas of policy: resource allocation, community care policies, producing health care (relationships between state, management and the major producer interests in the NHS), the commercial health sector, the commercialisation of health authority activities, and the relationships between centre and locality in the NHS.

4

Spatial Resource Allocation: Local Difficulties, Technical Adjustments and Political Solutions

An extended discussion of the geographical impacts of resource allocation policies might seem marginal to the concerns of this book. However I argue that it is crucial to a consideration of the NHS reforms. Firstly, having decided to restrict growth in the HCHS from 1983, it was inevitable that severe pressure would be imposed on individual DHAs. Not only did this produce a chorus of complaints from inner city areas, it also provoked protests from constituencies denied growth. It was also clear that problems being experienced by health authorities (notably, running out of funds before the end of the financial year) would not be resolved by minor adjustments to resource allocation formulae. The internal market potentially offered the government a chance to kill two political birds with one policy stone: (alleged) overprovision (relative to need) and concentration of hospital services in London, and the difficulties of developing services in the growth areas (and Conservative heartlands) of South East England. So whatever the technical merits of the internal market solution, these are inseparable from the political difficulties facing the government at the time of the reforms. To appreciate this it is necessary to consider the historical background to geographical inequalities in health service provision under the NHS.

The NHS inherited considerable spatial inequalities in the distribution of health care resources (Abel-Smith, 1964; Nuffield Provincial

Hospitals Trust, 1946), but at first little was done to remedy this situation; the distribution of health care resources was in effect 'frozen' and spatial inequalities became 'entrenched' (Webster, 1988, pp. 292–8). The Resource Allocation Working Party (RAWP) formula (DHSS, 1976) identified the relative needs of the 14 RHAs in England by taking account of the age and sex structure of the population, weighted by the all-cause standardised mortality ratio (SMR). Having regard to existing patterns of resource distribution and expenditure, it then determined how far each RHA was from a theoretical 'revenue target'. In this chapter I consider the impacts of the RAWP policy, focusing less on the technical weaknesses of the RAWP formula itself (see Mays and Bevan, 1987), than on the way the policy was implemented by successive governments. Introduced ostensibly as a means of achieving redistribution through growth in resources, during the 1980s RAWP arguably meant equality of misery, as revenue growth disappeared, with particularly severe consequences for the most 'overfunded' regions and districts.[1] This was due to a combination of the limited overall pace of growth of NHS resources, rapid shifts in the geographical distribution of revenue resources, and a plethora of other initiatives in the NHS (summarised by Birch and Maynard, 1986) that severely constrained the autonomy afforded to regions and districts.

The consequences of the ensuing budget restraint are all too apparent: rapid rationalisation of the hospital stock, intensification of patient throughput and increased waiting lists, to name but three. These were not just local difficulties, inevitable in a complex, centralised service: they were national problems that required national solutions, though crucial political pressures emerged from the South East. The government attempted to manage the problem by reviewing the RAWP formula, but this was a largely symbolic gesture that merely fine-tuned the formulae used. The case made by the review for taking account of social factors was soon overwhelmed by the government's determination to carry out a fundamental review of the NHS. Here, I argue that the White Paper's proposals were shaped by a clear awareness, on the government's part, of the political geography of the impacts of different resource allocation proposals, and of the way in which the internal market offered scope to challenge professional autonomy in London, one of the key sources of opposition to redistribution of funds. Finally the chapter demonstrates some of the effects of the White Paper on the distribution of financial resources to health authorities and considers the attempt to mitigate the consequences of the internal market through the Tomlinson Report.

RAWP under austerity: from differential growth to equality of misery?

According to the original RAWP calculations, the Thames RHAs, covering London and South East England (Figure 4.1) were deemed to be considerably 'overfunded' in relation to their revenue targets; conversely, RHAs in the north and west of England were held to be considerably below target levels of revenue. Figure 4.2 shows the position as of 1979 and the subsequent moves by RHAs towards their 'targets'. It can be seen that, over a relatively short period, there was a degree of convergence between the 14 regions; the consequences of this apparent convergence will be returned to later. The key to this apparently equitable policy was, of course, the determination of the revenue target and there was controversy over the appropriate criteria to be used (see Widgery, 1988; Woods, 1982). Also crucial to RAWP was the pace of implementation: the net transfer of the resources involved could hardly be accomplished overnight. At first the proposed method was one of differential growth: while all regions were to receive increases, in real terms, in their budgets (that is, after allowing for inflation plus some 1–2 per cent per annum to cope with increased needs), some were to grow faster than others. Even this limited redistribution caused some problems in the late 1970s. Whereas disparities between regions (in relation to revenue targets) were large, those between districts within regions were even greater, and in order to eliminate such inequalities rapid intra-regional transfers were instituted. Initially the Conservatives accepted that RAWP's aims should be achieved through levelling up rather than levelling down[2] but this acceptance did not last long.

The 1983 general election marked a decisive turn in the pace at which RAWP was implemented. Within a month of the election health authority budgets were cut by 1 per cent (effectively a 1.5 per cent cut, as it took place one-third of the way through the financial year). Revised long-term growth assumptions for regional revenue allocations meant that the Thames RHAs were to lose, in real terms, between 0.3 and 0.5 per cent of their budgets each year over the (then) ten-year planning cycle. The equity-oriented principle of RAWP was only maintained, therefore, at the direct expense of cuts in the budgets of 'overfunded' RHAs. Despite this, one Conservative health minister, Ray Whitney, argued that these annual reductions could 'be regarded in no sense as undue or immoderate haste or pressure'.[3] Table 4.1 gives the long-term growth assumptions built into RHA budgets from 1983, and subsequent annual resource assumptions up to 1990.[4] The 1987–8

Figure 4.1   RHAs in England, 1974–94

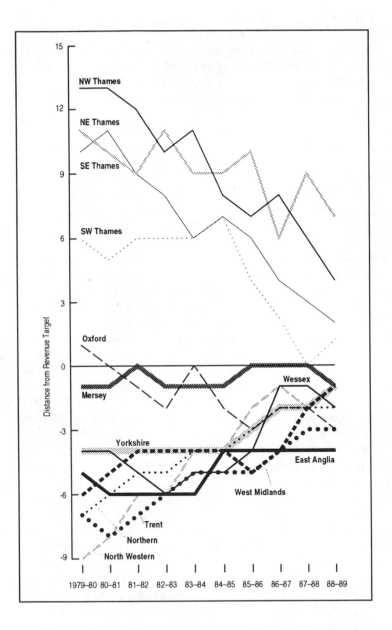

Figure 4.2 Regions' distance from RAWP revenue targets, 1979–80 to 1988–9

financial year saw a move away from actual reductions in the Thames regions; in addition, in the 1986–7 and 1987–8 financial years the government was forced by mounting media concern and political pressure about the NHS to allocate additional funds (£30 million and £90 million respectively) to those RHAs deemed to be suffering from 'transitional problems' over the implementation of RAWP.[5]

That there were indeed serious pressures on authorities in the Thames regions is clear from Table 4.2 which summarises trends in regional revenue allocations over the period 1983–7, together with estimates provided by the DoH of the impacts of these trends on RHAs' ability to develop services as planned. The actual purchasing power of the resources available to the Thames RHAs fell in each of the three years from 1984–5 to 1986–7. While these RHAs had some resources available for service development, this was only because of the effectiveness of their cost-improvement programmes. Even this, however, was limited, falling below 1 per cent in some of these regions, especially in 1984–5 and 1985–6. Only the East Anglian RHA received growth monies, which permitted its purchasing power to grow by more than 1 per cent in each of these four years (ranging from 2.9 per cent to 1.4 per cent); Trent's purchasing power grew by between 0.8 and 1.5 per cent per annum. Of course, when the effects of cost-improvement programmes were added into the equation, rapid growth was sustained in these regions: on the basis of these figures the East Anglian RHA increased by 11 per cent and Trent by 9 per cent in terms of purchasing power over this period. Conversely the South-East Thames RHA on these figures saw its purchasing power increase by only 2.5 per cent between 1983–4 and 1986–7, and without CIPs it would have registered a reduction of 2.2 per cent in the resources available to it. In other words, CIPs to some extent offset the effects of the net reductions in resources announced by the government in 1983. A more sobering statistic is that, for these four years and fourteen RHAs (a total of 56 cases), in only 17 instances did an RHA receive in *cash* terms more than 1 per cent growth in funds. Even after allowing for CIPs, however, there were 18 cases in which RHAs did not have available at least a 1 per cent margin for service development for the 1983–7 period. The conclusion is inescapable: without the resources generated by health authorities' own internal efforts at increasing efficiency, RHAs would not have been in a position to keep up with rising demands for health care.

But the problems were by no means confined to the regional level. The variability in distance from revenue targets was much greater within regions than between them. The Social Services Committee

Table 4.1 RHAs' distance from revenue targets, long-term revenue growth assumptions and financial increments, 1983–91

	(1) Distance from target Jan. 1983	(2) Long-term growth 1983–4 to 1993–4	(3) 1985–6	(4) 1986–7	(5) 1987–8	(6) 1988–9	(7) 1989–90 Lower growth	(7) 1989–90 Upper growth	(8) 1990–1 Lower growth	(8) 1990–1 Upper growth
			Resource assumptions for financial years							
Northern	−4.98	0.5	1.3	1.3	0.8	1.1	1.0	1.2	0.6	1.1
Yorkshire	−5.94	0.8	1.4	1.4	1.0	1.1	1.1	1.3	1.2	1.7
Trent	−7.55	1.1	1.9	1.9	1.8	1.7	1.5	1.7	1.9	2.4
E Anglia	−9.46	1.6	1.9	1.9	2.2	2.1	1.9	2.1	3.0	3.5
NW Thames	10.43	−0.5	−0.3	−0.3	0.0	0.0	0.4	0.6	0.9	1.4
NE Thames	8.44	−0.3	−0.3	−0.3	0.0	0.0	0.4	0.6	0.2	0.7
SE Thames	5.71	−0.3	−0.3	−0.3	0.1	0.1	0.5	0.7	2.0	2.5
SW Thames	6.06	−0.3	−0.3	−0.3	0.1	0.7	0.7	0.9	2.6	3.1
Wessex	−7.06	1.4	2.5	2.5	1.5	1.6	1.4	1.6	3.1	3.6
Oxford	−1.41	1.4	1.7	1.7	1.7	2.0	1.7	1.9	1.7	2.2
S West	−6.04	1.3	2.1	2.1	1.3	1.5	1.1	1.3	2.0	2.5
W Midlands	−5.13	1.0	1.7	1.7	2.0	1.7	1.3	1.5	0.7	1.2
Mersey	−2.60	0.2	0.6	0.6	0.3	0.6	0.7	0.9	0.5	0.0
N Western	−5.33	0.4	1.2	1.2	0.4	0.9	0.8	1.0	0.3	0.2

NOTES:
1. All figures are percentage increases in real terms, after allowing for the government's estimates of inflation.
2. In 1989–90 and 1990–1 RHAs were instructed to plan on the assumption that they would receive increases in funds within upper and lower growth limits.

SOURCES: Cols 1, 2: DHSS Circular HC (83) 4; Cols 3, 4: DHSS Circular HC (83) 16; Cols 5–6: DHSS Circulars HC (84) 23, (86) 2; Col. 7: DHSS Circular HC (88) 43; Col. 8: DoH Circular HC (89) 24.

Table 4.2 Trends in actual current expenditure on the HCHS, English RHAs, 1983–7

	1982–3 to 1983–4				1983–4 to 1984–5				1984–5 to 1985–6				1985–6 to 1986–7			
	A	B	C	D	A	B	C	D	A	B	C	D	A	B	C	D
Northern	6.4	1.2	1.6	1.2	5.9	0.1	1.5	0.8	5.7	0.4	−0.3	1.3	7.2	0.4	3.8	1.7
Yorkshire	6.2	1.0	1.4	1.0	6.1	0.3	1.7	1.4	6.4	1.1	0.4	2.6	6.9	0.0	3.6	1.6
Trent	6.6	1.4	1.8	1.4	7.1	1.2	2.6	2.3	6.0	0.8	0.0	2.4	8.5	1.5	5.0	2.8
East Anglian	8.1	2.9	3.3	2.9	7.3	1.4	2.8	2.4	6.8	1.6	0.8	2.4	8.7	1.7	5.3	2.9
NW Thames	5.1	0.0	0.4	0.0	5.4	−0.4	0.9	1.1	3.9	−1.2	−1.9	0.7	6.7	−0.2	3.3	1.9
NE Thames	5.1	0.0	0.3	N.A.	4.8	−1.0	0.4	0.4	3.7	−1.4	−2.1	0.4	6.8	−0.1	3.4	1.6
SE Thames	5.6	0.4	0.8	N.A.	4.4	−1.3	0.0	0.6	4.6	−0.6	−1.3	1.2	6.1	−0.7	2.8	0.8
SW Thames	5.4	0.3	0.7	N.A.	4.9	−0.9	0.4	0.3	3.8	−1.4	−2.1	−0.1	6.9	0.0	3.5	1.7
Wessex	7.3	2.1	2.5	2.1	7.5	1.6	2.9	2.5	5.0	−0.2	−0.9	0.7	8.3	1.3	4.9	3.0
Oxford	5.4	0.3	0.7	0.3	8.3	2.3	3.7	3.3	5.3	0.1	−0.6	1.3	7.8	0.9	4.4	2.0
S Western	6.5	1.4	1.8	1.4	5.7	−0.1	1.2	0.8	5.6	0.4	−0.3	1.0	7.8	0.8	4.3	1.8
W Midlands	6.4	1.2	1.6	1.2	6.7	0.9	2.2	2.4	5.9	0.7	0.0	1.9	7.8	0.8	4.4	2.1
Mersey	4.7	−0.4	0.0	−0.4	5.9	0.1	1.4	1.4	5.1	−0.1	−0.8	1.6	6.9	0.0	3.5	2.0
N Western	5.4	0.3	0.7	0.3	5.9	0.1	1.4	1.0	5.6	0.4	−0.3	2.0	7.2	0.3	3.8	1.9

KEY: A = Cash increase (%); B = Change in purchasing power (allowing for inflation) (%); C = Change in real terms (%); D = Margin for service development (after CIPs) (%).
SOURCE: Social Services Committee, 1988d, Table 3.1.

documented the situation of DHAs in four selected regions in relation to their revenue targets. Within the North East Thames RHA the range in 1983–4 was 44 percentage points, ranging from Islington (25 per cent over its revenue target) to Southend (19 per cent below its revenue target; six other DHAs were below their targets). By 1987–88 the disparities had been reduced to 27 percentage points as Southend was only 11.1 per cent below target while Newham remained 16 per cent above it. To achieve these transfers some DHAs had their budgets reduced in cash terms (that is before allowing for inflation) (Social Services Committee, 1988d, table 5.3.1, p. 65), while others simply did not receive increases in funds sufficient to keep pace with inflation. Conversely, at the other end of the spectrum in resource terms, the North Derbyshire DHA (in the early 1980s the most underfunded DHA in the most underfunded region) enjoyed an expansion in its funds of 47 per cent in cash terms between 1983–4 and 1987–8, representing a real-terms increase, after allowing for inflation, of some 14 per cent (Social Services Committee, 1988d, table 5.3.2).

This situation has, on the whole, put health authorities under considerable financial pressure. At the regional level some went so far as to abandon subregional redistribution of resources, while others slowed down greatly the pace of subregional redistribution; this was why 'insensitive sub-regional RAWPing' was cited as a cause of difficulties.[6] At the DHA level, authorities responded, depending on local circumstances and opportunities, by adopting some or all of the following measures: rationalisation of acute hospital capacity; intensification of patient throughput; restricting the numbers of non–emergency admissions; a number of measures designed to protect current levels of spending (for example capital-to-revenue transfers, deferring payments to creditors); efficiency savings of various sorts; and drawing on private sources of funds. The varied responses of health authorities are described in detail in the annual surveys of the National Association of Health Authorities (NAHA, 1987, 1988a; see also the next section).

The most publicised response by health authorities has been to rationalise hospital capacity. The impact has been sharply differ-entiated between health authorities (Figure 4.3). Of those 150 (out of 190) DHAs where comparable figures are available for the years 1979–89, 25 lost over 25 per cent of their acute beds while a further 29 lost over 20 per cent (note that some areas, such as inner London, experienced higher reductions in bed capacity, but this is disguised by the lack of comparable statistics). Note that RAWP implicitly assumed that certain geographical areas, especially those with high levels of access to services (principally inner London) made excessive use of the NHS, so that some reduction in use was desirable. However, as various reports on London made clear, despite reductions in bed provision, there remained high levels of demand for hospital services (partly a consequence of poor levels of primary care in the capital) (King's Fund, 1987; King's Fund Institute, 1992), while some contended that London was not, in fact, overprovided with hospitals in relation to its needs (Jarman, 1993). Ministers have been at pains to stress that local management decisions rather than aggregate levels of funding have been responsible for bed reductions. But such survey evidence as was available, together with anecdotal material such as press reports and documents from monitoring and campaigning organisations (for example ACHCEW, 1987; BCRNHS, 1987; CCHMS, 1988; New-castle Health Concern, 1986) provided ample information concerning temporary closures, five-day wards, temporary closures of wards and operating theatres, other reductions in services (for example freezes on operations in certain specialties) and underutilisation of newly built capital assets. Nonetheless no systematic survey was carried out by the government on the effects of financial stringency on health service provision, which the Social Services Committee (1988a, para. 26) regarded as 'extraordinary'.

While bed numbers have decreased dramatically, increased through-put and/or greater use of day surgery can help compensate for this. There is evidence of both reductions in length of stay and increases in patient throughput (summarised in OHE, 1992; see also Chapter 1 above). Not all of these increases in discharges are simply efficiency gains, since technical changes, principally in non-invasive techniques, have allowed operations to be done with much shorter recuperation periods, thus reducing turnover intervals. Paradoxically this has meant that health authorities have on the one hand been applauded for increasing the numbers of patients they treat, and on the other berated for keeping hospital beds empty; the resolution of the paradox is that treating more patients necessarily costs more money, which has posed problems within a cash-limited budget and which was one technical rationale for the White Paper's reforms because of the 'efficiency trap' into which health authorities fell.

There are also hidden costs of changes on this scale. Firstly, admission thresholds are said to have risen. This is because fewer beds are available and therefore there is less flexibility for hospital managers to admit patients. When this is combined with mounting financial crises, many DHAs have been forced to declare limitations on the numbers of non-emergency cases admitted to hospital. These have been

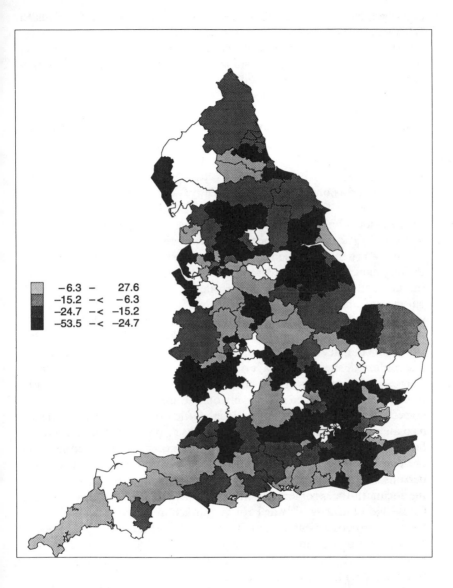

	−6.3 − 27.6
	−15.2 −< −6.3
	−24.7 −< −15.2
	−53.5 −< −24.7

Note: 25 per cent of DHAs in each quartile. Blank areas: no data due to 1982 boundary changes

Figure 4.3   Percentage change in DHA acute beds, England, 1979–89

described by pressure-group organisations such as London Health Emergency (1986; 1987a). They include 'yellow alerts' (admitting only a certain proportion of non-emergencies) and 'red alerts' (admitting emergencies only). It has for some years been apparent that gaining admission at all is extremely problematic: Beech *et al.* (1987) demonstrate the consequences of rationalisation of acute hospital capacity on the ability of GPs to obtain admission for their patients for routine elective surgery, raising questions about the extent to which the NHS is in fact a 'comprehensive' service (see also Langman, 1987).

A national crisis or a little local difficulty?

The pressures on the local levels of the service came to a head in the winter of 1987–8 when it became evident that the rationalisation of services was denying patients treatment, most notably in the case of the Birmingham Children's Hospital. This prompted public criticisms of the government from the Royal Colleges, and a spate of debates in parliament and the press about the NHS 'crisis',[7] usually illustrated with graphic details of the difficulties of individual health authorities. A frequent response from government spokespersons throughout the 1980s was the view that problems in the service were local in character and reflected specific managerial difficulties. For instance Kenneth Clarke had argued in 1984 that the Labour spokesman on health, Michael Meacher, relied excessively on anecdotal evidence, and that (in respect of one specific issue) 'a local difficulty has been exaggerated into an alarmist statement to boost his case'.[8] However the difficulties faced by the NHS can certainly not be regarded as a 'little local difficulty'. Firstly, they were not confined, as government spokespersons claimed, to selected 'problem' localities. Secondly, and of more significance, the problem of limited redistribution of funds to the Conservative heartlands was kept very much in the government's mind by its own backbenchers, and it seems likely that this influenced its chosen path to reform.

A little local difficulty?

The Social Services Committee (1988b) investigated the difficulties being experienced by DHAs under the headings of bed closures, reduced service provision, underutilisation and the 'efficiency trap', and longer-term problems (for example the effect on medical research and teaching, the lack of estate maintenance and delays in priority areas such as community care). Examining bed closures in particular, due to the high public profile of closures, the Committee drew the following revealing statement from a DHSS official:

If you had been having this discussion with us two years ago it is unlikely that any of us would have thought that closures of this kind would have been anything other than a reflection of particular local difficulties. *There is no evidence to suggest in the light of the evidence in this financial year that one can just dismiss it as difficulties in a few localities*, as one might have done at an earlier stage.[9]

The Social Services Committee assessed the situation of four districts in RHAs that either gained or did not lose under RAWP. Though only one reduced services for financial reasons during 1987–8, the others 'had been pushed to the limit' (Social Services Committee, 1988b, p. vii); all were anticipating service reductions for 1988–9. The NAO (1989) studied the responses of nine DHAs to financial difficulties. It noted the adverse effects of some measures taken by regional health authorities: the diversion of funds intended for service development; redistribution among DHAs in one region to create a fund for lending to more severely hit DHAs; delayed payments to suppliers, with some DHAs increasing trade creditors 'up to the limits of supplier acceptability' (para 2.33); and capital-to-revenue transfers on a scale that could delay progress towards estate rationalisation. Several points were made concerning the inability of health authorities 'to undertake full and detailed analysis of the available options' because of the lack of contingency plans identifying areas for 'pruning' and because of delays in availability of financial information (para 4.14). As a consequence health authorities had been forced to rely on short-term measures to avoid overspending during the financial year. While some problems had arisen from limitations in financial management and control within the districts, the crisis-prone nature of the responses by DHAs, and the generalised nature thereof, hardly lends credence to a view that these problems could be regarded as transitional, or local in character, nor does it suggest that they could entirely be resolved by managerial action without impacting on the quality of services being delivered.

More comprehensive data on the local impact of national policies are provided by the NAHA surveys on the financial position of DHAs. These usually cover around 40–50 per cent of all DHAs in England and Wales. They reveal the steps taken by the DHAs to limit expenditure and to attempt to remain within their cash limits. For illustrative purposes, Figure 4.4 shows the total number of health authorities that indicated they would have to adopt the measures shown in order to remain within their cash limit in the 1987–8 and 1988–9 financial years.[10] In both years at least a fifth of health authorities were applying each of these measures. The proportion either reducing services or (particularly) deferring or deleting planned service developments (43 per cent in 1987–8; 30.8 per cent in 1988–9) is noteworthy. In addition, at least a quarter of respondents stated that they would either draw upon reserves or transfer funds from capital to revenue accounts in both financial years. When combined with the practice of delaying payments to creditors[11] it was evident that health authorities were adversely affecting their liquidity, so storing up problems for the future (NAHA, 1987, p. 8).

The value of the NAHA data is that they were collected independently of any hypotheses about associations between geographical area or RAWP-status on the one hand, and the financial difficulties of DHAs on the other. The small numbers make it difficult to generalise about patterns, but it seems that the difficulties reported by NAHA were being experienced across the board in all regions. It seems implausible that they can be dismissed as local difficulties. One might argue about the fact that DHAs in all regions were experiencing financial difficulty – it might be claimed, for instance, that this merely reflected the processes of subregional resource allocation, which produced winners and losers. However a disaggregation by 'RAWP status', an admittedly imperfect guide to the resource position of the DHAs, shows no evidence of any association between RAWP status and the financial difficulties of the DHAs. In other words, problems were being experienced even in those DHAs receiving growth in resources (Mohan, 1990a). The NAHA data may even underestimate the significance of the difficulties faced by some districts and regions, since there were virtually full returns from some regions benefiting from RAWP but relatively few from some of the regions commonly thought to be experiencing the greatest problems (that is, the Thames RHAs). The assertion that the financial difficulties faced by health authorities were merely local in nature did not seem to stand up to serious scrutiny, given the kind of evidence presented here.

The territorial politics of RAWP: slow growth in the Conservative heartlands?

The NAHA data can also be supplemented by analyses of Opposition day and, particularly, adjournment debates within parliament concerning the impact of NHS financial policies on local commu-

87

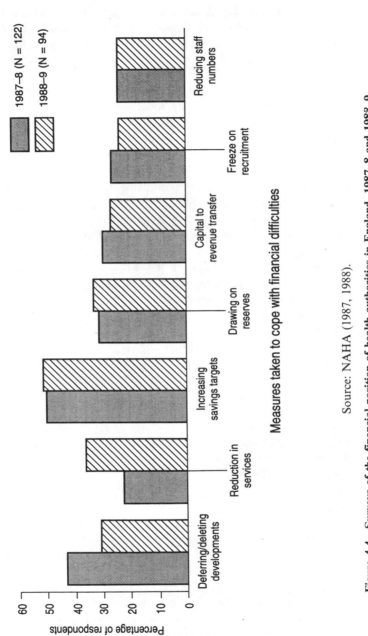

Figure 4.4 Surveys of the financial position of health authorities in England, 1987–8 and 1988–9

nities. Opposition day debates are generally characterised by opposition MPs using territorial pleading to advance their case against the government, and are clearly partisan. However the range of constituencies affected is considerable, as many debates have shown, notably during 1987–8. Adjournment debates are somewhat less adversarial, although opposition members make party-political points in attributing the closures of local hospitals to underfunding and stressing the particular social needs of inner city areas. In contrast Conservative MPs have raised constituency matters largely to criticise the local effects of national policies. In the mid-1980s numerous debates were initiated by MPs from South East England and elsewhere in which the mechanisms and implementation of resource allocation policies began to be questioned.

Several MPs argued that the pace at which RAWP was being implemented was having severe effects. Thus Sir Philip Goodhart (Beckenham) argued that his local health authority was 'being strangled by the guidelines of RAWP . . . [if these] continue to be enforced so enthusiastically we shall be faced locally with a perpetual crisis'. In the same debate Roger Sims (Chislehurst) urged 'a substantial slowing down of the effect of RAWP, or an abatement of it'.[12] Others drew attention to the inability of health authorities to maintain existing services or commission new capital developments because of revenue shortages.[13] Edward Heath (Bexley) stated that 'I am in favour of equalisation but not at the cost of refusing to use the modern facilities that we already have. . .. It is intolerable that Bexley should have its modern services damaged because new services are going to be made available in other parts of the country'.[14] John Redwood (Wokingham) argued strongly that imbalances were developing between the growing populations of the outer South East and the pattern of public services:

by allowing the recent growth in Wokingham without making the resources or plans available for improving local health services, schools and the road network, grave problems are presented locally. At the same time pitiful problems of decline are produced in our inner urban areas from which people are busily migrating. We then reach the ridiculous position where there is insufficient hospital and school accommodation in the high-growth areas. We then incur the financial and political costs of closing schools, hospitals or wards of hospitals in inner London and even in urban centres elsewhere in the South East.[15]

This speech was clearly hinting at the technical inadequacies of the existing system of funding, a view with which Julian Critchley (Aldershot) would concur:

> the rapid increase in population has outstripped the provision of facilities [creating] frustration and concern . . . the recent population increase without matching funding to develop services has meant there has been a cut in provision . . . the DHSS cannot cope with, or keep up with, the Department of the Environment [who had approved plans to accommodate increased population in the area]. *Is it not high time that my Right Honourable friends got their act together?*[16]

Similarly a Kent MP commented that 'We have depopulated London. We are moving people out of London, yet we are still building hospitals in London'; he also questioned whether 'the high site values of the London teaching hospitals qualify them to be where they are',[17] thereby anticipating by several years one of the White Paper's ideas.

Another line of criticism has concerned the government's commitment to redistribution of resources, especially into Essex and Kent, but also into the Trent RHA. Various MPs from constituencies both within and outside the South East argued that the government should not be diverted from its redistributive path because of the strident demands of inner London DHAs. In a debate about the suspension (for exceeding allotted expenditure) of the members of Lambeth, Lewisham and Southwark AHA(T) in 1979, several members representing Kent constituencies claimed that inner London health authorities were being allowed to get away with defiance of cash limits; as David Crouch (Canterbury) put it, 'Peter was being robbed to pay Paul. The Kent and East Sussex AHAs had their figures altered in front of me . . . to meet this overspending'.[18] Some years later, especially after 1983, adjournment debates on health matters affecting South East constituencies began to make more regular appearances on the Commons agenda and the apparent inability or unwillingness of the government to implement RAWP decisively was criticised by several MPs. Thus Sir Julian Ridsdale (Harwich) requested that ministers should 'take a far tougher line with London'.[19] D. Spencer (Leicester South) noted that while RAWP was being re-examined 'some people fear that the shrill battalions from London and the Home Counties will succeed in persuading the government that they should have a greater share'.[20] For others the apparent reluctance to redistribute funds was associated with what they perceived as the vested interests of the consultant lobby:

'the fifteen or so teaching hospitals in London were all built within a cabride of Harley Street. That mix of interests still distorts NHS provision . . . it is wrong to allow the great consultants' dependency on their private practices to slow down or thwart the transfer of (medical) teaching from the great cities to places where people now live'.[21]

Others began to suggest that RAWP be replaced by a system perceived as more advantageous to their health authority. Thus George Gardiner (Reigate) noted that despite the efficiency of his local health authority, hospital beds were being closed and managers being encouraged to run the hospital at less than capacity because of the certainty that they would overspend their budget. Without questioning the justice of RAWP, he suggested that a system in which 'money follows the patient' would be more appropriate.[22] Marion Roe (Broxbourne) argued that rapid population growth in Hertfordshire required local hospital provision, yet the DHA had little chance of acquiring it and therefore had to continue to send patients into London: 'the present funding arrangements . . . mitigate against local decisions being taken locally . . . the lack of resources prevents local people having a proper say in health care'.[23] Robert Jones (Hertfordshire West) pointed out that in view of the difficulties being experienced by authorities with growing populations, such as his own, there was 'a growing case for closing at least one of the teaching hospitals in the centre of London to enable those resources to be more readily redistributed elsewhere'.[24] Richard Ryder (Mid-Norwich) asked the government to consider whether a new incentive system could be built into RAWP 'by which hospitals and districts which perform well can be rewarded'.[25]

The response of government spokespersons to these issues was generally to dismiss them as failures of management and therefore capable of resolution by local managers. This allowed the government to shift the blame for difficulties away from the centre to the locality. Answers to adjournment debates are replete with comparisons between the performance of the relevant DHA and that of other DHAs in the same region, the clear implication being that the district can and should sort itself out. At other times ministers have referred to the 'difficult transitional problems' of the Thames regions and pointed to the convergence between DHAs therein, while an alternative approach has been to shift the terms of reference of the debate and argue, as Kenneth Clarke did, that RAWP has produced 'a change in the way services are provided . . . and not a cut in patient services'. Indeed the government claimed credit for its determination to implement RAWP, against what it saw as shroudwaving lobbies: 'now that we carry out the policy . . .

the Opposition make shallow party political points and cite anecdotal evidence about changes . . . which have inevitably followed the more sensible redistribution' of funds. [26]

This evidence draws on a cross-section of constituencies and DHAs from the South East and highlights the concerns of Conservative MPs about the state of their local health service and the limited action being taken to rectify it. It shows clearly the sort of electoral pressures to which the government might have been subjected if nothing was done. It suggests that a solution was needed that reflected the needs of such constituencies and would benefit them, and that any review of the RAWP formula would be carried out very much against the background of growing political pressure from particular localities.

Technical solutions: from RAWP to weighted capitation

The RAWP review: a technical fix?

The difficulties being experienced by some DHAs, added to the inter regional convergence towards RAWP revenue targets, led the Social Services Committee (1984) to conclude that 'it may be unwise to expect the RAWP process to go much further'. One attempt to resolve the political difficulties being generated by the government's policies was to review the factors used within RAWP for assessing the relative needs of health authorities. However, excluded from the remit of the review was the *pace* at which redistribution of resources was to take place, even though the Social Services Committee (1986) had highlighted this as one of the fundamental difficulties facing the NHS. Certainly there were a number of technical difficulties with the RAWP formula;[27] perhaps most importantly, RAWP did not allow for the effects of social deprivation on the need for health care (Mays and Bevan, 1987).

The caucus supporting inclusion of a deprivation factor embraced some unlikely partners, including senior hospital consultants concerned to defend the budgets and viability of London's hospitals, and London local authorities who argued that London's needs were not reflected in existing formulae (GLC, 1985). Their argument was that even after allowing for variations in age structure and mortality levels, inner urban areas exhibited a greater need for health care (expressed in terms of high levels of utilisation of health facilities). A major technical problem here is that the analysis of 'need' for health care is complicated by the effects of supply of facilities on their utilisation. Urban areas traditionally exhibit high levels of hospital utilisation and social deprivation, but they also have high levels of provision of hospital services (see Abel-Smith, 1964; Pickstone, 1986). Any proposal to introduce a deprivation factor into RAWP had to disentangle the relationships between these factors. The review recommended that a factor be introduced into RAWP to allow for social deprivation, on the basis that the analysis had shown that there existed a clear relationship between social factors and utilisation of services after allowing for the confounding effects of accessibility to facilities. The consequence would have been to stem the net flow of funds from the South East to the north of England. Under the system recommended, the Thames RHAs would have gained; by up to 3 per cent of their revenue budgets. In contrast Trent and the West Midlands, previously beneficiaries of RAWP, would have lost over 2 per cent (DHSS, 1988, table 8.2).

The proposal to include a deprivation factor was perhaps surprising given the declared views of the then secretary of state for Social Services, John Moore, that concepts such as poverty had ceased to have any policy-relevant status, the view of the Prime Minister that there was 'no such thing as society', and Kenneth Baker's statement to the 1987 Conservative Party conference that the 'pursuit of egalitarianism is over' (quoted in Johnson, 1990, p. 126). The government did not have to square this particular circle for very long, however, as the White Paper, which followed some six months after the RAWP review's final report, initially made no allowance for social factors in its proposals for resource allocation at regional level.[28]

However, the report did have severe technical limitations. By basing its analysis on existing hospital utilisation rates, it was open to the charge of preserving the status quo, since those areas with highest levels of supply were bound to experience the highest utilisation (Carr-Hill, 1990; Beech, Bevan and Mays, 1990; Mays, 1990). Even before the review was completed Mays (1987) claimed that the deprivation arguments concealed a defence of the status quo from those with an interest in its maintenance, especially in view of the lack of hard evidence about exactly how social deprivation translated into need for health care. Additional criticisms suggested that the research was structured in such a way as to produce a conclusion acceptable to the government – one that minimised disruption but did not concede too much to the deprivation lobby.[29]

The White Paper and spatial resource allocation

The principal proposal of the White Paper was the abolition of RAWP in England, on the grounds that 'the government has applied it to such effect over the years that the major differences have gone and it is no longer necessary' (para. 4.10). Certainly, compared with positions in relation to abstract revenue targets, gaps had generally narrowed; and the government had indeed applied RAWP to dramatic effect, notably by reducing the overall levels of growth in the HCHS while pursuing the redistributive aims of RAWP. However, it is arguable that some form of redistribution was still required; certainly most RHAs were approaching revenue target levels, but there remained substantial inequalities between DHAs. Whether RAWP had achieved greater *equity* is a question tackled by Powell (1991) and Beech *et al.* (1990); this is a complicated issue as one is dealing with moving targets – estimated levels of need can shift, as can levels of resources, so apparently 'underfunded' regions can move further away from their target revenue.

In contrast with the RAWP methodology, in which funding was still determined largely by historic patterns of provision, the White Paper introduced a methodology based on per capita allocations, weighted by using the SMR with a weighting factor of 0.5; Carr-Hill (1990) suggested that this had been introduced on the grounds of 'ease of communicability to the non-numerate', since the research for the RAWP review had suggested a weighting of 0.44. The Thames RHAs were to receive a 3 per cent addition to reflect the additional costs of providing care in the capital, which would mitigate the effects of the new system on London. No mention was made of deprivation factors in the new national formula, reflecting both the government's apparent abandonment of concern with social inequality (the RAWP review's recommendations were never formally adopted) and the move towards other forms of financing public services (such as the Poll Tax) that did not differentiate between people's ability to pay above a certain income level. There was also the need for a resource allocation system that reflected quickly and accurately the changing population distribution rather than being distorted by the revenue costs of facilities in locations where populations had declined. Arguably the new system showed an awareness that the problems of the NHS were moving into the Conservatives' electoral heartlands (see above). Hence Barry Jones described the White Paper as a 'Home Counties solution to health service problems' and as 'another example of the divisive cabinet politics of the South East of Britain'.[30] In a further attempt to produce redistribution of resources away from high-cost urban locations, the government pro-posed the introduction of capital charging into the NHS. Other things being equal, this would make it difficult for hospitals located in high-cost areas to compete in the internal market, since their prices would have to reflect capital charges. This meant that an ostensibly *national* service could be undermined by the emphasis on transferring resources away from the highest-cost areas, places which, despite the losses of population they had suffered, still required local hospital provision.

Whatever the technical arguments in favour of the reforms, then, they seem to have been motivated, at least in part, by awareness of the (increasingly polarised) political geography of the country (on which, see Gamble, 1989; Jessop *et al.*,1988; Lewis and Townsend, 1989). The areas likely to benefit most were clearly going to be the Conservative heartlands,[31] and with growing awareness of the problems of congestion and pollution in the South East (see Breheny and Congdon, 1989), the government seemed well aware of the need to avoid damaging publicity about the NHS's problems in those areas. By forcing all hospitals to compete in the market as quasi-autonomous enterprises, the White Paper allowed the difficulties experienced by health authorities or hospitals to be represented as failures to compete rather than a result of lack of funds. In principle this seemed to offer a way of abdicating responsibility for service reductions and achieving a market-led reduction in capacity in London without excessive political damage.

The potential impact on revenue budgets of the White Paper's proposals is shown in Figure 4.5, from which the general thrust of the proposals is clear: some authorities stood to lose up to 50 per cent of their budget, reflecting their high dependence on cross-boundary flows of patients.[32] Thus, by moving to a situation where DHAs' initial budgets would be determined substantially by their resident popula-tions, a number of districts, notably those with large acute general hospitals in locations that had experienced population decline, would have to attract substantial amounts of business in order to make up their budgets to their pre-White Paper levels. Freed to place contracts where they wished, the decisions of purchasers could clearly destabilise the acute hospital services in places such as inner London. Urban hospitals would be forced to compete in a Darwinian struggle for survival. Whether this represented a rational way of restructuring the pattern of services remained to be seen.

Planning versus the market: Tomlinson and beyond

The White Paper therefore implied major net transfers of funds within RHAs in particular, promoting the rapid rationalisation of hospital capacity in those areas that failed to compete in the new marketplace

(Figure 4.5). While the first year of the reforms was intended to be one in which a 'steady state' applied (purchasers were encouraged not to switch contracts excessively) as the brakes were released, Home Counties purchasers began to switch contracts away from the high-cost central London facilities. This prompted the following comment from the Health Committee (1991b, p. xviii):

> given the acknowledged overcapacity prior to the introduction of the reforms, to say that financial viability is likely to prove 'difficult' for many London hospitals after the introduction of the reforms is likely to prove an understatement.

Partly because of this, the White Paper's implementation was marked by the announcement of a 4 per cent floor in revenue growth to all RHAs, in what was described as 'the clearest indication yet that the implementation of the reforms is being diluted on political grounds'[33] (though it must be acknowledged that to move immediately to a capitation-based system would have had an even more dramatic impacts on the service; some form of transitional protection was required). William Waldegrave informed the Committee that 'we will have to plan and manage our way through the changes . . . When exactly the NHS executive and I, as Secretary of State, intervene is a matter of fine judgement' (Health Committee, 1991c), though the impending general election seemed to provide ample stimuli for such intervention. The government announced an inquiry into the problems of the London hospitals, under the chairmanship of Professor Bernard Tomlinson, former chairman of the Northern RHA, once it became clear that the closure of at least one teaching hospital was a distinct possibility, attracting damaging publicity in a pre election period. The emphasis had clearly swung back to *planning* the change in London's hospital system rather than leaving it to market forces. As reports circulated about the financial viability of numerous London hospitals it was clear that some form of coordination would be required if *ad hoc* closures were not to undermine a comprehensive acute hospital service and seriously weaken key provider units and centres of medical excellence. Thus the age-old conflict between medical priorities, professional autonomy and social needs (Rivett, 1982; Smith, 1981) surfaced again. Of course the announcement of the Tomlinson Inquiry represented a major volte-face for the government. If there existed surplus capacity in the health service (which opponents of the changes doubted), London was the one place where genuine competition would exist due to the existence of so many proximate alternatives with which

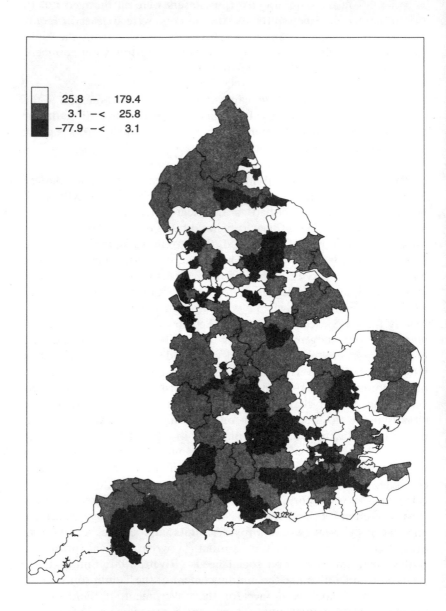

Figure 4.5   English DHAs: percentage change in budgets if White Paper system in operation

to place contracts. Furthermore, the market would, in theory, succeed in rationalising hospitals, in a situation where the implacable opposition of the teaching hospitals and professional elites had been a stumbling-block to change for nearly 100 years. The government had arguably backtracked once before by conceding above-average levels of resource growth to the Thames RHAs immediately prior to the implementation of the White Paper;[34] now it did so again, much more publicly, implicitly acknowledging the political consequences of its reforms and attempting to minimise their costs. And if some degree of planning was required in London, why not elsewhere? London was not the only location where inner-city hospitals were threatened by major reductions in revenue.

The central arguments of the Tomlinson Report were that London consumed an excessive share of the resources devoted to the NHS, and that inner-London residents were overprovided with hospital beds, which they used at above-average rates: the situation was therefore inequitable. Critics challenged the basis on which these conclusions had been drawn.[35] Nevertheless, according to Tomlinson (1992), change was inevitable – purchasers were already withdrawing funds (totalling approximately £50 mn in 1992–3) from central-London hospitals, and still greater reductions were anticipated in subsequent years. It was therefore suggested that a managed rationalisation of the London hospital system could minimise the adverse consequences of adapting to this new situation, but (almost in the same breath) that change would have to be swift to avoid blighting the future of several units. Leaving aside the specifics of the report – which hospitals were deemed viable and which not, or the likely future of numerous small institutions and the debates over the appropriate units with which they should be linked – the philosophical contradiction at the heart of the inquiry was explored by the Health Committee, drawing comments such as the following from Sir Bernard Tomlinson:

> It has indeed been said [that] *the best thing that could have happened was to allow the internal market to carry on and destroy a few hospitals* and then people would have put their problems right very quickly. . . . The danger in the process of *indiscriminate reduction* of hospitals in London is so great . . . that we believe the process . . . has to be a carefully and . . . *a firmly managed process.*[36]

Returning in subsequent questioning to this issue, Labour MP Hugh Bayley pointed to the apparent inconsistency evident in the report's proposals: 'Are you saying that the day to day decisions are best left to the market but the big strategic decisions need *something more than market forces?*' In response Sir Bernard agreed that: 'it is a philosophical difficulty, is it not, to have managed change in a market that is intended to produce change'.[37] The stability and indeed viability of London's hospital system rests on how this tension between planning and the market is resolved. At the time of writing, press reports almost daily highlight hospitals in deficit or otherwise vulnerable to the switching of contracts for patient care, or having to cancel non-urgent treatment of patients, while there has been ministerial intervention to prevent purchasers from switching contracts from hospitals that might otherwise close.[38] But it remains hugely ironic that since one purpose of the reforms was to eliminate overcapacity and inefficiency in the system, it has proved politically impossible to do so in London, of all places the location where the internal market was supposedly most necessary. More to the point, perhaps, while the internal market may well have the effect of reducing hospital provision in London, this will do nothing to improve community services there; whether planned or not, this is only a partial solution to a mismatch between services and needs. It may serve a political goal of reducing expenditure, but it does not stand as a viable *health* policy. Planning is confined to managing the decline of hospitals while minimising protests; it does not extend to guaranteeing the availability of alternative, community-based services.[39] Moreover, if as Jarman (1993) implied, there was no technical case for a reduction in acute hospital services in inner London, the only conclusion that could be drawn was that the government was not prepared to sustain those hospitals because of their high *costs* rather than because they were not *needed*.

Concluding comments

As with the material covered in much of this book, there is evident tension between the 'national' and the 'local'. For example, despite the government's insistence that the financial difficulties faced by health authorities were 'local' in character, much of the evidence implies that funding problems were generalised across the great majority of regions and districts. This tension is important in another sense: because RHAs have had discretion about the precise ways they allocate funds, the factors used in subregional resource allocation formulae have varied. This has led to complaints from MPs that while their region received no additional funds to cover the needs of its deprived inner-city districts, those districts in rural or suburban areas lost out – relative to comparable places in RHAs that chose to ignore deprivation factors – as the regional distribution was skewed away from them.[40] Though this is inevitable, given the government's decentralist stance, it throws some doubt on its commitment to equal treatment of places in equal need, and rather undermines the case for capitation funding, namely its transparency, simplicity and equity.

The foregoing discussion should be considered in relation to both technical and political criteria. The technical difficulties involved in designing an allocation of health care resources that is responsive to social need are immense. Much debate correctly focuses on factors that can serve as proxies for measures of health status in populations, or on social factors thought to influence the need for health care. For example, one might draw the conclusion that social deprivation generated need for hospital care because patients' recuperation was inhibited by inadequate community support, poor housing and so on. But if this is so the logical conclusion is that a wider programme of social and economic policy is required, which would obviously be anathema to the Conservatives. It was far simpler to ignore those difficult political choices by relying on the transparency of a capitation formula, which has its own rough and ready element of equity. But to do so is itself to make a political judgement, which is that health policy is confined to expenditure on health services. The reforms are not able to guarantee the development of community-based services, nor are they – without some imaginative purchasing, jointly with local authorities – likely to enable health authorities to do much about the social causes of ill health.

If the transparency of capitation was so attractive, why then did the government apparently accept the case for a social deprivation factor as recommended by the RAWP review? One reason has already been hinted at: it seemed to offer one way to stabilise the situation in the Thames RHAs, itself an outcome of the government's vigorous pursuit of redistribution within a minimum-growth budget, pending the outcome of the thinking on the NHS reforms that was under way at the time. Because such a measure would staunch the flow of funds away from London, perhaps the government felt it would help avoid a repetition of the events of the winter of 1987–8.

However we are less likely to explain post-1979 developments in resource allocation formulae and policies in terms of technical issues than in relation to political considerations. Whatever the merits of various criteria for the RAWP formulae, the basic problem was the pace at which RHAs were required to effect net transfers of resources between and within regions. This was what eventually provoked territorially based claims for funds, claims that suggested RAWP was not delivering the funds promised to its supposed beneficiaries. In addition, something as needs-based as RAWP may well have offended those who believed the government should abandon the pursuit of egalitarianism. Instead a cruder notion of justice pervades the reforms: levelling-down areas of high-cost provision will release funds to be spent elsewhere. Hence the internal market represented a quicker way of shifting resources away from the capital, and (arguably) a less politically visible one. Whereas prior to 1991 protests could focus on low levels of growth in the service (and thus implicitly on central government funding), under the new system the failure of a hospital is also a failure to compete, rather than the failure of the government to provide funds.

The market is also spatially selective. The electorate of suburbia and the outer South East benefit most under capitation (and indeed from the presence of high proportions of fundholding practices – see Chapter 8). Crucially, the reforms ensure that, in this zero-sum game, such locations will not lose out. The post-White Paper formula can best be regarded as a solution that maximises the purchasing power available to the outer Thames districts. In this context it is appropriate to consider how best to interpret the government's policies. The post-1979 governments have undeniably promoted the uneven development of Britain and relied, to a large degree, on a limited part of the country for electoral support. The logic of this would be to connect the availability of welfare resources more explicitly to the economic performance of particular places – for instance through an insurance system or via a greater degree of local finance for services. However to do so would invite the charge that the government is *denationalising* the service. Were this to happen the geographical pattern of services would rapidly begin to look very different, as the distribution of private care (Chapter 7) or of pre-NHS voluntary hospitals (Powell, 1992) makes clear. Instead the rationale for the internal market can be seen as a politically functional one for the government: the invisible hand serves the government's purpose of withdrawing resources from the high-cost inner-city hospitals, which can then be redistributed to an increasingly suburban and rural electorate. As such the reforms are inseparable from the political geography of Conservative governments' strategies since 1979: the need to protect core support in the South East appears central to the complaints voiced about subregional resource allocation and to the subsequent proposals.

5

Imagined and Imaginary Communities: Rhetoric and Reality in Community Care Policy

'Community' is and has been one of the most overused and least defined words in the social science lexicon; 'community care' may well occupy a similar place in the social policy literature. The confusions about the meanings of the term community defy simple summary, so it should be no surprise that community care has 'confused boundaries' (Land, 1991). Among the confusions of community care are whether it means care in or care by the community; the distinction between health care and social care; and the fact that, despite its title, effective community care does require the availability of inpatient treatment facilities. Given that the main responsibility for community care now falls on local government, it may seem out of place to include an extended discussion of it. However, given that adequate community-based services are necessary for those discharged from hospitals, consideration of community care policies is relevant to discussion of the NHS reforms (which are predicated on an increase in efficiency and the discharge of patients not requiring hospitalisation). Furthermore important issues are raised by community care, notably the boundary between the responsibilities of the health and social services.

The debates over community care often replay arguments rehearsed many years ago. Thus institutions for those with learning difficulties were only transferred away from local authorities when the NHS was set up; arguably they should not be a health service responsibility since the residents do not require medical treatment on account of their condition alone (Heginbotham, 1990). Changes consistent with the pursuit of community care policies have sometimes resulted from external influences. Thus the rapid decline in the population of mental institutions in the 1950s had much to do with labour shortages, an effect of which was the discovery that many inpatients need not be hospitalised at all. Technical developments, such as the discovery of psychotropic drugs, have also had a major influence on policies. However Chapman *et al.* (1991) suggest that the claims against institutionalisation and for community have both been overstated.

Community care has been subject to new twists and turns in the 1980s: for the right, the 'community' has been seen as the first port of call for those in need, whereas for the left, the practice of community care has been an index of the government's indifference to the welfare state, or more accurately to welfare *statism*, if by that we mean the notion that the state should provide for all. Perhaps more than any other policy arena, community care exemplifies the ideal world of welfare pluralists (cf. Johnson, 1987), in which the state's role is reduced to that of mobilising and coordinating individuals and communities in their efforts to care for the chronically sick, the mentally ill and those with learning difficulties or physical disabilities. A primary reason for this is precisely the indifference of the state to those unable to articulate and press claims upon it, whether they be professional lobbies or patients and their advocates, in contrast with the well-organised producer interests defending acute hospital provision. The invisibility of those to be cared for in the community, the nebulous nature of 'communities', and indeed the very invisibility to history and social policy of the 'carers' – primarily women – all help to account for the slow progress towards a coherent policy. But they do not, on their own, explain the neglect of community care and the absence of commitment to it during the 1980s.

Community care also raises the questions of how the rights of citizens are to be met in the case of groups that may be incapable of articulating their case, and of the obligation of those not requiring care to meet the 'needs of strangers' (Ignatieff, 1984). Community care is an area of substantial hidden and/or unmet need, and debates have focused on how resources are to be made available for the development of community care, and on how clients establish their rights to have their needs met. In respect of the mentally ill and people with learning difficulties, the implicit presumption has been that rationalising the historic asylums would release the resources to develop community-based facilities. For the elderly, the government's preference is for a market in formal sources of care and for preventing needs becoming translated into demands on formal services through reliance on informal care. At least initially the government repudiated the norms-based approaches of the priorities documents of the 1970s in favour of empowering individuals in the market via the expansion of social security payments. But this raised questions about how best to regulate such a mixed economy of care. Recognising these difficulties – notably the fact that social security expenditure was effectively demand-led and poorly targeted – may be one reason for the introduction of a greater degree of 'planning' into community care policy from the 1989 White Paper, *Caring for People* (Secretary of State for Health, 1989b), although the delays over implementing the community care reforms suggest that political expediency played a greater role in determining the character of the reforms to be implemented. In community care as in so many areas, then, the interaction between ideology and rationality is important.

This chapter is divided into five main sections. I first examine some of the diverse meanings of community care, noting the ideological appropriation of the term 'community' and summarising some of the commentaries on the hidden assumptions that underpin notions of community and caring. The main dimensions of change since 1979 in services for the main groups of people being referred to here – the mentally ill, people with learning difficulties, and the elderly – are then reviewed. A brief history is then presented of community care policies prior to 1979, noting some of the technical and political difficulties in implementing policy. The next section develops this account in a discussion of recent policies towards services for these groups, and the final section draws out the most important themes to emerge in the implementation of the community care reforms.

The ideological appropriation of community

There are three issues here: the translation of notions of community from academic and popular discourse in ways that may confuse as much as clarify; the reliance on unpaid carers to buttress government policy; and the promotion of a mixed economy of welfare in the guise of welfare pluralism.

The term 'community' continues to resist easy definition. It carries warm, nostalgic overtones of something we have lost (Titmuss, quoted in Land, 1991); it is normative as well as analytic and descriptive, so that it refers not only to society as it *is* but to social elements valued in the past, present or in a hoped-for future, and because of this it is open to use and abuse for rhetorical and political purposes. The term perhaps had strongest analytical utility in the context of small, geographically circumscribed communities (such as mining villages) where economic circumstance forced families to develop dense neighbourhood networks, quite literally as a matter of survival. But there are great difficulties with transplanting this vision of community to the late twentieth century, especially as a basis for social policy (Bulmer,1987). Firstly, few such work-dominated communities now exist, while rapid economic change, the growing segmentation of labour markets, and increased physical and social mobility all mean that localities and communities are much more heterogeneous while associations, or communal ties, are more transient. Changes in family structures mean that it cannot be assumed that family members will be available to assume the burden of care for those in need. Finally, social life is becoming more privatised, which reduces interactions with immediate neighbours and diminishes a sense of responsibility towards them (Newby *et al.*, 1985). Abrams' observation that the capacity of the community to care is 'typically volatile, spasmodic and unreliable' (quoted in Chapman *et al.*, 1991) seems apposite, and the evidence that communities are positively willing to become more involved in community care is in decidedly short supply.

Secondly, it is impossible to discuss community care without acknowledging that policies are structured by certain presumptions about gender roles. Dalley (1988) suggests that the assumption that the burden of caring will be borne largely by female relatives of those being cared for has invariably underpinned community care policies and is not unique to the Conservative administrations since 1979. A familial ideology, structured by patriarchy, constructs caring as 'women's work' and as a labour of love: it conflates caring *about* someone with caring *for* them and does not acknowledge that these can be separated, and gives menial tasks relating to caring for a person the same status as affective feelings associated with caring about someone. This has been strongly emphasised by Conservatives, with Margaret Thatcher referring to the 'immense sacrifices' that people will make for their relatives for example. But there has rarely been as explicit a statement as the 1981 White Paper, *Growing Older*, which suggested that 'care *in* the community must increasingly mean care *by* the community' (DHSS, 1981c, p. 3). But recent economic changes, notably the growth in participation by women in paid work as male unemployment rose and as emphases on owner occupation and consumption increased the pressures on household budgets, have severely restricted the pool of potential carers. There is a contradiction between an 'economy that increasingly depends on women's labour and a restructured welfare state making the same demands' (McDowell, 1991, p. 412). Other things being equal, pressures on carers are probably exacerbated by the increases in the pace of patient throughput and reductions in length of stay during the 1980s, so that patients are being discharged at an earlier stage of convalescence, thus requiring more attention at home. Hence the increased efficiency of the acute sector creates problems for the community sector, yet further increases in the acute sector's efficiency depend on viable community support for discharged patients.

In practice the cost-effectiveness of community care depends on not putting a cash value on the unpaid and often unaided contribution (financial, social, emotional) of carers (Wicks, 1985). Around 14 per cent of people aged 16 or over help the elderly, sick or handicapped in some way, suggesting approximately six million carers; however Parker (1992) suggested that a figure of 1.3 million carers 'heavily' involved (over 20 hours per week) in care would be a more useful basis on which to develop policies. If a cash equivalent were calculated for this work, at the average rate of pay for, say, a home help, it would probably run to billions of pounds. The vast majority of carers are female relatives and the proportion of non-relatives involved is small, especially for personal and physical care (Twigg, 1992). There are also variations in the potential availability of informal carers: the extent to which women participate in the labour force varies considerably between geographical areas (Duncan, 1991; McDowell, 1991), and the growing flexibility and insecurity of employment militate against combining work with caring.

Finally, discourses about community care have made much of a rhetoric of partnership and pluralism, the implication being that responsibilities of care are shared equally and that individuals are in a position to exercise meaningful choice (Johnson, 1987; Pinker, 1992). The promotion of the mixed economy of welfare would be unexceptionable if all providers of care (formal, informal, voluntary, statutory) were operating on a level playing field. Successful community care self-evidently demands the involvement of a range of partners; the issue is who is involved and on what terms. For example, at the same time as central government extended choice in the private sector by permitting residential accommodation to be financed from the social security budget, it contradicted this by heavily constraining local government finance, thus limiting the development of public sector services. Furthermore the insistence of the government that, following the community care reforms, a certain proportion of community care funds should be spent in the private sector, again contrasted with its decentralist rhetoric and with its belief in choice. Welfare pluralism had perhaps become welfare privatism, and suggesting that this has arisen independently of political decisions seems at best naïve (see Walker, 1992).

Thus community care is defined implicitly in several different ways: as deinstitutionalisation and community-based care; as care by the community; and as something carried out by non-state providers of care. Official definitions are less easy to come by. The Royal Commission saw it as a policy to provide care in community settings rather than institutions (para 6.26) but went no further than this. For the mentally ill it noted the desirability of providing psychiatric units within District General Hospitals but observed that this would leave a class of incurable, behaviourally disturbed, old and demented patients in psychiatric hospitals (para 6.44). Other definitions are confined to shifting some resources away from institutional settings (for example DHSS, 1977a). Perhaps most would agree that complementary community services enable health providers to concentrate on clinical needs, and that community care implies a shift both in the balance of care and in the balance of agency responsibilities (Wistow, 1988, p. 153).

Needs, expenditure and services

The most obvious source of need for community care derives from the growing proportions of the elderly, especially the frail elderly (those over 75), in the population, and from the decline in traditional sources of family support for those in need. Harding (1992) describes survey evidence that suggests the gap between levels of need and levels of services is wide and may be growing. In particular, the number of the over-85s unable to undertake basic tasks will double between 1980 and 2001. She also points to other estimates of the costs of, for instance, treatment of mental illness, which show very considerable unmet need.

Detailed data on expenditure trends are not easily available. Annual memoranda from the DoH to the Social Services Committee show expenditure in the NHS on the HCHS but the categories included in community care have changed over time, so determining precisely what is expenditure on 'community' health services is problematic. The Health Committee (1993a) states (para 6) that the 'proportion of HCHS expenditure on community services has increased from 9.5 per cent in 1980–1 to 14.6 per cent in 1990–1', and in the next paragraph suggests that expenditure on the community health services accounted for 8.7 per cent of total HCHS expenditure in 1980–1, increasing to 13.5 per cent in 1990–1. However if one examines the resources allocated to mental illness services alone, the proportion of the HCHS budget devoted to this sector has hardly changed at all, being slightly over 11 per cent throughout the 1980s, though falling to 10.6 per cent for 1990–1 (Lelliott *et al.*, 1993, table 1). This hardly seems consistent with the supposed priority attached to such services by successive governments, even allowing for the fact that community care may not require some of the overheads of long-stay hospitals.

The same memorandum provides details of expenditure in core services for community care from 1986–7 to 1990–1, although only from the 1988–9 financial year are figures available for the NHS. Discontinuities in the data mean that earlier years' figures are unreliable as a basis for year-on-year comparisons. These data comprise expenditure on NHS community services, local authority domiciliary and residential care, housing and various social security benefits. Although total expenditure in support of community care objectives grew by 15 per cent from 1988–9 to 1990–1, 64 per cent of this growth was due to the continuing expansion of income support payments, which rose by £617 mn. NHS community health expenditure grew by some 9.3 per cent over the same period. However NHS expenditure is still heavily dominated by inpatient treatment: for mental illness services 84.7 per cent of spending was on inpatient services in 1989 compared with 87.9 per cent ten years earlier; for those with learning difficulties the figure was 61.7 per cent compared with 74.4 per cent (Social Services Committee, 1990a). At the same time, expenditure on local authority residential care was virtually static in real terms, and in fact spending on the elderly declined, while local authority spending on domiciliary care grew by some 11 per cent, again concealing variations in expenditure trends (to the extent that these can be identified over such a short timespan). So expenditure growth is still led by income support payments, which may not be the most rational way to distribute funds for this purpose.

Furthermore there are substantial variations in spending by social services agencies, who are now the lead agencies in delivering community care. Figure 5.1 maps expenditure on social services per head of population aged over 65. There is a more than fivefold variation between authorities, from £809 to £122. These variations bear little relation to need (Audit Commission, 1988; Harding, 1992, pp. 25–7).

Some indication of trends in service provision is given in figures 5.2–5.4. Looking at the balance of care for the elderly, the most important feature has been the expansion of the private sector, which has grown more than fourfold since 1979 and provides the majority of residential places for those over 65. Local authority provision, in contrast, has declined per capita by nearly 40 per cent.

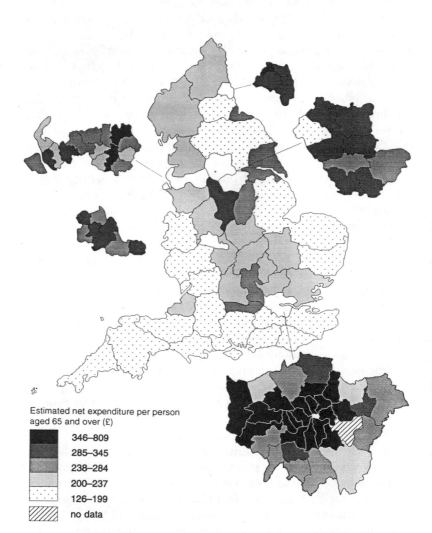

Estimated net expenditure per person
aged 65 and over (£)

346–809
285–345
238–284
200–237
126–199
no data

**Figure 5.1   Per capita net expenditure on personal social services,
England, 1990–1**

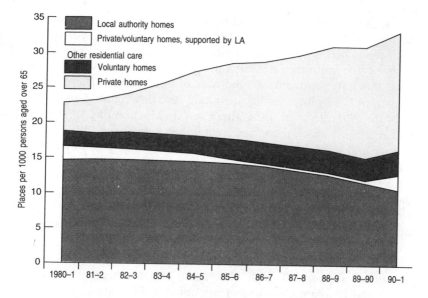

Figure 5.2 Balance of residential care for the elderly, England, 1980–1 to 1990–1

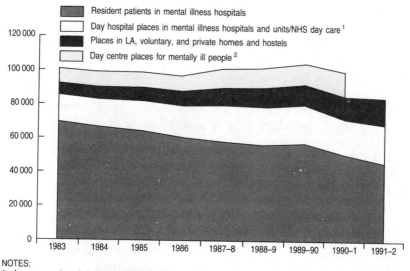

NOTES:
1. Average number of places available daily.
2. Day centre places not available for 1992.

Source: Health Committee, 1993.

Figure 5.3 Provision for persons with mental illness, England, 1983–92

For the mentally ill, the rapid rundown of mental illness hospitals (a decline from 69 000 beds to 45 100 from 1983–92, or 35 per cent) has not been matched by a corresponding absolute growth in private, local authority or voluntary homes; though these have grown by 107 per cent, this only represents an increase of 7026 places. There was also growth of 6307 places in day hospitals, and day centre places rose by 6424 (to 1991). In total, then, there was a reduction of 23 930 hospital places, against which there was a combined increase of 19 757 places in private and local authority residential institutions, plus day care and day hospital facilities. If, therefore, one assumes that those who no longer live in NHS hospitals are now cared for by either day hospitals, day centres or other residential accommodation, *but not by more than one of these*, then reductions in the mental hospital population have not quite been balanced by growth in community-based services. However it is more likely that some of those in non-NHS residential accommodation could not have been discharged without being given additional support through day care, and are therefore living in residential accommodation and attending a day care centre. Consequently, using only these figures, the presumption should probably be that the increase in community-based services has not accommodated the reduced mental hospital population. However figures produced for the Health Committee (1994), using a broader definition of community-based facilities than that given here, imply that the decline in hospital facilities has in fact been matched, numerically if not qualitatively, by the growth of community-based services.

However this does not necessarily mean that enough facilities are available. In an attempt to compare existing levels of provision with various government and clinical recommendations, Lelliott *et al.* (1993, p. 992) found that current provision for acute hospital services for mental illness was approximately four fifths of that recommended by the Royal College of Psychiatrists, while the availability of non-NHS residential facilities was some two thirds of the level recommended by, for example, the National Schizophrenia Fellowship. They also found clinical evidence to suggest that, due to the shortage of available places, nearly one third of patients who had been in hospital for more than six months were inappropriately placed in acute wards. Nearly half of these could not be transferred to more appropriate accommodation either because suitable facilities did not exist or because available services were full. Such patients occupied only 9 per cent of acute hospital beds, and represented only a fraction of the demand for community-based residential accommodation. Lelliott *et al.* (1993) therefore predicted the development of a vicious circle: discharge from hospital would become more difficult; community services would be under pressure since short-term hospital admissions, of value in the management of mental illness, would be harder to obtain;[1] health authorities might have to respond by creating or preserving medium- and long-stay beds at the expense of further community developments, for the lack of which pressure on acute facilities would increase.

Finally, analysing provision of residential care for those with learning difficulties is somewhat eased by a longer run of official data on provision, dating from 1974 (Figure 5.4). The population of hospitals for those with learning difficulties fell from 50 900 in 1974 to 19 600 in 1992. As can be seen, *total* provision in residential care fell only slightly, however, due to the rapid growth in local authority and, in particular, private and voluntary homes, especially after 1983, but there has been a welcome shift away from hospitalisation.

It must also be noted that deinstitutionalisation policies are caught by a scissors effect for, as hospitals are run down, unit costs per patient rise with declining occupancy. But because those patients with the least severe disabilities are discharged first, the longer the policy goes on, the higher the costs of (presumably more complex) community care for those who are discharged later. Thus the unit costs of hospital inpatient care for the mentally ill and those with learning difficulties increased

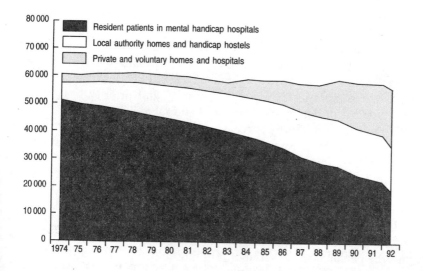

Figure 5.4 Residential provision for persons with learning difficulties, 1974–92

between 1979 and 1989 by 47 per cent and 58 per cent respectively (Social Services Committee, 1990a). Adequate bridging finance is therefore essential if non-institutional alternatives are to be developed, as repeated investigations have commented (Social Services Committee, 1985a; Health Committee, 1994).

While some of these statistics may give comfort to supporters of the community care ideal, institutionalisation can take place just as easily in a small facility as in a large one. Few studies have successfully traced those discharged from psychiatric hospitals (for an exception, see Tomlinson, 1991), so we do not know whether community care has been a success. Furthermore, change may be more apparent than real: in many cases facilities have become categorised as 'private' or 'voluntary' by administrative *legerdemain*, as statutory authorities have transferred legal control of services to trusts in order to maximise income from social security rather than from cash-limited or rate-capped sources. The buildings remain the same.

The development of community care policies: themes and assumptions

Debates about community care and deinstitutionalisation are hardly new. The problems of long-stay institutions were recognised during the 1950s (Ham, 1981); there were proposals for the integrated development of acute hospital and community facilities for mental illness and those with learning difficulties (MoH, 1962a, 1962b); and scandals about conditions in long-stay facilities led eventually to the Labour government's consultative document (DHSS, 1977a), which proposed a shift of resources in favour of community and priority services. The development of community care was undoubtedly affected during the 1970s and early 1980s by successive NHS reorganisations, and by the restrictions on local government expenditure by both Conservative and Labour governments (Murphy, 1991, 67).

Initial statements by Conservative spokespersons both anticipated a shift in responsibilities for community care and cut some of the ground from under the feet of those responsible for it. Thus Patrick Jenkin optimistically anticipated an enhanced role for the voluntary and informal sector. He made a clear distinction between the health service and the personal social services, arguing that:

when one is comparing where one can make savings one protects the health service because there is no alternative, whereas in the personal social services *there is a substantial possibility and, indeed, probability of continued growth in the amount of voluntary care, of neighbourhood care, of self help* (Social Services Committee, 1980a, pp. 99–100 – emphasis added).

However the Social Services Committee was concerned that this might mean that 'aspiration would be mistaken for achievement' (1980a, p. xiii).

At the same time detailed target levels of service provision were abandoned. *Care in Action* (DHSS, 1981a) no longer included benchmarks against which to measure progress towards national policies and priorities. This document, as well as *Growing Older* (1981c), was described as the 'high water mark of an anti-statist bias which [was] naive in its conception no less than its execution' (Wistow, 1988, p. 136). Whether naive or not, the anti-statist bias led to reductions in the level of local authority spending in 1979–80 and 1980–1, and to severe restrictions on spending thereafter, which gave little comfort to those who felt the public sector's role should be more than residual. Klein (1989) suggests this antistatism and decentralisation were the result of disillusionment with 'planning', but an equally plausible explanation seems to be a sloughing-off of responsibility from central to local administration.

Three reports in the 1980s pushed community care up the political agenda. The Social Services Committee (1985a) reported on the progress of the closure of long-stay hospitals. This was followed by the Audit Commission's (1986) report, *Making a Reality of Community Care.* Among the principal difficulties identified by the Audit Commission were the failure of community-based services to keep pace with the rundown of long-stay institutions, particularly for the mentally ill; the uneven pattern of local authority provision, so that the care received by individuals was 'as much dependent on where they live as on what they need'; and the fact that over 300 000 people lived in inappropriate and costly residential settings (Audit Commission, 1986, p. 2).

The Audit Commission highlighted the technical and political problems attending community care policies. Firstly, mechanisms for achieving a shift in funding consistent with government priorities were inadequate. Secondly, local authorities were penalised for developing community care services where this brought their spending above central government targets, and there were no incentives to develop services (domiciliary care, for instance) that might save public funds by preventing inappropriate placements in residential accommodation. Thirdly, bridging finance was inadequate to bring community services on stream in advance of the rundown of institutional provision. Fourthly, the effects of central government formulae, designed to promote the equitable distribution of public funds, were outweighed by the unplanned growth of social security payments, which dramatically altered the distribution of winners and losers under RAWP: the South Western RHA, the fifth highest beneficiary of RAWP, became the second highest gainer; even more perversely, the SW Thames RHA, one of the main relative losers under RAWP, overtook Yorkshire and the West Midlands (Audit Commission, 1986, table 19). Fifthly, responsibilities were excessively fragmented between agencies with different priorities, styles, structures and budgets (Audit Commission, 1986, pp. 2–3). The Audit Commission's recommendations included the first suggestion from a public body that a purchaser/provider split should be introduced for services for the elderly. It also sought to clarify the responsibilities for health and social care of health and local authorities, with local authorities being suggested as the lead agents for those with learning disabilities while health authorities would be responsible for mental illness provision.

The government's response was to appoint Roy Griffiths to conduct a review of community care policies. Griffiths (1988) was less optimistic than the Audit Commission that the necessary resources could be generated through increased efficiency; on the contrary, he suggested that service providers 'felt that the Israelites faced with the requirement to make bricks without straw had a comparatively routine and possible task'. Without discussion of available resources and timescales, talk of policy amounted to 'theology rather than purposeful delivery of a caring service'. Community care was 'everybody's distant relative but nobody's baby', and the system could almost have been 'designed to produce patchy performance', so one minister had to be clearly and publicly responsible for community care; finance should be provided through a central government ringfenced grant; social service authorities would have a strategic, enabling (rather than providing) role, being responsible for needs assessment and then for 'making the maximum use of voluntary and private sector bodies to widen consumer choice, stimulate innovation and encourage efficiency'; and health authorities would restrict services to health care and not include social care. Some of the strengths of the Griffiths Report were its emphasis on accountability through the electoral process, its clearer definition of the role of health authorities, and its stress on ring fencing, though it was open to the criticism that the performance of local authorities was variable. Although Griffiths reported in early 1988, it was some 16 months before his report was debated in parliament and the implementation of the community care White Paper was eventually postponed until April 1993.

The government's White Paper, *Caring for People* (Secretary of State for Health, 1989b), began by acknowledging that by far the greater part of community care was provided by friends and neighbours, and asserted that:

> The *decision to take on a caring role* is never an easy one. However, *many people make that choice* and it is right that they should be able to play their part . . . [but] carers need help and support if they are to continue to carry out their role (para 1.9, emphases added).

One might suggest that taking on the caring role is not just a matter of choice. Responding to the various critiques of their policies, among the key objectives were the promotion of domiciliary care to enable people to live in their own home as long as possible, attaching priority to services for carers, promoting the development of the independent sector, introducing assessment of need as a 'cornerstone' of policy, and clarifying agency responsibilities, to improve accountability. The two principal changes were making local authorities the lead agencies for needs assessment and developing care plans, and integrating social security expenditure on residential care with that of statutory agencies, thus removing the financial incentives towards residential care. However a further key recommendation of the Griffiths Report, that of ringfenced spending on community care, was rejected (Chapter 9). Nor did *Caring for People* set national norms or propose appointing a minister for community care; consequently the government's commitment to a *national* policy could be called into question.

Implementing community care: incompetence or malice?

The two principal dimensions of community care policies have been the attempt to replace long-stay institutions for the mentally ill and those with learning difficulties with community-based provision, and the development of community-based services to enable increasing proportions of the elderly to remain in their own homes.

Community care for the mentally ill and people with learning difficulties

The decline of the Victorian asylum was of course to be welcomed. Isolated, massive, often enclosed, such facilities were perhaps concerned less with providing a therapeutic environment than with social control and segregation; they were certainly not noted for innovation or, in general, for high-quality care (Murphy, 1991). However, smoothly and simultaneously replacing such institutions with community-based alternatives posed considerable challenges. The 1981 Care in the Community initiative (DHSS, 1981b) was intended to promote the discharge of long-stay hospital patients by enabling DHAs to transfer funds to local authorities and voluntary organisations in order to support experiments within the community. But the policy was intended to be cost-neutral, the presumption being that resources released could finance appropriate community care. The reality was rapid growth in other forms of residential care, or, to borrow a term coined in the USA, transinstitutionalisation.

The historical development of the asylum system constrained the development of alternatives. Many included listed buildings, and a number were in land protected by Green Belt restrictions. However there were central government pressures to dispose of as much land as possible (DHSS, 1983b), and given the potential for substantial windfalls from property transactions, especially in the South East, authorities were surely tempted to realise as much of their assets as possible. The Social Services Committee suspected that authorities were attempting this before alternative facilities had been provided, noting that the minister for health had been pressing authorities to close hospitals within specified time periods (Social Services Committee, 1985a, p. xxi), which was potentially dangerous in the absence of equivalent pressures to develop alternatives. Furthermore, bed reductions or discharge of patients did 'not reveal anything of the quality of community services. *Some authorities have adopted a policy of racing ahead and damning the consequences*' (p. lviii). And reliance on the property market had limitations: for some authorities land sales might ease the problem as the hospital could be in the ' "right" place in terms of its financial attraction to a property developer' (Social Services Committee, 1990a, p. xv). This would not help authorities in areas where property prices were low, but the government rejected any notion of subsidising authorities in that position; instead bridging finance was made available only for projects where there was an 'early prospect of receipts from sales of land' (ibid., p. xvi). Thus the development of community care was partly determined by market criteria affecting the receipts from property disposals.

Furthermore, depending on the position of an authority with respect to RAWP, the pressures to release resources through closures could vary greatly, as could the ability of a region to provide the revenue to develop alternative services (Social Services Committee, 1985a, p. xx; see also Chapter 4). Community resistance was perhaps predictable (see Dear and Taylor, 1982). More specifically, however, reliance on private provision meant that care providers sought out property that would maximise their returns, which meant that 'private establishments may cluster in locations where suitable domestic properties are available' (for example large houses or former hotels), so that services were on offer 'in an unplanned location and in an unplanned quantity' (Social Services Committee, 1985a, p. lxiii; see Eyles, 1986, for a local study). The resultant 'clustering' of homes could put pressure on community acceptance of facilities and also on available day care services. Sudden localised expansion of private accommodation was unlikely to be paralleled by rapid growth in necessary support facilities in the prevailing climate of local government finance. Drastic reductions in public housing expenditure and stocks constrained the development of community-based alternatives to institutions and meant that what was developed was a 'patchwork' (Social Services Committee, 1985a, p. lxvi).

Policy on community care for the mentally ill is also affected by debates on the most appropriate location for treatment, and specifically whether or not there remains a place for the asylums. The Social Services Committee (1985a) pointed out that if 'asylum' is taken to mean a 'place of shelter or refuge' then that is one function that has to be replicated for those in need of it; as the Health Committee (1994, para. 12) remarked, new community developments had not replicated the asylum functions of the old hospitals. However, emerging concern at the presence and plight of the homeless mentally ill on the streets, especially in London, had led to speculation that at least some places might be kept open for containment of that population.[2] But did this reflect genuine concern for appropriate treatment or a desire to reduce the visibility of one of the consequences of the government's policies? *Caring for People* had stated that hospital closures would not be approved without a demonstration of the availability of adequate alternative care; which could be taken as an acknowledgement of the failures of community care programmes to that date. The Social Services Committee believed this would result in a 'slowing down of the closure programme and the continuing institutionalisation of those who were capable of being discharged', and queried whether the government (1) was monitoring the discharge of patients to 'adequate alternative' care, and (2) actually had a definition of what was meant by 'adequate alternative care' (Social Services Committee, 1990a). The government's response was that what constituted appropriate care was a matter for local judgement rather than central prescription. But when this meant that a policy of national importance was not being monitored centrally, to the point where the government's knowledge of the progress of hospital closures lagged behind that of campaigning groups, it hardly inspired confidence in the government's policy.[3]

Caring for or warehousing the elderly? The nursing home and residential care business

This form of service provision has been largely state-funded, with changes in the provisions for the payment of Supplementary Benefit permitting the costs of accommodating the elderly to be met from the non-cash limited funds of the DHSS, in cases where no suitable public sector accommodation is available. From being insignificant in the early 1980s, expenditure has grown enormously: income support payments now account for around 20 per cent of community care expenditure (£1.59 bn out of some £7.6 bn – Health Committee, 1993c). The ostensible rationale for this policy was to increase choice by ensuring that individuals were not debarred from receiving private care by virtue of their inability to pay for treatment. It was also assumed, implicitly, that provision in the public sector would not be expanded, reflecting the government's ideological predispositions.

One justification for this policy was a consumerist one – to increase choice for the elderly – but it is debatable whether choice has actually increased. There has been little attempt consciously to stimulate alternatives to residential care. As a result, evidence to the Health Committee (1991c) suggested that up to 50 per cent of those supported through social security payments in residential care could have remained at home with appropriate support. Moreover the elderly were at the mercy of proprietors from whose point of view it was sensible to admit patients who were easy to manage: they could be admitted on grounds of their ability rather than disability (Andrews, 1984, p. 1520). In any case, the elderly are a socially and economically diverse group, and 'the inequalities with which individuals approach the market affect their abilities successfully to manipulate the market in their own best interests' (Vincent *et al.*, 1987, p. 459; see also Social Services Committee, 1988b).

A second implication is the question of control and regulation. There is extensive anecdotal evidence of substandard care (for example Holmes and Johnson, 1988; West Midlands County Council, 1986), though scandals about standards are not confined to private homes.

Regulation posed an ideological dilemma for the Conservatives. Private nursing homes are archetypical small businesses, for whom the government was anxious to minimise the regulatory burden. But greater regulation would implicitly compromise the independence of these small businesses (Phillips and Vincent, 1986). Although privatisation has meant that the state has been rolled back, the demands of regulation may require it to be rolled forward in another direction (Day and Klein, 1987) in order to protect the vulnerable. The Registered Nursing Homes Act of 1984 was one response. But there were reports during 1986 that the deregulatory instincts of Lord Young, then secretary for employment, who was seeking to remove or relax regulations on small businesses, were seen to be potentially in conflict with the need to protect the elderly. In practice these fears proved groundless as no deregulation took place.[4] By 1993, however, it was again being suggested that the regulations governing private nursing or residential accommodation be reviewed, in line with general government directives to reduce the burden on small businesses.[5]

Some forms of regulation may have had adverse consequences in terms of providing care for those in need of it. Before November 1983 the level of income support payments was by and large locally determined; local maxima were then introduced but these varied enormously (for nursing homes, between £80 and £290 per week). The limits were frozen in 1984 and national limits were introduced in 1985, though with higher limits for Greater London (Social Security Committee, 1991, p. v). This produced an upward drift in prices:

> there was some abuse because the local office limit-setting system was subject to charges being set by reference to the highest residential charge and *there was a lot of upward movement* (Social Services Committee, 1986, p. xl – emphasis added).

From 1987 there were complaints from the nursing home sector that benefit limits were too low, so that old people either had to fund the difference between what the DHSS would pay and the fees charged by the homes, or had to leave the homes and be supported by relatives. The Social Services Committee recommended that the secretary of state acknowledge the 'gap which it will be unreasonable or impossible to expect relatives to meet' (Social Services Committee, 1990b, para. 6), and suggested that topping-up payments from the DSS or local authority Social Services Departments should be permitted. The government rejected this, and the perception that the government had produced an iniquitous situation led to a rare Commons defeat, on the principle that social security payments to residents of private nursing homes should cover the full costs of their accommodation. The moral point at issue, argued critics, was that many elderly people had entered residential care believing that social security payments would continue to be adequate, yet they had no means of bridging the gap as benefit limits had failed to keep pace with charges. Although 58 per cent of residents were in homes where weekly charges were within benefit limits (Social Services Committee, 1990b, para 25), 42 per cent were not and had to make up the difference in some way. Furthermore, *Caring for People* had created a position in which those already in residential care prior to its implementation would be treated less well than those entering care after the Act was implemented, since they would still be dependent on an increasingly inadequate income support system whereas those present-ing for assessment of their needs after implementation would have their costs met (to the extent that they were not required to make means-tested payments) by their local authority.

Among the difficulties identified in a debate on a motion to preserve the rights of those in residential and nursing home care prior to the implementation of *Caring for People* were the extent of variability of treatment of elderly people according to where they lived and the costs of their accommodation relative to income support limits. But:

> what makes many of these cases so perverse is that they involve elderly people who were placed in private residential care by NHS hospitals who were desperately anxious to recover the beds that were being occupied. Time and again these people, having been placed in that care, are left in an impossible financial situation.[6]

Health authorities had, not unreasonably given the incentives to do so, sought to unblock beds by discharging patients into care whenever possible, which would help improve the efficiency of the hospital sector in general. But the consequences for residents could be severe, depending on the cost structure of the establishments in which they were accommodated. In turn this was influenced by geographical variations in property prices. As Ann Widdecombe put it, it was 'not insignificant that many Conservative members who first started to draw attention to the problem have come from areas where property is expensive'.[7] As with the lobby focusing on the need for a reform of RAWP, interests had been structured around a territorially based claim for resources. Of course some of the blame for this could be laid at the door of other aspects of the government's strategy, which had produced tremendous property and house price inflation.

Among the more general political issues raised by the differential treatment of those in residential care, Frank Field emphasised the rights of citizenship:

we are talking about people who . . . have paid all their rates and taxes. One of the benefits which they thought would result from the contract struck with the state was the certainty that, if they needed to go into hospital or have nursing care, they or their relatives would not be faced with a bill.[8]

However he did not emphasise that the availability of those citizenship rights varied capriciously as a result of variations in charges for residential accommodation.[9] Despite the strength of feeling revealed by that debate, the government rejected a suggestion (Social Security Committee, 1991) that local authorities could top up fees, suggesting instead that local authorities could use their purchasing power to drive down prices from the independent sector through aggressive bargaining. However, the Health Committee (1993c, 21) was not sanguine about this, and the possibility of large bulk contracts appeared to contradict the notion of choice.

Geographical variability in costs clearly meant that what was, in principle, a national policy could be implemented unevenly due to reliance on relatively inflexible limits on charges that would be met by social security.[10] One response to such variations in costs was some relocation of patients to cheaper regions. A Health Advisory Service report on Bromley commented that 'frail elderly people face exile in homes far from Bromley' (quoted in Social Security Committee, 1991), but perhaps more controversial was the deliberate effort of one health authority to decant patients from a long-stay hospital in Hackney, East London, to nursing homes in Yorkshire.[11] One effect of this variability in costs and in the pattern of provision was that when finally implemented, community care funding was based to a large degree on the existing pattern of social security payments. Thus, localities with low levels of private residential provision – largely, high-cost urban areas – were relatively disadvantaged in funding terms.

A third implication of these developments concerns defining the boundaries between public and private provision. Several health authorities and local authorities have attempted to transfer responsibilities for long-term care for the elderly into the nursing or private residential home sector; the growth in social security-funded private accommodation has been matched by a decline in publicly funded accommodation, especially in the local authority sector (Figures 5.3

and 5.4). In some cases this has been via establishing nursing homes as 'social security-efficient' charitable trusts, which transfers the burden of financing from the NHS or local authorities to the DSS. While 'virtually every metropolitan authority'[12] had tried this, the loophole had been closed by regulations that ensured that the status of residents transferred remained unaffected – that is, they remained the responsibility of the local authority. Now one could welcome this as an honest attempt to draw boundaries between the responsibilities of health authorities for health care and those of local authorities and other statutory providers for social care, and argue that it enables the NHS to concentrate on what it does best. Government ministers have drawn a distinction between the role of the NHS, which is to provide treatment, and the role of the private sector, which is to provide long-term care, in an effort to justify these developments, but the distinction seems a fine one, especially for those suffering from long-term, degenerative conditions. However this had occurred by default rather than by deliberate decision. Authorities have on occasion been roundly criticised for withdrawing from long-stay care. Thus in 1991 NAHAT informed the Social Security Committee that it did not regard the provision of nursing home care to be a function of the NHS, which the Committee regarded as:

> an extraordinary statement . . . the obligation on health authorities to provide nursing care for those who cannot or do not wish to pay for it *should be strictly enforced . . . health authorities should not evade what are their proper responsibilities* (Social Security Committee, 1991, emphasis added).

However a number of horses had already bolted through that stable door, and there remained a need to establish a consistent national policy; without this there would be 'a failure of services to provide the requisite level of care' (Social Security Committee, 1991, p. xxiii). This was likely to lead to a narrowing of the scope of a free service. If health authorities were discharging into nursing homes people whose incomes were above income support levels, those people would find themselves paying for nursing care that they really should have been receiving as of right.[13] This narrow distinction was challenged by the DSS, which in 1993 successfully argued that a patient discharged from hospital to a nursing home was not entitled to income support because the judge ruled that they had been placed in a 'hospital or similar institution' and that the health authority concerned was therefore financially responsible.[14] The fact that this case had been pursued suggested that the government was seeking to limit its commitment to supporting alternatives to hospital-based care through the benefits system. Without clarification of responsibilities, the logical course of action for health authorities would be to preserve (cheaper) institutional patterns of care, which no one would presumably want. Subsequently the discharge of patients to nursing homes was criticised by the health service ombudsman, who ruled that a health authority had wrongly stopped treating a stroke victim on the ground that nothing more could be done for him. The ombudsman recommended that the health authority compensate the patient's family and accept the future costs of his care.[15] The difficulty for the health service was that large numbers of health authorities had reduced their continuing-care beds, on the assumption that income support payments would cover the costs of former NHS patients; clearly, if patients in nursing homes were to become, once again, a charge on the NHS, there would be major cost implications for health authority budgets.[16]

Caring for People: delays and unresolved questions

There were two sets of delays in implementing the government's community care policies: those inherent in producing the white paper; and those that followed its announcement. The government's antipathy to local authorities was well known, so it was widely assumed that the delay was due to an unsuccessful search for an alternative to local government control (Henwood *et al.*, 1991, p. 6). The delay in reacting to this second Griffiths Report contrasted sharply with the swift move to implement the first Griffiths Report, on general management. Furthermore this delay was compounded by the postponement of implementation because of the impact of community care on the community charge (Henwood *et al.*, 1991, p. 9): originally scheduled for April 1991, the community care reforms were postponed to 1993. Consequently the social security bill (control of which was a key reason for official concern about community care policies) continued to rise since the incentives for social security efficient provision were still in place.

The issues left unresolved by the changes to community care include whether or not to ringfence funds for community care, the assessment of unmet need, and the extent of choice for users of services. The first of these continues an established theme – of the tension between centre and periphery – that runs through the issues considered in this book, and so is considered in Chapter 9.

Unmet need

The debates over whether or not to ringfence community care funds raised the more general question of precisely what those in need of community care are entitled to under the new legislation. Social services authorities must carry out a formal assessment of need on persons who 'appear' to be in need of care, from which they then decide what services should be provided. It is easy to see that this could open up a Pandora's box of unmet need, and ministers have stated that needs assessment is not an exercise in drawing up a wish list against a background of finite expenditure (Secretary of State for Health, 1993), suggesting that the intention is to cash-limit community care expenditure. However local authorities suggest they have been substantially underfunded for community care,[17] by up to £135 mn, and some charitable agencies argue that the fog of unclear guidance will permit local authorities to continue to avoid their legal responsibilities. Given the uncertainty surrounding the likely costs of *Caring for People* it might have been expected that some contingency funds, similar to those made available for the restructuring of the health service, would have been on offer, but this was rejected because local authorities were expected to allow for 'contingencies . . . except when there are unforseeable and significant effects on expenditure';[18] but it was difficult to see how the new system could be viewed as entirely unforseeable or insignificant. The Health Committee also recommended that there be no restriction on the ability of local authorities to make a 'full assessment of unmet needs', but the government's view was that assessing unmet need was 'potentially subjective and divorced from reality' (Secretary of State for Health, 1993, 4), again indicating the priority attached to cost containment.

But if needs were assessed and found to be unmet, what then? Various local authorities were concerned at the legal ramifications of the assessment process, in particular the possibility that they could be challenged in the courts. The government's initial advice had been not to disclose to clients whether they had been assessed as being in need, but local authorities approached the problem in diverse ways, with some recording all unmet need and others not telling clients what they were entitled to.[19] At the time of writing this issue is still unresolved. The logical product of a system of needs assessment, in a situation where resources are finite, would be a community care waiting list analogous to that of the NHS (Health Committee, 1993c). However only an irrepressible optimist would believe that the government would attach the same priority to such a list as they do to the waiting list for acute hospital treatment.

Choice

The question of choice, in a cash-limited system, was also a thorny one for a government committed to consumerism. *Caring for People* saw choice developing through the assessment process (para 3.2.6) and through the emergence of a more diverse range of non-statutory providers (para. 3.4.3). The main determinants of choice would be the overall level of resources, the personal resources available to individuals, the relative costs of specific services in particular places, and the political priorities of local authorities. Three points are relevant here.

Firstly, authorities were to spend prescribed proportions of the funds transferred from social security on *private* residential and nursing care, presumably to avoid destabilising this sector, but that hardly contributed to the development of a range of alternative services from which to choose or to expanding the availability of domiciliary care, despite the optimism of one Conservative MP that the availability of funds would 'summon forth domiciliary services'.[20] Secondly, it was likely that the poorest local authorities would provide least choice, yet they were often the authorities with the highest levels of chronic and mental illness (Social Services Committee, 1990d, p. vi). The official view was that it was open to clients to select appropriate services of their choice, provided that the authority 'is not called upon to meet greater expense than it considers justified for their reasonable care need' (Secretary of State for Health, 1993). If local authorities do not offer a choice that clients deem appropriate the decision can be challenged, but the review process is only able to consider cases on an individual basis, with regard to whether they have been properly dealt with within the framework of existing procedures. Clients in different authorities may be treated differently and (potentially) inequitably, although one early decision did go in favour of a client.[21] Thirdly, choice between residential and domiciliary forms of care was also very much dependent on the support of carers and the availability of alternatives. Despite the government's assertion (Social Services Committee, 1990e, p. xv) that 'we are giving as much help to carers as we can', the Social Services Committee's recommendations for a package of proposals costing £200 mn were rejected (note that this sum was less than 10 per cent of the amount being spent on income support payments).

Concluding comments

Jordan (1987, p. 197) suggests that 'if there is an underlying moral basis of society one would expect it to show itself most clearly in the way people care for and help each other'. What conclusions can be drawn from this brief review of community care policies?

Firstly, there are some technical reasons why recent policy changes have been introduced. In particular, community care has had confused boundaries for too long, and the attempt to clarify the divide between health care and social care is important if it leads to circumstances in which the obligations of health and local authorities are made explicit and prevents various agencies offloading responsibilities onto one another or on to the private sector. Hence the *principles* enshrined in the 1989 legislation are generally welcome.

Secondly, it would be unwise to impose the template of an undifferentiated 'Thatcherism' on the range of policies pursued since 1979. In the first period of office one might identify a period of benign neglect and wishful thinking, encapsulated in the assumption that informal care would take up the slack but also evident in the belief that community care policies could be financed through releasing resources from the long-stay hospitals. Subsequently there were moves towards an unregulated pluralism, as finance was made available, through the social security system, for long-stay facilities, but this was unsustainable because it was demand led and eventually unacceptable because of the problems of regulation it posed. The eventual community care legislation sought to rectify some problems associated with both the above strategies. However it is a skewed and cash-limited market, with an emphasis firmly on the private sector, and seems likely to lead eventually to some of the same problems faced by the pre-reform hospital services, particularly as regards unmet need. As with other policies, this does not seem to add up to a coherent vision, pursued steadfastly over time. Rather, some consistent ideological themes can be traced: the stress on devolution, even when this apparently means that central government lacks information on the progress of an ostensibly national policy; the removal of local authority nomination to health authorities and the continuing absence of integration between health and local government, despite what might appear to be the evident need for collaborative action; belief in the importance of the 'community', against evidence that current economic changes reduce the community's capacity to care; the belief that generating funds internally would solve the problems of the service; and faith in the private sector and market forces as responsive providers, against the evidence that the imperfect markets operating in community care seem unlikely to promote much in the way of innovation, and against the evidence that consumerism is weakly developed in community care.

Even though there is a degree of all-party consensus on the principles and desirability of community care, critics question the substance of the government's commitment to it, pointing to its prevarication (the delayed response to the Griffiths Report), vacillation (over the existence and extent of ring fencing) and political manipulation (postponing implementation due to the effects on Poll Tax levels). The overwhelming desire seems to be to cap the expenditure on community care: major policy initiatives have been introduced largely in response to concerns about the apparently demand-led nature of spending.

In addition, the decentralist rhetoric of the government means that there are no mechanisms for monitoring progress and ensuring that all authorities perform to acceptable standards. This has been a feature of policy since the abandonment of norms-based planning in 1981, and it has recently been evident in various responses to criticisms from the Social Services Committee (Secretary of State for Health, 1990, 1991). Consequently, 'where in Britain the patient lives is probably the most significant factor in determining the quality of care he or she receives' (Murphy, 1991, p. 61). Groves (1990) consequently calls for a comprehensive 'atlas' of need for and provision of community care services. The variable performance of local authorities leaves much room for improvement and unless there are efforts to establish meaningful ways in which those in need can make effective claims on statutory agencies, that situation will persist. Furthermore there is evident variability in support services available in the community from the voluntary and commercial sector, so while it might be desirable that local authorities see themselves as entrepreneurs in a mixed economy, if non-statutory resources are not available they cannot be conjured up from nowhere and the vision of the enabling state may be no more than wishful thinking (Cochrane, 1993). It follows that the extent of unmet need and the ways in which needs are met (for example the extent of charging for services) will depend on the resource position and policies of the local authorities in question and on other factors such as local demographics, economic circumstances and availability of other services. There will be no absolute standards, and the 'principle of autonomy for local decision-making has taken precedence over the principles of fairness and equity' (Doyle and Harding, 1992, p. 71). Thus, whether a national, consistent policy exists is debatable. The Health Committee (1994) referred to the government's penchant for 'motherhood statements' about community care, and questioned whether mechanisms existed to ensure that these were translated into practice, noting in particular the absence of a means of guaranteeing some priority for – in this case – mental-health services in purchasing decisions (paras 22, 48, 71).

There is also a need to clarify the notion of the mixed economy of welfare because it is not clear that the playing field is level. The signals have been clearly set at green for the private sector for some years: if the economy was genuinely mixed local authorities would be able to compete, and they are not; it is the structuring of market relations that is important. For example, will there be genuine competition, or will block contracts dominate, limiting choice and replacing one set of institutions with another? Will local authorities be left with residual care for those who cannot afford private services and for those whose needs are greatest? What will be the consequences for local authorities of local monopoly businesses that then fail, for whatever reason? How far is the rhetoric of choice achievable in practice, given limited resources? These questions suggest several potential weaknesses of the market-based strategy adopted by the government. This is unfortunate because some commentators envisage a progressive alternative scenario, in which the community itself, rather than state institutions or large commercial organisations, takes on a greater responsibility for community care. Indeed some argue that strengthening the voluntary sector's role is a way of rebuilding the community (Heginbotham, 1990; Donnison, 1991) as part of a wider project of empowerment and participatory democracy. This will have to be coupled with a greater degree of awareness of the consumer voice in community care: at present user involvement could consist of 'no more than an occasional survey among users together with minimal individual consultation at the point of assessment' (Walker, 1992, p. 221). It will also require greater provision of independent arbitration for those in need (Doyle and Harding, 1992, p. 82) if their claims are to be given any substance; in this policy area, articulating consumer demands in a marketplace model is particularly fraught with difficulties.

6

Producing Health Care: Management, Labour and the State in the NHS

Health care is highly labour intensive: around a million people in Britain are employed in (public or private) health care; wages and salaries account for some 75 per cent of NHS costs. Given the government's determination to restrict growth in NHS spending, it was inevitable that cost-containment measures would bring government into conflict with professional interests and with trade unions. Decisions taken vis-à-vis different groups of staff demonstrate the political priorities of the government. As Clay indicates, the government has prioritised key sectors for reducing staff costs:

> Governments are exhausting, one by one, all the options to constrain and cut resources. Capital cuts, administrative reductions, new management arrangements, and new market disciplines imposed on ancillary staff, *bring the government closer, step by step, to the question of the use of the major resource in the service, the people who work in it, and their skills* (Clay, 1987, p. 15, emphasis added).

Clay's metaphorical journey to the heart of darkness of the public sector thus saw the government beginning with ancillaries and administrators, moving on to nursing and eventually, through the NHS reforms, attempting to tackle both the national systems of pay determination and the primary source of expenditure in the service – the clinical decisions of medical practitioners. This is a provocative characterisation and summary of a wide range of policy measures.

Three issues and debates seem central to this chapter. Firstly, to what extent do events in health care reflect the government's wider determination to increase the flexibility of the labour market, in line with its neoliberal principles?[1] It is often suggested that the character of employment is changing so that the workforce is divided between those regarded as 'core' staff and those seen as 'peripheral' (Leadbeater, 1987). In this scenario, employers prioritise those members of staff whose skills are in relatively short supply and who are in demand in external labour markets, by offering them rewards over and above those available to their 'peripheral' staff. By contrast those on the 'periphery' are regarded as dispensable and are subject to much poorer terms and conditions of service. There are clear parallels with some views of Conservative political strategy (Chapter 3). There is some evidence of this, but such principles have not been applied to all groups of staff, so it is necessary to analyse the reasons for this differential treatment. Related to this, this chapter considers the extent to which the notion of the 'flexible firm' (Atkinson and Meager, 1986; Pollert, 1988) is relevant either as an explanation of, or as a description of the *outcomes* of, government policies. This notion implies that businesses attempt to develop flexibility in two senses: functional flexibility (adjusting tasks to meet the changing nature of demand) and numerical flexibility (adjusting the size of the workforce to fluctuations in demand) (Atkinson and Meager, 1986, p. 3). Flexibility is said to be required to sustain productivity growth achieved by straightforward means (such as rationalisation of capacity) and to cope with uncertainty about external conditions. The kind of innovations introduced in the guise of flexibility include changing contractual patterns, changing working hours and occupational change.

Secondly, one of the defining characteristics of health care is the jealously guarded clinical autonomy of doctors. According to Elston (1991), in sociological terms medicine is the paradigmatic profession: a publicly mandated, state-backed monopolistic supplier, granted considerable autonomy and (for some commentators) intent on steadily enlarging its sphere of influence. In addition, the power of the medical profession to block change was almost legendary, so that it came to be regarded as the 'dominant structural interest' in the health-care policy arena (Alford, 1975). The extent to which policies since 1979 have challenged professional prerogatives is important here. Interestingly, the newest group of NHS staff is also the smallest – general managers – yet the group's importance is disproportionate to its size. This group arguably challenged traditional assumptions about professional autonomy: it was not just that managers were likely to come into conflict with doctors, but also questions were raised about whether they would indeed have the 'right to manage'.

Thirdly, the centralised systems of wage determination characteristic of the NHS were anathema to some Conservatives, fired with a vision of a localised, performance-related system of allocating rewards. Therefore the calls for localised wage determination should come as no surprise. These demands were initially confined to proposals affecting certain staff groups, and were given impetus by widespread recruitment difficulties, largely in, though not confined to, South East England. As with other chapters, the tension between national and local procedures and practices is relevant here.

It is important to keep these ideas in mind and to recall Allen's (1988a, 1988b) point that services are indeed 'produced': we should be aware of relations of control and conflict within the service. The nature of the NHS poses unique problems for both employers and workforce. The resources available to it, and the way they are used, depend directly on political decisions. Even so, the options available to a government wishing to cut costs are limited: capacity cannot be reduced indiscriminately without generating significant protests; relocation of services to lower-cost sites may be inconsistent with the notion of a *national* service.

If the employers have limited scope for manoeuvre, the same is true of the NHS workforce. Most health care employees are women and a large proportion of the workforce is part-time. The NHS workforce cannot, on the whole, be characterised as industrially militant, partly because of their pride in the collectivist ethos of the service (Manson, 1977, p. 211), partly because of the difficulty of taking industrial action without damaging the interests of patients – despite the size of the workforce there was relatively little industrial action before the 1970s. When it has occurred, industrial action in the NHS has been exploited by the government to mobilise popular prejudices against inefficient, strike-prone public sector workers. Furthermore, the sheer range of personnel employed in the NHS – from consultants to trainee nurses, from senior administrators to ancillary staff – implies that the class interests and locations of health care workers are very different (Carpenter, 1977; Widgery, 1976; 1988, pp. 125–49; see also Wright, 1985). The major divide is between the professional organisations (especially nursing and medical staff) and those organised into trade unions (notably the ancillary workers). Thus there is a distinction between the 'caring' professions, applying skills that take years of training to acquire, and dealing directly with people, and the 'support' staff, doing what Huws (1982, pp. 60–6) describes as 'other people's housework', which by implication can be done by anyone with experience of running a home. Constructed, then, as women's domestic labour and lacking in skill, such tasks can the more easily be subjected to market forces.

This chapter is about the effects of policies pursued since 1979 on the health care workforce, in terms of absolute levels of employment and terms and conditions of service. It focuses more explicitly than other commentaries on the distributional consequences of decisions taken which affect the NHS workforce. The chapter is divided into five main sections. Firstly, a review is presented of aggregate trends in employment in the NHS. This provides the context for the next section, a discussion of policies pursued towards various sectors of the workforce. Next the differential treatment of staff covered by pay review bodies (PRBs) and those not so favoured is discussed in relation to the distinction between the 'core' and the 'periphery' in the labour market; this section also considers the changing relationships between doctors and the state resulting from the various internal reorganisations in the NHS. The obverse of the benefits enjoyed by these groups is the subjection of non-review body staff to the discipline of the market via competitive tendering for ancillary services, and discussion of the origins and effects of this policy form the next section. The penultimate section considers the recruitment difficulties faced by the service during the 1980s and their effects on service delivery, which leads into the debates on what became known, somewhat inaccurately, as 'geographical pay', and it is logical to follow this with a discussion of the post-White Paper situation in which NHS trusts were much freer to vary the terms and conditions of their staff.

Aggregate trends in the NHS workforce

The Royal Commission contended that the NHS had never given much consideration to developing a 'manpower' (*sic*) policy as such (para. 12.57), despite the need for forward thinking about the likely future form of the service and its personnel needs (see also Wilson and Stilwell, 1992). The crude nature of some of the policies followed from 1979 – such as the manpower ceilings – was therefore nothing new: staff cuts had been imposed in the 1950s. The bluntest instrument of all has been the simple expedient of not funding pay awards adequately and of cash-limiting the service. The PRB recommendations[2] were evidently regarded as inflationary by the government, but under-funding seems to have been used deliberately to reduce staff expectations: as the government put it, promising to fund pay awards fully 'would create a wholly unrealistic framework for negotiations'.[3] Cash limits constrained the scope for negotiation and affordability criteria – as defined by the government – predominated: as a DoH management side representative explained, 'at the end of the day it [a pay settlement] has to be done within the amount which has been made available to meet it' (Social Services Committee, 1989, p. xvi). So while officially disavowing incomes policies, the government clearly operated one in the public sector.

The other perceived advantage of underfunding from the government's point of view was that of stimulating greater efficiency. However this imposed differential pressures on authorities, depending on the accuracy of inflation estimates used in reaching pay awards, the financial position of the health authority and the extent of local staff recruitment difficulties. Even in 1986 it was recognised that eventually it would be necessary to agree on pay settlements that 'do retain and do take account of the need to recruit, retain and motivate existing staff' (Social Services Committee, 1986, p. xxii). Nevertheless Barney Hayhoe, the then minister for health, laid the blame for service reductions on excessive pay demands: 'if an *unreasonable* settlement emerges that must *always have its effect on the level of service provision*' (Social Services Committee, 1986, p. xxii, emphases added).

The strict financial discipline imposed on the service led to an emphasis on greater productivity as a means of achieving service developments. Hence the following, which laid heavy stress on generating resources for service development internally to the service:

services should develop faster than revenue and, *as productivity improves, revenue faster than manpower*. Any growth in staff numbers should continue the existing trends of *concentration on those groups who deliver services direct to patients*. Any increase in staff numbers over the agreed base line *must be explained by reference to improvements in services which cannot be achieved by improvements in performance or redeployment elsewhere* (DHSS, 1984, emphases added).

Precisely how far productivity has increased is evident from a comparison of increased throughput against declining staff numbers. A substantial increase in activity and throughput has been achieved with next to no net growth in staff. In England for the 1981–91 period[4] the largest absolute increases were in professional and technical staff, administrative and clerical staff, and general managers (the latter being a category that did not exist in 1981), though the growth of 7600 (18.6 per cent) in medical and dental staff should also be noted (Table 6.1). Conversely nursing staff grew by only 4400 (4.4 per cent), while the ancillary workforce was reduced by slightly over 50 per cent (86 300 jobs), largely as a consequence of competitive tendering, though many of these staff will have been re-employed, albeit usually on poorer conditions of service, by private contractors.

Patient throughput increased over the same period by approximately 1.7 per cent per annum: total admissions increased from 5.76 million to 7.20 million and day-case activity more than doubled, from 714 000 cases to 1.55 million cases. Another way of capturing the intensification in activity is by looking at average cases per available bed, which nearly doubled from 1981–91 and in the acute sector rose from 30.8 cases to 51.8 cases per available bed. On any count, then, staff were bearing the brunt of a rapidly increasing workload, treating growing numbers of patients in declining numbers of beds.

However internal improvements to efficiency were not enough. There had been criticisms, from both parliament and external organisations such as the CBI, that staff numbers in the NHS were continuing to rise (Harrison, 1988a) and the Griffiths Report was originally called for as a response to this situation. After the 1983 election, the emphasis switched to a much more prescriptive approach to manpower targets, in which each RHA was told to ensure that it kept staff numbers below centrally-determined ceilings. Ministers

Table 6.1 Change in NHS staffing by main staff groups 1981–91 (Whole-time equivalents)[1]

	1981	*1991*	*Change*	*% Change*
Nursing and midwifery	391 800	396 200	+4 400	+1.1
Medical and dental	41 000	48 600	+7 600	+18.6
Professional and technical (excl. works)	65 200	86 500	+21 300	+32.6
Ancillary	172 200	85 900	−86 300	−50.1
Admin and clerical	108 800	127 400	+18 600	+17.1
Maintenance and works	27 200	18 300	−8 900	−32.5
General/senior managers[2]		13 300	+13 300	N/A
Ambulance	18 200	18 200		−0.2
Total employed staff	824 400	800 500[3]	−23 900	−2.9

NOTES:
1. From 1987 figures include statutory authorities such as the HEA and Public Health Laboratory Service, so are not strictly comparable. All figures rounded; changes calculated on unrounded figures.
2. Did not exist in 1981.
3. Includes 6100 persons classed as unspecified 'other'.
SOURCE: Health and Personal Social Services Statistics.

considered that 'whilst resources were running pretty level manpower was continuing to creep up' (Public Accounts Committee, 1984, p. vi), indicating the 'reluctance on the part of some health authorities to tackle one of the basic .problems of the NHS'. Staff reductions were *imposed* in September 1983, partly following the refusal of some RHAs to agree to proposed ceilings. Though a reduction of 4800 jobs was requested, imposed differentially in line with RAWP principles (Mohan and Woods, 1985, describe the disputes over this issue in more detail), eventually some 10 000 jobs were cut from the NHS in the 1983–4 financial year.[5] These cuts were criticised as being a 'sharp and crude corrective adjustment' (Public Accounts Committee, 1984) and as being 'inappropriate and unnecessary' (Social Services Committee, 1984, p. xviii) and the specification of precise overall numbers was soon dropped, though close scrutiny of some grades of staff continued (e.g. NAO, 1985; Public Accounts Committee, 1986, 1987).

Authorities were also told, as a matter of policy, to emphasise the distinction between 'frontline' and 'support' staff. The best example here is administrative staff. Thus Norman Fowler emphasised in 1983 that his proposed staff reductions should be directed to the 'administrative tail' of the service.[6] Recruitment of additional personnel had to be justified by a demonstration that resources could not be better spent in ways that would improve services to patients (DHSS, 1984). This was an extension of the ideas underlying the 1982 reorganisation of the NHS (DHSS, 1979a), namely that the service was over administered and under managed; yet by the early 1990s government spokespersons were defending the rapid increase in management and of their salary bill on precisely these grounds. The government could justifiably claim that the proportion of personnel engaged directly in patient care had increased greatly, though this had less to do with dramatic increases in nursing and medical staff than with the rapid fall in ancillary numbers.[7] But the divisive nature of these policies was belatedly recognised – as Sir Duncan Nicholl, chief executive of the NHS, subsequently admitted: 'We went through the phase of dividing the sheep from the goats and saying in some fashion . . . that there were lesser people, unnecessary people'.[8] However merely suggesting to health authorities that they should separate the sheep from the goats in this way was by no means as divisive a measure as some other policies pursued, such as competitive tendering, which will be discussed below.

Furthermore, the 1980s were marked by a rapid growth in part-time employment in health care. The available published statistics disaggregating full-time and part-time employment incorporate both

NHS and private sector providers. However, almost all the growth in employment in hospitals, nursing homes and similar establishments[9] was accounted for by part-time staff (133 900 out of a total increase of 135 800), and by far the greatest element of this was the growth in female part-time employment, from 351 000 to 466 600. To some degree this mirrored developments elsewhere in the economy, where part-time female employment has been the most rapidly growing element of the labour force. However, whereas in 1992 the proportions of part-time workers for Great Britain were 23 per cent (all employees) and 45 per cent (women employees), for health care the corresponding figures were 43 per cent and 49 per cent.[10] The corresponding proportions for 1981 were 36 per cent (all employees in health care) and 43 per cent (female employees in health care), indicating that the health sector had led – not followed – the expansion of part-time work.[11]

In short, the broad context of the 1980s and 1990s was a general intensification of NHS workload, coupled with policies that, to a greater or lesser degree, prioritised 'frontline' staff over others working in the service. In this sense some of the ideas in vogue in the early 1980s laid the foundations for some of the rather more radical notions advocated when the NHS reforms were introduced, though the NHS did not proceed far down the road of dividing its workforce into a 'core' and 'periphery' prior to the reforms.

The 'core': medical staff and the recasting of administrators as managers

The primary concern here is with medical staff within the NHS, and with attempts to exert greater managerial influence over them. Related to this is the introduction of what represented an entirely new group of staff into the service, namely general managers, with the avowed purpose of increasing the efficiency with which resources were managed within the NHS. These measures raised the important issue of the contradiction between notions of professionalism, which stress the autonomy of clinicians, and notions of managerialism, which stress accountability and control (Harrison, 1988a; Elston, 1991). Largely for reasons of space, issues relating to nurses are not discussed here, although nurse recruitment and retention are dealt with later in this chapter in an analysis of broader recruitment difficulties.

Clinical autonomy

The autonomy of the medical profession from the state was a central feature of the NHS. The clinical freedom of medical staff to determine treatment has always been held up as a *sine qua non* that guarantees treatment according to need and clinical priority, rationed only by waiting lists and times. To what extent did policies pursued after 1979 constitute a challenge to this prerogative? Perhaps constraints on resources produced a *de facto* rather than a *de jure* limit on clinical autonomy.[12] Indeed this was welcomed by some clinicians, who felt it would force doctors to examine the effectiveness of the methods they used.[13] In addition, the numerous initiatives and targets specified for health authorities (for example target numbers of operations per 100 000 population) meant that the ways in which they spent their money had fewer degrees of freedom, representing an indirect constraint on clinical autonomy.

One of the first initiatives introduced in 1979 was a relaxation of consultants' contracts, giving them more scope to practice privately (DHSS, 1979b), and permitting 'whole-time' NHS consultants to practice privately for the first time, subject to an earnings limit. This relaxation provided a sweetener to doctors after the paybed battles of the 1970s and was part of the government's wider strategy to expand private health care. But it opened up its own small Pandora's box: by 1990 the National Audit Office (NAO) had concluded that any further growth in private practice would be at the expense of the NHS commitments of consultants unless there was an increase in consultant numbers or a change in the type of contracts they held (NAO, 1990; see also Chapter 7). Nor was any attempt made to reform the potentially lucrative system of distinction awards to consultants, which awards were and are virtually self-appointed without any attempt to assess contribution to improved health (Scambler, 1992). In respect of these developments, at least, the privileged position of sections of the medical profession was confirmed. If further evidence was needed for this, some of the salary awards to doctors – for instance the 1983 award, which was more than twice that offered to nurses in the same year – indicated the priorities of the government. Permitting consultants to undertake more private practice was not without its ironies, since ministers occasionally voiced their belief that doctors were abusing the freedoms extended by the government in 1979.

Expanding opportunities for private practice was arguably a distraction from what was really necessary: gaining control of clinical costs. There was emerging evidence of considerable variations in the 'performance' of different staff and hospitals (for example Public Accounts Committee, 1981). While such variations could arguably be contained while resource growth was sustained, once the pace of growth slackened in the 1970s it became likely that clinician autonomy would be challenged, regardless of which party was in power (Coles, 1988). Politically, attempts to introduce general management offered some hope of being able to generate resources internally to the service. But the Griffiths Report became, for a while at least, the focus of some determined opposition. Early reactions from the BMA and from some of its committees deplored the 'progressive reduction in the influence of the medical profession . . . [the Griffiths Report] would further this trend'.[14] However a more conciliatory tone was eventually adopted. The BMA cautiously welcomed the report, though it was still concerned about how clinicians' views were to be considered, while there continued to be concern at the exclusion of doctors and nurses from management positions.[15] Proposals such as the resource management initiative (RMI) can be seen as efforts to develop ways of including hospital doctors in the management process, and one criticism advanced of the subsequent NHS reforms was that the RMI had not been given sufficient time to work.

It was not until the proposed new contract for GPs, and subsequently the NHS reforms themselves, that what began to look like decisive efforts to challenge clinical autonomy began to be pursued. One can identify three strands of policy, which might be characterised as anticorporatism, antiprofessionalism, and proentrepreneurialism.

The deliberate exclusion of the medical profession from discussions on the NHS reforms contrasted sharply with the privileged status it had enjoyed since the NHS was established. Indeed it was probably this, as much as the proposed reforms themselves, that initially drew the wrath of the BMA, which campaigned against the secretary of state's unwillingness to listen to advice[16] and failure to consult the profession. Kenneth Clarke's refusal to countenance pilot schemes may also have offended those used to the protocols of clinical trials; he had suggested that the need for reform was self-evident.[17] In addition, the exclusion of professional representation on health authorities and trusts, while defended on the grounds that health authorities were managerial not representative organisations, was seen as further weakening the influence of the profession over policy.[18]

Furthermore, the government's tactics reflected a wider Conservative critique of the potential for professional organisations to pursue their own interests rather than those of the people they served. Thus one BMA correspondent saw the reforms as being of a piece with other attacks on, for example, teachers and the legal profession. Clarke portrayed the profession as a conservative, reactionary force.[19] He drew on consumerist images to suggest that the medical profession was insufficiently responsive to external demands and had determinedly resisted progressive changes, even accusing it of having objected to the concept of a national health service in the first place.[20] Clarke linked this to the fact that the NHS was a *public* service:

> *After forty years of a state system* it is the doctors and teachers who are now represented by people suspicious of consumer choice, competition, rewards linked to performance, and managerial efficiency.[21]

He frequently referred to the BMA pejoratively as a trade union, while his comments about doctors 'reaching nervously for their wallets' at the mention of change were hardly likely to endear him to the profession.[22] He also insisted that good doctors had nothing to fear, suggesting that the primary aim was to remove variable standards of practice.

The pro-competitive stance of the government served to fragment medical opposition. The more hospitals became self-governing, or applied for self-governing status, and the more GPs took up fundholding, the less the medical profession spoke with one voice. It is arguable that the government sought to get consultants in major hospitals on its side by seeking to 'ingratiate them with the silver of opting out'.[23] Indeed Clarke at times hinted that he had sought to divide and rule in this way:

> I am putting a lot of effort into the top of the profession, the academics, the research people, the Royal Colleges *whom I think need have no problems over the reforms and ought not to be engaged in all this unseemly punch-up that the rough end of the trade engages in.*[24]

If this was a deliberate strategy, the pursuit of fundholding general practices also had the effect, unintentionally or not, of establishing a section of the profession with a vested interest in the progress of the reforms. Doctor seemed to be set against doctor, and the subsequent evidence of priority admissions to the patients of fundholders seemed incompatible with the 'corporate sense of continuity which distinguishes a professional from an entrepreneurial career'.[25] Yet for non-fundholders autonomy was circumscribed as the block-contract system limited their freedom of referral. Although limited funds were available for 'extra-contractual' referrals these accounted for a very small proportion of health authority budgets. It was not surprising, then, that much adverse comment in the medical press concerned the emerging evidence of a two-tier health care system, particularly the distortion of treatment according to clinical need by the fundholding system.

It is doubtful whether doctors had ever felt as excluded from the bargaining table as in the early days following the review announcement, though once Clarke departed as minister for health a less confrontational approach was evident. But clinical autonomy has been challenged through the purchaser-provider split, which calls units and doctors to account in ways hitherto unheard of in the service, and this may be one of the more welcome elements of the reforms, although more information on the costs and benefits of different forms of treatment is still needed.

From administration to management?

One attempt to control clinical costs was through the strengthening of management within the service that followed the Griffiths Report. Though originally conceived as an inquiry into staffing levels – the announcement of the inquiry followed the imposition of manpower ceilings in early 1983 – this was arguably the product of a simplistic fixation with the number of people employed by the service. It followed the persistent scapegoating of NHS bureaucracy, and, at Griffiths' instigation, the inquiry's remit was broadened to an investigation of management. The four central diagnoses of the Griffiths Report were (1) that decisions were taken on a lowest common denominator basis, with no one perceived as being in charge; (2) there was no concern with the implementation of policies; (3) there was no orientation towards performance or change, so that decisions were largely incremental adjustments to existing services that did not challenge vested interests; and (4) there was little attention to consumerism (see Harrison, 1988b; Harrison *et al.*, 1990; and Cox, 1991, for commentaries). In industrial relations terms the report marked the introduction of elements of performance-related pay and short-term contracts. The service may not have got the managers it wanted originally – there were numerous complaints about superannuated former military personnel (Petchey, 1986) – but Griffiths led to grade inflation because of the relative shortages of skilled managerial talent in the NHS. As the subsequent reforms created extra tiers of management and bureaucracy, this process accelerated and a generation of managers advanced quickly up the salary scale.

The consequence was that the number and cost of management increased substantially. The Public Accounts Committee's conclusion – that implementation of the Griffiths recommendations might actually require 'more, better and . . . more costly management' (1984, 16) – proved prescient. In 1975 there were 91 870 administrative and clerical staff in the service; by 1991 this had risen to 127 370 and there were, in addition, 13 370 general managers.[26] This represented a 53 per cent increase and it was somewhat ironic that such a rapid increase took place, given that the Royal Commission had suggested that the service had excessive layers of administrative fat. Perhaps more controversially, from the introduction of the Griffiths reforms the total salaries of general managers alone had risen to some £380 million by 1992–3. Even if the net increase was actually somewhat less than this because the introduction of general managers had led to the replacement of administrators at various levels whose salaries would have to have been paid anyway, this sum represented over 1 per cent of the NHS budget. It was also evident that this had not necessarily led to appropriate management personnel and methods being introduced. It is too easy to trivialise the issue by dismissing these developments for introducing 'commercial' management methods. But as reports circulated of 'nights of the long knives', when managers were summarily dismissed or reshuffled[27] and as health authorities engaged in entrepreneurial schemes of doubtful value (Chapter 8), it became apparent that for all the improvements in 'efficiency' in the service there had been a serious conflict of values as a consequence of the Griffiths Report. This was evidenced in a dramatic fashion when the first chair of the NHS management board, Victor Paige, resigned, being unable to operate within the political constraints imposed on him. His resignation was followed by that of several early appointees to general management positions within DHAs. This raised questions about management's right to manage within the public services. In many respects the changes introduced into the service, notably the loosening of accountability through the introduction of general management, can be seen to have weakened the public service ethos of the NHS (see Chapters 9 and 10). Had Florence Nightingale actually returned, and searched for the person in charge as Griffiths suggested, it may not be too great a caricature to suggest that she might have found a virile, macho figure, armed with the latest computer systems and filofaxes – the antithesis of the legendary nurse. The problem with this particular staff group is not so much the desirability of management as such but rather the way it was introduced, namely as a means of imposing central government targets on the service, and a costly one at that.

The contrasting treatment of these groups of staff is revealing. Whereas in the early years of the Thatcher governments administrators were blamed for all the service's ills, they were rehabilitated as dynamic figures whose skills would stimulate great increases in efficiency and thus stave off the decline of the service. Doctors, on the other hand, for most of this period went relatively unscathed: the Griffiths Report had relatively little impact since it was not accompanied (apart from financially based performance indicators) by guidance as to how to challenge medical autonomy, so it was not until the NHS reforms themselves that the government engaged in a confrontation with the one group of staff whose decisions had the most influence on health care spending. This was in contrast with the approach adopted in respect of the Whitley Council staff.

The 'periphery': Whitley Council staff

It could fairly be said that such conflicts as emerged between medical staff (whether doctors or nurses is irrelevant) and the government resulted less from a deliberately confrontational stance on the part of the government towards these professions *per se*; rather conflicts emerged from the implications of other reforms for the status of those professions. The same could not be said for the government's attitude to those staff covered by Whitley Council agreements, and especially the government's *bêtes noires*, the ancillary workers.

The government's emphasis on the separation between frontline staff and those not so regarded was reflected in their attitude to industrial relations in the service. Although the Conservatives honoured the recommendations of the Clegg Commission (which had reported just after the 1979 election) on public sector pay, they were evidently keen to break the link between NHS pay and external comparators. This they did in 1980 and 1981, when settlements for Whitley Council staff fell behind those of their external counterparts such as civil servants. Furthermore, differential pay awards widened internal relativities. Thus Norman Fowler stated that he would make no apology for 'seeking to make some distinction between staff groups on the grounds of recruitment, the degree of skill and qualifications required'.[28] This was his justification for the much lower pay awards offered (in 1982) to ancillary staff (4 per cent) than to nurses (6 per cent). The government was also criticised, during the 1982 dispute, for appearing to suggest that 'the nursing profession was acting responsibly . . . *while implying that the health service unions did not have the same attitude to patients or the same strength of feeling for the NHS'*.[29] In short the government was seeking to open up differentials between staff groups on the basis of a distinction based on skill levels and professionalism, and on a presumed equation of the work of the 'support' staff with unskilled and peripheral labour, which could thus be more easily subjected to market forces.

The more general question to be resolved related to the future of the Whitley Councils, the mechanism set up when the NHS was established, adopting a structure similar to those in place for local government and the Civil Service. The Whitley Councils negotiated settlements on a national basis, which was desirable because 'standardised, centrally determined terms and conditions promote the unity of a national service and relieve staff and management of the complexities of local bargaining' (Royal Commission, 1979, para. 12.16). However the Whitley Council system had other technical deficiencies, which led to suggestions that pay review bodies should be introduced throughout the service.

Despite such criticisms and the government's agreement to a PRB for nurses (in 1983, following an agreement that nurses would eschew strike action), no PRB was forthcoming for other staff groups and there was no replacement of the Whitley Council mechanism. The differentials between PRB staff and Whitley Council staff became more apparent and subject to criticism, especially when the government took steps to widen such differentials by instituting competitive tendering after the 1983 election.

The ostensible aims of competitive tendering were to reduce costs and promote competition, but the not-so-hidden agenda seems to have been to weaken trade union power and prepare the ground for the introduction of market-based determination of wage levels. The pamphlets produced by various Conservative think tanks (for example Adam Smith Institute, 1981, 1984) demonstrate that the coercive powers of trade unions and the vested interests they represented were seen as a major obstacle to the government's strategy of weakening trade union power. Indeed the government issued a controversial circular, *If Industrial Relations Break Down* (DHSS, 1979c), indicating that it was not prepared to tolerate a repeat of the NHS industrial action of 1978–9. In preparing contract specifications for competitive tendering, fair wages legislation was to be ignored and the scope for health authorities to insist on particular terms and conditions of service was steadily reduced (IPM/IDS, 1986). The principal sources of cost savings have been increased use of part-time staff, often for under 16 hours weekly (this is the time threshold below which employment protection legislation does not apply), and reductions in bonuses, holiday and sick-pay entitlements (HM Treasury, 1986, 1991). The effect of competitive tendering is to divide and rule the workforce, as the direct labour force is drawn into accepting reductions in hours worked and fringe benefits as the price for preserving jobs. Faced with the aggressive pricing behaviour of private companies they have little alternative. As a result NHS ancillary workers, among the lowest-paid workers in the country (Coyle, 1985), have experienced sharp reductions in employment, wages and the terms on which jobs are offered. Total ancillary service employment in the NHS in England fell from 172 200 full-time equivalents in 1981 to 85 900 in 1991 (Table 6.1), and while a large proportion of this reduction can be accounted for by the transfer of staff to private contractors, there have still been redundancies, estimated at around one third of the total job losses, or approximately 29 000 jobs. Of much wider significance are the alterations to workers' terms and conditions of service, the impacts of which has been felt in a particularly acute form by minority groups, notably those from the New Commonwealth (Coyle, 1986; Cousins, 1988; NAO, 1987; Paul, 1984; Whitfield, 1992). This may be counterproductive: as ancillary jobs became less attractive, serious problems of staff turnover and recruitment were experienced by both health authorities and contractors across the South East and indeed over much of England (Social Services Committee, 1986; NALGO, 1989) – a clear case of market failure?

Nevertheless, in the new macho management climate of the 1980s some managers were prepared to contemplate pushing the market to its limits. As a NUPE representative explained to the Social Services Committee, the union had asked a member of the Whitley Council management side how low he thought wages could be pitched as a result of competitive tendering. He had replied: 'As far down as you can take it while you've got people coming in to work for you'.[30] The consequence of this was that money saved by one branch of the government was being spent by another:

> We actually have [union] members within the NHS who get two pay packets. They get a pay packet for working in the NHS as a worker, and they get another pay packet from the DHSS in social security payments. . . . This really is nonsense, and does not give people any feeling they are being properly treated'.[31]

The morality of taking advantage of enormous geographical variations in unemployment to enforce such market-dictated conditions was also a point raised by union representatives, and the Contract Cleaning and Maintenance Association (CCMA) (the main trade association) argued that reliance on market forces alone would permit the entry of irresponsible firms offering low wages to poor quality staff; they therefore objected to the withdrawal of the Fair Wages resolution. However the minister for health, David Mellor, dismissed such arguments, stating that if there is low pay 'that means there are too many people doing too little work'.[32]

Competitive tendering, then, began to exacerbate differentials between staff groups in the NHS and between staff working for the NHS and those employed by contractors; indeed it led to the replacement of middle-aged women with domestic responsibilities and commitments by younger, single and unencumbered women who were able to get by on the limited wages and were sufficiently desperate for work to accept the conditions upon which it was offered (Pulkingham, 1992). Conceived as a demonstration of the potential impact of competition on labour costs, it arguably succeeded, although perhaps not to the extent the government had hoped, and brought with it problems of its own in terms of staff shortages. It also impacted on nurses as debates grew about the extent to which nurses were undertaking 'non-nursing' duties, and as the valuable social and therapeutic function of ward-based ancillary staff was lost (for example Harrison, 1986).

Recruitment difficulties and 'geographical pay'

The primary purposes of the national system of wage negotiation in the NHS were to facilitate mobility, prevent poaching of staff and promote unity and pride in the service (TUC, 1981). It also facilitated central control over the pay bill and removed the possible perverse incentive that staff operating in a national labour market might migrate to areas where higher rewards were available (NAHA, 1986). Any widening of regional variations in living costs was therefore likely to affect the ability of the service to recruit staff. This was the case in the 1980s as regional divisions widened substantially (see Martin and Townroe, 1992). Unemployment rates fell in the late 1980s to below 3 per cent in much of the South East of England; simultaneously, rapid economic growth and the promotion of owner occupation led to extremely rapid house price inflation, pricing many low-paid personnel out of the housing market. An important question was therefore what effects such regional variations and recruitment difficulties had on service delivery, and whether they could be best dealt with through some form of geographical variations in pay settlements.

Staff shortages were significant and often severe. National surveys undertaken for the nurses' PRB showed vacancy rates by geographical area for 1989–92, but unfortunately these surveys were begun only when the regional inequalities in housing costs were beginning to level out and after the generous 1988 pay settlement; in other words, after recruitment difficulties peaked. In 1988 up to 11 per cent of established posts were vacant for *over three months* in the London area and in the special health authorities (SHAs), and the rate for the Thames RHAs was over 8 per cent (Table 6.2). Though there have always been problems in certain specialities irrespective of location (for example the long-stay hospitals, where recruitment difficulties were exacerbated by deinstitutionalisation programmes), the sharp regional differences are still startling. At the DHA scale, a (somewhat imperfect) indication of shortages is given by expenditure on agency staff.[33] Nursing agencies must pay identical hourly wage rates to those of the NHS; agencies supplying other staff (such as secretaries) are not bound in this way. For England, expenditure more than doubled between the 1983–4 and 1986–7 financial years, rising from £67.3 mn to £140 mn at 1986–7 prices. Expressed as a proportion of their revenue budget, 13 DHAs in London spent over 4 per cent of their budget on agency staff in that financial year and four spent over 5 per cent (Mohan and Lee, 1989). At current prices, agency staff expenditure in England reached £297 mn in 1989–90 (2.2 per cent of the revenue budget), though it had fallen again to £234 mn by 1991–2.[34]

Thirdly, with regard to the direct effects on patient care, several health authorities throughout the South East produced a substantial amount of evidence (summarised in Mohan and Lee, 1989). For example, various DHAs referred to turnover levels of 25–30 per cent per annum (SWTRHA, quoted in Buchan, 1989). The Royal College of Nursing (RCN) found that vacancy levels for trained nursing staff in inner London DHAs were between 20 per cent and 25 per cent. Such shortages had both direct quantitative (ward closures) and qualitative (staff morale) impacts. Much of the evidence, and media coverage, related to nursing, but it was abundantly clear that shortages of other staff affected the delivery of care (Social Services Committee, 1989). Explanations for staff shortages included low pay nationally (not just in the South East) (NUPE, 1987; NALGO, 1989), poor working conditions and increased throughput (Waite and Hutt, 1987) and competition from the growing private sector (Thomas *et al.*, 1988). One consequence was that health authorities were compelled to pay staff at a higher rate than those agreed nationally for their level of skills and responsibilities, a phenomenon known as 'grade drift'. This undoubtedly increased the unit costs of providing services; administrative and clerical costs were substantially higher in London and the South East than elsewhere in the country (NAO, 1991a). A further response was

**Table 6.2 Vacancy rates for qualified nursing staff by region, 1989–92
(vacancies that lasted over three months, as percentage of funded establishment)**

Region	1989	1990	1991	1992
Northern	1.5	1.0	1.1	0.7
Yorkshire	1.9	1.4	1.2	1.0
Trent	2.2	2.3	1.5	1.4
East Anglia	3.7	3.5	2.6	2.1
NW Thames	7.9	6.9	6.1	2.8
NE Thames	9.9	8.7	5.4	3.9
SE Thames	9.1	8.0	5.3	4.4
SW Thames	8.0	8.5	4.5	5.0
Wessex	1.9	0.8	1.1	2.0
Oxford	4.4	4.0	2.2	1.9
South Western	2.6	1.8	0.6	0.4
West Midlands	2.7	2.5	2.2	1.6
Mersey	1.8	1.6	1.6	1.1
North Western	2.3	2.5	2.2	1.8
England	4.1	3.6	2.5	2.1
Wales	1.8	1.1	1.7	1.3
Scotland	2.4	2.0	1.8	1.7
SHAs	11.3	10.6	3.2	3.3
Inner London[1]	11.1	9.1	5.4	4.4
Outer London[1]	9.2	8.7	6.0	5.3
London Fringe[1]	7.2	8.3	5.3	3.9
Rest of GB	2.6	2.2	1.7	1.4

NOTE:
1. These three areas (inner/outer London, and the London 'fringe') are areas in which different levels of London supplements were payable. Full definitions of the areas covered are given in the 5th Report of the Review Body for Nursing Staff, Midwives, Health Visitors and Professions Allied to Medicine, Appendix C.

SOURCE:
Review Body for Nursing Staff, Midwives, Health Visitors and Professions Allied to Medicine, 7th, 8th, 9th and 10th Reports on Nursing Staff, Midwives and Health Visitors.

the granting of additional increments to staff, which was acknowledged by the DoH in late 1987 when it made available £65 mn to health authorities to help cope with such costs. Against such a background it was inevitable that a debate would open up on breaking up national pay agreements, or 'geographical pay'.

Proposals to introduce some form of decentralised pay bargaining had been advocated by senior NHS management on more than one occasion,[35] and NAHA (1986) favoured the principle, although it wished to retain a national spine, within which local management would have some flexibility to reward staff differentially. By late 1988 Edwina Currie was convinced that 'more flexibility and some form of regional pay' were the only ways to resolve the problems of 'recruitment and retention of essential staff in various parts of the country'.[36] David Mellor expressed his frustration with national pay bargaining: 'the monument to Whitleyism is the fact that we cannot fill vacancies in a number of key grades in a number of key parts of the country'. He dismissed union arguments that the problem was a national one of low pay: 'We have a certain problem in some areas of the country which we believe should be addressed by an element of local flexibility, not the kind of across-the-board increase that the unions put forward, *the consequence of which would simply be that there was less money available for service development*'.[37] A prominent advocate of 'geographical pay' suggested that national pay awards would not provide enough funds to 'tackle the problem in the South East' and they would be 'too expensive of scarce resources by unnecessarily increasing NHS costs elsewhere' (Dyson, 1990). Despite these arguments the nurses' PRB rejected DoH proposals for local pay supplements as 'premature'.[38] More detailed proposals were put by the DoH in 1988–9, to which the PRB agreed, including supplements of up to £1000 per post.[39] However the 1992 report of the PRB suggested that a reduction in vacancies was accounted for almost entirely by the cutting of vacant posts rather than by the positive effect of supplements, and also by the onset of recession.[40] However the precise form to be taken by 'geographical pay' was problematic, and the issues were sharpened by the creation of NHS trusts.

The White Paper and beyond

The White Paper was prefigured by various efforts to transfer staff from the NHS and its associated terms and conditions to the private sector; these demonstrated that entrepreneurial managers and health authorities were seeking to cut their teeth on the issue of local pay determination (Chapter 8).

One of the principal attractions of NHS trust status was said to be the freedom to determine staffing and wage levels – to adjust the staff mix and numbers to fluctuations in demand for care. This was heralded as a radical change in NHS pay policy: it would act as a catalyst in ending the national structure of pay bargaining, and staff shortages in the South East would force hospitals to 'shape contracts that would be more attractive' to scarce staff (Dyson, 1989). However its actual impact has been rather less dramatic. Dyson (1992) suggested two principal strategies available to managers: changing the skill mix of staff, and distinguishing between 'core' and 'contract' staff. He identified two elements of a human resource strategy: a remuneration strategy, and a labour utilisation strategy. While the former had been attempted through such initiatives as competitive tendering and was implicit in putative departures from national wage agreements, it was only when the two elements of the strategy were combined that the 'opportunity arises to achieve greater reductions in unit labour costs' (Dyson, 1992 p. 2). Changes in skill mix were essential because existing demarcations and hierarchies were 'fiercely defended' on the basis of 'tradition and long usage'. But changing patterns of service delivery would require a different staff profile. In addition, because demand would have peaks and troughs, and because NHS staffing was always geared towards the peak workload of any given establishment, the distinction between 'core' and 'contract' staff would allow 'staffing and labour costs to vary more in proportion with patient/client flow' (Dyson, 1992, p. 5).

Dyson stressed the benefits to staff as well as to the trusts: these benefits included tailoring their work commitments to their personal circumstances and maximising the time spent on the tasks for which they have been trained; if this happens, their 'bonding with the Trust is stronger, their commitment to the post is stronger, and their commitment to their professional work task is stronger'. He drew on the growth of agency work to make his case: far from reflecting chronic staff shortages, this growth was interpreted voluntaristically, as evidence of staff choosing more flexible hours of work. But his guard slipped on some crucial points: personalised, flexible labour utilisation offered trusts the opportunity to be 'released from *all the on-costs associated with employee status*', including superannuation, holiday pay, sickness benefits and other employment costs. While employees might benefit if some of these cost savings were used to increase the hourly rate of pay for those staff on a flexible, hourly paid contract, such employees would have to finance those 'on-costs' themselves. There is an obvious parallel with competitive tendering (HM Treasury, 1986), except that Dyson is presenting this as a progressive strategy that is to the advantage of the employee. The advantages to the workforce are presented as a matter of *choice*, and are linked to workforce *requirements* – that there is potential for management to use personalised contracts as a divisive tool is ignored. But Dyson suggests that 'the hospitals that continue to ignore [the need to change patterns of labour utilisation] may not survive in their present form' (p. 11); in other words, the workforce will have little option but to comply.

Precisely how far the NHS will depart from its national wage rates and terms and conditions is uncertain. EC regulations governing workers transferred from one employer to another will prevent radical departures and may spark off compensation claims by thousands of workers affected by competitive tendering. Within the NHS, the departure from the National Health Service Management Executive (NHSME) of Eric Caines, a vigorous advocate of pay decentralisation and performance-related pay, seems to suggest that the pace of such change has been slowed down.[41] Buchan (1992, pp. 17–24) noted some evidence that trusts were considering departures, in various ways, from nationally agreed frameworks, but he felt that unless the financial position of trusts was very secure they were more likely to remain within the national framework. He also observed some evidence that local cartels or informal agreements on wage levels were emerging. But perhaps the most fundamental criticism of market-based salary determination for nursing staff was made by the nurses' PRB, which had commented that the logic of market forces would:

> suggest that pay levels need be set only marginally above the point at which significant losses [of nursing staff] would occur. . . Those who commit themselves to a professional career such as nursing *may reasonably expect that wider considerations than this will be taken into account in setting their pay*.[42]

The difficulty of a decentralised, market-based solution is that there will be both winners and losers in a game circumscribed by the funding made available nationally for the service, and as a result worthy objectives of fairness and stability will take second place to issues of cost control (Buchan, 1992, pp. 36–7; Fatchett, 1989). In fact reports suggest that the Treasury has been unwilling to permit a greater degree of decentralisation, not least because centralised wage bargaining facilitates cost control. Consequently ministers are reported to have 'backed away' from abandoning nationally agreed pay deals, despite the urgings of NHS trusts and their representatives.[43]

Concluding comments

The foregoing discussion needs to be set against the difficult demographic situation facing the NHS. Some years ago Conroy and Stidston (1988) characterised the situation facing the NHS as a 'black hole', because several factors (technological change, increased competition for staff, service sector growth, reduced female unemployment, increased part-time working) would make it virtually impossible for the NHS to retain the requisite numbers of staff. The recession has not defused the demographic timebomb: competition for relatively well-educated female school leavers, from whom the NHS draws many of its recruits, is intense as the service sector trawls the same group of people (Wilson and Stilwell, 1992). It remains to be seen, therefore, whether the strategies described here will prove a stable solution to recruitment difficulties in the long term.

In terms of interpreting the changes described here, the NHS seems almost a paradigm example of the so-called 'flexible firm', with its growing polarisation between core and peripheral staff. To suggest that – for example – the growth of subcontracting in the public sector merely reflects, in a straightforward way, developments elsewhere in the economy is to ignore the 'central political thrust' of public sector subcontracting, 'which is to dismantle *public* service' (Pollert, 1988, p. 290 – emphasis in original). Furthermore there may be similarities – overtime/agency working might be regarded as evidence of numerical flexibility, for example – but these may reflect responses to financial circumstances and recruitment difficulties rather than a deliberate managerial strategy. Finally, and more importantly, the model of the flexible firm confuses what are largely the effects of occupational and sectoral restructuring – such as the expansion of services and the feminisation of the labour force – with developments in state policy (such as privatisation of services). In short the political background to and motivations for labour market changes need to be given prominence. Furthermore, while working practices may have become more flexible, to the benefit of some groups of staff, decentralisation to trusts makes it seem likely that flexibility will be introduced as part of a managerial attempt to control the workforce rather than to shape work patterns to the needs of staff. This raises the question of flexibility for whom? (Hudson, 1988).

The promotion of flexibility has clear political origins and consequences. In terms of creating constituencies for the government's policies, and in terms of fragmenting opposition, this is almost textbook statecraft, though not without some limits (for example the staff shortages and recruitment difficulties). For it has been the ancillary and other Whitley Council staff who have been accused of being an unproductive burden on the service, and the nursing staff whose salary settlements have been underfunded, forcing authorities to trade off improved efficiency for increased pay. For some ministers, national pay settlements symbolised an outmoded collectivist and corporatist era: as the secretary of state said in 1989, 'I do not like centralised pay bargaining. I do not like national pay bargaining. I do not think it is good for management and staff'.[44] As the biggest employer in the country it may not be surprising that the NHS is used as a demonstration project in this way, but it rather gives the lie to suggestions that the NHS is merely following what are supposed to be secular trends. Instead, policies seem to be *designed* to divide the workforce into a secure, well rewarded, compliant core and a part-time, underpaid periphery. In fact some commentators (for example Deakin, 1992; Michie and Wilkinson, 1992) suggest that it was in the public sector that the most dramatic changes in labour market organisation took place during the Thatcher years. If the consequences in terms of staff numbers and redundancies have been unspectacular by the standards of the former nationalised industries, the impact on the terms and conditions of employment of substantial numbers of staff is highly significant. If this is a new era of labour market regulation, it seems to exemplify the 'palaeoliberal, hire and fire labour market' described by Jessop as symbolising the post-Fordist ideal. But whether it can also deliver quality services is perhaps another question.

Two spatialised discourses can be discerned with regard to government policies towards health care personnel: a discourse of core and periphery, and one of localisation. On the former point, the government has emphasised a distinction between 'productive' and 'unproductive' staff, which reflects its wider deployment of a 'two-nations' rhetoric (Jessop *et al.*, 1988). A contrast is drawn between 'frontline' and 'support' staff, and the two groups have been treated in sharply contrasting ways. Thus 'support' staff have been pilloried as an unproductive burden and subjected both to strict numerical controls and to market disciplines. However this proved counterproductive, with evidence of market failures and adverse effects on service quality. In contrast consultant medical staff were at first permitted to undertake additional private practice. Granting the nurses a PRB was intended as a reward for their eschewing industrial action. The position of managerial staff is ambiguous. The imposition of strict controls on administrative staff numbers and costs in the 1982 reorganisation suggested that these were seen as supernumerary, but more recently the emphasis has been on the importance of determined and effective management to achieve the government's wider goals. The high rewards available to such staff signal the importance attached to them. Even so, charges that expenditure on management is excessive continue to provoke disputes.[45]

The localisation of wage bargaining continues to elude the government to the frustration of some of its leading advocates. It is ironic that one reason why decentralised wage bargaining became a prominent issue was the difficulty of recruiting caused by the government's own spatially selective policies for promoting economic growth, which led to labour market inflexibilities. However the precise form to be taken by 'geographical pay' remains uncertain. Given the decline of the regional tier in the service (Chapter 9), and the self-evident fact that RHAs were not natural labour market areas, pay negotiations will probably not be devolved to that level. Since the great majority of NHS staff are now employed by trusts, a number of scenarios are possible. Depending on local labour market conditions, hospitals would be in competition with one another for scarce staff, which could lead to inflationary awards. Alternatively, pay could be driven downwards in areas of high unemployment. A third possibility is the emergence of informal agreements between trusts on local wage rates. None of these will go very far, however, without relaxation of central control, which seems unlikely at present. Nevertheless, whereas national wage bargaining was originally seen as essential to promoting the unity and integrity of a national service, it is now regarded as an obstacle. While mass unemployment remains, recruitment difficulties may ease, but this hardly seems a long-term solution in the case of skilled staff. Surely, in a system of national importance, such personnel deserve better than to be subject to the caprice of local labour-market conditions, potentially leading to differentiation between areas in terms of their ability to provide services. The deregulated labour market beloved of the Conservatives may prove incompatible with – indeed unable to deliver – a comprehensive, *national*, service.

Blurring the Boundaries: Health Care Outside the NHS

The 1970s and 1980s were marked by rapid, though not uninterrupted, growth in commercial health care. I say 'commercial', in opposition to the more usual 'private' or 'independent' health care, since the dominant feature of the growth of health care outside the NHS has been commercial medicine. In addition there is nothing in the appellation 'private' to distinguish the health care that is actually provided from that in the NHS (apart, perhaps, from the privacy afforded individual patients); nor is health care outside the NHS really 'independent' in view of its close interrelationship with developments in the NHS (Griffith, Mohan and Rayner, 1985; Griffith, Iliffe and Rayner, 1987). The term 'independent' has been deliberately promoted by the private sector: it at once attempts to rebut criticisms that the sector depends on the state for recruitment and training personnel, and suggests that the sector is self-reliant. Williams (1989, p. 75) observes a similar strategy in private education: 'it is much easier to sell "independent" schools to the public than it is to sell "private" ones. As a title "public" is dangerous: it now has disturbing connotations of privilege, while carrying disconcerting memories of just why schools were so called'. Just as public schools have deliberately emphasised their so-called 'independence' so too have private and commercial hospitals sought to distance themselves from any criticism that they draw resources away from publicly-funded health care.

However markets do not operate independently of specific institutional conditions and frameworks (Hindess, 1987): the growth and development of commercial health care in Britain is inextricably bound up with state policies towards both the private sector and the NHS. Consequently I seek to chart the recent growth of the commercial sector and to demonstrate its close relationship to state policy decisions, whether these be concerned with the rate of growth of NHS resources, the relationship between the NHS and the private sector, or the regulation of private practice. I also focus on two key aspects of recent developments in this sector: the commercialisation and internationalisation of the 'independent' sector. Aspects of the very rapid growth of the nursing home business, which has been a direct result of state policy decisions, are considered in Chapter 5. Finally I consider the implications of future growth in the private sector, both for the future geography of health care and, more generally, for public attitudes to the NHS. Not considered here are the growth of other forms of private health care, such as alternative medicines and therapies (Sharma, 1991), and progressive examples of private care, such as the hospice movement. The reason for the focus on acute care is that it is provided by both the NHS and the commercial sector and its growth provides a test case of to what extent market-driven health care is likely to succeed. In contrast the overlap between the NHS and 'alternative' medicines is, almost by definition, minimal, so the growth of such treatments more genuinely reflects consumer dissatisfaction or frustration with the NHS. However the issue of consumerism is returned to in the concluding section.

Historical background: state policies and private sector growth

Ironically, perhaps the greatest single stimulus to the growth of independent acute hospitals was the 1974–9 Labour government's attempt to eliminate private practice from NHS hospitals. This manifesto commitment did not, however, extend to abolishing private medical care altogether: there was some cabinet concern that, if private hospitals were not allowed to develop, 'we should lose a lot of revenue from rich overseas patients' (Castle, 1980, p. 704). Labour established the Health Services Board (HSB), which oversaw the phasing-out of paybeds and set size limits on the development of hospitals outside the NHS. The withdrawal of paybeds was pursued steadily if unevenly. Some rural areas were virtually exempt because paybeds could not be withdrawn from NHS hospitals if there was thought to be insufficient demand locally to support a private hospital, while most of the beds withdrawn were under-utilised anyway.[1] The intention was substantially to reduce private beds in the NHS, and as a result those involved in the private sector had to attempt to provide independent facilities for private medical treatment. Thus Labour's policies, perhaps paradoxically, produced a climate in which the private sector arguably knew exactly where it stood in relation to government policy, in contrast with what has sometimes been regarded as a vacillating policy (at least prior to the 1989 White Paper) pursued by successive Conservative governments (Mohan, 1986a).

The Royal Commission still concluded that the private sector 'is too small to make a significant impact on the NHS, except locally and temporarily' (Royal Commission, 1979, p. 294). The Conservatives were apparently determined to change this, but while they have encouraged private health care, they have not satisfied all the demands of the private sector. The steps taken to encourage private sector expansion have been limited and indirect. Until 1989 there was no relief from taxation on private health insurance policies, something for which the major insurers, such as BUPA and PPP had lobbied regularly for several years.[2] However medical premiums paid for workers earning less than £8500 were exempted from tax in the 1981 budget, which also permitted companies to set private medical insurance premiums – paid on behalf of employees – against corporation tax.

Of rather more significance were the relaxation of controls on private practice by NHS consultants, and various related measures that have given the private sector greater scope for manoeuvre. In 1979 'whole-time' NHS consultants were permitted, for the first time, to undertake limited private practice, and to receive professional fees up to a limit in gross annual earnings of 10 per cent of their NHS whole-time salary. If undertaken outside NHS hospitals, this practice must be so arranged as to minimise the amount of time spent travelling to and from private commitments. In addition, whereas 'maximum part-time' consultants had previously been paid 9/11 of a whole-time salary (on the basis that they worked nine 'notional half days' per week), the maximum part-time contract was increased to 10/11 of a whole-time NHS salary, on the basis that consultants work ten 'notional half days' (DHSS, 1979b).

In line with the government's deregulatory policies, the HSB was abolished in 1980, and the size thresholds below which private hospitals did not require authorisation were increased to 100 beds outside London and 120 beds within the capital (DHSS, 1980b). The Royal Commission had recommended that the powers of the HSB be extended to cover situations in which the impact of the *total* number of private beds in a locality could be assessed (rather than just the effects of *individual* hospital developments), but the government rejected this proposal. Furthermore, only reserve powers were left to the secretary of state to intervene if it were believed that the growth of private hospitals was interfering with the NHS in any given locality. This, Patrick Jenkin said, was 'very much a long stop' power[3] requiring the specific request of a health authority for designation as an area wherein all future private hospital developments would require authorisation by the secretary of state. This legislation proved toothless: at the time, the few DHAs with over 120 beds were mainly in inner London and were unlikely to attract much further investment, given market conditions throughout the 1980s. In practice no DHA ever received 'designated area' status. Thus such legislation as existed to control commercial hospital development was virtually neutralised after 1980 and was removed with the 1989 reforms. The only other legislation to impinge on private hospital development was that relating to planning permission, but such controls were eased during the 1980s. Thus the Department of the Environment emphasised that the planning considerations of which a local authority should take account excluded such matters as the appropriateness of a private hospital to the health care needs of the local population; nor were health authorities to express views on or offer guidance to local authorities regarding the need for private hospitals in their area (DoE, 1980). Local opposition to proposed hospitals has therefore to be confined to narrowly technical planning grounds, and where authorities sought to use planning legislation to voice opposition this was ruled inadmissible (Mohan, 1984).

In addition, as part of a more general move towards a mixed economy of health care (Chapter 3), health authorities were encouraged to take account of existing and planned capacity in the commercial sector: since 1981 they have been able to place contracts with commercial hospitals (DHSS, 1981d). With hindsight this might be seen as a first step towards an internal market, in which private and NHS hospitals compete with one another on the same terms. However, a NAO (1990) study reported that health authorities considered the private sector only in the absence of any immediate in-house alternatives (for example to overcome capacity constraints).

Perhaps the most important influence on commercial sector growth, however, has been the continued exhortations to individuals to take out insurance against the cost of treatment, in the context of (at best) minimal growth in the NHS. A substantial number of individuals have taken out insurance policies (although this is far less significant than the main area of growth – company-paid premiums) but individuals do not, presumably, make such decisions without considering whether or not the NHS can provide for their needs. There has been a consistent ideological message since 1979, consisting of two related propositions. Firstly, the Conservatives have emphasised that growth in the NHS is inherently limited by the state's finite resources, and so future growth in health care has to depend substantially on the independent sector; they have further insisted that spending on health care is relatively low *because of* low spending on private health care. Secondly, the government has argued that individuals who take out insurance are not only exercising freedom of choice, they are also relieving the NHS of some of its burden. One might challenge this in relation to the unwillingness of the private sector to diversify beyond short-term acute surgery, but the more significant point is that individual decisions have been taken in a climate in which the NHS is widely seen to be in serious difficulty (see Chapters 1 and 3). It seems difficult to dispute the contention that the NHS's difficulties are at least a proximate cause of individuals taking out private insurance against the cost of treatment in the commercial sector.

In short, while commercial sector growth cannot be entirely attributable to the policies of the Conservative government, nevertheless its overall policies towards the NHS have done much to create an atmosphere in which to 'exit' (Hirschman, 1970) is seen as the only feasible option for many people, especially in localities hit hardest by expenditure restraint.[4] In addition, a whole range of policies have undoubtedly helped establish a climate conducive to commercial sector expansion. The NHS reforms were a step further along the road to the more complete integration of the commercial sector with the NHS, but they were not a truly radical departure, for many of the steps proposed in the reforms have long historical roots.

Dynamics of change in the commercial sector

The insurance market: spatial and social divisions of welfare

The main motor of growth in commercial medicine is the insurance market. Insurance can be obtained in three ways: by individually-paid subscriptions; through workplace-based 'group' schemes, in which discounts are offered in proportion to the number in the scheme, though the employers do not contribute to the costs of insurance; and 'company-paid' schemes, in which employers pay all or part of the premiums on behalf of their employees. Insurance schemes are usually arranged through one or other of the 'provident associations', which are non-profit distributing organisations (they do not pay a dividend to shareholders; instead, surpluses are retained for reinvestment). The provident associations cover 75 per cent of those with insurance policies, and their moral authority as non-commercial bodies has allowed them scope to criticise the entry of commercially-oriented organisations in both insurance and hospital provision.

Some 7.2 million people (around 13 per cent of the population) are now insured against the costs of medical treatment, an increase of 320 per cent over the mid-1970s figure of 1.7 million. However an expansion of coverage to 25 per cent of the population, as predicted in 1980 by Gerald Vaughan, then Conservative health minister, seems highly unlikely. These figures compare with proportions of around 4 per cent (which was the figure for much of the 1970s), and between 7.5 and 8.5 per cent which is the range that applied from 1982 to 1987 (Laing, 1993). The most rapid area of growth has been that of company-paid schemes, which from 1977–91 increased by 350 per cent (from 424 000 premiums to 1 911 000)[5], compared with the overall growth of 139 per cent (Laing, 1993, Table 3.6). This highlights the significance of state policies (the major stimulus to growth having been the Labour government's restrictive incomes policies), and also arguably undermines claims that insurance growth is simply and solely the result of individuals making unconstrained choices in the free market. Thus Conservative claims, often repeated in parliament, that the most rapid increases in private insurance followed the industrial action of the 1978–9 'winter of discontent', are somewhat wide of the mark. Company-paid schemes now account for 44 per cent of those covered (32 per cent are wholly paid by employers, 12 per cent are partly paid by employers – OPCS, 1989), and for 59 per cent of all policies (compared with 40 per cent in 1977 – Laing, 1993).

Given the importance of company-paid schemes, social divisions are clear: some 27 per cent of those in managerial and professional occupations, and 23 per cent of employers/managers, have at least some insurance cover, compared with only 2 and 1 per cent respectively for the semi-skilled and unskilled manual socio-economic groups. Changes for 1982–7 do not indicate that insurance is spreading to lower socio-economic groups, as the proportion insured remained constant for the intermediate/junior non-manual, semi-skilled manual, and skilled manual socio-economic groups over that period. (Table 7.1a; OPCS, 1989).

Geographically, the most recent figures relate to 1987, the last year in which the *General Household Survey* asked about private health care[6]; the following statistics refer to the Standard Regions used for statistical purposes. Insurance coverage ranged from some 16 per cent of the total population in the Outer Metropolitan area, to under 4 per cent in Wales and Scotland and 3 per cent in the Northern region (Table 7.1b); some 13 per cent of the population of London were

Table 7.1 Private medical insurance coverage, 1982 and 1987: (a) Private medical insurance by socio-economic group, Great Britain; (b) Private medical insurance cover by standard region (percentages)

		Insured		Percentage Point Change	Percentage Change in Proportion Insured
		1982	1987		
(a)	Professionals	23	27	+4	+17
	Employers/managers	19	23	+4	+21
	Intermediate and junior non-manual	9	9	0	0
	Skilled manual/own account professional	3	3	0	0
	Semi skilled manual and personal service	2	2	0	0
	Unskilled manual	2	1	−1	−50
	All persons	7	9	+2	+28
(b)	North	3	3	0	0
	Yorkshire/Humberside	7	6	−1	−14
	North West	7	7	0	0
	East Midlands	5	7	+2	+40
	West Midlands	7	8	+1	+14
	East Anglia	6	10	+4	+66
	Greater London	10	13	+3	+30
	Outer Metropolitan	13	16	+3	+23
	Outer South East	9	15	+6	+60
	South West	8	8	0	0
	Wales	3	4	+1	+33
	Scotland	3	4	+1	+33
	Great Britain	7	9	+2	+28

NOTE: Subsequent *General Household Surveys* have not sought data on private health insurance.
SOURCE: *General Household Survey*, 1982, 1987.

insured. Growth in the proportion insured has been greatest in the prosperous southern regions of England: the proportion insured rose from 6 per cent to 10 per cent in East Anglia from 1982–7, and from 9 per cent to 15 per cent over the same period in the Outer South East, while remaining static in the Northern, North West, and South West regions. Individual areas within South East probably have much higher insurance coverage than these region-wide statistics would suggest: given their social composition, up to 30–35 per cent may not be unreasonable estimates for parts of Berkshire and Buckinghamshire for instance. This may reflect continued outmigration from London as well as the generally buoyant economic fortunes of the areas surrounding South East England. Coverage in London and South East England was substantially higher than would be expected from the socio-economic composition of these areas; conversely, in the Northern region it was substantially below the expected levels (OPCS, 1984).

There is an emergent spatial division of welfare here: the distribution of employer-paid benefits, such as medical insurance, is skewed between the north and south of the country. Access to such benefits depends increasingly on one's position within the division of labour, with key personnel within firms being able to avail themselves of a range of subsidies in the health, housing, educational and transport fields (see, *inter alia*, Forrest and Murie, 1988; Bradford and Burdett, 1989; Whitelegg, 1984). The presence of large numbers of branch plants carrying out largely routine assembly tasks in the regional economies of Scotland, Wales and north-east England, may mean that few employees in such locations receive perks such as medical insurance as part of their salary package. In contrast executives, management and research and development staff in areas where most corporate headquarters are located, such as South East England, will be more likely to receive such fringe benefits. This may be regarded as a crude dichotomy but it is nevertheless recognised in analyses of regional problems in Britain (for example Martin and Townroe, 1992). These social and spatial divisions raise important questions about attitudes to welfare, political alignments and consumption sector cleavages that are taken up in the concluding section.

The independent hospital sector: commercialisation and internationalisation

Two key trends have marked the independent sector since 1979: the increased significance of commercial organisations (Rayner, 1986), and the growing presence of transnational corporations. These have determined the direction of the sector and have led a market-based restructuring of provision, financing and ownership. Overall growth has been rapid: there are now 11 416 beds in independent acute hospitals, an increase of 71 per cent over the 1979 figure of 6671 (IHA, 1993).

A substantial private sector remained after the NHS was established. Some 300 hospitals were disclaimed by the minister of health, principally because they were inappropriately located and/or required extensive modernisation. They were usually owned by charitable or religious organisations, and in many cases they treated (and still treat) NHS patients on a contractual basis. The unpredictability of charitable sources of funds, however, has meant that these institutions play a declining role in the private sector: only 8 per cent of private acute beds are now owned by charitable organisations.

Clearly charity was not a stable, long-term basis for the industry. Hence BUPA, the major provident association, established Nuffield Hospitals in 1957 with the aim of dispersing private hospital capacity across the country and thus attracting new insurance business. Nuffield Hospitals is, however, a non-profit organisation with relatively little access to capital. Consequently the market situation in the 1970s was ripe for commercial development. Firstly British companies became involved, often on a small scale in alliance with groups of consultants, but also including BUPA Hospitals, a commercial hospital development company established by BUPA. Perhaps the most controversial single development was BUPA Hospitals' acquisition of the HCA's (Hospital Corporation of America) British facilities, which raised the question of conflict of interest given BUPA's position as a leading insurer. Despite being referred to the Monopolies and Mergers Commission (1990), the takeover was permitted. The entry of multinationals into the commercial health care scene can be explained in terms of diversification in the USA: faced with a tougher domestic regulatory and competitive environment, US hospital corporations scoured the globe in search of profitable locations for future development (Berliner and Regan, 1987). The perception of the NHS as a system in 'crisis' was influential: opportunities for expansion were 'brightest in countries with ailing health care systems, such as England' (*sic*) (Federation of US Investor-Owned Hospitals, 1983, quoted in Griffith, Iliffe and Rayner, 1987). One might add that the willingness of the Conservatives to promote the internationalisation of the British economy post-1979 was a contingent factor.

Foreign corporations, notably from the USA, saw the NHS as a system in crisis. But there was also little serious competition from indigenous commercial organisations. In the mid-1970s the British private sector was seen as being 'in some disarray and therefore unable to unite, expand and repel the American invasion' (Rowell, 1983, p. 225). In the absence of a tradition of commercial health care provision in Britain, few indigenous firms could exploit the opportunities created by the 1976 Health Services Act. Hence firms such as American Medical International and Hospital Corporation of America were well positioned to develop hospitals in Britain.

The most notable development since 1979, then, is the increased significance of multinational organisations within a sector characterised by greater competition since the slow-down in the growth of the insured population in the mid-1980s. This competition has been intensified by the decline in the number of patients from abroad seeking treatment in British hospitals, as many Middle Eastern states have established their own hospital facilities. The impact of greater competition is apparent from an examination of survey data from the Independent Healthcare Association (IHA). Commercial hospitals accounted for 63 per cent of all beds in private hospitals in 1992, compared with 29 per cent in 1979 (IHA, 1993). Within this overall commercialisation, US-owned corporations were initially particularly active in acquiring British-owned hospitals and some 22 per cent of all private hospital beds were at one point US-owned, though more recently there have been entries into the market from European groups (accounting for 16 per cent of total beds), including the takeover of AMI's (American Medical International) British hospitals by the French company, Compagnie Générale de Santé, a takeover said to be influenced by the fact that the British market was 'uniquely liberal' in Europe.[7]

There are also indications of a shakeout of hospital capacity, with 45 hospitals closing between 1979 and 1992, most of these being charitable, religious or single-hospital organisations (IHA, 1993). Furthermore, and perhaps more surprisingly given their access to capital, an important development in the late 1980s was the departure of US-owned hospital chains, itself a reflection of determined federal government and corporate efforts to reduce medical bills. AMI was forced into asset sales to reduce debts while the HCA decided to 'shrink its operations in the face of a tougher US market.[8] This, added to the motives attributed to the French company noted above, indicates the significance of the international regulatory environment within which global corporations in the service sector operate.

The geography of commercial health care

The availability of commercial health care is uneven, both between and within regions. Figure 7.1 shows the location and ownership of independent hospitals in Britain in 1992. Note the dispersed distribution of the not-for-profit hospitals, especially those owned or managed by Nuffield Hospitals. The map does not, however, bring out the extent of the contrast between the Thames RHAs and the rest of the country. Thus the NW and NE Thames RHAs, with 36 and 46 beds per 100 000 population respectively, contrast sharply with the Northern RHA and Wales, with six and nine beds per 100 000 population respectively. Similar geographical divisions are evident in the commercial hospital market. There has been rapid expansion in regions that previously had little private hospital capacity, notably in the East Anglian and Wessex RHAs while, relatively speaking, growth was slower in RHAs such as NW and SE Thames. Within the Thames regions, while London remains dominant, there has been a relative shift of capacity to the Outer Metropolitan area, which has the highest concentration of the insured population and has benefited more than almost any other area in Britain from the economic growth of the 1980s. However the focus of the whole industry remains Harley Street in west-central London, located for proximity to major rail termini in the nineteenth century and for access to the hospitals in which major consultants practised, but now very much part of an international health-care economy.

Considerations such as the insurance market, the availability of local sources of finance and, perhaps crucially, access to NHS consultants influence the spatial pattern of commercial facilities (Mohan, 1985). The distribution of commercial facilities is skewed towards the most prosperous areas of England, compounding rather than eliminating inequalities in the distribution of resources. This concentration is also an institutional barrier to change in the hospital system, because many consultants with large private practices are also employed in the London teaching hospitals and might therefore be expected to resist relocation of such facilities. In addition, the pattern of services available in the private sector has the potential to influence considerably the operation of the internal market, depending on where spare capacity is available (see below).

The distribution of the commercial hospital sector is mirrored in the distribution of its workload, both by geographical area and in terms of the kind of procedures carried out. The sector's workload is primarily in elective surgery for non-life-threatening conditions. There has been a

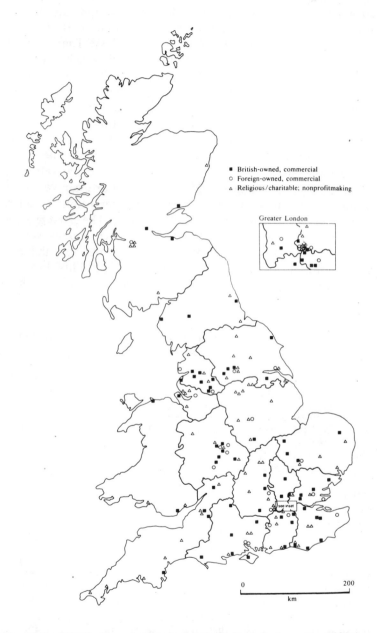

Figure 7.1 Distribution of acute hospitals in the private sector, 1992

substantial increase in the proportion of operations carried out in the private sector (Table 7.2). In 1986 approximately 31 per cent of all operations carried out in the NW Thames and SW Thames RHAs took place in private hospitals or in NHS paybeds (Nicholl *et al.*, 1989a, 1989b), followed by NE Thames (22 per cent) and Oxford (21.8 per cent) against a national figure of 16.7 per cent. While the most rapid growth of private acute hospital capacity has taken place in RHAs outside London, the proportion of operations in elective surgery carried out privately has increased dramatically in the Thames RHAs – by up to 71 per cent in the case of NE Thames. The differentials between regions in the proportions of activity in the private sector may reflect differential changes in NHS activity. For example, at a time of overall expansion in the private sector, the proportion of elective work done privately actually fell in the Trent RHA. The rapid growth in the contribution of the private sector in the Thames regions was therefore probably a combination of private sector expansion and a lack of corresponding expansion in NHS activity. This indicates the significance of the private sector in certain types of procedures, and

Table 7.2   Contribution of the private sector to elective surgery, 1981 and 1986
(percentages)

	Caseload treated in private sector 1981 1986		Percentage point change	Percentage change in proportion
Northern	5.2	6.3	1.1	21.1
Yorkshire	10.8	11.4	0.6	5.5
Trent	10.2	9.8	−0.4	3.9
East Anglia	12.3	13.9	1.6	13.0
NW Thames	21.8	31.2	9.4	43.1
NE Thames	12.8	22.0	9.2	71.8
SE Thames	13.6	19.0	5.4	39.7
SW Thames	21.7	30.8	9.1	41.9
Wessex	14.6	19.0	4.4	30.1
Oxford	18.5	21.8	3.3	17.8
S Western	13.6	15.1	1.5	11.0
W Midlands	13.1	16.8	3.7	28.2
Mersey	9.3	15.0	5.7	38.0
N Western	10.3	14.2	3.9	38.2
All Regions	13.2	16.7	3.5	26.5

SOURCES: Nicholl *et al.*, 1989b; Williams *et al.*, 1984a.

it is interesting to speculate what the political pressures on the government might have been had this safety valve not relieved some demands on the NHS.

Diversification and change

The growth of the private sector has not been unproblematic, and not all the optimistic statements of the early 1980s have been borne out. In the insurance market there has been steady growth, but in both 1991 and 1992 subscriptions fell by an estimated 1.5 per cent and 4 per cent respectively. Indeed in 1991 the number of company-paid policies dropped by 3 per cent, the first time since the mid-1970s that there had been a reduction in the number of such policies (Laing, 1993). Individual subscriptions continue to grow slowly, but they are likely to be affected by recession, while group schemes have declined steadily; initially these were priced very competitively in order to attract a wider range of subscribers, but this was associated with a high claims incidence, rendering them unviable.

In the hospital sector, reports of overcapacity have been rife for some years. One effect has been a limited shakeout of hospital provision, especially in the non-profit sector. There has also been some diversification into new areas of activity. Originally this was limited to certain specialised forms of treatment – such as AMI's head injuries treatment centre – that were simply not available on the NHS and which were financed largely by contracts from NHS authorities. The private sector has also introduced innovations in the form of screening programmes that parallel developments in the USA, where there are clear corporate interests in reducing health care bills because these are financed largely by business itself (Rayner, 1987). The private sector also sees itself having a role in a managerial sense, possibly taking over NHS units such as paybeds and running them to make profits for itself and the DHA concerned. Several initiatives in this vein have been attempted and they are being extended in the shape of joint-development schemes between the private sector and the NHS (Chapter 8). In the longer term, recessionary conditions may limit growth, but they have allegedly had a perverse short-term effect: Laing (1993, p. 63) suggests that many people with insurance policies have accelerated their treatment for fear of redundancy and consequent loss of insurance. But the reduction in subscribers in 1991 and 1992, the impact on profit margins of reduction in lengths of stay, and growing competition from the NHS (see below) will increase competitive pressures.

Government–industry relations and the effects of the NHS reforms

The development of the commercial sector has depended heavily on state action or inaction in order to create the conditions for a market to operate in the health sector. However relations between the private sector and government have not always been cordial. The continued presence of NHS paybeds and the absence (prior to the NHS reforms) of capital charges for NHS property meant that the private sector was not convinced that there was a level competitive playing field. Furthermore, divisions within the private sector have inhibited the development of policy.

Divisions within the private sector were evident in the lack (until 1986) of a single representative organisation and in the numerous antagonisms within the industry: between commercial and non-commercial operators, between British-owned and American-owned organisations, and between insurers and providers. Private hospital interests were represented until 1986 by the Association of Independent Hospitals (AIH) and the Independent Hospitals Group (IHG). The former took over the functions of the British Hospitals' Association (which had represented the voluntary hospitals in the pre-NHS days); the latter was established to campaign against Labour's plans to eliminate private practice in the mid-1970s. Serious proposals for more cooperation with the NHS, although encouraged by the government, arguably did not get off the ground until the single umbrella organisation, the Independent Hospitals Association (subsequently the Independent Healthcare Association), was formed in 1987.[9]

One reason for this disunity was British opposition to the influx of foreign-owned, commercial hospital chains. BUPA's chief executive argued in 1986 that the pursuit of profit led to inflationary pressures, especially given the American corporations' orientation towards high-technology medicine.[10] In response, American corporations have criticised BUPA's ambiguous position as both insurer and provider of health care, especially following the acquisition of HCA's UK hospitals. However the Monopolies and Mergers Commission (1990, p. 67) argued that even this was not a monopoly since BUPA still had only a limited share of the hospital market, operated its hospitals at 'arm's length' from its insurance business and was unable to 'divert' subscribers to its own hospitals.

These divisions provoked criticisms of the apparently contradictory position of the government vis-à-vis the commercial sector, and also calls for greater regulation. Oliver Rowell, then chair of the Independent Hospitals Group, claimed that if the HSB had 'remained a non political body, it could have been used to mastermind . . . the integrated development of health services'.[11] This was ironic because of the implicit recognition that the absence of controls on private hospital location had contributed to the private sector's overcapacity problems in the mid-1980s. More generally, the private sector had vigorously opposed the proposals of the HSB: although according to Barbara Castle (1980, p. 557), the private sector could see its value in 'helping to secure a better distribution of private facilities', they objected strongly to the actual size limitations above which independent hospitals would require certificates from the government (p. 695). Thus despite the IHG's initial opposition to regulation, only a few years later there were calls for greater state intervention, and other criticisms from the private sector reinforce this view. For example the government was persistently criticised by the private sector for permitting unfair competition by not forcing NHS authorities to charge the full economic cost of paybeds, and by allowing health authorities to reintroduce paybeds.[12] The continued existence of paybeds has been cited as a cause of overbedding in the commercial sector, since many hospital developers had 'assumed that NHS paybeds would be phased out'.[13] The reintroduction of paybeds (currently there are some 3 000 in England, or approximately 600 more than when the HSB's last set of proposals were carried through – Laing, 1993) was unquestionably a response to increasingly severe financial constraints, but this action only served to increase competitive pressures on the commercial sector. In short, the relationship between the private sector and the Conservative governments was not always harmonious, with the private sector consistently calling for greater support from the government.

A number of changes in the White Paper impacted on the relations between the government and the private sector. The proposal for capital charging on NHS buildings and property would help to put commercial and NHS facilities on a comparable footing for the first time, removing what the private sector regarded as an implicit subsidy to the NHS. The impact of this would be felt if contracts for treatment moved from the NHS to the private sector on a large scale, though so far there is little evidence of this. The most controversial innovation was the granting of tax relief on health insurance policies for the over-60s. This was criticised as the only example of new money for care of the elderly in the White Paper[14] and take-up has been limited. But its introduction perhaps owed less to its likely effects on health care (the Social Services Committee, 1988c, p. xxxiv, concluded that the concession 'cannot be demonstrated to extend the total availability of health care', and that it would reduce the total public expenditure from which NHS resources were drawn while also narrowing down the tax base) than to an ideological attempt to sustain Conservative support among the middle-aged beneficiaries of health insurance. Opponents argued that the relief was not well targeted and would subsidise an already wealthy group of the population. This expansion of the middle class welfare state would also be socially divisive; obtaining it would be much easier than being subject to the 'full panoply of state supervision and regulation' associated with claiming other welfare benefits.[15] Conservative spokespersons claimed, in contrast, that the measure was designed to encourage individual responsibility and that it was to be bracketed with their support for home ownership and enterprise formation, but if this was the case then the government was being inconsistent since it had not supported other measures (tax relief on childcare for instance) that might help families dependent on welfare to obtain employment.

The net result has been that individuals who already have insurance have benefited from tax relief, subsidised by the taxpayer. Little new business has been generated and the idea that such a scheme could be self-financing by reducing demands on the NHS has been shown to be hopelessly optimistic (Laing, 1993). Perhaps that was never the intention – the appearance of action may have been what was required. But the limited take-up of tax relief (which was introduced in advance of the main body of the NHS reforms) led William Waldegrave, while health secretary, to speculate in October 1991 that it might be abandoned – a speculation he was quickly advised to retract.[16]

Other developments may have been a mixed blessing for the private sector as they have opened up to competition from the NHS markets that were previously largely the province of the private sector. The best example is the growth in paybeds: the 1988 Health and Medicines Act freed NHS paybed units to charge commercial prices with a view to making profits, and this prompted several authorities and hospitals to upgrade their private wings and/or develop paybed units[17] (during the 1980s the throughput of paybeds had declined as consultants deserted NHS paybeds in favour of independent facilities – Laing, 1991, p. 81). As a consequence paybed income more than doubled, from £77 mn in 1988–9 to £157 mn in 1992–3.[18] Much of this would have been through diversion of demand from neighbouring private hospitals, but some paybed units have been established in towns that previously had no private inpatient facilities (Laing, 1993, pp. 67, 88).

Fundholding GPs were another potential source of private sector income, but there seems little evidence to date that the private sector has received many contracts from such practices. The end of the 'steady state' of the first year of the NHS reforms was not marked by any major shift in the direction of the independent sector. In fact at least one RHA has recognised that, in localities where insurance coverage is high, fundholding GPs can potentially gain because they are able to refer patients to private hospitals for treatment without it being a charge on their NHS allocations. Consequently consideration is being given to making allowances, in allocations to fundholders, for the proportions insured privately.[19] This echoes the earlier suggestions of several commentators (for example Klein, 1982b; Nicholl *et al.*, 1989a; Williams *et al.*, 1984a) that account should be taken of private facilities in any revision of RAWP (see also Chapter 4). However one result would appear to be that this would reduce the financial advantages of fundholding.

Finally, the principles of the internal market and their differential impacts may affect the private sector in diverse ways, depending on location. The major redistribution of funds away from central London may force hospitals there to compete aggressively with the commercial sector for cold surgery. This could disadvantage the private sector since it lacks the backup facilities of major acute hospitals; on the other hand the private sector in central London may be oriented more towards international markets. Against this, one could argue that overcapacity in the private sector may permit providers to offer contracts for patient care at marginal cost, so purchasers in some localities may benefit considerably.[20] Finally, continued growth of private health care may, as was suggested by the NAO (1990), be to the detriment of the NHS unless the number of consultants' posts is expanded, as existing consultants expand their private commitments. Recognition of this possibility has already prompted one NHS trust to consider requiring its consultants to carry out their private work in the hospital's private facilities,[21] and this may be an indicator of conflicts to come.

Wider implications

Whatever the Royal Commission said in 1979, there is little doubt that the private sector is now a major element in the British health care scene, and this is in part testimony to the success of the government's policies designed to promote it. Whether these have involved direct subsidy, deregulation or ideological exhortation, the result has been that not only are a substantially greater proportion of people insured or treated privately, there is also a greatly increased number of people with a material stake in the continuance of the private health sector. This creates a substantial political lobby in favour of the private sector, and this bloc of support would be difficult to erode. The regionally differentiated nature of this is also important: from some perspectives, policies aimed at promoting the private sector (for example tax relief) are part of a strategy of consolidating the Conservatives' core support, especially in those areas in which its parliamentary seats are concentrated (Jessop *et al.*, 1988). These policies also represent an ideological gesture rather than a real contribution to meeting health care needs, because of the risks of adverse selection and because they prioritise ability to pay rather than medical need. In fact, given the contribution made by the private sector to elective surgery, it may have had the effect of defusing criticism of the government's policies, especially in the South East. It is thus a safety valve not just in terms of relieving some pressure on the NHS, but also in terms of helping reduce electoral pressures on the government.

Furthermore, since the reforms the private sector has been potentially enmeshed more firmly into the totality of health care provision in a way that was perhaps unthinkable fifteen years ago. In principle, all private hospitals can now compete for NHS business, while there are no restrictions on NHS purchasing agencies deciding to establish contracts with private institutions. In addition, competition is arguably on an equal footing. It is not surprising that private sector analysts see its future as being one of steady expansion, nor that the 'limits the NHS sets to its responsibilities are seen as key determinants of independent sector involvement' (Laing, 1991, p. 61) – another clear recognition of the importance of the state in setting the parameters within which markets work. However this growth has not been without conflict between the government and the private sector, especially as regards permitting health authorities to reintroduce paybeds – which is regarded as unfair competition by the private sector – and (though to a lesser extent) controls on the location of facilities.

In considering the wider consequences of this expansion, it is helpful to relate this to the debates about the significance of 'consumption cleavages' as a source of social stratification and a basis for political alignment. Busfield (1990) has recently considered the importance of private medical care in this context, and several years ago Crouch (1985) argued that the growth of the commercial sector could presage a situation in which 'many people . . . become accustomed to building up a mixed bundle of welfare', much as they now do for housing, transport, pensions and so on. The implication was that this would undermine the strength of the lobby for collective provision of services.

However Busfield suggests that this is unlikely to happen to the same extent as in housing or education, because the scope for gaining advantage through the purchase of private health insurance is less than in those services, and also because many of those with private insurance also make use of the NHS (Taylor-Gooby, 1989; OPCS, 1990), so that there can be no clear demarcation between public and private in consumption terms. The only obvious advantage of using the private sector is convenience and quality of hospital accommodation; health insurance does not constitute the same sort of investment in longer-term advantage that housing and education offer (Busfield, 1990, p. 93). In a study of the use of and attitudes towards private health care, Calnan *et al.* (1993) echo these broad conclusions. They reported that the decision to take out health insurance could not be explained by general dissatisfaction with the NHS: their respondents showed general support for the NHS, but other factors (for example the social relations and settings of private care; loss of time and money from waiting and unplanned hospitalisation; the provision of insurance as a 'perk') were all-important. Finally, national surveys of social attitudes indicate that while opposition to private medicine is less overt than in 1979, there is great concern that the NHS should not be eroded (Taylor-Gooby, 1991). Hence it seems unlikely that the expansion of insurance as a way of financing health care will reappear on the political agenda in the foreseeable future.

What is not known is whether the precise nature of provision of *publicly-financed* health care (that is, whether treatment takes place in public or private, non-profit or commercial facilities) is a matter for serious ideological dispute. In this context it may be that the public is indifferent to who provides facilities, so long as they are available, and the White Paper and its advocates seem to support this view. The key issue will then become not whether private medicine will remain but whether the consequences of having a greater proportion of *publicly funded* health care provided *privately* will include adverse selection and even non-availability of services for certain sections of the population. For example, purchasers may be able to negotiate contracts that use private sector spare capacity at attractive rates, from the purchaser's point of view, but if this means that clinically more urgent conditions go untreated it will clearly be of concern. In this sense the post-reform developments need to be closely monitored since they appear to indicate a blurring of boundaries in which access to services may depend at least in part on locally-available, non-state resources. If so the consequences for the equity of this 'mixed economy' could be serious.

8

The Entrepreneurial State: Commercial and Charitable Activities by Health Authorities

The Royal Commission was adamant that the NHS should remain funded through direct taxation. It observed that the possibilities of generating additional sums of money for the NHS were limited since 'trivial additions . . . might be disregarded by those who control NHS expenditure, but would not assist an underfinanced service, while a substantial addition would probably lead to a reduction in funds made available from the Exchequer' (Royal Commission, 1979, p. 338, para. 21.24). The Commission argued that increased charging would not discourage frivolous use of the service; sources such as lotteries would 'be at the very best marginal in a national context'; voluntary efforts would not contribute 'significantly' to NHS funds, while there were technical objections to hypothecated taxes (paras 21.28–21.34). Nonetheless the subsequent years have seen numerous initiatives designed to raise funds from non-exchequer sources and, by exposing parts of the NHS to commercial disciplines, to improve the internal efficiency of the service. The growth of such initiatives betokens not just efforts by the government to shift the boundaries between public and private sectors (for example prescription charges, income generation, competitive tendering), it also symbolises the problems facing individual health authorities, who have seen little alternative but to raise funds either internally, through more 'efficient' ways of working, or externally, through drawing on sources of private finance, charity or joint arrangements with commercial operators of health services. Hence this chapter seeks to document and assess the significance of efforts by health authorities to raise funds to supplement those provided by the state.[1]

174

There are various possible interpretations of the initiatives described here. Firstly, and perhaps most crudely, they have been characterised as a strategy of 'privatisation from within' (Haywood and Ranade, 1989). Given that there was no scope to reprivatise the NHS, attempts were made instead to impose market-based disciplines as and where appropriate or feasible. This somewhat economistic interpretation is mirrored by the transparently political motives evident in some government strategies, such as compulsory competitive tendering. According to this view the savings or funds generated were marginal and did not justify the amount of political capital invested therein, so policies could only be interpreted as class politics by another name.

Neither of these rather one-dimensional interpretations capture the range of measures and the diversity of the motivations for them. In a more subtle account, Stoker (1989, p. 141) interprets the Conservatives' policies towards public services as efforts to transform the 'production process, the pattern of consumption and the arrangements for political management' in ways compatible with the enterprise culture, a two-tier welfare structure and the flexible economic structures associated with the transition towards flexible accumulation. The steps described here could perhaps be represented as transplanting into the NHS the model of the 'flexible firm', in which organisations specialise in their 'core' functions while leaving to subcontractors the 'peripheral' elements of their business (Atkinson and Gregory, 1986). In the NHS's case this would imply concentrating on patient care while divesting itself of other 'peripheral' activities, which could be left to commercial organisations. As Pollert (1988) points out, flexibility in the public sector has to be seen as part of a political strategy, not merely a technical administrative response. In the commercial sector, organisations are generally forced towards greater flexibility by competitive pressures; in the NHS prior to the White Paper the key determinant has usually been central government initiative, allied to innovative and entrepreneurial managers seeking to demonstrate managerial flair. More recently Osborne and Gaebler (1992) have extended such arguments in their bible for the entrepreneurial manager, *Reinventing Government*.

In outline these arguments seem a reasonable description of change in the public sector and the NHS, but such change cannot be reduced to a strategy for mimicking an ideal-typical model of the private sector. Jessop (1993) places these changes in the context of a wider transition towards a 'Schumpeterian workfare state', in which, broadly speaking, social policy is subordinated to market needs. There is an emerging concern, therefore, with the promotion of flexibility and competitiveness in social policy (Jessop, 1993, p, 18). Related to this, Jessop points to the relegation of concern with 'planning' in favour of an emphasis on flexibility and entrepreneurialism (p. 19). This is legitimated in several discursive strategies: contrasts between the arcane institutions of state socialism and the need for perestroika (see Chapter 3); the lionising of managers as driving the service to ever-higher levels of efficiency (Chapter 6); and discourses which stress the need for entrepreneurship and initiative (Chapter 8) and the importance of local flexibility and freedom from excessive supervision (Chapter 9). Thus we are dealing with an attempt to transform the terms of debate about public management.

Analytically, a distinction is made between activities that involve expansion of the role of voluntary or charitable activity and those that entail greater levels of commercialisation. In the former category the main innovation has been in the form of proposals for the transfer of hospitals to charitable trusts, and the establishment of community care facilities as nominally-independent organisations eligible for charitable status and therefore gaining some tax exemptions as well as being eligible for payment of social security monies to their patients. In the latter category one could place the income-generating activities of health authorities, joint arrangements with commercial providers of services, and competitive tendering for ancillary services. This distinction also ignores issues dealt with elsewhere. Thus community care could be regarded as a form of privatisation as it transfers the burden of caring away from the state and onto families and communities, and especially onto women within them (Chapter 5). The chapter concludes with an examination of self-governing hospital trusts and GP fundholding as flagship examples of the new entrepreneurialism in the NHS.

Back to the future? Charitable fund raising and charitable trusts

Trust fund income

Charitable sources of funding for the NHS did not disappear following the 1948 Act (see Fitzherbert, 1989, and Williams, 1989, for the legislative background). While the state took over ownership of virtually all existing hospitals, it did not preclude charitable effort, but it was anticipated that the future role of charity would be small, being confined largely to providing 'comforts' for patients and staff, funded by 'small tokens of appreciation', refusal of which would be churlish.

Little effort was made to encourage health authorities to expand charitable income until 1980, when the Conservatives, via the Health Services Act, permitted health authorities to organise their own charitable appeals and to use Exchequer funds to do so; these costs were to be repaid from appeal proceeds. Though presented to parliament as a 'modest extension of the existing powers' of health authorities, the subsequent circular (DHSS, 1980c), coupled with ministerial statements (Chapter 3) offered a much more positive defence of charitable and voluntary effort. This proposal was not vigorously attacked by the opposition, but it received substantial criticism from the voluntary sector as an undermining of the independence of voluntary organisations. Perhaps for this reason, health authority activity on these lines was at first limited. However the funds available to health authorities from charitable sources expanded rapidly in the 1980s, from £57 mn in 1985–6 to £220 mn in 1990–1, which, even when inflation is allowed for, reflects great activity by authorities and appeal organisers. The rapid increase in appeals launched by health authorities (from around 12 per annum in the 1970s to about 50 per annum in the late 1980s – Lattimer and Holly, 1992) suggests that authorities saw themselves as having little choice but to seek funding for services that might previously have been provided through the state. The total assets held by health authorities amounted to some £683 mn in 1990–1, though this concealed major variations between health authorities and hospitals (Lattimer and Holly, 1992). While there was some evidence that health authorities in the northern regions and in some inner-city areas lacked access to these funds, there was no obvious geographical pattern, itself a reflection of the haphazard historical development of hospital provision, in which specialist hospitals, mainly the teaching hospitals – located in what are now deprived inner city areas – retain quite substantial funds for reasons of historical accident. Thus some of the major London hospitals have annual incomes of several million pounds from their endowments.

In relation to the total hospital budget, the sums involved are marginal. Their ideological significance is greater: have such schemes gone beyond what some would regard as an appropriate use of charitable funds? A statutory authority should not use funds raised through charitable sources for purposes that would otherwise be met out of rates, taxes or other public funds (Fitzherbert, 1989). But what was formerly the 'use of funds to purchase exceptional and experimental machinery had developed into routine buying of standard equipment', such as scanners, which are not particularly unusual now (Williams, 1989, p. 102; Fitzherbert's 1989 study revealed nine appeals for whole-body scanners). In addition, mainstream capital expenditure projects are now regularly funded, at least in part, by charitable appeals. Furthermore, while no health authorities have openly said that they are using trust monies to supplement their revenue budgets, Fitzherbert (1989) claims that it is difficult to see what else health authorities could be doing with the sums available to them, and some have launched appeals to supplement their revenue budgets.[2]

Major appeals

So far the expansion of charitable activities seems of limited significance, but there have emerged measures that take the role of charity much further than its traditional preserves of fund-raising to promote patient welfare or research. These involve the raising and application of charitable funds for major capital projects, and the transfer of hospitals to hospital 'trusts' independent of the NHS, as well as the establishment of community care facilities as independent organisations to take advantage of social security benefit regulations. The best-known examples in this regard have both been connected to the Great Ormond Street Children's Hospital (GOS), though note that some Conservatives urged the government to pursue the possibility of transferring more facilities to the voluntary sector.[3]

The Tadworth Court branch of GOS was saved from closure and reopened as a trust in 1983, on condition that it developed alternative sources of income from charity and fundraising. The trust insisted that the wages it could afford would depend on the funds available to it, and in so doing it arguably pioneered moves away from national determination of wage rates in the NHS (Sherman, 1984). While a local MP, George Gardiner (Reigate), praised the arrangement as a 'new and positive approach to health care', newspaper editorials criticised the move as an abrogation of the principles of the NHS, pointing out that most hospitals in difficulties lacked Tadworth's 'political pull'.[4]

Much more publicised was the decision to pursue a national fund-raising campaign for GOS itself in 1987–8. The supposed rationale was the government's limited resources for capital development: the DoH was to contribute some £30 mn to the development leaving some £25 mn to be found through charitable donations – at the time the NHS's total capital programme was of the order of £1000 mn per annum. The appeal emotively portrayed the difficulties in which GOS found itself, and its title – the 'Wishing Well' appeal – carried certain semantic overtones: the idea that GOS's financial difficulties would be 'wished away' might have had attractions for government ministers, but was obviously wishful thinking, while not all hospitals could be 'wished well' in this way.

The appeal easily exceeded its target, but the government's contribution to the development was somewhat illusory: the hospital's general manager, Sir Anthony Tippett, candidly admitted that he had agreed a 'secret deal' with ministers that *made it look as if the government had put up £30 mn* towards the hospital's redevelopment'; in fact this £30 mn was for (presumably rather less publicity-worthy) remedial work. He justified this on the grounds that 'the cause we had undertaken was greater than the morality'.[5] The appeal implicitly pitted hospitals in different areas against GOS for appeal funds: in Manchester, fund-raisers for GOS clashed on the streets with people attempting to raise money for their 'own' local children's hospital.[6] The relationship between charities and the state is in question here, for fund-raisers have sometimes been placed in the position of having raised large sums of money for a particular project only to be told that the project will go ahead in another location, or not at all. A good example from the North Western RHA was a proposal to build a new children's hospital in central Manchester – with public appeal funds topping up RHA capital money – when around £1.5 mn had already been raised for equipment for a children's hospital in North Manchester. Perhaps more embarrassing for the government was the announcement that the £140 mn Philip Harris House at Guy's Hospital, one third of which had been financed by charity, would not be used for its original purpose due to the impending closure of the hospital.[7] These examples demonstrate the clear limitations of reliance on charitable funds.

There have been several other examples of communities attempting to save their hospital by relying on charitable fundraising or volunteers;[8] one RHA actually proposed establishing hospitals as charitable trusts (SE Thames RHA, 1985). Community groups have often actively proposed such schemes when it has appeared that the scope for 'saving' their hospital in any other way is limited. Of course there are important advantages of community effort in health care delivery; privatisation can have a progressive potential (Donnison, 1985). However the principal impression gained from reports of charitable appeals to retain health service facilities is that this is the last resort to which communities have recourse and that they see little alternative. It appears that the profile and impact of charity on the service is increasing and will do so as long as – for example – major appeals continue to be launched for essential capital developments within the NHS. If these developments would not reproduce the inequalities of pre-NHS days (Powell, 1992), there is little doubt that they would take the NHS further in that direction than at any time since 1948, distorting priorities in favour of high-technology, high-profile specialities.

The entrepreneurial welfare state: commercialisation of health authority activity

Underpinning much of the government's strategy towards the public sector has been the belief that considerable resources can be generated internally by policies designed to produce greater efficiency, thereby sustaining growth without increased resource inputs. Thus central government policies requiring health authorities to generate cash-releasing efficiency savings, or deliberately underfunding pay awards, were intended to force health authorities to review critically their activities. Three specific developments – competitive tendering, income generation and collaboration with the private sector – are reviewed here. These illustrate attempts to stimulate entrepreneurship within the service. In different ways these are not just examples of 'Thatcherite' policies; they also prefigured measures introduced more widely in the NHS reforms.

Competitive tendering for NHS ancillary services

From the late 1970s onwards several Conservative-controlled local authorities (notably Wandsworth and Southend) experimented with the use of commercial contractors for the provision of ancillary services. Vociferous lobbying by right-wing think tanks, plus the government's anger at the ability of large public sector unions to use their market muscle in the 1978–9 and 1982 industrial disputes, help explain the timing of the competitive tendering initiative. Most decisive was the government's re election in June 1983, with an enhanced majority (Chapter 3). Competitive tendering for ancillary (cleaning, catering and laundry) services was therefore introduced from the autumn of 1983 (DHSS, 1983c), facilitated by the rescission of the Fair Wages Resolution of 1946, which had required private contractors working in the public sector to comply with public sector terms and conditions. As an indication of the importance attached by the government to this issue, it intervened on several occasions to ensure that private contractors won contracts (see Chapter 9).

The primary motivation for competitive tendering was the desire to deploy market disciplines to weaken the producer monopoly created by strong unions. An undoubtedly influential factor in this was the gender composition of the workforce in NHS support services – primarily female and part-time – such work being socially constructed as particularly 'suited' to women. The use of women as a reserve army of labour left those working in ancillary services particularly vulnerable to competitive tendering (Coyle, 1985; McDowell, 1989). Privatisation is not gender-blind; the workforce, generally, is less unionised and easier to exploit.

Four points may be made about competitive tendering. Firstly, it has had an uneven impact between sectors of the service and between geographical areas. Sectorally, domestic services (largely cleaning) have seen the greatest private involvement, partly because of barriers to entry in laundry and catering. Geographically there is some evidence of greater activity in southern and rural DHAs, with activity being greatest in those parts of the Thames RHAs that lie outside London. These patterns can be accounted for in terms of barriers to entry, local labour market conditions, the strength of union opposition, the political composition of DHAs and the degree of intervention by central government (Ascher, 1987; Mohan, 1986b; JNHSPRU, 1990; PSPRU, 1992).

Secondly, the impact on cost savings is disputed. An early evaluation (Social Services Committee, 1985b, p. xx) suggested that the initiative had 'not brought home the bacon', but as it has expanded, substantial savings in direct costs to the NHS have been achieved – of the order of £140 mn per annum up to 1991 (DoH/OPCS, 1993, figure 19). However, in order to assess the net savings to the Exchequer it would be necessary to estimate the additional costs involved due to severance pay and increased social security payments. Since there are now some 80 000 fewer ancillary workers in the NHS than in 1983, such costs are probably substantial.[9] If the aim is to produce a 'flexible' workforce (Atkinson and Meager, 1986), the costs are borne by some of the poorest-paid members of the public sector workforce (see also Cousins, 1988).

Thirdly, there has been little demonstrable growth in competition. The great majority of contracts have been won by in-house tenders. Few companies actively compete for NHS business: some 60 per cent of all NHS domestic service contracts held privately are in the hands of two firms, and national, if not multinational, firms dominate the market. McGregor (1990, p. 671) suggested that 'skewed and distorted markets have emerged along duopolistic and oligopolistic lines'. There is little evidence of new business formation and recent entrants have themselves largely been multinationals (Mohan, 1991; PSPRU, 1992).

Finally, the impact of competitive tendering has been most marked upon in-house tenders. It produced the 'increased readiness of in-house teams to compile cost-effective tenders' (NAO, 1987, p. 2), usually by specifying exceptionally intensive rates of work, making large reductions in the staff required to carry out a contract, and cutting out meal breaks, holiday entitlements and so on (London Health Emergency, 1987b; McGregor, 1990). However, as Pollock and Whitty (1990) note, this has been 'at the expense of service provision, the patient and the employee with grave implications for quality'. This is why opposition to privatisation has recently focused on the implications for quality control of competitive tendering (PSPRU, 1992).

Despite the savings, then, competitive tendering has experienced its own problems of market failure, in particular limited new entrants and a failure to penetrate the whole country. Furthermore, labour supply problems have beset contractors offering low wages (Social Services Committee, 1989), and even industry representatives have baulked at the removal of fair wage legislation. If the real motivations of the government had been to safeguard service quality, this is something that should have been written into tender specifications from 1983, not an afterthought, as it appears to be. Competitive tendering seems to have been the Trojan horse through which localised wage determination could be introduced into the NHS (see Chapter 6). Perhaps this indicates that the motivations for it were, after all, political rather than technical, but if so, European Community legislation, which protects the terms and conditions of workers when they are transferred from one employer to another, may yet prevent this goal from being achieved.

Income generation in the NHS

The primary motivation for the national income generation initiative was undoubtedly the criticisms of the underfunding of the NHS, and during parliamentary debates in the mid-1980s many Conservative members pointed to the need to raise funds by other ways than direct taxation (see Chapter 3). Building on the ad hoc activities of individual DHAs, the 1988 Health and Medicines Act gave health authorities greater powers to raise income from the sale of their activities or from activities carried out on their premises. The Act empowered DHAs to exploit their assets more fully, including the charging of private patients and overseas visitors at commercial rates, and giving them 'basic powers to acquire, produce and provide, for a charge, goods, land, accommodation and services, including training'.[10] One implicit problem with the Act was the possibility of conflicting with the activities of existing voluntary fund-raisers, including hospital Leagues of Friends and other organisations. Edwina Currie sought to minimise this possibility, suggesting that health service managers should 'not ride roughshod over the League of Friends . . . and other organisations which might already be working in the area' and encouraging managers to liaise with voluntary organisations to ensure that volunteers were redirected to different forms of help, 'rather than restricting voluntary effort to raising money when in many cases more could be raised through commercial activity'.[11] What the Act therefore implied was a rather closer relationship between voluntary activity and that of the NHS.

The exercise seemed largely symbolic. Some £70 mn was to be raised per annum, one third of 1 per cent of the NHS's budget, and as one prominent DGM said, 'in terms of what the NHS needs, the sums we are raising are peanuts. It's just that at the moment, peanuts are bloody useful'.[12] Survey evidence suggests that the majority of projects have been limited in both scope and the returns on them, which represent very limited additions to DHA budgets (NAHA, 1988b; see also NAO, 1993). In general their distribution is related to both the entrepreneurial skills of particular general managers and/or the availability of assets that can be exploited: laundries with spare capacity, or historic buildings pressed into service for entertainment or conference purposes. However critics have pointed out that these schemes distort priorities and lead to effort being concentrated on schemes that will make a profit, rather than on those most needed (Brotherton and Miller, 1989).

Indeed the enthusiasm for income generation schemes seems to have largely evaporated. Even by late 1989 it was reported that ministers had overestimated the amounts that might be raised.[13] The central income generation unit at the DoH was wound up in 1992 (NAO, 1993, p. 1). The total sums raised in England amounted to £51 mn in 1990–1, or approximately 0.3 per cent of the NHS's revenue budget. Expressed as a proportion of RHA budgets the sums raised varied from 0.15 per cent to 0.7 per cent (calculated from Health Committee, 1991b, table 11.5), and it was recognised that only seven of the fourteen RHAs had taken 'positive steps' to pursue the initiative (NAO, 1993, p. 6). Perhaps the aim was not so much to raise large amounts of money as to open managers' eyes to the possibilities that existed for offering new services, and in this sense further stimulate an entrepreneurial culture within the service.

Joint public-private deals: health authorities as flexible firms?

The possibility of greater collaboration with commercial organisations was not neglected by health authorities during the 1980s. Health authorities had been encouraged to consider the benefits of closer links with the independent sector in various contexts, notably the possibility that private facilities might be used for treatment of NHS patients. A 1983 circular argued that the benefits of collaboration with the private sector were 'disproportionate to its size' and discussed several options open to health authorities.[14] Collaboration took various forms – partnerships between private developers and the NHS, staff buyouts of NHS services, the establishment of NHS divisions as trading agencies – and arguably the self-governing trusts epitomise these developments, free as they are to arrange their business without reference to standard NHS terms of service or organisational structures.

A common form of partnership between the NHS and commercial companies has been to develop hospital or nursing home capacity. Illustrations include links between NHS hospitals and private companies who develop or manage paybeds;[15] the various proposals for joint hospital developments; and the transfer of long-stay facilities to nominally-independent 'trusts' or to other non-profit organisations such as housing associations. Joint capital schemes were proposed in several health authorities, the rationale being a combination of limitations on NHS capital, the land available in NHS ownership (which meant that private health care development did not constitute a change of use under planning law) and the alleged speed with which the private sector could build hospital developments.[16]

Several authorities also established various long-stay care facilities as charitable trusts in order to transfer the cost of accommodating patients to the social security budget. Thus by January 1989 all but two DHAs in the South Western RHA had established trusts to provide shelter outside hospitals for mentally ill or mentally handicapped people; by the same date 18 DHAs had established trusts for long-stay patients.[17] Elsewhere some health authorities had sought to transfer certain long-stay services direct to management by housing associations, which would deprive staff of NHS pay agreements and employment protection.[18] Numerous health authorities sought to transfer long-stay beds to privately funded operators.[19]

Finally, several authorities extended the logic of competitive tendering by establishing parts of their service either as trading agencies, providing services to the authority on the basis of 'service-level agreements', or as fully independent commercial businesses, sometimes formed through management buyouts. Examples included information services,[20] estate management, architecture and pathology.[21] Such decisions led to a conflict of interest between the emerging commercial culture and the values appropriate to a public service, notably the decline in public accountability under the cloak of commercial confidentiality, and raised questions about the extent to which those involved in management buyouts could adapt to a commercial culture while still retaining their commitment to public service. The *Health Service Journal* commented that 'open debate must be the first condition of sale', and asked whether it was 'the proper domain for NHS managers to explore ways of reshaping the service, with the main incentive to make money for themselves?',[22] an issue relating to the corporate governance and ethos of the service (Chapter 9).

Self-governing hospital trusts, GP fundholding and the post-White Paper organisation of the NHS

It is important to stress the continuities between national policy initiatives to develop contracting out and links with the private sector, the steps taken by individual DHAs to supplement their financial resources, and the measures taken in the White Paper to promote this entrepreneurial ethos throughout the NHS. Without the various initiatives described above, the ground for the NHS reforms would have been much less well prepared. In an environment in which health authorities had honed their managerial and entrepreneurial talents through various initiatives, grafting the enterprise culture onto the NHS was much less problematic. Specifically, the proposals for self-government of provider units and for fundholding by general practices together signalled moves from a top-down version of planning to a model in which the decisions of individual entities were presumed to produce the allocative efficiency associated with the free market. They also betoken a system in which the managers of the service are given very clear financial incentives, not just through performance-related pay, but – in the case of GPs – through the direct rewards that accrue to them as individual practitioners when they achieve their targets. This section outlines the nature of the proposals, the measures taken to operationalise them, the ways in which they represented a logical extension of Conservative philosophy, and some of the early difficulties associated with this new system.

Self-governing trusts

Dissatisfaction with many of the supposed 'inflexibilities' of the NHS – in this case, excessive constraints on local management – lay at the root of this proposal. The rationale for the proposal was to 'encourage a stronger sense of *local* ownership and pride, building on the enormous fund of goodwill that exists in local communities . . . it will encourage local initiative and greater competition' (Secretary of State for Health, 1989a, para. 3.3 – emphasis added). Kenneth Clarke stressed that such units would have 'far more freedom to take their own decisions on the matters that affect them most without detailed supervision'.[23] This extended the devolutionary emphasis of *Patients First* down to individual units; indeed one Conservative MP argued that the establishment of trusts represented an attempt to give to every hospital the freedoms that Aneurin Bevan had granted to the teaching hospitals.[24] These freedoms included departing from nationally agreed wage rates, autonomy in acquiring and disposing of assets, the borrowing of capital and the generation of surpluses (DoH, 1989a, pp. 5–6). Trusts were seen as major potential sources of innovation in the NHS, and Clarke further claimed that they would 'encourage other hospitals to do even better in order to compete'. Notably, however, they were to be insulated from excessive public scrutiny and permitted to 'determine whether [they wish] to open [their] routine meetings to the public', because much of their business would relate to the confidential consideration of contracts and personnel issues (DoH, 1989a, para. 3.7). Through the cloak of commercial confidentiality, the allocation of public funds was transformed into a private, managerial matter.

Proposals to establish hospitals as trusts were invited within weeks of the announcement of the reforms, and there was evidently considerable pressure placed on hospitals to put themselves forward, most famously Guy's Hospital, at one stage the flagship of the reforms but now contemplating closure.[25] There was limited consultation over proposals for trust status: indeed a leaked DoH circular suggested that hospitals needed to be freed from 'petty consultation' and that it would be 'convenient if the regulations were changed as soon as possible . . . which would, *inter alia*, exempt all trust applications from the statutory requirement to consult CHCs'.[26] Ballots on self-government were rejected, according to the government, because there was no way of identifying the 'natural constituency' of hospitals, which contrasted sharply with the government's ostensible aim of increasing local involvement (note also the rights of parents of schoolchildren to be balloted on school opt-out decisions). Although most responses to consultation had been negative, these were dismissed by Duncan Nicholl, NHS chief executive, as being opposed to the principle of trusts rather than offering constructive comments.[27] The decision to allow these to proceed was taken despite advice that most of the business plans prepared by the putative trusts had uncertain financial viability.[28] The government was clearly determined to transfer at least some prominent units out of the direct control of DHAs as soon as possible, perhaps with an impending general election in mind. The trusts were initially given some favourable financial treatment; thus their capital programmes increased by 20 per cent for 1991–2 compared with 14 per cent for the NHS as a whole.[29]

Trusts are now the dominant form of health care provision in the NHS, covering some 95 per cent of all provider units, and their development raises a number of questions. Those concerned with changing labour utilisation practices and the extent of trust autonomy are discussed elsewhere (Chapters 6 and 9 respectively). Secondly, trusts have produced an army of authority members and bureaucrats: even allowing for the reduced number of members of health authorities, to call into existence several hundred trusts, with five non-executive members each, and associated management staff, hardly seems consistent with the declared intention of reducing bureaucracy. In this context the government's attacks on RHAs as bureaucratic and inflexible seemed somewhat misplaced.[30] Related to this, do not trusts, in common with any bureaucracy, have a vested interest in their own survival? Yet this could conflict with desirable policy goals: a logical implication of community care programmes would be that, as hospital-based facilities are run down and closed, some trusts would go out of business, but recent press reports suggest a reluctance among trusts to plan themselves out of existence,[31] so that inappropriate services may remain in place.

Fourthly, trusts have not yet been permitted (as was originally envisaged) to borrow on the private market (due to Treasury restrictions); should they do so capital funds raised from commercial sources will require a rate-of-return on assets and this will mean that trusts will be forced to generate profits on their trading accounts. The experience of the USA suggests that, in the absence of strong regulation, hospital development is determined less by social need than by access to capital (Berliner, 1987). It is unlikely that there will be quite the competitive and duplicative development characteristic of the pre-NHS era or that found in the USA, nor the degree of exploitation of local monopoly powers. There would seem to be a risk of adverse selection (Scheffler, 1989) of patients by NHS trusts, especially where hospitals have particular areas of medical expertise that they are in a position to exploit. The reforms do give trusts an interest in seeking contracts from whatever source – an early indication was the announcement by the Christie Hospital, Manchester, that it would reopen a closed ward if purchasing authorities were willing to contribute to it, in return for which they would be guaranteed priority admission for their patients.[32] This report confirmed the fears of those who felt that trusts would respond to purchasing power rather than social need. The persistent reports about the two-tier system of admissions, differentiating between patients from fund-holding and non-fundholding GPs at the expense of the latter, are a natural corollary of the fragmentary system that has emerged. Trusts are also active in seeking other sources of income: their income from private patients totalled £58.5 mn in 1992–3, out of an NHS total (in England) of £157.3 mn.[33] Although this partly reflects the change of status of formerly directly managed units, the paybed income of RHAs and SHAs had dropped by only £19.4 mn since trusts were established in 1991, clearly indicating the attention trusts were giving to private patients.

Finally, because the entire reforms are predicated on a major increase in the efficiency of the acute hospital services, it is essential that proper coordinative mechanisms are in place to ensure that appropriate community facilities are available to support patients upon discharge. The fragmentation of the service into directly managed units (DMUs), trusts and budget-holding practices seems unlikely to facilitate this, and the opposition to 'whole-district' trusts, though apparently intended to ensure that community services have a separate voice, would seem likely to promote further fragmentation. Furthermore, if long-term trends towards concentration of hospital services continue, competition will be reduced and local monopolies will develop (apart from in larger cities). This suggests that, to the extent that competition has been responsible for improvements in efficiency, those improvements may not be sustainable once that competition no longer exists. In addition the success of trusts depends on them winning contracts to treat patients. If this is a stimulus to efficiency it has its negative consequences, because withdrawal of contracts, especially where major purchasers are involved, can undermine the position of a trust. This is important where specialist services, which require the support of several purchasers, are being considered, since the withdrawal of one purchaser of a trust's services can threaten the viability of the services, forcing patients to travel elsewhere.[34] This is very much the antithesis of the hierarchical vision of planning that formerly characterised the NHS; although bureaucratic, it at least meant that patients could be reasonably sure of the availability of services within their region.

Budget-holding general practitioners

The White Paper initially announced that GPs would be allowed to become budget holders if their practices exceed 11 000 patients, though this threshold was lowered and in many cases practices have combined into large consortia. The twin philosophies that inform much of government policy – decentralisation and competition – were clearly in evidence in this proposal, the logic of which was to give GPs, as purchasers, an 'opportunity to improve the quality of services on offer to patients, to stimulate hospitals to be more responsive to needs of GPs and patients, and to develop their own practices for the benefit of their patients' (DoH, 1989a, para 1.2).

Central to the process of developing fundholding were the criteria whereby practices were to be funded. The demonstrable risk that practices would select particular patients (compare Health Maintenance Organisations (HMOs) in the USA – Petchey, 1987) meant that funding needed to be linked very closely to the likely use of resources by age, sex and social status. The government initially proposed that the hospital services component of a practice budget would be determined by comparing the costs of the hospital services used by that practice's patients with the district average, making allowance for the age, gender and health status of patients. However budgets would 'not underwrite high referral rates for which there is no demonstrable cause' (para 4.5). In the long run the aim was to move towards some form of capitation allowance. But because hospitalisation rates and costs varied within and between RHAs, the highest-spending fundholders had twice as much to spend on each patient as the lowest, and Day and Klein (1991) argued that this demanded a move towards a capitation-based system, even though this would result in substantial transfers of resources, thereby removing some of the potential attractions of fundholding.[35]

The most controversial issue continues to be the possibility of patients of identical clinical need receiving differential treatment because of the nature of the practice with which they are registered. There have been many press reports of provider units giving preference to fundholding practices, and the General Manager of City and Hackney DHA was quoted as having said that:

> *this does mean that the question of equity has gone out of the window, but this is the reality* of GPs holding their own practice budgets for

elective work. *If we do not respond they will spend the money elsewhere.* [36]

This prompted the government to issue guidance to the effect that common waiting lists should be used for all urgent or seriously ill patients, and that waiting times stipulated in contracts covering non-urgent patients should allow for relative clinical need; otherwise hospitals should not offer contracts to one purchaser that would disadvantage patients from other purchasers.[37] The wider problem that arises, however, is how to make the purchasing intentions of fundholders compatible with those of DHAs, especially in localities where fundholders are in the majority, since their decisions and priorities may not coincide with those of the purchasing authorities.

Finally, what is not really known yet is just where fundholding practices are and who benefits from them.[38] One criticism was that a system rather like HMOs would develop: fundholders in relatively healthy, suburban and middle-class areas could find it straightforward to make surpluses. Another reason for this is that the proportion of the population having private medical insurance in such areas is high, so a large proportion of GP referrals to hospital will not be paid for out of their practice budgets. This would generate surpluses for fundholding GPs. Again these are precisely the Conservative 'heartland' areas in which the government must consolidate its support and reassure the electorate that the NHS is indeed safe with them, but if this is why the government has pursued this approach it must be recognised that the possibility of a two-tier GP service clearly exists as a result of these reforms. Finally, according to recent reports, the guidance on fundholding practices has not been followed for there is still evidence of hospitals giving preferential admission to patients registered with fundholders. Thus, of the 173 short-stay units to which the BMA sent a questionnaire on this subject, 73 (42 per cent) offered arrangements to the patients of fundholders that were not available to the patients of other purchasers, while 41 (24 per cent) offered accelerated admissions.[39]

Internal reorganisation of health authority services

Fundholders and trusts were the real novelties of the reforms, and one consequence was a change in the character of health authorities, at both district and regional level. Regions were most under threat as the

White Paper announced that the NHSME would review all regionally managed services, approving retention of services at regional level only where cost effective and encouraging DHAs to ask 'whether they can provide more of these services themselves or purchase them from the private sector' (Secretary of State, 1989a, para 2.9). Regions therefore attempted to identify those services which should not be part of their 'core' activities and which should no longer be part of their core management structure. Implicit in the recent review of RHAs is their establishment as, essentially, monitoring and strategic agencies of the DoH (NHSME, 1993). Their responsibilities will include formulating regional strategies, monitoring and performance review; stimulating and appraising major investments; and providing a strong account-ability link to the NHS management executive. They will achieve this through a combination of devolving of services to district or unit level, establishing trading agencies, transferring services to commercial agencies and establishing NHS trusts (for example ambulance services). This might establish RHAs as paradigmatic 'flexible firms', with clearly distinguishable 'core' and 'periphery' staff (with the associated labour market consequences), and with many of their functions performed under contract by subsidiary agencies. As health authorities have almost lost their provider role, and as a larger proportion of their budgets are taken over by fundholders, one can expect similar changes on the part of DHAs. Davies' (1987) vision of the entrepreneurial, coordinative health authority of the future seems to have come to pass. Three potential consequences are a loss of accountability and control of public money, a greater degree of centralisation of authority, and alterations to the terms and conditions of employment of staff.

Concluding comments

A central argument of this chapter has been that important continuities exist between what might have appeared as small-scale one-off initiatives to keep hospitals open or to develop alternative sources of funds, and what are increasingly coming to be regarded as the cornerstones of the new NHS. Broadly what has emerged is an entrepreneurial state, in which managers and doctors have steadily been either freed from the shackles of excessive bureaucracy or fragmented into an atomistic, divided service, according to one's point of view. It is certainly possible to read into this the argument that the health service is merely following developments elsewhere in society: as business becomes organised on more 'flexible' lines, health authorities are approximating more closely to the 'flexible firm' in their activities, with an emerging distinction between the core and peripheral functions of authorities, an expansion of buying in services from outside the NHS and a flattening of hierarchies (Kelly, 1991; Osborne and Gaebler, 1992; but see also Pollert, 1988).

Nevertheless the parameters within which health authorities work are set by government constraints on resources, so we cannot just dismiss these developments as technical or managerial responses to localised funding difficulties. It is surely no coincidence that the number of NHS-related charitable appeals rose dramatically between the mid-1970s and the late 1980s, nor that there were many proposals to establish hospitals as charitable trusts by communities concerned at the inability of their local health authorities to retain them.[40] In other cases the hand of the government was clearly behind the policies pursued. To interpret the developments described here in any other way than as part of a wider political strategy to shift the terms of debate on the NHS rightwards, and to begin to transform public attitudes, would be naive at best, and at worst misleading. But does this mean that we can attribute the changes described here to a *coherent* strategy, designed ultimately to lead to (something like) the white paper's proposals? The evidence points in two, perhaps contradictory, directions. On the one hand, taking various measures individually, they can all be seen as separate initiatives, with little or nothing in common, representing ad hoc, opportunistic and piecemeal change. Thus Patrick Jenkin's nostalgia for charity and the voluntary sector (see also Chapter 3) seems naively optimistic; the GOS appeal was perhaps a unique opportunity to redevelop a unique hospital because of the public's sentimental attachment to it; the motivations for competitive tendering were largely political; while the income generation initiative was a symbolic gesture, designed to appeal to managerial instincts. On the other hand, there has arguably been a progression: from measures to supplement the resources available to health authorities through community support; to the first signs of a commercial culture via competitive tendering and income generation, though not directly affecting clinical services; to the establishment of trusts and GPs as competitors in a marketplace. There are elements of broad strategy here, but they read more like efforts to divide and rule potential opponents and to build blocs of support. Arguably the Thatcherite governments have been both acutely aware of their political opponents and particularly astute at neutralising them, but they have been less capable of constructing a viable programme for the development of the British economy. Thus, seeing these changes as the imposition of a hypothetical post-Fordist blueprint (Chapter 2; see also Mohan, 1994) oversimplifies an interesting case.

These developments have clearly taken the NHS some way from the top-down versions of planning that characterised it after the 1974 reorganisation. Instead there are a growing number of autonomous units – principally self-governing trusts and fundholding practices, but also various agencies or independent firms depending on NHS business, and several thousand private nursing homes. In the light of growing 'entrepreneurial' activities in the health and personal social services, Kelly (1991) suggests jettisoning the notion of privatisation in favour of analyses that demonstrate how commercial and market-inspired principles have changed the 'tradition of thinking in terms of statutory provision' – the challenge to traditional management and professional practices in the state sector is the really crucial impact of privatisation. For Jessop (1993) the discourses of entrepreneurship are sweeping through the public sector, reflecting a wider transformation from administration to management. However the new types of enterprise being created are of interest. What does not seem to be happening in the NHS is a growth in *innovative* voluntary schemes (with the exceptions, perhaps of the hospice movement and of innovations in the care of AIDS patients), and the voluntary sector is being used to shore up the NHS's deficiencies. While some authors highlight the progressive potential for democracies of community control and participation (Donnison, 1991; Hirst, 1994; Lipietz, 1992) there seems little evidence of this in the NHS to date. This is partly because of the internal market, which does not provide an environment in which alternatives to highly capitalised, commercial providers can flourish.

The issues raised here are also of significance when compared with the utterances of government spokespersons who suggest that greater community involvement is something members of the public have been deprived of for too long and that it is a necessary check on the power of impersonal bureaucracies. Increased commercial and charitable involvement in the NHS has not increased local control: those who have raised funds for hospitals have not been in the happy position of influencing health policy decisions, and hospital closures have been implemented despite the often considerable efforts of communities to keep them open. Active citizenship takes place on the state's terms (Kearns, 1992): at the same time as central government has ostensibly declared its aims of devolving responsibility locally and has celebrated the role of communities in financing and delivering health care, community input into health policy issues has been greatly circumscribed, and it seems that the state is demanding fund-raising without representation in its active citizenship strategy (see also Chapter 9). Moreover, even were a future government inclined to reverse the NHS reforms, the post-1979 changes have created a substantial number of individuals with vested interests in private provision in various forms. The real significance of various forms of privatisation from within may therefore be in eroding support for collectivism.

Finally, Jessop and others have spoken of the subordination of social policy to market criteria under the neoliberal Schumpeterian workfare state. This has not happened directly under the Conservatives. Instead the capacity of health authorities to deliver services is linked, to a greater extent, to their success in competitive markets: their ability to make savings through competitive tendering, dispose of property,[41] strike beneficial deals with the private sector and so on. Patterns in these various activities may or may not reinforce one another. The important point is that health authorities have had little alternative, given little overall growth in funds. There are three principal problems with this kind of strategy. Firstly, what happens in cases of market failure – for example, when appeals, land sales or property deals fail to produce the necessary returns, or when labour shortages impinge on the quality of ancillary services? Some strategies will have diminishing marginal returns and they cannot be sustained indefinitely. Secondly, what happens when market principles conflict with the ethics and values of the NHS, in cases where entrepreneurial individuals push beyond acceptable boundaries? Thirdly, where should the boundary be drawn between, for example, the state and the charitable sector? Since 1948 charitable activities have generally been confined to providing that which it would not be reasonable to expect the NHS to offer, but the scope of what users of the NHS can legitimately expect from statutory funding has been restricted (see the debates about long-stay care – Chapter 5), while simultaneously the scope of medical capability continues to expand. Though in some respects the NHS is a victim of its own success, what is needed is an open debate about what can be expected of the public sector. National appeals for major capital projects also call into question the government's willingness to dig further into the public purse for NHS hospital investment. Fitzherbert (1989, p. 3) consequently argues that the distinction between the statutory and charitable sectors is fast disappearing under day-to-day funding pressures. Furthermore, the charitable sector is concerned about the possibility of being swamped by NHS appeals, which would clearly have considerable market power. Collectively the issue raised by this chapter is the extent to which the market-oriented service can deliver comprehensive services on a national, equitable basis. The more the capacity of health authorities to provide services is related to market criteria, the less likely we are to be able to speak of a national service.

9

Powers, Responsibilities and Accountability: Organisational Reform and Local Autonomy

Local administration of health care has always been fragmented. Resistance to local authority control by the medical profession was partly responsible for the separation of the NHS from local government, and rivalries within the medical profession secured a privileged status for the hospital services; even within this, teaching hospitals retained a separate identity until 1974. Despite various reorganisations, this tripartite division largely persists, though the 1974 reorganisation sought some coterminosity between AHAs and local authorities, and introduced local authority nominations to health authorities. The question that remains to be answered is: what form of local administration would best secure the delivery of health care?

Historically this question has been answered through some form of hierarchical regionalism (Fox, 1986) focussed around hospitals, with teaching hospitals at the apex of each region, and with each region containing subregional units, themselves organised around hospital catchments. Whether such arrangements will continue to operate seems questionable. For commentators such as Jessop (1993) the nation state is being 'hollowed out' by globalising and localising tendencies, both economic and political, which are displacing power upwards and downwards (and in some cases sideways) from the nation state. This new localism has been embraced by the Conservatives, for example in articulating the need for minimal interference from above in the activities of the 'autonomous communities' or 'little platoons' that sustain social cohesion through voluntary activity (Kenneth Baker, former Conservative Party chairman, quoted in Kearns, 1992, p. 23).

However, while the government has enunciated a great deal of antistatist rhetoric about devolution and community control, this has been within parameters set and firmly enforced by the central state. Therefore whether Jessop is correct in suggesting a resurgence of local and regional government is somewhat debatable in the context of the NHS.

Other writers suggest, perhaps more optimistically, that bureaucratic, centralised, hierarchical modes of service delivery are inflexible and unresponsive (Stoker, 1989; Osborne and Gaebler, 1992). In the future, they contend, public agencies will become entrepreneurial, coordinative, enabling, flexible and responsive. On the assumption that this goal itself is desirable, what changes in the local organisation of what is still a national health service might be necessary to achieve it? The notion of an enabling role for health authorities has some merits, but not if conceived as a new territorial code for the centre (Rhodes, 1992), whereby central government abdicates responsibility for levels of funding or hands over responsibility for the NHS to a semi-autonomous agency. Nor is the Conservatives' decentralist rhetoric easily reconciled with their practice, which has often involved a prescriptive approach, particularly on issues to which the government attaches high priority. It might be helpful, therefore, to consider whether decentralisation involves decentralisation of responsibilities or devolution of genuine powers.

British health care policy has been marked by oscillations between 'firm central control and permissive local discretion' (Harrison *et al.*, 1990, p. 86). While ministerial accountability must be preserved, excessive central review of decisions at the periphery is a recipe for sclerosis. On the other hand, because funds for the NHS are raised centrally and spent locally, those administering the service do not have to concern themselves with the consequences of their decisions for levels of local taxation, for instance. So there emerges a fundamental incompatibility between central control and local autonomy. The way this is tackled sheds considerable light on the priorities and strategies of the government (see below). Organisational reforms also raise the important question of the accountability of the service to its local community and parliament. The principal debates about health service organisation have been concerned with the spatial organisation of the service and the distribution of power between different levels of it, and the criteria for membership of health authorities, where the main tension has been between whether members should be appointed in a representative or managerial capacity.

Against the background of these debates, this chapter begins by describing the principal organisational reforms affecting the NHS since 1979 and the arguments for and against them. It then reviews the ways in which the balance of power and responsibility between central and local tiers of the service has been altered, in some cases as explicit policy, in others as an effect of other decisions. Finally, the effects of the NHS reforms and of subsequent developments are analysed.

Organisational reforms

In discussing the changing organisation of the NHS and the balance of powers between tiers of it since 1979, it would be a mistake to focus exclusively on organisational reforms such as that of 1982 or the rapid process of mergers of health authorities since the White Paper. Much of what has happened since 1979 in the sphere of central–local relations can be related directly to measures such as the introduction of legally binding cash limits, performance indicators and processes of annual review of performance, rather than to service reorganisation *per se* (Paton, 1993). Rigorous enforcement of cash limits constrains the scope for manoeuvre of local agencies, and these were made legally binding in 1980. While this could be presented as closing a legal loophole, the fact that the legislation enabled the secretary of state to remove health authority members who exceeded allotted expenditure gave a revealing insight into the government's views. Indeed the precipitate action of Patrick Jenkin, who as secretary of state for social services appointed commissioners to run the Lambeth, Lewisham and Southwark AHA in 1979, seemed to indicate the government's determination to impose firm central control. In some ways requiring health authorities to pursue privatisation policies (and other initiatives such as income generation) has also reduced their autonomy. Performance review and the specification of central government targets (for example on waiting lists and times, or on numbers of operations in specified categories) dictate how authorities should spend their budgets, though performance indicators were criticised for giving excessive weight to easily measurable financial criteria rather than to needs-based assessments of outcomes (Pollitt, 1986). The impetus for such measures arose to a considerable degree from criticisms from the Public Accounts and Social Services Committees that there was little effective central monitoring of health care expenditure and policies.

Turning now to those changes that have taken place, we should note that 'administrative maps are much more than mere spatial structures' (Taylor, 1991, p. 319): they touch on issues of legitimacy and accountability. In health care the notion of hierarchical regionalism has a long history (Fox, 1986), being regarded as the optimal way to ensure linkages between levels of a service hierarchy of increasing specialisation, and to secure some degree of egalitarianism in the distribution of specialist services. But regionalism in Britain has derived largely from bureaucratic, not democratic, impulses. As implemented in the NHS it involved limited local accountability since (between 1948 and 1974) there were no formal links between regional hospital boards and local government. Some such links were introduced via the 1974 reorganisation, but the multiplicity of operational and strategic tiers produced by that reorganisation were widely regarded as unsatisfactory. The Royal Commission stressed the importance of a regional tier for strategic reasons. It recommended the abolition of one tier of authority below that level (paras 20.45, 46) and argued that FPCs should be abolished to facilitate integration with health authorities (para 20.57). It also saw 'no reason for departing from the principle that there should be representation of local authority members as well as health workers and the public at large' (para. 20.63). On the second of these points there was general agreement. Labour spokespersons had little difficulty criticising the 1974 reorganisation, for which none of them had been responsible. However the government was evidently unwilling to pursue a policy that might embroil it in conflict with the medical profession, and it did not endorse the proposed integration of health authorities and the family practitioner service.

Patients First, the government's consultative document on the 1982 reorganisation, captured the decentralist philosophy of the first Conservative administration and stressed the virtues of localism and small scale. Patrick Jenkin, the first secretary of state for social services, was convinced of the merits of a hands-off approach, often showing a touching faith in the ability of communities to support and run their local services.

Insisting that 'the closer decisions are taken to the local community and those who work directly with patients, the more likely it is that patients' needs will be their prime objective' (foreword, para. 3), the government stated that it was 'determined to have more local health authorities whose members will be encouraged to manage the NHS with the minimum of interference by any central authority'. Authority boundaries were based around hospital catchments: the proposed DHAs would have populations of between 150 000 and 500 000, though several had populations above and below these upper and lower limits. Local authority nominations were reduced from one third of the authority membership to a total of four, so that they would have between one fourth and one fifth of the membership of the new authorities. Coterminosity with local government was rejected because 'local authority boundaries do not necessarily bear much relation to the hospitals to which people look',[1] which seemed both to indicate the hospital-centred nature of the reorganisation and, together with the removal of local authority representation, to signal reduced emphasis on facilitating collaboration between the health service and local government. In this sense it denoted a move away from many reform proposals of the 1960s and 1970s that had attempted to achieve greater local democratic accountability in the service. *Patients First* gave no hint of the Griffiths-inspired internal reorganisation of NHS management that was to follow shortly after the 1982 reorganisation; indeed it rejected the notion of a chief executive for health authorities on the ground that this would compromise professional autonomy. But for all its decentralist rhetoric, its philosophy was applied inconsistently: some decisions, such as resource allocation, would become more centralised since the intermediate AHA tier had been removed; central government limits on management costs were retained; and FPCs were retained while multidistrict AHAs were broken up (Nuffield Centre, 1980).

Fortunately for the NHS there were no further formal reorganisations before the White Paper, but a series of measures, beginning with the Griffiths Report, swung the centralism / devolution pendulum back in the direction of centralisation. The introduction of general management held individual managers accountable for scrutinising the operation of those activities for which they were responsible, and for determining how best to develop their services, stimulated by performance-related pay and annual reviews. Managers became responsible for achieving a range of targets that were largely to conform with national priorities, often specifying precise numerical targets for particular types of operation. The introduction of general management served the helpful function of allocation of responsibility, but it also arguably permitted ministers to disavow their own responsibility for problems in the service. Paton (1993) makes a similar point about the introduction of mechanisms such as medical audit and clinical budgeting into the service: unobjectionable in themselves, they become so when introduced as a means of ensuring conformity. Furthermore, when politically sensitive issues, such as waiting lists and times, were important to the government, centralism – Stalinism, for one commentator – was the order of the day, with managers being left in no doubt as to the importance of achieving centrally determined targets.[2]

Despite these measures and other areas in which central government rhetoric has not matched reality, the White Paper stressed localism and local management in the provision of services. Problems of service delivery were dismissed as the result of inefficient management, or of management being unable to manage. This could be avoided if local managers were freed, as far as possible, to make their own decisions – free from interference from RHAs, the government and local authority and trade union members of DHAs, from nationally agreed wage rates, from controls on acquiring and disposing of assets, and so on. What would also flow from this devolution would be a marked political gain for government because fewer problems would require ministerial attention; they would instead be dealt with locally.[3]

In short, the White Paper sought to establish a system in which responsibility was decentralised from central government to local managers: given the right people, and the right incentive structures, and ministers would be able to absolve themselves from responsibility for local difficulties. Instead, through their entrepreneurial skills, managers would be able to prevent the crises of funding that had beset the system in recent years. But what form would the new service take, and precisely how would it be accountable to local communities?

The government's antipathy to local government being well known, it was not surprising that local political influence over the NHS, never very strong anyway, was eliminated. The few local authority and trade union nominees on DHAs were replaced by people nominated for the skills they could bring as individuals to management. This was nothing new: in 1980, opposing the proposals for the reduction in local authority nomination rights to health authorities, Labour had insisted that there must be some 'democratic representation that is not solely at the behest of the Minister'.[4]

In other words the White Paper represented the continuation of an attack on local democracy in the running of the service. This was partly an attack on special interests (professional rights of membership of authorities was also abolished) and partly an attempt to facilitate the managerial agenda for the NHS. But perhaps a clue to the real motivations was given by Kenneth Clarke:

> recently there has been a growing tendency, sometimes by supporters
> of my party and frequently by supporters of the Labour Party, to put

on local authority members who are mandated to pursue local political aims and then to remove them *when changes of political control or nuances in the local Labour Group determine that a new political input must be made.*[5]

Whatever political motivations might be imputed here, the removal of local authority nomination rights to DHAs did not seem consistent with the greater co-ordination that had been envisaged between the services provided by the two sets of authorities. Few trusts and DHAs have preserved the frequency and openness of pre-White Paper meetings and evidence from press reports suggests that much information is now kept secret on the ground of 'commercial confidentiality'. Taxpayers may fund the service, but they are not, it seems, allowed to conduct their own inspections and form their own conclusions about how it is performing. ACHCEW's annual report showed that two thirds of health authorities met between four and six times annually, compared with 10–12 meetings annually before the reforms, so that the amount of public information available had been substantially reduced.[6]

Direct control of decision making was strengthened still further by a ministerial propensity to veto the appointment of individuals not seen as sympathetic to their views, or to impose on health authorities known Conservative supporters. That the White Paper allowed for Ministerial power of appointment over many health service bodies was a natural extension of this and led to heightened suspicion that central control was being pursued. The implication seemed to be a return to pre-NHS days, when hospital management was carried out by paternalistic local elites. The likely problem is the extent to which consumer interests will be represented, and the extent to which co-ordinated planning of services with local authorities and community health services will be possible. Nor is it obvious that appointees to health authorities and trusts have their roots in local soil: strong Conservative leanings and connections seem more the order of the day.[7] Even if the presence of local authority nominees in health authorities is no guarantee of competence, it would at least ensure some responsiveness to and knowledge of the community.

It is here that the critique of the new magistracy, as expressed by John Stewart and Vernon Bogdanor, is most relevant. If public body appointments are carried out by government ministers, such bodies become agencies of central government rather than organisations able to implement policies formed by representatives accountable to the local community. While they may therefore be held accountable for their success or otherwise in meeting centrally determined targets, then, they are never put in the position of having to respond to the local community, apart from the requirement that at least one meeting a year should be open to the public.[8] The fact that the appointment process is open to accusations of patronage raises the question of standards of conduct in public life: the scandals in the Wessex and West Midlands RHAs, the windfall profits made by some senior health authority officials who have engaged in buyouts of NHS activities, and the lucrative moves made by some professional staff both within the NHS and from the NHS to outside firms and consultancies all raise the issue of the standards to be expected from a public service. At one level the increased mobility of senior managers reflects a shortage situation in which premium rewards are available to those with the requisite talents. At another level the new breed of entrepreneurial managers in the public sector run the risk of taking decisions for purely managerial reasons, without justifying them properly to their 'constituency' or following the required procedures. They are enabled to do so by the background of the new members of health authorities, whose experience of non-commercial cultures and understanding of public service values are limited. At another level still the possibility that some individuals are benefiting substantially from their involvement in a public service raises serious questions about the values now infiltrating the NHS from a commercial culture. This was belatedly recognised in the NHS by the establishment of a task force on corporate governance, which produced guidelines designed to promote public service values and accountability throughout the NHS.

It is instructive to compare the proposals of *Patients First* with those of the White Paper. In only nine years the government had decisively shifted away from efforts to democratise the service and from top-down planning within a framework of hierarchical regionalism. Despite the emphasis on devolution, the size of some of the merged authorities if anything took decisions still further away from the local community. Although the reforms were proclaimed as a form of perestroika in the NHS (see Chapter 3), critics charged that extent of government control over appointments to the service would produce a 'board of management *that will exist to implement central policy –* exactly the sort of machinery of the clapped-out, centralised state that is being dismantled all over Eastern Europe'.[9] The fragmentation that seemed likely to emerge appeared to mitigate against successful planning and placed a question mark against the future of the regional tier in the service. Should the reforms lead to the demise of this tier, this would be consistent with the abolition of other bodies with a regional focus since 1979 – bodies such as regional economic planning councils were among the first to go, being tainted both as quangos and by their association with 'planning' – and with the government's neglect of the regional dimension to policy making. Thus in many areas of public policy what has emerged is a succession of *ad hoc* bodies with a narrow geographical or issue-based focus and/or a limited timespan, exemplified by the recent history of urban policy (see Keith and Rogers, 1991). In health care policy, what has been evident instead is a plethora of various task forces – for instance the waiting list initiatives or the community care task force – while the process of policy formulation itself has been removed from the realms of democratic consultation via reports by individuals (the Rayner scrutinies or the two Griffiths Reports) or secretive government cabals (the NHS review). Even where there might have been a case for a strong regional organisation to plan the future of London's services, the Tomlinson Report shied away from any notion of a pan-London health authority. This may have been because of guilt by association with the GLC, but the consequence has been the perpetuation of the task-force mentality, with an appointed 'London Implementation Group' set up to drive through the proposals of Tomlinson. For some commentators this approach reflects the government's overwhelming stress on the politics of national interest to the neglect of sub national interests (Taylor, 1991); for others it is a deliberate strategy to remove any semblance of local democratic accountability and potential resistance to government policy (Duncan and Goodwin, 1988). It also surely reflects a reactive approach to social policy rather than a proactive one.

Centre versus periphery

Tension between central and local administration has been endemic to the NHS, while conflict between local authorities and the Conservative government has been an enduring feature of the post-1979 years. On the one hand the government has been determined to place the blame for problems firmly on the shoulders of local tiers of the service; on the other hand there is ample evidence of a dirigiste, centralising tendency on the government's part. This section focuses on some of the issues on which central government has asserted its authority and occasionally behaved in a way that flatly contradicts its declared preference for decentralisation. Events since 1979 amply vindicate Gamble's (1988, p. 231) claim that the government had diagnosed one of the key problems of the public sector as being the lack of central government control of its activities, therefore impelling the government towards intervention.

A great deal of health care policy on the part of the Conservative government can plausibly be explained as reflecting a desire to push responsibility as far as possible from central government down to the local tiers of the service. Though certainly rational from the point of view of a minister wishing to be shielded from constituency pressures, this has often appeared to be a strategy designed to insulate the government from criticism that service reductions at the local level were due to insufficient funds being allocated at the national level. Parliamentary debates are replete with references by ministers to the variations in performance between and the apparent inefficiencies of health authorities, sending a clear message that the amount of funds and their distribution are irrelevant – health authorities must sort out their own problems. So at the same time as the government claimed record levels of resources and restricted the autonomy of health authorities, it appeared to contradict this by devolving responsibility for problems with service development to the same authorities. Nevertheless, when it has suited the government's purpose, depending on the strategic significance of the issue in question, it has been prepared to intervene in local decisions.

Symbolic politics: staff reductions and competitive tendering

Two major clashes between centre and locality occurred in late 1983 when health authorities were requested to reduce staff numbers by between 0.75 per cent and 1.0 per cent; almost simultaneously the government declared a national programme of competitive tendering for ancillary services.

It was the first time in over 30 years that NHS staffing had been reduced, and it led to unexpected resistance.[10] Several DHAs openly refused to carry out the reductions – the first to do so was Brent, in North West London. Thirteen of the fourteen RHAs also objected, although in some areas resistance was muted (Mohan and Woods, 1985; Small, 1989).[11] In an effort to override Brent's resistance, the RHA chair wrote to all DHA members requesting their support for the proposals and threatening the termination of their appointments. The DHA challenged the legitimacy of this step in the High Court, and although the RHA's action was upheld, the judge said that 'one approaches with a certain amount of distaste a system that envisages that the junior body is just a bunch of yes men' and criticised the RHA for attempting to 'stampede a subordinate body into following its wishes'.[12] Subsequently the DHA members who had voted against the cuts were threatened with dismissal,[13] and their resistance was broken when the RHA appointed several Conservative members to the DHA. The government's approach here was associated with other initiatives, such as specifying ceilings for numbers of particular types of staff, which contradicted its declared aim of increasing local autonomy and indicated its determination not to be faced down. Such central control inhibited innovation at the periphery: personnel ceilings limited the scope for transfer of staff from long-stay hospitals to community-based settings, for example (Social Services Committee, 1985a, p. lvi).

As for competitive tendering, DHAs were merely requested (not compelled) to provide a timetable for submitting their services to competitive tendering. The government had attempted to remove barriers to competition between private and public sectors, notably by providing for an automatic refund of VAT on contracts placed with outside organisations, and had also rescinded the Fair Wages Resolution. To facilitate the private sector winning contracts the government insisted that private tenders be sought for all laundry developments of more than £500 000 before they could proceed. As with staff reductions, there was resistance to competitive tendering: some authorities delayed implementing it or refused to comply; others voted to reinstate fair wage clauses. In the first round of tendering 14 DHAs did not comply and 26 decided to maintain Whitley Council pay rates and conditions of service;[14] a further 55 did not follow the government-directed timetable. Apparent dissatisfaction with the progress of the initiative, especially in peripheral regions, led to directives being issued to authorities in Scotland and Wales to speed up their programmes of competitive tendering.

There is extensive evidence of the government's willingness to intervene in the process of competitive tendering. In one case a DHA was prevented from tendering for a service in a nearby authority, not because its tender was not competitive but because it would have involved recruiting ten additional staff, thereby taking the authority above the government's manpower target. The Cornwall and Isles of Scilly DHA was compelled to accept a private tender against evidence suggesting that the in-house tender would have been cheaper.[15] Given the firm's market position in this relatively isolated part of the country, they were being set up as *de facto* monopolists, contradicting the declared intention of opening up scope for competition. Because all laundry contracts involving capital expenditure by the NHS had to be put to tender, the plan of two DHAs in Yorkshire to build a joint laundry were rejected, even though it would have saved £250 000 in running costs annually.[16] In similar cases capital improvements to NHS laundries had to be costed into tenders, thereby wiping out their cost advantages[17] (in contrast private contractors were unlikely to tender for NHS laundry services unless they already had spare capacity). Finally, the resistance of some authorities was allegedly broken by RHA threats to cut finance for new capital developments – such tactics were difficult to resist by DHAs faced with major resource reductions.[18]

Central government, then, did not openly direct all DHAs to privatise ancillary services. However the way the tendering process is organised, especially as regards capital investment provisions, limited the chance of success of in-house tenders. Other decisions have involved the acceptance of private tenders that cost more than in-house ones, which flies in the face of the apparent rationale behind the programme: the cutting of costs. This aroused fears that the exercise was less about costs and market discipline than about the break-up of the powerful public sector unions and the assertion of central government control.

Ringfencing of funds for community care

The debates on this issue seem to suggest that the government was prepared to maintain its ostensibly decentralist stance even when the interests of vulnerable client groups were at stake. Ringfencing was seen by a substantial body of opinion as providing the only way of guaranteeing some degree of priority for community care and ensuring that funds were not raided for other purposes. This was especially important at a time when local government finance was to be restructured, creating uncertainty, and given that proposals by local authorities and health authorities would expose areas of unmet need. Griffiths (1988) had suggested that ringfencing be applied not only to central government support (the element of DSS money, for instance, transferred to community care; see Chapter 5) but also to that proportion of expenditure supported from local taxation. When this proposal was rejected, Griffiths stated that:

> I had provided a purposeful, effective and economic four-wheel vehicle, but the white paper has redesigned it as a 3-wheeler, leaving out the fourth wheel of ringfenced funding (Social Services Committee, 1990f, p. v).

The evidence considered by that committee led it to express dismay that the government had refused to ringfence local authorities' resources for community care. The government's evidence suggested three reasons for its refusal: (1) the disruption it would cause (being introduced immediately after the poll tax); (2) the contradiction between, on the one hand, announcing a substantial specific grant for one purpose and, on the other hand, promoting the community charge as an instrument for enhancing local accountability and asking local authorities to take on community care as an acknowledgement of their flexibility and responsiveness; and (3) – though this was partly supposition by the Social Services Committee – that ringfencing would require the government to specify with some precision the level of community care activity it required social service authorities to sustain. There were also disputes between the centre and those local authorities that were convinced the government did not know how much the reforms would cost (Henwood *et al.*, 1991, p. 10).

While not ruling it out at first, the government's response to demands for ringfencing could hardly have been clearer: Virginia Bottomley suggested in evidence to the same inquiry that ringfencing 'dictates central control . . . [and] leads to conservative, reactionary, fossilised provision'.[19] But the Social Services Committee (1990f, p. xi) remained unpersuaded, arguing in its report that ringfencing could also be liberating and safeguarding, and that the government's position was inconsistent (not least because it had approved central government grants in some areas, for instance mental health):

> It is difficult to escape the conclusion that specific grants are acceptable vehicles for enabling central government to achieve its own priorities but not to safeguard the capacity of social services authorities to secure their own.

By refusing to ringfence the government laid itself open to the charge that there was no national policy on or commitment to community care. Certainly this was Griffiths' own view: ministerial control and monitoring was the only policy consistent with the claim that there was a national policy. Eventually the government did accept that some elements of community care funds, such as transferred income support payments, might be ringfenced, but this was coupled with the prescription that at least 75 per cent of funds so transferred should be spent on the independent sector, which, offering as it did predominantly residential care, was not conducive to the development of domiciliary provision. Furthermore, in a surprising *volte-face*, the government reneged on its earlier intention of ringfencing services for drug and alcohol abusers.[20] Tim Yeo indicated that the government regarded excessive ringfencing as 'inconsistent with the principle of individualised assessment of clients',[21] but the failure to protect such services would leave open the possibility that local authorities would prioritise elderly and more 'deserving' clients over 'undeserving' ones whose own actions had rendered them in need of community care.[22]

This led to a second set of criticisms, that by refusing to accept ringfencing, and thus to accept responsibility for specifying the level of resources required to make a reality of community care, the government was passing the buck to local authorities, who would be identified as responsible for any gap between the funds available and the fulfilment of need – the potential 'Pandora's box' of community care.[23] Again, while the government was seeking to obtain credit for promoting community care, it was refusing to estimate what the full cost of its implementation would be, and local authorities would be accused of failing to meet what clients would perceive as obligations. At the same time, however, the government did specify in some detail just how local authorities should spend those funds that were ringfenced, a prescription that, while justified in terms of stability for the independent sector, contrasted somewhat with the need for local innovation in non-residential forms of provision: as Hudson (1992) commented, the absence of non-residential private sector alternatives in some localities meant that no choice existed between residential and domiciliary satisfaction of needs.

The examples given here illustrate the contradictory nature of some of the policies pursued since 1979. Ostensibly decentralist in philosophy, in practice – where issues perceived by the government as strategically significant have been at stake – the government has not been afraid to impose its will. Elsewhere, as in community care policy, its attitude has been ambivalent, accepting some degree of ringfencing almost against its better judgement.

Paradoxically, despite the reduction in direct local influence, DHAs' scope for local initiative has been expanded, notably through the Health Services Act of 1980 and the Health and Medicines Act of 1988. Consequently, health authorities and individual managers (or groups thereof) have had greater scope to test the boundaries of legitimate or acceptable activity with limited interference from above. This has attracted ministerial censure when taken too far in a particular context – witness the request to health authorities to cease transferring long-stay provision into autonomous trusts (Chapter 5). But it has also meant that profitable privatisations have gone ahead without restraint. To focus on the morality of the individuals involved in such scandals as the failed privatisation of the West Midlands RHA's information services division is to miss the point, therefore: to do so would be to ignore the climate created by government pressure to privatise, its limited will to regulate former public bodies, and its decentralist philosophies.

Beyond the reforms?

It would be hazardous to speculate how the geographical organisation of the NHS will develop as the reforms continue to work their way through, nor would it be sensible to speculate how relations between centre and locality will develop. However the three main issues seem to be the degree of autonomy to be accorded to NHS trusts, the future of the RHAs, and the process of mergers among health authorities and between health authorities and other agencies.

NHS trusts

Given the political priority the government attached to NHS trusts, a key question was bound to be whether the government would intervene in their affairs once set up. The government certainly put pressure on local tiers of the service to put forward hospitals for trust status, so would they be allowed to fail? Certainly the government was keen to see applications come forward and rejected proposals for extensive local consultation (the Labour Party focused on the question of opting out of the NHS) on the ground that it was impossible to identify 'who on earth the electorate would be in those decisions; hospitals do not belong to any particular section of the public' [24] (in contrast with school opt outs, where parents had to be balloted).

Within weeks of the April 1991 starting date, redundancies at Guy's Hospital and the Bradford Hospitals trust were announced, primarily because anticipated revenue levels would not permit the hospitals to retain their existing numbers of personnel. This generated a fierce debate about the extent to which the minister of health should or should not intervene in the decisions of such organisations. William Waldegrave argued that he would not intervene to bring a trust's budget into balance or to stop job losses: 'that would not be of itself evidence that something had gone wrong'. [25] Criticised for appearing to disclaim responsibility for the cuts at Guy's and in Bradford (and thereby adding weight to the criticism that the hospitals were indeed 'opting out' of public control), Waldegrave went on to say that if he had accepted responsibility for them and intervened, it:

> would have been a dreadful signal to send . . . it did not mean that I do not take responsibility for the fact that we have set up a system of devolved management, but that does not mean I am going to interfere in every management decision.[26]

This issue also provoked a dispute within the Health Select Committee over the type of criticism they could publish of self-governing trusts, with some (Conservative) members arguing that a report based only on two case studies hardly represented a solid base of evidence. The Committee therefore resolved to pursue the question of trusts at a later date. However the need for supervision of trusts subsequently led to proposals for six regional outposts of the Department of Health, whose function would be to monitor the plans and finances of trusts to avoid further public criticism of such bodies. This in turn led to questions being raised about the future of the regional tier of NHS management, for if the majority of provider units were in future to have trust status, what role did that leave for the RHAs?

Mergers of health authorities

In addition to the above, the reforms were not accompanied by any prescription for the spatial organisation of the service. This was to be largely governed by local circumstances, in contrast with the formalised blueprints of 1974 and 1982. A number of interesting permutations and mergers developed, although note that several mergers had taken place in the years prior to the reforms. These have had the effect of reducing further the representativeness of the authorities concerned and increasing their remoteness from the population, especially where mergers have also led to the elimination of a community health council (CHC). We can distinguish three types of consolidation of health authorities: formal mergers, consortia, and joint purchasing arrangements (see Exworthy, 1993). Formal mergers have taken place in all DHA activities and were the usual way in which consolidation took place prior to the reforms (for example the Paddington/Brent merger to produce the Parkside DHA). Consortia have been developed for purchasing purposes, that is to enhance the leverage available to purchasers vis-à-vis providers, and thus the Northern RHA proposed 7 purchasing consortia covering its 15 DHAs. Joint purchasing refers to establishing links between DHAs and FHSAs for purchasing purposes, and indeed in one or two instances between DHAs and local authorities, which in some respects is a logical development of the community care reforms, even if not formally stated as an expected goal of the NHS review. This at least opened up the possibility of greater accountability if, in the long term, such authorities were to merge into joint commissioning agencies, substantially controlled by local government. Elsewhere consortia within the health service have been realigned so that their boundaries are coterminous with those of local authorities or groups thereof, though interestingly this often reinvents shadow versions of the AHAs abolished in 1982. From 192 DHAs in 1982, reduced by two mergers to 190 by 1990, the number of health authorities in England had fallen to 146 by early 1994. Now while some elements of these developments are to be welcomed, they also mean that opportunities for consultation and local involvement are at risk of being lost. For example, when mergers reduce the number of CHCs, scrutiny of the activities of providers and the plans of purchasers is even more difficult, though as yet the number of CHCs has not declined as rapidly as the number of DHAs. Furthermore the merger process has produced some very large consortia (deemed necessary to given sufficient leverage to purchasers in negotiating contracts) such as the North Yorkshire HA, the maximum dimensions of which are 120 and 90 miles, rather larger than the former Mersey RHA or the Thames RHAs. Precisely how authorities of this size develop procedures for consultation with users, or for taking local needs into account, remains an open question. Likewise the fragmentation of the NHS into over 400 trusts, some 140 DHAs (at the time of writing, though the numbers are reducing steadily) and several hundred fundholding GPs raises the question of what sort of mechanisms exist for ensuring that some form of coordination of activities takes place.

The above questions are particularly pertinent to the reorganisation of community care. Although *Caring for People* implicitly entailed a greater degree of planning, the range of trusts and agencies involved is considerable and they do not all share the same boundaries. Griffiths (1988) felt that collaboration would be *helped* by restructuring and coterminosity but to attempt this would create 'turmoil under a semblance of action'. However coterminosity between local authorities and health authorities was lost in the 1982 reorganisation (DHSS, 1979a) and the spate of health authority mergers and the emergence of purchasing consortia since 1991 has not always reproduced it. The Social Services Committee (1987b) proposed greater integration between DHAs and FPCs, and subsequently suggested that opportunities be taken to align the boundaries of health authorities and local government (Social Services Committee, 1990c, xv). The former will happen as a result of the recent Langlands review (NHSME, 1993); the latter may happen on an *ad hoc* basis. A logical outcome might be some form of integration between the NHS – or at least its purchasing role – and local government in order to achieve better collaboration and improve local accountability, but this seems highly unlikely at present.

Regional outposts and the future of RHAs

The regional outposts, or 'zonal monitors', were set up 'almost by accident' when the NHSME found it could not cope with the volume of work needed to check trust business plans.[27] Initially six (later, eight) were established, covering all the trusts within particular regions. The role of the outposts was to monitor the trusts' finances, assess their business plans and ensure that NHS corporate objectives were delivered. This was a technical justification. However a more obviously 'political' one may have been the complaints from trusts and the NHS Trust Federation (NHSTF) that RHAs were interfering directly in operational matters: the NHSTF had argued for a direct line of accountability to the NHSME because 'some RHAs were finding it a little difficult to take their hands off'.[28] The NHSTF had also suggested abolishing the RHAs and replacing them with six to eight review boards, half of whose members would be trust chairs. But this, if anything, was a self-perpetuating oligarchy (compare Crossman, 1972, on RHBs and boards of governors of teaching hospitals). Duncan Nicholl, NHS chief executive, informed the Health Committee that he did not think 'RHAs are sympathetically inclined to help the trusts at all' (Health Committee, 1992, p. 9), and Virginia Bottomley foreshadowed the demise of RHAs when she stated she would not permit the NHS to 'slip back into the old ways of monolithic, oppressive overplanning'.[29] William Waldegrave had assured trusts that their proper accountability was to the secretary of state, which appeared to place a question mark against the future of the RHAs, not least because trusts had to make a case for capital to the NHSME rather than to RHAs.

Partly in response to such criticisms, the review of NHS management (NHSME, 1993) abolished RHAs, replacing them with eight regional offices of the NHS Management Executive (Figure 9.1). The review followed an earlier criticism that RHAs were redundant and a request from government that all RHAs reduce their staff to a figure of 200 (again, a somewhat symbolic exercise given the disparities in size between RHAs, but symbolising the government's distaste for what it regarded as bureaucratic encumbrances on the internal market). The new regional offices are to be a hybrid, merging the monitoring of providers (the role of the outposts) and strategic planning (the RHA role). Formally they will be purely operational agencies, with no public access to meetings or local nomination rights, so while they drew back from the notion of establishing the NHS as a 'next steps' agency, formally separate from parliament, they are at some remove from any notion of democratic accountability, fuelling fears that their primary purpose is to act as transmission mechanisms for central policy. For example, the regional offices will be accountable direct to the NHS chief executive rather than to the region in which they are located, so any semblance of local accountability will be lost, while staff will technically be civil servants, responsible to ministers, as opposed to employees of the NHS, responsible to RHAs. If this is not enough to weaken public accountability, the size of these units alone almost guarantees difficulty of access (for example the HQ of the North East and Yorkshire office, in Leeds, is some 150 miles from the most distant parts of the region; the new South West region, incorporating the former Wessex and South Western RHAs, is also enormous and internal distances very great). In fairness, one progressive aspect is the proposed merger of DHAs and FHSAs, which will facilitate the joint commissioning of health services, but there is no sign of further integration with local government, nor is it apparent how the intentions of fundholding practices can be better integrated with those of health authorities. The overwhelming impression is one of centralisation and weakened representation. However the fact that a regional tier has been retained in some form indicates some recognition of the dangers of unregulated markets within a public service.

Concluding comments

It is important to distinguish those changes that have been the intended outcome of deliberate legislation (such as the 1982 reorganisation) from those that have emerged almost as a by-product of the NHS reforms (such as the merging of health authorities) and from those that have resulted from an *ad hoc*, reactive approach to policy making. In the latter category we can include the various task-specific agencies and inquiries as well as the growing role of the state as a regulator of a mixed economy. Even that role has emerged not deliberately but out of

Figure 9.1   Areas to be covered by proposed regional units of the NHS Management Executive

decisions to expand the private sector at a breakneck pace in some instances, with the need for regulation being recognised belatedly.

However, if the state's role is reduced in some respects, the centre's grip at the local level has tightened. The directive style of policy making clearly circumscribes local autonomy, as in the emphasis on achieving highly visible political targets – such as waiting list reductions and restricting staff numbers – and intervening to ensure that strategic initiatives (competitive tendering) are carried through. The appointments system for health authority membership has helped to ensure the government's will is done, while limiting the scope for alternative views to be voiced, the careful vetting of members has ensured that dissent is limited, and the abolition of local authority nomination rights has removed the service further from democratic politics. It is clear that decisions are not being taken closer to service users, especially now that health authorities are merging to form substantial consortia. While the post-1982 DHAs were planned to coincide, as far as possible, with hospital catchment areas, the post-White Paper authorities cover much larger areas and populations (not least because of the technical requirements of the purchasing process and because of the expansion of the catchments of hospitals). In short there seems to be a substantial gap between the claims made by the government for decentralisation, and the actual outcome of its policies. Accountability to collectivities is not developing at all in the NHS. Instead accountability is treated as an individual matter: users of the health service are treated as individual consumers (hence the Patient's Charter), who have the option of complaining (if minimum standards are not maintained) but little else. Health authorities are required to hold open meetings, but these are largely for presentational purposes and are confined to reporting the activities and plans of the authority or trust. Although local consumerism is being developed (focus groups and surveys) it is not clear that this provides an effective means of counterbalancing the weight of executive and managerial influence.

If the so-called 'hollowing out' of the state heralds new possibilities for local autonomy, this is certainly not apparent in the NHS, where a clear chain of command has been established to implement central policy. Hierarchies have certainly been reduced and ostensibly there is greater scope for health authorities and trusts to operate without interference, but for some this means these bodies are part of a quango state, spending large amounts of public money while enjoying limited accountability and control. It remains to be seen whether there will be any repetition of the financial controversies that surrounded the West Midlands and Wessex RHAs, and it is noteworthy that these happened when the traditional regional structures were still in place. For the moment, then, changes in the NHS indicate a greater degree of centralisation and more limited local accountability than hitherto, strengthening the claims made by several critics of the Thatcher governments that, despite being elected on a decentralist and antistatist manifesto, they were all too ready to limit local autonomy when it suited their broader political programme (Duncan and Goodwin, 1988; Gamble, 1988; Jessop, 1991a).

Although this is a somewhat depressing conclusion, for some commentators the reforms have had the unintended consequence of opening up quite radical possibilities for reform. The reforms owe less to antipathy towards local control or to efforts to impose a managerial agenda on the service. Rather they are 'desperate attempts to prop up an unsound system' when what is really required is the integration of the NHS and local government (Hunter and Webster, 1992). Bevan (1952) regarded the administrative structures devised in 1948 as a temporary expedient and looked forward to the day when the NHS would be subject to local government. Among the reasons why the local government option has resurfaced, Hunter and Webster suggest that: (1) the community care reforms demand the integration of health and local government if the two sets of authorities are to avoid becoming embroiled in continual 'frontier disputes' between 'health care' and 'social care' (see Chapter 5); (2) any coherent public health strategy demands the active participation of local government; and (3) because the purchaser/provider split involves questions of values and political judgements (regarding priorities) this must be a matter for elected representatives. Unitary local authorities could provide a local democratic base to articulate health strategies, overcome the difficulty of separate funding bases for health and social care, and avoid major organisational turbulence (Hunter and Webster, 1992). However such a solution is some distance from the political agenda at present: the difficulties and delays in accepting the widely-shared view that community care should be the responsibility of local government (Chapter 5) indicate the problems that might attend any serious proposal to integrate the NHS with local government. Furthermore the current review of local government is taking place without reference to the realignment of health authorities; conversely, those realignments and mergers are taking place in advance of the recommendations of the Local Government Commission.

Whatever the spatial organisation of the service, there remains a need for national decisions to be taken and implemented on questions of priorities and rationing. It would simply be inconsistent with a national health service if patients were to be denied access to certain forms of treatment in one authority while in a neighbouring authority the purchasers were continuing to fund that treatment. It would be disingenuous of the government to leave such decisions to local purchasers while seeking to maintain the claim that local managements everywhere would be able to guarantee access to agreed levels and types of service. Central government's role in maintaining standards must go further than the relatively limited consumerism of the Patient's Charter, to prescribing what forms of treatment shall be available and to whom. Even if such decisions were to be legitimated locally by reference to the electorate, the danger would be, as with the Oregon experiment in the USA, that voters' preferences may be influenced by their perceptions of who is and is not 'deserving' of treatment. This question is taken up in the concluding chapter.

10

Conclusions: In What Sense a *National* Health Service?

In this concluding chapter I summarise some of the key debates that have been thrown into relief by the NHS reforms. The first is the extent to which geographically uneven development now means that to talk of a *national* service is arguably inapt. In fact, as one doctor pointed out within months of the publication of the White Paper, 'the word "national" is pointedly lost in the White Paper on the health service'.[1] Secondly, I discuss the question of 'market failure' in health care delivery. Thirdly, there will be on-going 'boundary disputes' about what a health care system can and cannot be expected to provide and about who should be responsible for providing services, which raises the question of just what is meant by a 'national' health service. Finally, I consider some alternative directions in which the service might develop. But first I comment on the limitations of some of the explanatory perspectives I have drawn upon and criticised.

Explanatory pitfalls

The empirical chapters of this book ought to suggest clearly that identifying changes in health policy since 1979 merely as rational responses to technical or administrative weaknesses in the NHS is, to put it mildly, a gross oversimplification. Change took place within carefully circumscribed parameters: on the one hand the collectivism and public expenditure programmes of the Black Report were ruled out; on the other hand individualism and private finance were welcomed and a steady succession of measures taken to promote them. Thus, in focusing largely on developments internal to the health service, the government has neglected the wider determinants of ill health and ruled out a collective response to them. Health policy has thus been equated with health care policy: the promotion of public

219

health has been marginal to the Conservatives' political agenda and those who advocate preventive measures are dismissed as living in 'cloud cuckoo land'.[2] Instead health inequalities have been reduced to questions of lifestyle and morality. Within the service the stress has been on the need to increase efficiency in order to reduce claims on public funds. Simultaneously, however, enormous amounts of public money (North Sea oil revenues, privatisation proceeds) have been used to fund tax cuts, the effect of which has been highly regressive. Such actions reflect political priorities and create a climate in which there appears to be no other solution than to generate funds internally to the service, and to draw to a greater degree on private sources of finance, as well as implicitly relying on informal and unpaid sources of care to cope with the burden of community care and the increased throughput of patients. This is not the autonomous 'end of collectivism'– as de Swaan (1988) might suggest – but a deliberate political choice. The parameters of health and health care policy were thus clearly demarcated shortly after the 1979 election. *Within* these parameters one can perhaps identify measures on which there was some consensus – for instance the need to remove administrative tiers, or the promotion of community care – but even on these there was evidence of the government pursuing ideologically inspired reforms (Chapters 5 and 9).

It would be equally naive to represent post-1979 changes as merely the restructuring of state welfare in the interests of capital, or the replacement of an era of 'disorganised capitalism' by one of 'organised capitalism'. Such grand sweeps of history do not help much either. Thus Lash and Urry's argument (1987, p. 231) – that, as capitalism moves from an 'organised' to a 'disorganised' phase, it will replace centralised, bureaucratic modes of service delivery with localised, variegated modes of provision – may be descriptively accurate, but it does not automatically follow that changing patterns of service organisation can be read off from the development of 'disorganised capitalism'. If health care delivery systems such as Britain's have moved towards greater commercialisation and decentralisation, this is because of specific conjunctions of political forces that seek to mediate external economic conditions. One contribution of this book has been, I hope, to show that events in the NHS are not simply the result of the service mirroring and mimicking developments elsewhere in the economy, but instead are the result of the working out of deliberate political decisions. Of course there are parallels between the ways in which the service now operates and putative models of contemporary corporate structure. These are evident, for instance, in terms of the more flexible deployment of labour (Chapter 6), and the expansion of various forms of subcontracting and/or dividing authorities through the development of arm's-length trading agencies (Chapter 8). But these resulted partly from central government diktat, (Chapter 9) or were responses to funding crises, themselves related to the relative political priority attached to health care (Chapter 4) – to suggest that they can be explained in isolation from such developments seems naive. There have also been persistent political pressures for changes, that involve a greater degree of commercialisation of health authority activity (Chapter 3).

If we reject such transition models, what of the argument that there is emerging a 'Schumpeterian workfare state', representing the best possible political shell for a post-Fordist regime of accumulation? The evidence seems mixed. A cardinal principle of such a state would be to establish a clear link between labour market position and access to welfare, including health care: this clearly has not yet happened, despite the growth of private health insurance. Arguably, as long as the NHS is financed substantially from direct taxation rather than from charges or insurance, it is incompatible with Jessop's (1993) putative Schumpeterian workfare state. The 'hollowing out' of the nation state has not been associated with opening up spaces for autonomy, for the central state has kept a tight grip on the local tiers of NHS administration, which seems set to continue. If anything, one could make a case for regarding the latest reorganisation of the regional tier (NHSME, 1993) as the end of a long history of regionalism in the NHS (for that history, see Fox, 1986; Webster, 1988) rather than its revival. Market principles have certainly been introduced, but they have also led to market failures and calls for new forms of intervention (see, for instance, Chapter 4), and it is difficult to envisage internal market principles being extended to encompass the full commodification of primary and community care (Chapter 5).

Given those caveats, it is difficult to view the various changes in the NHS as the systematic imposition of a coherent blueprint by the government: pragmatic and tactical considerations have affected the timing of particular measures and there has been a constant process of market testing. Indeed some measures have simply been inconsistent or symbolic, tax concessions on private health care being the classic example of a measure that owes nothing to the development of an accumulation strategy and everything to opportunism. However extension of market principles to include the commodification of primary care or of care of chronic conditions would seem to be virtually impossible. One feature contributing to the durability of the internal market may be its uneven impact: crucially, the fact that the rationalisation imposed on the NHS by the reforms of acute hospital care is concentrated largely in inner city areas while many suburban locations have benefited from the net transfer of funds, means that the negative consequences of the reforms are partly hidden from the core constituencies that are relied upon to deliver unto the Conservatives a fifth election victory. That motivation – the selective prioritisation of certain key geographical locations – may plausibly be seen as underpinning the government's strategies in other areas too (Chapter 7). Given that, it may be best to see the post-1979 changes in the NHS largely as political manoeuvres rather than as elements of fully worked out accumulation strategies, especially given the massive centralisation of authority necessary to ensure that the government's political will is done.

Geography, locality and welfare

Noting Lash and Urry's (1987) views, and the suggestion by Davies (1987) that health authorities have been recast in an entrepreneurial, coordinative capacity, to what extent are we moving away from a national health system and towards a collection of local systems? This relates to two sets of arguments about the future of welfare provision. Firstly, individuals are becoming accustomed to building up their own packages of welfare, much as they do in housing, education and transport (Busfield, 1990; Crouch, 1985; Taylor-Gooby, 1989). Consumption divisions, structured according to access to private sources of welfare, are, according to some commentators, more significant than those based around social class. This may fragment support for collectivist provision since many people will not be exposed to the failings of the NHS: they can either opt out of the NHS through the private sector, or their particular locality is reasonably well-served by the private sector, thus minimising pressure on the NHS.

Secondly, developing Davies' (1987) case, there are clear spatial differences in the capacities and resources of localities. This is manifest in the public-private mix of care (Chapter 7), the rejection of resource allocation formulae incorporating social factors (Chapter 4), variations in family structures that might facilitate or inhibit community care (Chapter 5), and the variable support authorities obtain or are able to generate through their charitable or entrepreneurial activities (this is itself a function of the economic health of a locality; for an American parallel, see Wolch, 1989). But divisions of welfare are also, in principle, widened by, for example, the move away from national wage bargaining (previously recognised as central to the concept of a national service – Chapter 6), the decentralist philosophies of the government, and the virtual withdrawal of ministerial responsibility for what happens locally, even when under ministers' nominal jurisdiction (Chapter 9). Other influences constrain or enable the capacities of health authorities: Strong and Robinson (1990) note that the single most important influence on health authority activity has been its historical legacy of capital stock, a legacy that is very unevenly developed. While this may no longer be the case as the NHS relies less on major capital projects, it is still significant. The ability (or otherwise) of health authorities to dispose of this legacy through the property market, in order to fund capital developments, has been a further destabilising factor, especially in those regions where the property market collapse has been most acutely felt. Fundholding general practices, which in some localities cover over 50 per cent of the population, are another potential force for destabilisation, through demands for priority treatment, while the presence of fundholders in areas with a high proportion of people with private health insurance means that the purchasing power of those fundholders is potentially enhanced. (It might be argued that formerly DHAs would have benefited in the same way since they might have spent a lower proportion of their funds on treating public patients. The consequence of fundholding, however, is that any benefits are confined to a smaller group of patients.)

Perhaps the most significant aspect of this new localism is the question of rationing. Should access to treatment depend on where one lives, or on decisions taken by individual authorities as to what they can and cannot afford? The various reported proposals by individual purchasing authorities or health authorities to cease providing or purchasing specific forms of care – such as the NE Thames RHA's proposals to cease various forms of non-urgent or cosmetic surgery, and the decisions by health authorities that long-stay care shall be provided entirely in the private sector – are cases in point. If the concept of a national system, meaning equal treatment for those in equal need, is to be sustained, such decisions cannot be left to the whims of individual authorities.

It may be rational for purchasers, faced with limited resources, to take decisions of this kind, but the present system of appointing health authorities (Chapter 9) is such that those decisions lack a base in democratic accountability. Closer integration with local government might not necessarily solve this problem, since decisions might be made for electoral reasons in order to please a particular constituency.

Another example is community care. The uneven development of the private sector, different levels of spending by local authorities, their different approaches to means testing and their respective financial positions could mean an inequitable diversity of policies and standards. Do the trends being witnessed in the welfare state now signal widening 'divisions of welfare' (Ginsburg, 1992)? Pinker (1992) suggests that this might be nothing new, because the 'misconception' of Britain as a 'unitary welfare state' was promulgated by collectivists, who mistook their own aspirations for reality, and by individualists, whose anxieties and resentments made them exaggerate the collectivist elements in the welfare state. It is possible to suggest that the effect of the NHS reforms, and of numerous changes over the past decade, has been to fragment interest groups within the service and to expand a constituency with a vested interest in private provision outside the service. Such divisions are complex: they include not just different groups of staff, but also divisions between groups of staff (fundholding versus non-fundholding GPs), consumers (those with and those without private insurance), and other producers (those with a stake in the continuance of the private sector, such as owners of private care facilities, or those participating in management buyouts or who have become self-employed as a result of change in the NHS). So how long a national consensus on collectivist welfare provision can last is debatable. The effect of welfare pluralism depends on how it is developed as a political strategy. In one vision, statutory sources of funding support a variety of service providers: a modified version of an institutional model of welfare. In another, new pluralities are developed as an alternative to statutory funding, with the 'ultimate goal of privatising as much as possible of the system' (Pinker, 1992, p. 279). Celebrating pluralism as contributing to diversity or to consumerism might miss the point that collective and comprehensive services are under attack. What perhaps is needed, Pinker argues, is a communitarian version of pluralism – participatory, democratic, community-based – the moral and behavioural dynamics of which would be very different from bureaucratic models. Notions of obligation, entitlement, rights and responsibilities have to be taken on board here, though a cautionary observation might be in order: communities can oppress and exclude, and community cohesion may be more often presumed than observed.

Related to this is the idea that communities can in some way be responsible for their own salvation by providing resources over and above those made available by the state. This links to the notion of local proactivity stressed by investigations of uneven development in

Britain during the 1980s, which suggested that in some circumstances local coalitions, cutting across conventional political alignments, could secure the economic fortunes of places affected by economic restructuring (see Cooke, 1989). While this may have had some benefits for some places at some times, the idea that anything more than a marginal contribution to services as expensive and complex as health care can be made by local initiative seems politically extremely dubious. There is simply no escape from state funding at a level that permits all to enjoy basic services that have come to be regarded as the rights and entitlements of citizenship. When commentators such as Bennett (1989; see also Bennett and Krebs, 1991) advocate a future role for the local state as simply developing proactive coalitions to entice investment, in what they term a 'post-welfare agenda', they implicitly acknowledge that some will miss out in a territorially based competition for resources. In so doing, such commentators deny any conception of universalism or of universal and enforceable rights to services, seeing them as the natural outcomes of a market order. But an analysis of the pre-NHS situation would clearly show how closely access to services was determined by the economic fortunes of particular regions and towns (Powell, 1992). Do we wish to return to that situation, or to produce Jessop's (1993) 'Schumpeterian workfare state', wherein the welfare 'packages' available to individuals would depend substantially on the success of their 'place' in competing for economic activity? (cf. Cochrane, 1992, on local government.) It is not too many years since Patrick Jenkin advocated a greater degree of local financing and suggested greater involvement by local people in delivering services, whether on a voluntary basis or in terms of fund raising (Chapters 3 and 8). The political difficulty with such analyses is that their localist prescriptions open up considerable scope for unequal access and provision.

Markets, planning and ethics

It is often suggested that markets have developed in health care because of the expression of consumer preference; hence the growth of private medicine is said to reflect individual decisions to purchase insurance policies. But this growth has in part resulted from deliberate government decisions – for example to facilitate private practice by NHS consultants, subsidise insurance coverage for the elderly, and pay for long-stay residential care through social security. Markets arise in specific institutional and political contexts (Hindess, 1987); what matters is the way the rules are established. The various attempts to expand the role of market forces in the delivery of health care raise numerous questions concerning equity, ethics and market failure.

Taking the last of these first, there are numerous instances in which markets can be said to have failed – or at the very least to have provoked calls for greater regulation. These include the surprising demands for greater regulation of private acute care and for examination of the basis on which NHS paybeds compete with the private sector (Chapter 7); the tightening-up of standards in long-stay private and public care; the contractors' failures exposed repeatedly in the privatisation of ancillary services (Chapters 6 and 8); the collapse of the property market, bringing down with it the capital programmes of various RHAs (Chapter 8); the production of chronic staff shortages, in part due to central government macroeconomic strategy, which generated serious regional differentials in living costs (Chapter 6); and, possibly the ultimate example of market failure, the realisation that the NHS reforms demanded careful, strategic management if they were not to have catastrophic consequences in certain locations (Chapter 4). Other initiatives, such as the imposition of charges for certain diagnostic tests for eyes and teeth, will be counterproductive if, as expected, they deter people from having checkups. On occasion, as in the introduction of the latter charges or in the failure to make good the benefits gap in income support payments to residents of long-stay establishments, market failures have proved politically damaging to the government, though not to the extent of challenging its parliamentary majority. Perhaps even more controversially, the internal market has meant that fundholding GPs are able to distort priorities by requesting preferential admission for their patients, leading to accusations of a two-tier system. Some predicted forms of market failure have not, so far, emerged: for example there is little sign of the competitive, duplicative and wasteful development of hospital facilities characteristic of the American situation, which may be connected to the Treasury's refusal (*contra* the government's initial statements made about the reforms) to permit substantial private borrowing to finance the capital aspirations of trusts.

What is also not recognised in evaluating the benefits of markets is that while many post-1979 developments have, on a narrow definition, increased efficiency, this has been at the expense of displacing problems onto other people. This applies to the concentration and centralisation of services, and to the increased speed of discharge from hospital, both of which depend on relatives, friends or local social services agencies coping with discharged patients (Chapter 4). Market signals encourage managers to displace costs: the disputes between health and local authorities over community care responsibilities, and the decanting of long-stay patients into unsuitable accommodation, have resulted from managers taking decisions in the short-term interests of their employers that displace the costs of care elsewhere (Chapter 5). Likewise competitive tendering has meant that the cost of additional social security for those on casual labour contracts are met by another branch of the government (Chapter 6), so that savings on the NHS budget appear as additional costs elsewhere. Consequently many efficiency savings and cost improvements should be regarded as cost displacements rather than improvements *per se*.

As a consequence, what has emerged is a qualitative change in the forms of state regulation of the service. Whereas in 1979 the role of market forces in the service was marginal, that can no longer be said. Whereas in 1979 the state's role was primarily that of provider, increasingly it is involved in the regulation of commercial and voluntary sector provision and is engaged in partnerships with a range of agencies. The difficulty here has been policing standards and ensuring that ethical codes of conduct consistent with a public service are followed. The concentration of power in health authorities, now entirely appointed by the secretary of state or his/her appointees (Chapter 9) has contributed to this situation, for it has meant that opportunist managers or authority members are subject to little scrutiny: expanding the autonomy of managers was the intention of successive reforms, but several scandals about financial control have shaken faith in the system. It might be argued that health authorities have moved away from accountability (as if that alone guarantees the maintenance of correct standards), and that this has allowed a situation to develop in which windfall gains can be made from public service.

This links to the question of ethics and public service. Only belatedly has it been recognised that the opening up of the NHS to market forces, and its various administrative reorganisations, has meant that decisions are taken by very few people and without proper scrutiny. Hence the recent controversies about misuse of public funds in the Wessex and West Midlands RHAs. It is essential that the discussion on corporate governance currently taking place in the NHS covers both public and private providers of health care and ensures that the use of public funds is properly scrutinised. This has not always been the case, so enforceable codes of practice are essential (see also Public Accounts Committee, 1994).

The more fundamental question raise by the reforms, of course, is whether clinical need has now been superseded by financial criteria in determining access to services, as the disputes about the priority given to patients of fundholding GPs indicates. This is profoundly inequitable and it is not surprising that medical opposition has been vociferous. Questions of equity are also raised by the evident differences between health authorities in their priorities – most notably in relation to rationing decisions, so that where one lives can have an important impact on the probability of receiving treatment for a given condition. Reliance on the mixed economy of care, especially with regard to community care (Chapter 5), also raises the possibility of individuals in similar circumstances being treated differentially according to locally available resources.

Boundary disputes

Many developments since 1979 have had an effect on the boundaries or divisions of responsibility and power in health care. Most notably, the boundary between private and public health care is considerably more fluid, not merely in terms of the proportions insured privately or using private hospitals, but also in terms of the role of private finance in the delivery of services. Thus the role of charity has expanded (Chapter 8; Lattimer and Holly, 1992), raising the question of how far equipment, services and medical research should depend upon such sources of funds. This concerns both charities themselves (who may now have to compete with prominent NHS appeals) and the charity commissioners (regarding the correct use of charitable funds). Debates about the private sector were, in the early 1980s, largely confined to localised competition for NHS staff from the concentration of hospital developments in particular localities (Chapter 7), but its contribution to elective surgery is now considerable. But its expansion may not be without cost, for if the number of consultants is not increased the availability of consultants for their NHS commitments may be in question, a point to which at least one hospital trust has attempted to respond by proposing that all its consultants carry out their private work in situ rather than at nearby private hospitals. Again, none of these issues should come as a great surprise. Private sector expansion has been partly the product of legislation and partly the product of other concessions, but it will continue to prove contentious.

Similarly the boundary between health- and local-authority responsibilities, and between what is regarded as 'health' and 'social' care, will continue to be a focus of debate as the community care programme develops. Vesting responsibility in the hands of one authority should mitigate the perverse process whereby – for instance – health authorities have a financial interest in decanting patients into long-stay care because their costs will then be met by the social security budget, regardless of whether this is in the best interests of those so transferred (Chapter 5). Ministers have stated on several occasions that long-stay care was becoming the province of the private sector, but no formal decisions were taken on this point, and the *ad hoc* decisions of individual authorities have led to an unsatisfactory situation. Legal challenges mounted by the DSS to clarify this situation may, however, have the perverse result of saving money on social security but forcing authorities to reduce the pace of the rundown of long-stay institutional provision.

There have also been continuing debates about the appropriate roles for central, regional and local tiers of the service. How far should central government intervene in decisions taken locally in a service the size of the NHS? The answer has depended in part not on technical issues relating to the proper exercise of authority, but on the political priority attached by central government to the issues in question, notably on competitive tendering and manpower control, where an overtly centralist line was pursued (Chapter 9). In other circumstances devolutionist rhetoric has helped the government to shrug off its responsibility for problems, dismissing them as local difficulties to be resolved by local management (Chapter 4). The logic of the NHS reforms places the regional tier in question, but it remains to be seen whether the absence of firm controls between the DoH and individual trusts is the best way to ensure some of the NHS's traditional goals, such as equitable access.

Finally, the slow pace of resource growth, the advances in medical technology and the NHS reforms have together given rise to controversy over precisely what the NHS can be expected to provide. Traditionally, rationing has taken place implicitly, through devices such as waiting lists or through nationally specified lists of 'priority' services. What appears to be happening in the present NHS is the imposition of three additional forms of rationing: abandoning a service because it is deemed 'cosmetic' or not cost-effective; explicitly defining how much of which service should be provided, through the contract system; and balancing the competing needs of different categories of patient rather than types of service (for example rationing services according to age, or refusing treatment to people whose lifestyle seems likely to prejudice their ability to benefit from it, such as refusing smokers coronary bypass surgery).[3] The controversy surrounding some such decisions has largely been because they have been taken on an *ad hoc* basis by individual health authorities. But if the service is to continue to be a national one, it would seem appropriate for such decisions to be taken nationally. The difficulty then becomes how those decisions are to be justified. The Oregon experiment in the USA (Dixon and Welch, 1991) suggests there are some dangers: decisions to prioritise medical care can easily turn on prejudices about who does or does not deserve treatment rather than on informed debate on the relative cost-effectiveness of various interventions.

These recent developments raise the question of how far there can be said to be a genuinely *national* health service. In one sense it could be argued that the service has been national*ised*, by which I mean the removal of local influence from the service, and power over purchasers and providers being concentrated in the hands of central government appointees to authorities. Some of this would, in principle, be welcome if it meant the prospect of a 'NHS that actually lives up to its name – a national service whose local patterns of provision and activity actually reflect national policies' (Day and Klein, 1985, p. 1676). However, not only has this been achieved through a massive centralisation of authority and control, but ministerial refusal to guarantee standards locally has meant that we can arguably not regard what is on offer as a national service.

In another sense, though, there will be continued boundary disputes regarding the confused responsibilities described here. At the national level, the current public expenditure round is provoking at least the right wing of the Conservatives to argue against the perceived burden of state expenditure. In recent parliamentary questions the government has refused to either rule in or rule out the possibility of 'hotel' charges for inpatient stays, and the possibility of some contracting-out of state services has been advocated by the insurance industry. This would probably lead to 'cream-skimming' of profitable cases, leaving the state with cases of long-term illness and community care. It would, of course, also remove the possibility of cross-subsidisation, which is implicit in the way the NHS is financed and run, and in that sense would *denationalise* the service, leading to greater differentiation between areas in levels of access to health care.

Alternatives

The most important task of an alternative health policy is arguably to promote the public health. As less and less health care is delivered in hospital, and as the role of primary and community care grows in relative importance, more attention will need to be devoted to prevention, which will demand the involvement of many agencies other than the health service. The government has apparently rediscovered public health, with the publication of its *Health of the Nation* White Paper, though one criticism of this has been the lack of sensitivity to local variations in the interests of pursuing visible national goals. However, while that White Paper did suggest targets for improvements in health status, it did not commit itself to expanding the role of local government, nor did it pay more than lip service to the challenges posed for the health services by poverty, poor housing and unemployment. The major health challenges of the late twentieth century include AIDS, degenerative diseases such as heart disease and cancer, unhealthy eating habits, health problems caused by pollution and deprivation, and problems related to drug and alcohol abuse. Many of these are preventable, given investment in education, housing and other infrastructure, and given social policies that integrate citizens rather than marginalise them. But prevention cannot rest content on an individualist, voluntaristic approach that suggests that ill health is related to individual failings: low-income families may be unable to afford healthy diets or to travel to shops where they can purchase healthy food; and deprived areas may not have facilities for exercise. In addition children living in substandard housing are exposed to a greater risk of accidents and other health hazards. Class inequalities in health are substantial and persistent.[4]

Accepting the above, it is logical to suggest that local authorities should return to one of their original roles: the control of the environment in the interests of public health. Local authorities already pursue public health policies (though not necessarily by that name) through environmental protection and regulation, housing and planning, the personal social services, and leisure and educational services. These can all contribute to a social model of health, focusing on the health of the population, not on the health of patients (in a medical model of health). There is insufficient space here to examine the growing public health movement, and the activities of many local authorities through the WHO's Health for All Network, except to say that in principle such activities offer scope for democratic control and community participation. The growth of such activities, when added to the involvement of local authorities in community care, might suggest that health and social services purchasing responsibilities should be put in the hands of local government (Hunter and Webster, 1992). This may be anathema to Conservatives but would avoid the present duplication and conflicting interests of local and health authorities.

As well as the growing role of local government, what also needs to be examined is whether and to what extent the NHS reforms could operate in a progressive manner. The reforms could, in principle, help empower community organisations to develop localised models of service provision that are accessible and responsive to community needs, and that involve members of their local community in running such services. However at present there is growing commercial involvement in service provision but not many examples of community-based services. Even in community care, non-state provision is dominated by residential care with limited domiciliary service provision. The vaunted advantages (flexibility, low cost, localism, community involvement) of the voluntary sector have yet to be seen on a large scale in health care; privatisation's 'progressive potential' has yet to be realised (Donnison, 1985). Competitive bidding for contracts for service delivery will favour established organisations capable of sustaining short-term losses – what scope here for the voluntary sector?

Finally, the rights of citizenship seem to be back on the political agenda in two senses: promoting citizen involvement through the philosophy of 'active citizenship', and promoting the social rights of citizenship through giving people the right to redress. Active citizenship has been criticised as a flag of convenience rather than coherence; in other words, it was hastily patched together in response to a realisation of growing public concern at the individualism espoused by the Conservatives in the late 1980s. But the limited impact of active citizenship (see Kearns, 1992) is not surprising: it emphasises obligations and duties without a parallel extension of community control or citizens' rights. In the health sector public access to information is now more restricted and local democracy has been reduced, so the notion that this is a more participatory health service is false. Citizens are expected to contribute to a service whose policies, even on a local level, they have little chance of shaping. Although health authorities have been exhorted to take account of local opinions in developing policies, practice of this is variable, and in any case this is not the same as an input from a democratically accountable body. As far as rights are concerned, these need to be given far more legislative teeth than the limited rights (for example individual appointment times in outpatient clinics) in the Citizen's Charter. Standards of treatment, expected waiting times, levels of accessibility to services (it ought to be reasonable to specify maximum distances to be travelled, for instance), advocacy for patients (contra the government's refusal to implement legislation requiring such advocacy in community care), and the right to equal health outcomes irrespective of location all need to be examined in more detail. However what might have far more impact is thinking in terms of the right to freedom from hazards that are injurious to health, as the Commission on Social Justice is beginning to argue (though see the reservations of Montgomery, 1992). Any such initiative, however, would require a national framework of standards, a significantly greater degree of restraint of the competitive mechanisms now driving the service, and a much greater degree of accountable local supervision of service delivery. For if a national health service means anything, it means people having enforceable rights, and people with similar needs in similar places being treated in a similar fashion. This seems to be precisely the opposite direction to that in which the service is currently heading. The problems of market failure, lack of accountability and perverse incentives point to incompatibilities between the blueprints of the reforms and the ideals of a public, free and comprehensive health service.

Appendix: Chronology of Major Developments in Health and Health Care Policy since 1979

1979: Conservatives win general election.

Report of the Royal Commission on the NHS published: largely endorsed the structure and financing of the NHS. Did not support any switch from direct taxation as a means of financing the service, nor the introduction of Griffiths-style chief executives. Recommended abolition of one tier of administration below the RHA level.

Patients First published: consultative document on the reorganisation of the NHS. Accepted Royal Commission's recommendation that one tier of administration be abolished and proposed abolition of AHAs. Reduced local authorities' right to nominate members to health authorities. Rejected (as had the Royal Commission) the possibility of appointing chief executives, à la Griffiths, to health authorities.

Revised NHS consultants contracts published: consultants permitted to undertake more private practice; full-time consultants allowed to undertake private practice up to a limit of 10 per cent of NHS salary.

1980: *Inequalities in Health* (the Black Report) published (August): report of working group established by Labour government. Identified significant and persistent inequalities between social classes in health status. Recommended programme (costing £2 bn) of initiatives to attempt to deal with such inequalities. Rejected by Patrick Jenkin as unrealistic in current or foreseeable economic circumstances.

Social Security Act: DHSS offices given discretion to meet the costs of residential or nursing-home care from the social security budget.

Health Services Act passed. Made health authority cash limits legally binding. Abolished the Health Services Board (the body that had been set up to regulate the growing commercial sector) and weakened controls on private hospital development, reserving power to the secretary of state to decide whether a proposed development would interfere with the provision of NHS care in a locality. Empowered health authorities to establish charitable appeals to raise funds, the costs of such appeals to be repaid from the proceeds of appeals.

1981:   *Care in Action* published. This was the planning guidance for the new post-1982 DHAs. It refrained from setting national norms for services, regarding health service priorities as a matter for local discretion and decision. It envisaged a rather more 'entrepreneurial, coordinative role' (Davies, 1987) for health authorities, encouraging them to draw upon a range of resources available locally.

White paper, *Growing Older*, published. Considered the implications for health and social care of the growing proportion of elderly people in the population. Stated that 'care *in* the community must increasingly mean care *by* the community'.

Care in the Community (DHSS, 1981). Consultative document on transferring patients and resources from hospital settings into the community. Envisaged that disposals of surplus land and buildings would provide the funds to develop community-based services.

1982:   Central Policy Review Staff (CPRS) report leaked. Report reviewed options for replacing some welfare state programmes with private alternatives, including the possibility of an insurance system for health care. Disowned by the government after adverse public reaction. Thatcher then declares that 'the NHS is safe with us'.

NHS reorganisation. AHAs replaced by DHAs. Coterminosity between local authorities and the NHS lost in many places. Local authority and trade union nomination rights to health authorities reduced.

Rayner scrutinies introduced. These were examinations of the ways in which the health service could be made more efficient; named after Lord Rayner, the prime minister's efficiency expert, focused on specific areas of expenditure and were aimed at producing recommendations for swift, visible action.

NHS industrial dispute involved nursing, ancillary and administrative staff. Included short national strikes and a TUC day of action.

1983:   General Election. Conservatives returned with increased majority. Three weeks after the election a 1 per cent cut in the NHS budget was announced.

Davies Report published. Health authorities expected to investigate the possibility of disposals of surplus land and buildings; the proceeds were to be incorporated into capital programmes.

Performance indicators introduced into the NHS. Permitted district-level (and subsequently, unit-level) comparisons of resource use within the HCHS, though – initially at least – they were focused heavily on efficiency rather than on any other dimension against which the service might have been evaluated. There were few outcome indicators.

Competitive tendering introduced. DHAs expected to develop programmes for testing the competitiveness of their ancillary (catering, laundry and domestic) services by inviting tenders from the in-house workforce and commercial firms.

1983   Personnel cuts imposed. Target levels of staffing for RHAs and DHAs specified with a view to reducing the proportions of staff not directly involved in patient care.

Griffiths Report on NHS management published. Criticised lack of managerial accountability and the inefficiencies of consensus management in the service. Recommended introduction of general management from unit level upwards, highlighting the responsibility of individuals to deliver agreed results.

Pay Review Body for nurses established. Took nurses out of Whitley Council system of wage determination.

1984: Health and Social Security Act passed. Family Practitioner Committees (FPCs) constituted as separate authorities (note that the Royal Commission had recommended that they be integrated with health authorities).

Cost improvement programmes (CIPs) introduced. Health authorities expected to deliver specified proportions of their cash allocations in the form of cash-releasing CIPs.

1985: Social Services Committee report on community care published. Criticised deinstitutionalisation programmes for patients in long-stay hospitals. Main problems identified as inadequacy of resources for community-based services and the excessive pace of the run-down of institutions.

1986: NHS ceased to supply spectacles; vouchers introduced.

Resource Management Initiative launched at six pilot hospitals. Aimed to devolve budgetary responsibility to clinical directorates, giving doctors and nurses a greater role in the management of resources, and to relate workload and service objectives to financial and personnel allocations.

Audit Commission report on community care. Commented that, despite the sums spent on community care, notably through social security funds, progress had been slow and uneven across the country. Identified various obstacles to a coherent community care policy, including fragmentation of responsibility between local government and the NHS, difficulty of transferring funds from one budget to another, and the bias in favour of residential care imparted by the availability of social security funds.

1987: General Election. Conservatives won third term of office.

Great Ormond Street 'Wishing Well' appeal launched. Sought to raise funds to complement DHSS money for redevelopment of the hospital.

Income generation initiative. Health authorities encouraged to seek ways of exploiting their assets to raise funds and to generate income from commercial activities on their property.

Perceived crisis in the NHS. Wave of temporary / permanent bed closures in the NHS, with cancelled operations and rising waiting lists. Provoked unprecedented statement from Royal Medical Colleges denouncing the underfunding of the service.

Promoting Better Health launched. White paper on primary care. Gave GPs incentives to offer more preventive services in their surgeries (including payment for screening and for GPs operating in deprived areas) and introduced a contractual obligation to check the health of their patients regularly. Health promotion largely confined to GP surgeries, rather than applied in a wider context.

1988:   NHS Review announced. In a television interview the prime minister announced that a ministerial working group would review the NHS. Review process to be conducted in secret by a team composed largely of Treasury ministers.

Review of RAWP published. Recommended inclusion of factor for social deprivation in RAWP formula, as well as other modifications that would have benefited inner-city areas while reducing the weighting given to SMRs in the formula.

Griffiths Report on community care published. Endorsed many previous criticisms of community care programmes. Recommended appointment of minister for community care, some ring fencing of funds, and a lead role for local authorities in delivering community care. Report given little ministerial attention.

1989:   NHS White Paper published. Proposed the internal market as a basis for NHS reform. Separated providers from purchasers of care. DHAs given main purchasing role. Capital charging proposed to facilitate competition on an equal basis between NHS trusts (and between trusts and the private sector). Fundholding introduced for general practices above a certain size (initially 11 000 patients).

White Paper established NHS trusts as the principal providers of care, free of excessive consultation or supervision. Also abolished local authorities' right to nominate health authority members. Executive membership of health authorities introduced.

White Paper proposed tax relief on health insurance premiums for those over retirement age.

Community Care white paper published. Local authorities given lead role in developing policies.

1990:   NHS and Community Care Act received royal assent. White paper to be implemented from April 1991.

1991:   NHS reforms introduced (April). Reforms immediately controversial as two prominent NHS trusts announced major job losses. 'Steady state' ordered by government to avoid destabilisation of hospitals (which might have resulted from too many purchasers switching contracts).

Tomlinson review of London's hospital services announced. This was because of the impact of the internal market on hospitals in London. It represented an attempt by the government to produce an orderly rationalisation of facilities.

Health of the Nation white paper published. Set targets for health status. Criticised for making little mention of poverty and social inequality as causes of ill-health.

Community care reforms postponed to 1993. This was widely believed to be because of the effect the transfer of responsibility for community care to local authorities would have on the community charge (poll tax).

1992:   Tomlinson report announced proposals to concentrate London's hospital facilities, including the merger or closure of various prominent hospitals.

Regional outposts of DoH created to monitor NHS trusts, partly in response to complaints from trusts that RHAs were reluctant to let them operate in an autonomous fashion and were being restrictive.

1993:   Langlands Report on the future of regional health authorities published. Recommended creation of 'super-regions', which in all but two cases merged two RHAs together. These were formally regional divisions of the DoH, with no direct community or local representation. Their role is a strategic and enabling one, setting priorities and monitoring the activities of trusts and purchasers within their jurisdiction.

Community care reforms implemented (April). Local authorities given lead role in community care policies, in collaboration with the health service and the voluntary sector. Social security budget for residential care transferred to local authorities, though subject to specification that certain proportion should be spent in the private sector.

1994:   Public Accounts Committee report on various scandals and waste in the public sector published. This followed criticism of incidents in West Midlands and Wessex RHAs in which inadequate financial control over contracts and contractors had led to the waste of several million pounds, prompting concern about standards of probity in the NHS.

Notes and References

Chapter 1

1. In other words, levels of efficiency savings were not specified from the centre, but were agreed between regional and local tiers of the service. However, while centrally specified target levels of efficiency were no longer prescribed, the government's underfunding of pay awards had much the same effect. The government rarely accepted in full the recommendations of the Review Bodies for doctors, dentists and nurses; even when they had decided on the awards to be offered, they did not fund them fully, regarding this as a stimulus to efficiency on the part of health authorities.
2. The *Observer* (20 March 1994) reported the possibility of patients paying the full price for NHS dentistry, although it was also reported that a quid pro quo would be the reintroduction of free dental and optical checkups.
3. DoH / OPCS *Annual Report*, 1992, Cm. 1913, table 4. One of the reasons for the increase is the rapid rise in income from paybeds in NHS hospitals, which has followed from legislation that permitted health authorities to set paybed charges at commercial rates. This does not include capital receipts; at one point during the 1980s these accounted for some 20 per cent of NHS capital expenditure, though that figure has dropped sharply as property prices have fallen.
4. Health and Personal Social Services (HPSS) Statistics, 1991 and 1992, table 2.1.
5. Quoted in Social Services Committee, 1988a, para 14.
6. Treasury and Civil Service Committee, 1988, Evidence, Q 145.
7. Evidence to Health Committee, 1991c.
8. Social Services Committee, 1988a, para. 12.
9. Mr I. Todd, president of the Royal College of Surgeons, and Sir R. Hoffenberg, president of the Royal College of Physicians, in evidence to Social Services Committee, 1988a, Q3 and 4.
10. Sir George Godber (former Chief Medical Officer), letter to the *Lancet*, 12 December 1987.
11. HC Deb., 15 December 1988, v. 124, c. 918–921
12. DoH/OPCS (1992), *Annual Report* (Cm. 1913), figure 18. This indicated that CRES were to increase by £280 mn between 1990–1 and 1991–2.
13. DoH Statistical Bulletin 1993/2, *NHS Hospital Activity Statistics, England, 1981 – 1991–2.*
14. Data on temporary closures are not collected centrally because these closures do not require ministerial consent. The reports produced by local

campaigning groups, especially in London, give some idea of the extent of temporary or partial closures of services. London Health Emergency (1986, 1987a, 1988) document the extent of the problems suffered by DHAs in the capital, with virtually every DHA, in the 1987–8 financial year, having to take decisions to close, on a temporary basis, at least some beds or wards. On the question of new or replacement facilities, information is given on a regular basis in Social Services Committee reports about capital schemes approved in principle, but there is no summary of the number of beds that are provided as a result of such schemes.

15. Social Services Committee, 1988a, Vol. II, Evidence, Q408, and, more generally, Q408–432 on bed closures and the monitoring thereof.

16. Thus the number of non–psychiatric hospitals has fallen dramatically – in England, from 1609 in 1979 to 1147 in 1991. The greater part of this reduction was due to a fall in the number of hospitals with less than 250 beds from 1306 to 884; the mean size of hospitals rose from 151 beds in 1979 to 168 beds in 1990–1. Source: HPSS Statistics, 1991, table 4.2.

17. In psychiatric services for the 1979–91 period, the reduction in beds from 127 497 to 62 906 is largely due to community care initiatives. Large institutions have been substantially eliminated: while there were 31 psychiatric hospitals with over 1000 beds in 1979 there was one in 1991; 29 hospitals have over 500 beds, compared with 106; nearly half have under 50 beds compared with one third. Source: HPSS Statistics, 1993.

18. HPSS Statistics, 1993, table 5.12.

19. HPSS Statistics, 1991, table 4.3.

20. HPSS Statistics, 1992, table 4.5.

21. DoH Statistical Bulletin 1993/2, *NHS Hospital Activity Statistics, England, 1981 – 1991–2*; HPSS Statistics, 1993, table 5.12.

22. 'NHS Waiting lists reach record high', *Guardian*, 7 May 1994, p. 8. These figures only include individuals actually on waiting lists for treatment; they do not include those waiting for outpatient appointments prior to joining official waiting lists.

23. These years were chosen because in 1981 a reduction in the working week for nurses from 40 to 37.5 hours had the effect of increasing the WTE figure for nursing staff by approximately 31 000.

24. For example the 1987 Public Expenditure White Paper ((Cm. 56), vol. II, p. 225), commented that the 'number of staff providing direct patient care has increased both absolutely and as a proportion of total staff'. Subsequent white papers continued to stress this.

25. HPSS Statistics, 1993, table 7.1.

26. Health Committee, 1991c, Evidence, Q259, Q274; see also Health Committee, 1991d.

27. *HSJ*, vol. 104 no. 5393, (10 March 1994), pp. 32–33, 'Evaluating the Reforms'. The Department of Health published, early in 1992, a document that argued that, even at that early stage of the reforms, there were significant improvements in care and responsiveness to individuals, and better value for money. However a critical analysis of that publication (Radical Statistics Health Group, 1992) showed how the Department of Health had failed to compare changes with longer-term trends, and had not allowed for changes in age structure and data-collection systems.

Chapter 3

1. HC Deb., v. 212, c. 592–662, 22 October 1992. Note, however, that in May 1994 the government announced, as part of a review of the Health of the Nation targets, a working group to examine health inequalities. The BMA chairman suggested that this indicated that the government was 'willing to move towards a much broader agenda in tackling the problems of inequality and health' (*Guardian*, 4 May 1994), but whether the government will, in fact, act on the recommendations of such a working party remains to be seen.
2. HC Deb., v. 212, c. 600–601, 22 October 1992; HC Deb., v. 237, c. 566–630, 11 February 1994; 'Ban on smoking ads rejected', *Guardian*, 8 February 1994, p. 8.
3. HC Deb., v. 976, c. 662, 19 December 1979.
4. HC Deb., v. 976, c. 696, 19 December 1979.
5. For the debate on this issue, see HC Deb., 17 March 1982, v. 21, c. 411–451. In the first six months after the regulations were implemented, only £375 000 was collected in England (HC Deb., 16 November 1983, v. 48, c. 499–503.
6. HC Deb., v. 124, c.31, 7 December 1987.
7. Ibid., c. 83, emphasis added.
8. HC Deb., 1 November 1988, v. 139, c. 819, emphasis added.
9. HC Deb., v. 124, c. 46, 7 December 1987.
10. HC Deb., v. 124, c. 35, 7 December 1987.
11. HC Deb., v. 139, c. 854–922, 1 November 1988.
12. All these options were put forward in a Commons debate, v. 123, c. 397–480, 26 November 1987.
13. Edwina Currie, HC Deb., 1 November 1988, v. 139, c. 849.
14. Proposals for both alternative sources of funding for the NHS, and for reform of the internal organisation of the service, were reviewed at some length in Social Services Committee, 1988c, paras. 75–174. This included an examination of proposals for internal markets (Enthoven, 1985) and for variants of Health Maintenance Organisations (HMOs) in a British context. Some of the relevant proposals are contained in Letwin and Redwood, 1988; Whitney, 1988; Butler and Pirie, 1988; and Goldsmith and Willetts, 1988. For critiques, see NHS Unlimited, 1988; and Socialist Health Association, 1988.
15. Patrick Jenkin, HC Deb., v. 991, c. 75–6, 27 October 1980.
16. HC Deb., v. 59, c. 644.
17. Ibid., c. 646.
18. Ibid., c. 654.
19. HC Deb., v. 63, c. 496, 5 July 1984.
20. Patrick Jenkin, speech to the National Association of Health Authorities, 27 June 1980; quoted in Klein, 1985, p. 196. See also Deakin, 1987, p. 98.
21. HC Deb., v. 979, c. 1115–50, 26 February 1980.
22. HC Deb., v. 124, c. 92–3, 7 December 1987.
23. Speaking in a television interview in January 1988, former Health Minister Gerald Vaughan stated that 'We have known this would be crisis year since 1981' (quoted by Robin Cook, HC Deb., v. 125, c. 826, 19 January

1988). This was a reference to the limited growth in the hospital and community health services from the early 1980s onwards.

24. According to Frank Field, the then chair of the Social Services Committee – HC Deb., v. 146, c. 174, 31 January 1989. Indeed, the then Chancellor, Nigel Lawson, (a 'convinced fiscal purist' according to Thatcher (1993)) also opposed this subsidy. See Lawson (1992).

25. Kenneth Clarke, HC Deb., v. 163, c. 506, 7 December 1989 – emphasis added.

26. HC Deb., v. 163, c. 694–5 – emphasis added.

27. Editorial comment, *BMJ,* vol. 298 (4 February 1989), p. 275.

Chapter 4

1. Since the NHS's inception health authorities had largely been funded in relation to historic budgets, so there was considerable inertia built in to the system. As the populations of major urban centres began to decline, it was clear that such areas (notably London) appeared to have excessive concentrations of hospitals in relation to their populations. RAWP attempted to redistribute funds slowly, partly in relation to needs, partly having regard to the feasibility of bringing the most overfunded authorities closer to their 'target' levels of revenue.

2. Patrick Jenkin, HC Deb., v. 967, c. 1796.

3. HC Deb., v. 89, c. 742, 20 December 1985.

4. Allocations for 1989–90 were superseded in late 1988 by a decision to allocate to each region a minimum of 2.5 per cent revenue growth (after allowing for inflation), though four regions (Trent, West Midlands, East Anglia and Oxford) received slightly more than this. In announcing this Kenneth Clarke dismissed the need for further redistribution, which was somewhat surprising given that the large cash increase for the NHS announced in late 1988 would surely have permitted a greater degree of redistribution (*BMJ*, vol. 298, 28 January 1989, pp. 211–12.

5. Part of the problem was that health authorities in London and the South East were simply unable to recruit staff at the wages offered by the health service, in a context in which rising house prices and tight labour markets, themselves partly a product of the government's neoliberal economic policies, rendered NHS employment unattractive (see Chapter 6; Mohan and Lee, 1989). When this was combined with underfunding of pay awards and intra regional transfers of funds, the pressure on many authorities became unsustainable.

6. Barney Hayhoe (a former health minister), HC Deb., v. 123, c. 418, 26 November 1987.

7. The Social Services Committee (1988a, pp. v–vi) reported that within six months of the 1987 Election, 26 early day motions were tabled in Parliament drawing attention to service reductions and financial difficulties; there were nine debates on the subject (six adjournment debates and three full-scale debates); and prime minister's question time was regularly dominated by angry exchanges about the NHS.

8. HC Deb., v. 63, c. 481, 5 July 1984.

9. Social Services Committee, 1988b, vol. II, Evidence, Q419 – emphasis added.
10. These years are illustrative of the pressures on health authorities in the two years surrounding the NHS 'crisis' of 1987–8, and the announcement of the reforms. Previous surveys did not obtain the data in quite the same form so the comparison is not extended to years prior to 1987–8. However, note that in the 1985–6 financial year, of the 148 respondents to the NAHA survey, 48 (32.3 per cent) had deferred or deleted planned developments, 17 (11.4 per cent) were reducing service provision, 25 (16.9 per cent) froze recruitment, and 20 (13.5 per cent) reduced staff numbers (NAHA, 1985).
11. There was no specific question on this point but it was frequently mentioned in answers to a request to indicate any other measures taken by the authority.
12. HC Deb., v. 89, c. 739–44, 20 December 1985.
13. For example D. Evennett (Erith and Crayford) complained that his health authority was closing facilities that, had they adhered to their plans, would have remained open until the provision of replacement services – HC Deb., v. 106, c. 591–6, 28 November 1986.
14. HC Deb., v. 93, c. 769, 16 June 1986; see also HC Deb., v. 106, c. 591 on Bexley DHA.
15. HC Deb., v. 120, c. 623.
16. HC Deb., v. 39, c. 1248, 1250 – emphasis added. For similar complaints, HC Deb., v. 93, c. 421–6, on Essex or v. 90, c. 770–6, on Bexley. Part of the problem was that revenue budgets and targets were always based on population estimates that were (generally) about two years out of date. In situations where populations were growing rapidly, as was the case in the outer South East during the 1980s, this imposed severe pressure on health authorities.
17. HC Deb., v. 967, c. 339, 16 May 1979.
18. HC Deb., v. 980, c. 1184; see also HC Deb., v. 998, c. 1153–6 on the denial of funds to Kent because of overspending in London.
19. HC Deb., v. 87, c. 1181.
20. HC Deb., v. 113, c. 548–54; HC Deb., v. 113, c. 1281, 1298. For similar comments from MPs in the Trent RHA, see HC Deb., v. 976, c. 801–12; v. 979, c. 1263–74.
21. Andrew Rowe (Mid Kent), HC Deb., v. 93, c. 785.
22. HC Deb., v. 101, c. 1337–8.
23. HC Deb., v. 70, c. 270-6.
24. HC Deb., v. 63, c. 501, 5 July 1984.
25. HC Deb., v. 100, c. 985, 1 July 1986.
26. Kenneth Clarke, HC Deb., v. 82, c. 214, 2 July 1985.
27. For accounts of RAWP and criticisms thereof, see Buxton and Klein, 1978; Butts *et al.*, 1980; Mays and Bevan, 1987. Among the criticisms considered in the RAWP review were its use of SMRs as proxies for need for health care; its treatment of crossboundary flows of patients and the ways in which health authorities were recompensed for them, giving rise to perverse incentives to health authorities in terms of who they treated and from where; and its treatment of teaching-hospital costs (DHSS, 1988).
28. The white paper formula was introduced, it seems, largely on the grounds of simplicity and transparency, which may be one reason for the absence

of a deprivation factor. Another possibility may be that, for inter regional resource allocation, relative levels of social deprivation are not as significant as between DHAs. However, if that was what the government had decided it made no mention of it in debates on the white paper.

29. For example the deprivation index used (the Jarman index, after its originator) was criticised for having an inbuilt London, south-eastern and urban bias, for including census measures that were ambiguous, and for being more relevant to primary care (for which it was originally devised) than to hospital care. Furthermore one commentator suggested that the answer produced by the review was 'obviously extremely acceptable politically' since the review of RAWP was very much driven by 'problems experienced in London teaching hospitals and south eastern constituencies' (*HSJ*, vol. 98 , no. 5111, 28 July 1988, pp. 846–7).

30. HC Deb., v. 163, c. 571, 7 December 1989.

31. Thus Gillian Shepherd (Norfolk SW) stated that the abolition of RAWP would 'be welcomed in many areas with high population growth . . . that single measure will help East Anglian residents more than anything else' (HC Deb., v. 151, c. 237, 18 April 1989).

32. The potential impacts of the white paper on DHA revenue allocations were estimated using the criteria advanced in the white paper - capitation allowances for different age groups reflecting different consumption of resources, square root of the SMR, and differential allowances for 'high-cost' locations (the full analysis is reported in Mohan, 1990b). Substantial reductions (and in some cases increases) in DHA budgets were implied, although the analysis made no assumptions about present patterns of use of services and about cross-boundary flows of patients and resources, nor did it attempt to simulate the process of contracting in the internal market.

33. *Guardian*, 19 December 1990, 'Bed closures force health cash U-turn', p. 2.

34. See note 4 above.

35. Although the Tomlinson Report identified the high levels of social need in the London health authorities, it implied – in part relying on evidence produced by the King's Fund Institute (1992) – that these needs would be better met by community-based services; the issue of whether London's needs meant that its above-average provision of hospital services was *necessary* was not considered. The Tomlinson Report therefore accepted the proposition that reductions in beds were necessary and took the view that managing this in a planned fashion was essential. Jarman (1993) disputed Tomlinson's claims; he argued that the case for a reduction of hospital provision in London could not be justified in terms of hospital utilisation, the availability of hospital beds, nor considerations of relative efficiency. If areas comparable to inner London were examined, there were no significant differences in hospital provision or use, and London's acute hospital services were no less efficient than the national average (Jarman, 1993, p. 982).

36. Health Committee, 1993b, Evidence, Q5 – emphasis added.

37. Ibid., Q12 – emphasis added.

38. Such as Virginia Bottomley's intervention in the case of University College Hospital.

39. In fact the government's proposals for replacement community facilities were criticised as being an inadequate response to the needs of inner-London residents.

40. J. Whittingdale (Colchester South and Maldon, HC Deb., v. 235, c. 1093, 20 January 1994). This MP then demanded a uniform national formula, bypassing the regions and allocating funds direct to districts. However this was not a new complaint: much of the critical evidence submitted to the RAWP review from RHAs and DHAs focused on the process of allocating funds subregionally.

Chapter 5

1. This was echoed by the Health Committee (1994, para. 20) which commented that the pressure on acute services was such that voluntary patients were rarely admitted to hospital, thus leaving open the possibility that their condition would deteriorate, leading them to make heavier demands on acute services in due course.

2. This was provoked by the public reaction to incidents such as a murder committed by a discharged psychiatric patient, and the mauling of another by lions in London Zoo. It also led to suggestions for supervised discharge schemes as alternatives to continued institutionalisation, largely to allay public fears.

3. 'Closing mental hospitals: simple information about hospital closures is not available'. *BMJ*, vol. 306, pp. 471–2, 475. This reported on a survey undertaken by the National Schizophrenia Fellowship, which had shown that 45 hospitals were due to close between 1993 and 2000. However, Tim Yeo, the minister with responsibility for community care, had been unable to say how many hospitals in England were due to close, because no information was held centrally (HC Deb., v. 217, c. 387, 21 January 1993) (he had previously suggested that 29 mental illness hospitals were to close by 1997). Although the government had appointed a mental illness task force for a two-year period while it was monitoring the progress of community care initiatives the closure process would presumably continue.

4. While Tony Newton accepted the need for stringent controls, he drew attention to the excessive rigidity with which local authorities were imposing registration requirements on the private sector and argued that those authorities should not be seeking to apply standards higher than those that would apply to their own properties. The then minister for health, Barney Hayhoe, insisted that the government had no intention of relaxing regulatory standards (Social Services Committee, 1986, Evidence, Q 330–333).

5. The DoH had written to proprietors of nursing and residential homes asking whether current levels of inspection were too onerous and costly (*BMJ*, vol. 307 18 September 1993), p. 702.

6. R. Cook, HC Deb., v .169, c. 200, 13 March 1990.

7. HC Deb., v.169, c. 206, 13 March 1990.

8. HC Deb., v.169, c. 208, 13 March 1990.

9. The government was defeated in a Commons vote on this issue, with 32 Conservatives voting against the government. However, Labour's proposed amendment was not accepted due to a procedural technicality.

10. A government survey revealed variations in weekly costs for residential care that ranged from £143 to £217 per week (in Lancashire and Strathclyde respectively), or some 50 per cent, and evidence to the Social Security Committee (1991) showed large variations even within regions. Yet the government's view was that there was 'no pattern or basis which left us with the view that there was a secure basis for coming forward with a regional or local scheme' (Tony Newton, social security minister, in Social Security Committee, 1991, Evidence, Q262). This was strongly criticised; for example the National Association of Citizens' Advice Bureaux (1991) berated the government for adhering to 'this very crude national assessment' of maximum charges that would be met by social security.

11. This was the subject of a television documentary shown nationally in January 1992.

12. Social Security Committee, 1991, Evidence, Q89.

13. M. Henwood and G. Wistow, evidence to Social Security Committee, 1991.

14. *Community Care*, 2 September 1993, pp. 16–17, 'Who foots the bill?'

15. 'Care ruling could cost NHS dear', *Guardian*, 3 February 1994, p. 8. The man had been placed in a nursing home and although he continued to receive income support covering part of the fees, the shortfall on fees was some £6000 per annum.

16. 'Crumbling of care', *Guardian*, 4 February 1994, p. 19. This editorial commented that, in a survey carried out in 1990, 77 per cent of health authorities had reduced continuing care beds, and most authorities had not replaced them with contractual beds in the private sector. This ran counter to procedural guidelines issued by the DoH in 1989, which stated that patients should not be transferred to private nursing homes if it meant that they or their families would have to pay.

17. *Guardian*, 6 July 1993.

18. DoH evidence to Health Committee, 1993c, p. 37.

19. *Community Care*, 1 April 1993, p. 1.

20. HC Deb., v. 218, c. 1150, 11 February 1993.

21. *Community Care*, 5 August 1993.

Chapter 6

1. The Conservatives' policies towards the labour market since 1979 are reviewed by Deakin (1992) and Michie and Wilkinson (1992), while Rubery (1989) discusses labour market 'flexibility' in Britain.

2. Under the pay review body system, recommendations are made by the review bodies as to the appropriate level of salary increases for particular staff groups. The system is intended to limit the risk of industrial action in the NHS by reducing confrontation in wage negotiations.

3. Government response to Social Services Committee, Cm. 405, 1989.

4. Due to a reduction in the working week of nurses in 1981 (from 40 to 37.5 hours) the whole-time equivalent figures for nursing staff are inflated in comparison with years prior to 1981.

5. 'Health chiefs overshoot jobs cut by 10 000', *Guardian*, 9 May 1986, p. 3.

6. Speech to the Conservative Party conference, quoted in the *Guardian*, 14 October 1983, 'Fowler line on cuts quells party unrest'.

7. From 1987 the government began to publish, in the annual public expenditure white papers, figures indicating the distinction between what were regarded as 'frontline' staff (nurses and midwives; professional and technical [excluding 'works'] staff; and medical and dental [including locums] personnel) and 'other' or support staff (works/maintenance, administrative and clerical, ancillary, and ambulance). The respective proportions of frontline and other staff changed from 59 and 41 per cent in 1979, to 66.9 and 31.9 per cent in 1990, excluding general managers (1.2 per cent; given their symbolic importance, however, and their salaries, these should probably be included in the core staff, raising the proportion to 68.1 per cent). However this change is partly artifactual; many of those formerly employed by the NHS are now employed by private contractors, while the figures for nurses are inflated by the reduction in the working week in 1981.

8. Public Accounts Committee, 1990, Evidence, Q667–8.

9. The data that follow are drawn from the Census of Employment, standard industrial classification, activity 9510 (Hospitals, nursing homes and so on). However, since the NHS remains the dominant provider of health care, it can reasonably be assumed that the data broadly reflect developments within the service.

10. *Employment Gazette*, vol. 101 no. 5, (May 1993), p. 213; vol. 101, no. 4, (April 1993).

11. *Employment Gazette*, vol. 91 no. 12, (December 1993), Occasional Supplement, p. 10. The 1991 statistics may underestimate the proportions of health care workers classed as part-time. This is because many NHS ancillary workers whose jobs were transferred to contractors from 1983 will no longer be categorised as being employed in the health sector, even though they will continue to work in NHS establishments, and contractors have made savings largely by reducing the number of full-time employees.

12. Norman Fowler suggested in 1984 that no consultant could expect to practice as if resources were limitless (HC Deb., 4 May 1984, v. 59, c. 649). The Social Services Committee (1988c, HC-613) made the same point.

13. 'Clinical freedom is dead . . . if we do not have the resources to do what is technically possible, then medical care must be limited to that of proven effectiveness . . . clinical freedom should have been strangled long ago . . . [it] was a myth that prevented advance': J. Hampton (1983) 'The end of clinical freedom', *BMJ*, vol. 287, (29 October 1983), pp. 1237–8. A few weeks earlier a *BMJ* editorial had claimed that the 1983 cuts in NHS resources heralded the end of clinical freedom (vol. 287 [17 September], p. 780).

14. BMA, *Annual Report of Council*, 1983–4, p. 13 (included as an appendix to *BMJ*, vol. 288). Previously the BMA had expressed concern about the concept of an 'executive manager . . . taking decisions in conflict with professional advice' (*BMJ*, vol. 288 (14 January 1984), p. 165). Community physicians were seen as likely to be marginalised in the new structure, and the chair of the BMA's Central Committee for Community

Medicine and Community Health commented that 'if the general manager has no power to control medical activities he [sic] is almost certainly unnecessary. If he does, he represents an extremely serious threat to the independence of British medicine' (letter to the *BMJ*, vol. 287, p. 1473).

15. 'Administrator-dominated or management-efficient NHS?' *BMJ*, vol. 289 (17 November 1984), p. 1331; 'Not what the doctor ordered', *BMJ*, vol. 291 (28 September 1985), pp. 843-4.
16. One advertisement ran: Q: 'What do you call a man who refuses to listen to medical advice?' A: 'Mr Clarke' ('Healthy' was Clarke's own riposte!)
17. See Chapter 3, note 25.
18. *BMJ*, vol. 300 (28 April 1990), p. 1097. This was evident in other policy areas, notably in education, where the powers of professional organisations were reduced by changes affecting the composition of school governing bodies. The government deployed similar logic in first of all reducing and subsequently abolishing the rights of local authorities to nominate members to health authorities – Chapter 9.
19. One *BMJ* editorial suggested that the government aims 'to deride any professional complaints; in the case of the NHS, we are told, these come from Luddites, [from] a BMA that is out of touch with its members, and that has opposed any projected change in the NHS in the last 40 years': 'Steaming through the NHS', editorial comment, *BMJ*, vol. 298, pp. 619–20.
20. *BMJ*, vol. 300 (30 June 1990), p. 1727.
21. Speech to Tory Reform Group, reported in *BMJ*, vol. 298, p. 160 – emphasis added.
22. Quoted in BMJ, vol. 298 (11 March 1989), p. 704.
23. S. Lock, 'Steaming through the NHS', *BMJ* editorial, op. cit.
24. Interview in the *Independent*, quoted in *BMJ*, vol. 299 (5 August 1989), p. 348 – emphasis added. However the (anonymous) *BMJ* correspondent questioned whether the strategy of splitting the profession in this way would really work, suggesting that the divisions between the London-based specialists, exploited skilfully by Bevan, had been largely filled in, that 75 per cent of the profession were members of the BMA, and that the NHS was no longer an untried social experiment but a cherished national institution.
25. D. Taylor, 'The destruction of a welfare system', letter to the *BMJ*, vol. 299, p. 1304. Revelations about the surpluses being made by such practices, and the lack of information concerning the basis on which their budgets had been calculated, contributed to suspicions about favourable treatment for fundholders.
26. In fact the number of administrative staff grew every year following the 1974 reorganisation of the NHS, apart from 1981–2, if general managers are included. HC Deb, v. 221, c. 755w, March 1993.
27. During 1992 Duncan Nicholl, NHS chief executive, was reported to have voiced his concern about the 'macho management' culture that was infiltrating the NHS. *BMJ*, vol. 304, pp. 1586, 1588.
28. HC Deb., v. 25, c. 419, 10 June 1982.
29. Gwynneth Dunwoody, HC Deb., v. 25, c. 419, 10 June 1982 – emphasis added.
30. Quoted by Roger Poole, COHSE, Social Services Committee, 1989, Evidence, Q327.

31. Ibid.
32. Ibid., Evidence, Q. 414–422.
33. On the one hand agency staff expenditure partly reflects recruitment difficulties and problems experienced in certain specialties. However it can be advantageous for health authorities. Paying overtime is more expensive than employing agency staff at standard rates; although a commission is payable to the agency, it is not as expensive as paying overtime.
34. HPSS Statistics, 1993, table 7.9.
35. *Guardian*, 8 June 1986.
36. HC Deb., v. 142, c. 108, 22 November 1988.
37. Evidence to Social Services Committee, 1989, Q414 – emphasis added.
38. Review Body for Nurses, Midwives and Professions Allied to Medicine, 5th Report, para. 129.
39. Ibid., 6th Report, para. 117.
40. Ibid., 9th Report, para. 17 – 8.
41. Caines deplored the government's continued use of the Review Body system, which he viewed as an impediment to the development of a system of performance-related pay (*Guardian*, March 1994).
42. Nurses' Pay Review Body, 2nd Report, 1985, para. 57 – emphasis added.
43. *HSJ,* 19 November 1992, 25 March 1993, 5 August 1993.
44. Evidence to Social Services Committee, 1989, p. xxv.
45. As this book went to press (May 1994) there was evidence of disputes between some government ministers; John Redwood, secretary of state for Wales, had ordered an across-the-board reduction in management costs in the NHS in Wales, but some of his colleagues regarded this as a somewhat naive approach to the problem.

Chapter 7

1. See Health Services Board, Annual Reports (1978–1980) for details of the Board's activities. Over 1000 paybed authorisations were revoked between 1977 and 1980.
2. See BUPA Annual Reports, *passim*, for examples.
3. HC Deb., v. 976, c. 660, 19 December 1979.
4. It may be that the government expected the private sector to take up the slack with which the NHS was unable to deal in the low-growth years of the mid-1980s. Certainly some ministers – for example Gerald Vaughan, the Conservatives' first minister for health – expected substantial growth in the insured population: Vaughan expected that private insurance would eventually cover some 25 per cent of the population. If this had happened, some of the difficulties reported by backbench Conservatives in the mid-1980s might never have become political issues.
5. The figures are not strictly comparable as the 1977 data only include the principal provident associations whereas the 1991 figures include various other commercial operators. However the number insured by organisations other than the three main provident associations in 1977 was small.
6. It would be possible to estimate more recent figures by applying the GHS rates for specific socio-economic groups (SEGs) to census figures for the

distribution of these SEGs. However this would presume that the rates in the SEGs were constant nationally, which was not the case according to the OPCS (1984).

7. 'French group in AMI control bid', *Daily Telegraph*, 8 March 1990, p. 24.

8. 'AMI Healthcare likely to be sold after bid for parent', *The Times*, 11 July 1989, p. 24; 'BUPA to buy HCA's UK hospitals', *Financial Times*, 23 June 1989, p. 6.

9. 'The private sector has to make its case much more effectively', *Independent Medical Care*, vol. 3, no. 1, p. 2–4.

10. See *Independent Medical Care*, 'Choice, care or commercialisation?', vol. 5, no. 2, pp. 12, 14, 23.

11. *Guardian*, 15 February 1984.

12. There were several inquiries during the 1980s into the apparent failure of the NHS to recover the full cost of private treatment. See, for example, Public Accounts Committee (1985, vi–ix), which suggested that the NHS did not cost paybeds adequately, to some extent bearing out the criticisms voiced by the private sector's representatives.

13. *Financial Times*, 22 January 1986.

14. R. Cook, HC Deb., v. 146, c. 171, 31 January 1989.

15. HC Deb., v. 156, c. 1004–1030, 12 July 1989.

16. Some 350 000 people currently receive this tax relief, costing the Exchequer an estimated £85 mn. (1994–5) – HC Deb., v. 234, c. 16w, 6 December 1993.

17. Approximately 60 per cent of first-wave NHS Trusts were believed to have separate facilities for private patients, while the number of dedicated paybed units in NHS hospitals was estimated to have risen from 25 to around 50 in the first two years after the reforms – *HSJ*, vol. 103, no. 5347, (8 April 1993), p. 12; vol. 103 no. 5350, (29 April 1993), p. 5. Health insurance companies have responded by launching new products, with reduced premiums, targeted at the NHS paybed market.

18. HC Deb., v. 236, c. 531-2w, 31 January 1994 (figures at current prices).

19. 'GPs facing cash cuts for serving middle classes', *Guardian*, 26 November 1993, p. 3.

20. In fact this may be nothing new: in 1984 one regional treasurer was reported as saying that the NHS 'is rubbing its hands with glee at being able to take advantage of the overprovision of private beds at knockdown prices' as a consequence of overcapacity in the commercial sector (*HSJ*, 5 July 1984).

21. *HSJ*, vol. 103, no. 5340 (18 February 1993), p. 17; vol. 103, no. 5345 (25 March 1993), p. 20.

Chapter 8

1. Much information in this chapter is drawn from a detailed reading of the *Health Service Journal (HSJ)* which is a valuable source of reports about innovation in the NHS, though inevitably some innovations will not be recorded, so it may not be a comprehensive source.

2. For example, all new equipment in the Royal Manchester Children's Hospital had been provided by charitable sources for a whole year, prompting the Chair of the health authority to remark that 'renewing

equipment is the function of the NHS' – *HSJ*, 2 November 1989, p. 1327. Also the Worthing Waiting List Trust was established to raise funds to reduce waiting lists in the DHA – see *HSJ*, vol. 100 no. 5198 (26 April 1990), p. 623 (though it failed to raise more than a few thousand pounds – *HSJ*, vol. 101 no. 5240 [28 February 1991]), p. 5; and 'Healthaid' was established by the Barking, Brentwood and Havering DHA to concentrate all charitable income into a consolidated fund to be used for the DHA as a whole.

3. For example, within months of the 1979 election Patrick Jenkin spoke of the possibility of transferring hospitals to voluntary organisations at 'peppercorn rents' (HC Deb., v. 970, c. 1798, 18 July 1979). Subsequently Rhodes Boyson argued that denationalising hospitals and transferring them to the control of community-based organisations would enable them to raise 'vast amounts of money' (HC Deb., v. 125, c. 872, 19 January 1988).

4. *Guardian*, 15 March 1983, 22 March 1984; Tadworth Court Trust *Annual Report*, 1986–7

5. 'Pots of money at the end of the rainbow', *HSJ*, 19 July 1990, p. 1064 – emphasis added.

6. Ibid.

7. 'From pride and joy to £140M white elephant', *Guardian*, 11 February 1994, p. 2; a subsequent report (*Guardian*, 26 March 1994, p. 1) suggested that prominent donors had asked that their money be returned.

8. *The Sunday Times*, 9 October 1983; *HSJ*, 9 January 1989, pp. 20–21; 'Ambulance staff replaced by volunteers', *HSJ*, 18 October 1990, p.1537; 'Local hospital dream turns into nightmare', *Guardian*, 5 February 1994, p. 9. Other innovations reported included the use of volunteers to care for the elderly both in hospital, to ease shortages of nurses (*HSJ*, vol. 97, no. 5045, p. 406) and in the community (*HSJ*, vol. 99 no. 5163) pp. 972–3.

9. Milne and McGee (1992) consider the impact of severance payments and conclude that, nevertheless, competitive tendering has still produced substantial savings. However they neglected additional social security costs and loss of income to the Exchequer from reduced national insurance contributions (following from the greater use of part-time staff by contractors and, indeed, successful in-house tenders). See also Milne (1990).

10. Edwina Currie, HC Deb., v. 139, c. 849, 1 November 1988.

11. HC Deb., v. 139, c. 854, 1 November 1988.

12. Quoted by Robin Cook MP, HC Deb., v. 124, c. 48, 7 December 1987.

13. 'Whatever happened to income generation?' *HSJ*, vol. 99, no. 5204, 7 December 1989.

14. *HSJ*, 3 June 1983.

15. During 1990, for example, the *HSJ* reported various developments: see vol. 100 no. 5191 (8 March 1990), p. 347; vol. 100 no. 5204 (14 June 1990), p. 867; vol. 100 no. 5209 (12 July 1990), p. 1019; vol. 100 no. 5212 (2 August 1990). Prominent in this was the private hospital group, AMI, which was attempting to diversify from private acute hospitals (see Chapter 7).

16. Various references in the *HSJ* (1989 and 1990, passim) to such schemes included developments, or potential developments, with the following

health authorities: Bromley, Coventry, Crewe, Eastbourne, East Suffolk, Hillingdon, Gwynedd, Oxford and King's Lynn.

17. *HSJ*, vol. 99 no. 5133, (12 January 1989), p. 58.
18. *HSJ*, vol. 99, no. 5162, 3 August 1989, 'Brighton homes transfer criticised in Commons', p. 937.
19. *HSJ*, vol. 100, no. 5195, 5 April 1990, 'Green light for nursing homes', p. 498; *HSJ* vol. 100, no. 5201, 17 May 1990, 'Slow progress but lots of prospects', p. 727.
20. *HSJ*, vol. 100, no. 5192, 15 March 1990; 'RHAs poised to switch services to the private sector', *HSJ* vol. 100, no. 5197, 19 April 1990, p. 1497.
21. *HSJ*, vol. 100, no. 5200, 10 May 1990, 'Lab staff form company for private work', p. 687; 'IBH bring in cash for 3 health authorities', *HSJ*, vol. 100, no. 5209, 12 July 1990, p. 1089; vol. 100, no. 5219, 'Flood of pathology labs market services', *HSJ*, 20 September 1990, p. 1374.
22. 'Selling out to enterprise', *HSJ*, vol. 99, no. 5158, 6 July 1989, p. 809.
23. HC Deb., v.146, c. 169, 31 January 1989.
24. HC Deb., v. 217, c. 951, 26 January 1993. The MP was David Willetts, who had, when working at the Centre for Policy Studies, been an advisor on various welfare state reforms introduced by the Conservatives.
25. For example, it was suggested that Guy's Hospital might lose funding for the third phase of a redevelopment programme if it did not submit an application for self-governing status ('Stitch-up undone', *Guardian*, 17 May 1989, p. 25).
26. 'Secret plan to ease in hospital opt-outs', *Guardian*, 17 April 1990, p. 4.
27. 'Minister gambles on opt-out deals', *Guardian*, 5 December 1990, p. 3.
28. Ibid.; see also 'Ignored warnings that backfired', *Guardian*, 30 April 1991, p. 2.
29. 'Limits set on borrowing by opt-out NHS trusts', *Guardian*, 30 January 1991, p. 6.
30. As was pointed out by Alan Milburn, MP: HC Deb., v. 235, c. 1119, 20 January 1994.
31. *Guardian*, 26 October 1993.
32. 'Waldegrave backs plans of queue-jump hospital', *Guardian*, 27 March 1991, p. 4.
33. HC Deb., v. 236, c. 531–2w, 31 January 1994.
34. In the context of community care, for example, the government's refusal to ring-fence funds for drug and alcohol-related services was criticised as it would lead to precisely this situation, potentially threatening the viability of services covering several health authorities – see chapters 5 and 9.
35. Figures on fundholders' budgets by RHA showed that, even at the RHA level, per capita expenditure by fundholding GPs varied by around 35 per cent. In 1992–3 expenditure per patient registered with fundholding practices ranged from £100 in NE Thames to £134 in the Northern RHA (HC Deb., v. 218, c. 472–3w 8 February 1993).
36. 'Ministers retreat in NHS row', *Guardian*, 10 May 1991, p. 1 – emphasis added.
37. *BMJ*, vol. 302 (18 May 1991), p. 1172; vol. 302 (22 June 1991), p. 1486.
38. Between RHAs the proportion of patients covered by fundholding practices varied between 13.7 per cent (NE Thames) and 34.8 per cent

(Mersey); Yorkshire, Trent and Oxford RHAs also had over 30 per cent covered by fundholders. HPSS Statistics, 1993, table 6.17.

39. 'Fundholders patients are treated quicker, says BMA', *BMJ*, vol. 308, 1 January 1994.

40. Many initial proposals for NHS trust status came from communities concerned at the potential loss of cherished local institutions, often before alternative services had been provided, although the government refused to allow self-government to remain an option for facilities that health authorities had determined did not feature in their plans.

41. The impact of land sales on the NHS capital programme has not been considered here for reasons of space. However it is notable that during the 1980s the proportion of the NHS capital programme financed through land sales reached a peak of 24 per cent in 1989-90, having risen from less than 3 per cent in 1981–2 (Health Committee, 1991a, table 11.3). While it may be rational to dispose of genuinely surplus assets, for a capital programme to depend on the sale of such assets seems risky, to say the least. As property prices collapsed in the South East in the early 1990s, RHAs there were left with capital commitments they could not fulfil, and had to postpone some much needed schemes (NAO, 1991b) while concentrating their efforts on a few major projects.

Chapter 9

1. Patrick Jenkin, HC Deb., v. 991, c. 67, 27 October 1980.
2. C. Ham, 'Search for a vision', *Guardian*, 19.1.94, p. 17.
3. One could draw a parallel with the establishment of several government departments (or units thereof) as 'next steps' agencies, in which ministers were accountable to parliament only for the results of these organisations' activities, not for the ways in which they went about their business. Clearly such an approach had attractions for those Conservatives who believed that, in contrast with the time-honoured cliche, ministers should *not* have to be aware of every bedpan dropped in every hospital in the NHS.
4. Stan Orme, HC Deb., v. 991, c. 92, 27 October 1980.
5. HC Deb., v. 163, c. 507, 7 December 1989 – emphasis added.
6. *Independent*, 5 July 1993, p.7.
7. A succession of parliamentary questions during the summer of 1993 made public the available information about the background of appointees to NHS trusts and health authorities, while later figures showed that 60 per cent of all chairs of trusts in England, and 50 per cent of non-executive members, had a business or financial background, while only 4 per cent and 6 per cent respectively had any NHS background (HC Deb., v. 235, c. 1031, 20 January 1994).
8. See HC Deb., v. 224, c. 604–621, 10 May 1993, for opposition criticisms of this process. Note also the speech by Jack Straw, shadow environment spokesperson, to the Audit Commission on 5 March 1993, in which he criticised the much greater rewards available for health authority and trust chairs compared with those offered to council leaders, saying that 'what

offends against democracy is to offer greater incentives . . . to be selected
to serve the unelected state . . . than to be elected to serve the local
community'.

9. R. Cook, HC Deb., v.163, c. 519, 7 December 1989 – emphasis added.
10. 'Cuts may close hospital wards', *Guardian*, 20 September 1983.
11. Brent refused to implement 'horrendous' service reductions in order to lose
100 jobs, and cut spending by £250 000. 'Brent's resistance may crumble',
Guardian 11 October 1983; 'Stockport joins health cuts revolt', *Guardian*,
12 October 1983. The DHAs involved included Northumberland,
Stockport, Sheffield, West Lambeth and Islington, while the Richmond,
Twickenham and Roehampton DHA and the Wandsworth DHA both
deferred decisions on implementing the required reductions.
12. 'Rebel health authority defies cuts threat', *Guardian*, 18 October 1983.
13. 'Brent health rebels receive sacking threat', *Guardian*, 22 October 1983.
14. As of December 1984 – HC Deb., v. 70, c. 686–94.
15. *Guardian*, 23 March 1984.
16. *Guardian*, 9 September 1983.
17. Quoted in the *Newcastle Journal*, 4 May 1984, p. 1.
18. This is documented by the regular bulletins of London Health Emergency;
see also London Health Emergency (1987b), and PSPRU, 1992.
19. Social Services Committee, 1990f, p. ix.
20. HC Deb., v. 175, c. 404, 27 June 1990.
21. HC Deb., v. 220, c. 401–4, 3 March 1993.
22. Alan Milburn, HC Deb., v. 220, c. 416, 3 March 1993.
23. Social Services Committee, 1990c, p. xvii.
24. K. Clarke, HC Deb., v. 163, c. 512, 7 December 1989.
25. Evidence to the Health Committee, 1991c, Q158.
26. Ibid., Q167.
27. *HSJ*, vol. 102, no. 5392 (27 August 1992).
28. *HSJ*, vol. 102, no. 5287 (30 January 1992) p. 3.
29. 'Bottomley signals fresh NHS changes', *Guardian*, 27 June 1992, p. 4.

Chapter 10

1. D. C. Taylor, 'The destruction of a welfare service', letter to the *BMJ*,
vol. 299, p. 1304.
2. Patrick Jenkin, HC Deb., v. 991, c. 83, 27 October 1980.
3. There are numerous examples of health authorities reviewing their
priorities and deciding they will no longer purchase certain forms of
treatment. For example, the NE Thames RHA, in the months leading up
to the reforms, indicated it would no longer provide types of surgery that it
deemed of little value or of only cosmetic benefit. On the second point,
during early 1994 an elderly man was refused physiotherapy by a DHA on
the grounds that he was over 65, raising the spectre of rationing by age. On
the latter point, during 1993 a consultant refused to perform bypass
surgery on a middle-aged man who smoked – the patient subsequently
died.

4. As this book went to press there were reports that the government was to establish a committee to examine health inequalities as part of the monitoring of the targets included in the *Health of the Nation* (' "Health link to poverty" U-turn by Bottomley', *Guardian*, 4 May 1994, p. 8).

Bibliography

Abel-Smith, B (1964) *The Hospitals 1800–1948* (London: Heinemann).

Adam Smith Institute (1981) *Health and the Public Sector* (London: Adam Smith Institute).

Adam Smith Institute (1984) *The Omega Health Papers* (London: Adam Smith Institute).

Alford, R. (1975) *Health Care Politics: ideological and interest group barriers to reform* (New York: Basic Books).

Allen, J. (1988a) 'The geographies of service' in D. Massey and J. Allen (eds), *Uneven Re-development: cities and regions in transition* (London: Hodder & Stoughton), pp. 124–41.

Allen, J. (1988b) 'Service industries: uneven development and uneven knowledge', *Area*, vol. 20 no. 1, pp. 15–22.

Andrews, K. (1984) 'Private rest homes in the care of the elderly', *British Medical Journal* vol. 288, pp. 1518–20.

Ascher, K. (1987) *The Politics of Privatisation: contracting-out public services* (London: Macmillan).

Association of Community Health Councils for England and Wales (ACHCEW) (1987) *Mid Year Budget Cuts: Health Authorities in Crisis* (London: ACHCEW).

Association of Independent Hospitals (1988) *Survey of Independent Hospitals in the Acute Sector* (London: AIH).

Atkinson, J. and D. Gregory (1986) 'A flexible future: Britain's dual labour market' *Marxism Today*, April.

Atkinson, J. and N. Meager (1986) *New Forms of Work Organisation*, IMS report no. 121 (Brighton: Institute of Manpower Studies).

Audit Commission (1986) *Making a Reality of Community Care* (London: HMSO).

Audit Commission (1988) *Community Care: managing the cascade of change* (London: HMSO).

Bartlett, W. and J. Le Grand (eds) (1993) *Quasi-Markets and Social Policy* (London: Macmillan).

Bartley, M. (1992) *Authorities and Partisans: the debate on unemployment and health* (Edinburgh: Edinburgh University Press).

Baumol, W. (1967) 'Macro-economics of unbalanced growth: the anatomy of urban crisis', *American Economic Review*, vol. VII, pp. 415–26.

Beattie, A. (1991) 'Knowledge and control in health promotion: a test case for social policy and social theory', in J. Gabe, M. Calnan and M. Bury (eds), *The Sociology of the Health Service* (London: Routledge).

Beech, R., G. Bevan and N. Mays (1990) 'Spatial equity in the NHS: the death and re-birth of RAWP' in A. Harrison (ed.) *Health Care UK 1990* (London: Policy Journals).

Beech, R., S. Challah and R. H. Ingram (1987) 'Impact of cuts in acute beds on services for patients', *British Medical Journal*, vol. 294, no. 6573, pp. 685–8.

Bennett, R. J. (1989) 'Whither modelling and geography in a post-welfarist world?' in B. Macmillan (ed.) *Remodelling Geography* (Oxford: Blackwell).

Bennett, R. J. and G. Krebs (1991) *Local Economic Development: public-private partnership initiatives in Britain and Germany* (London: Belhaven Press).

Berliner, H. (1987) ' 'Bye state planning – hello what?', *Health Services Journal*, vol. 97 no. 5032, p. 38.

Berliner, H. and C. Regan (1987) 'Multinational operations of US for-profit hospital chains: trends and implications', *American Journal of Public Health*, vol. 77, pp.1280–4.

Bevan, A. (1952) *In Place of Fear* (London: Heinemann).

Bevan, G., R. Beech, and M. Craig (1985) 'Alternatives to RAWP', *Health and Social Services Journal*, vol. 95 no. 4964, pp. 1098–9.

Bevan, G. and J. Brazier (1985) 'Subregional RAWP – Hobson's choice?', *Health and Social Services Journal*, vol. 95 no. 4963, pp. 1064–5.

Birch, S. and A. Maynard (1986) 'Health and personal social services', in P. Cockle (ed.), *Public Expenditure Policy 1985–6* (London: Macmillan).

Birmingham Consultants for the Rescue of the NHS (BCRNHS) (1987) *Difficulty Admitting Acutely Ill Patients to Hospital* (Birmingham: BCRNHS).

Bloor, K. and A. Maynard (1993) *Expenditure on the NHS during and after the Thatcher years* (York: Centre for Health Economics).

Bosanquet, N. (1983) *After the New Right* (London: Heinemann).

Bosanquet, N. (1985) *Public Expenditure on the NHS: recent trends and the outlook* (London: Institute of Health Services Management).

Bow Group (1983) *Beveridge and the Bow Group Generation* (London: Bow Group).

Bradford, M. and F. Burdett. (1989) 'Privatization, education and the north–south divide', in J. R. Lewis and A. R. Townsend (eds), *The North–South Divide* (London: Paul Chapman).

Brazier, J. (1987) 'Accounting for cross-boundary flows', *British Medical Journal*, vol.295, pp. 898–900.

Breheny, M. and P. Congdon (eds) (1989) *Growth and Change in a Core Region* (London: Pion).

Brotherton, P. and C. Miller (1989) *Dismantling the NHS? Income generation schemes in City and Hackney DHA* (London: Greater London Association of CHCs).

Buchan, J. (1989) *Grade Expectations: clinical grading and nurse mobility*, IMS Report 176 (Brighton: Institute of Manpower Studies).

Buchan, J. (1992) *Flexibility or Fragmentation? Trends in nurses pay* (London: Kings Fund Institute).

Bulmer, M. (1987) *The Social Basis of Community Care* (London: Allen and Unwin).

Busfield, J. (1990) 'Social divisions in consumption: the case of medical care' *Sociology*, vol. 24, no. 1, pp. 77–96.

Butler, E. and M. Pirie (1988) *Health Management Units: the question of an internal market within the NHS* (London: Adam Smith Institute).

Butts, M., D. Irving and C. Whitt (1980) *From Principles to Practice* (London: Nuffield Provincial Hospitals Trust).

Buxton, M. J. and R. Klein (1978) *Allocating Health Resources: a commentary* on the Report of the Resource Allocation Working Party Research Paper no. 3, Royal Commission on the National Health Service (London: HMSO).

Calnan, M., S. Cant and J. Gabe (1993) *Going Private: why people pay for their health care* (Buckingham: Open University Press).

Carpenter, M. (1977) 'The new managerialism and professionalism in nursing', in M. Stacey, M. Reid, R. Dingwall and C. Heath (eds), *Health and the Division of Labour* (London: Croom Helm).

Carr-Hill, R. (1987) 'The inequalities in health debate: a critical review of the issues' *Journal of Social Policy*, vol. 16, pp. 509–42.

Carr-Hill, R. (1990) 'RAWP is dead – long live RAWP' in A. Culyer, A. Maynard, and J. Poskett (eds), *Competition in Health Care: reforming the NHS* (London: Macmillan).

Castle, B. (1980) *The Castle Diaries, 1974–76* (London: Weidenfeld and Nicolson).

Cawson, A. (1982) *Corporatism and Welfare* (London: Heinemann).

Central Committee for Hospital Medical Services (CCHMS) (1988) *NHS Funding: The Crisis in the Acute Hospital Sector* (London: BMA).

Chapman, T., S. Goodwin and R. Hennelly (1991) 'A new deal for the mentally ill? Progress or propaganda?', *Critical Social Policy*. vol. 11, no. 2, pp. 5–20.

Clay, T. (1987) *Nurses: Power and Politics* (London: Heinemann).

Cochrane, A. (1992) 'Is there a future for local government?' *Critical Social Policy*, vol. 35, pp. 4–19.

Cochrane, A. (1993) *Whatever Happened to Local Government?* (Milton Keynes: Open University Press).

Coles, J. (1988) 'Clinical budgeting as a management tool', in R. Maxwell (ed.) *Reshaping the NHS* (London: Policy Journals).

Conroy, M. and M. Stidston (1988) *The Black Hole* (London: SW Thames RHA).

Cooke, P. (ed.) (1989) *Localities: The changing face of urban Britain* (London: Unwin Hyman).

Cousins, C. (1987) *Controlling Social Welfare: A sociology of state welfare work and organisations* (Brighton: Wheatsheaf).

Cousins, C. (1988) 'The restructuring of welfare work: the introduction of general management and the contracting-out of ancillary services', *Work, Employment and Society*, vol. 2, pp. 210–28.

Cox, B. D., M. Blaxter, A. Buckle *et al.* (1987) *Health and Lifestyle Survey* (London: Health Promotion Research Trust).

Cox, D. (1991) 'Health service management – a sociological view: Griffiths and the non-negotiated order of the hospital', in J. Gabe, J. Calnan and M. Bury (eds), *The Sociology of the Health Service* (London: Routledge).

Coyle, A. (1985) 'Going private: The implications of privatization for women's work', *Feminist Review*, vol. 21, pp. 5–23.

Coyle, A. (1986) *Dirty Business: women's work and trade union organisation in contract cleaning* (Birmingham: West Midlands Low Pay Unit)

Crossman, R.M. (1972) *A Politician's View of Health Service Planning* (Glasgow: University of Glasgow Press).

Crouch, C. (1985) 'Can socialism achieve street credibility?' *Guardian* 14 February 1985, p. 9.

Dalley, G. (1988) *Ideologies of Caring: rethinking community and collectivism* (London: Macmillan).

Davey-Smith, G., M. Bartley and D. Blane (1990) 'The Black report and socioeconomic inequalities in health, 10 years on', *British Medical Journal*, vol. 301, pp. 373–7.

Davey-Smith, G. and M. Egger (1993) 'Socio-economic differentials in wealth and health', *British Medical Journal*, vol. 307, pp. 1085–6.

Davidson, N. (1987) *A Question of Care: The changing face of the National Health Service* (London: Michael Joseph).

Davies, C. (1987) 'Things to come: the NHS in the next decade', *Sociology of Health and Illness* 9, pp. 302–17.

Day, P. and R. Klein (1985) 'Central accountability and local decision-making: towards a new NHS', *British Medical Journal*, vol. 290, pp. 1676–8.

Day, P. and R. Klein (1987) 'The business of welfare', *New Society*, vol. 80, no. 1277, pp. 11–13.

Day, P. and R. Klein (1989) 'The politics of modernisation: Britain's NHS in the 1980s', *The Milbank Quarterly*, vol. 67, no. 1, pp. 1–37.

Day, P. and R. Klein (1991) 'Variations in budgets of fundholding practices', *British Medical Journal*, vol. 303, pp. 168–70.

DE (Department of Employment) (1986) *Building Businesses – not Barriers*, Cmnd. 9794 (London: HMSO).

Deakin, N. (1987) *The Politics of Welfare* (London: Methuen).

Deakin, S. (1992) 'Labour law and industrial relations,' in J. Michie (ed.) *The Economic Legacy, 1979–92* (London: Academic Press).

Dear, M. J. and S. M. Taylor (1982) *Not On Our Street* (London: Pion).

DHSS (1976) *Sharing Resources for Health in England* (London: DHSS).

DHSS (1977a) *Priorities for the Health and Personal Social Services* (London: DHSS).

DHSS (1977b) *Prevention and health: Everybody's Business* Cmnd. 7047 (London: HMSO).

DHSS (1979a) *Patients First: the reorganisation of the NHS* (London: DHSS).

DHSS (1979b) *Contracts of Hospital Consultants and Senior Medical Staff* (London: DHSS).

DHSS (1979c) *If Industrial Relations Break Down*, Circular HC (79) 20 (London: DHSS).

DHSS (1980a) *Inequalities in Health: report of a Research Working Group* (London: DHSS).

DHSS (1980b) *Health Services Act, 1980: private medical practice in NHS hospitals and control of private hospital developments*, Circular HC (80) 10 (London: DHSS).

DHSS (1980c) *Health Services Act, 1980: fund raising by NHS Authorities* Circular HC(80)11 (London: DHSS).

DHSS (1981a) *Care in Action* (London: DHSS).

DHSS (1981b) *Care in the Community: a consultative document on moving resources for care in England* (London: DHSS).

DHSS (1981c) *Growing Older*, Cmnd. 8173 (London: HMSO).

DHSS (1981d) *Contractual Arrangements with Independent Hospitals and Nursing Homes* (London: DHSS).

DHSS (1983a) *NHS Management Inquiry Report* (The Griffiths Report) (London: DHSS).

DHSS (1983b) *Underused and Surplus Property in the National Health Service: report of an inquiry chaired by Ceri Davies* (London: HMSO).

DHSS (1983c) *Competitive Tendering in the Provision of Domestic, Catering and Laundry Services* Circular HC(83)18 (London: DHSS).

DHSS (1984) *Health Services Development: resource distribution for 1984–5, services priorities, manpower and planning*, Circular HC (84)2 (London: DHSS).

DHSS (1988) *Review of the RAWP Formula: a report by the NHS Management Board* (London: DHSS).

Dixon, J. and H. Welch (1991) 'Priority setting: lessons from Oregon', *Lancet*, vol. 337, (13 April), pp. 891–4.

DoE (1980) *Development Control: policy and practice*, circular 22/80 (London: DoE).

DoH (annual) *Health and Personal Social Services Statistics for England* (London: HMSO).

DoH (Department of Health) (1989a) *Self-Governing Hospitals* (Working for Patients Working Paper 1) (London: HMSO).

DoH (1989b) *Practice budgets for general medical practitioners* (Working for Patients Working Paper 3) (London: HMSO).

DoH/OPCS (1992) *Departmental Report*, Cm. 1913 (London: HMSO).

DoH/OPCS (1993) *Departmental Report*, Cm. 2212 (London: HMSO).

Donnison, D. (1985) 'The progressive potential of privatisation' in J. Le Grand and R. Robinson (eds), *Privatisation and the Welfare State* (London: Allen and Unwin).

Donnison, D. (1991) *A Radical Agenda* (London: Rivers Oram).

Doyal, L. (1979) *The Political Economy of Health* (London: Pluto).

Doyle, N. and T. Harding (1992), 'Community care: applying procedural fairness' in A. Coote (ed.) *The Welfare of Citizens: developing new social rights* (London: Rivers Oram).

Duncan, S. S. (1991) 'The geography of gender divisions in Britain', *Transactions, Institute of British Geographers*, vol. 16 no. 4, pp. 420–39.

Duncan, S. S. and M. Goodwin (1988) *The Local State and Uneven Development* (Cambridge: Polity).

Duncan, S. S., S. Halford and M. Goodwin (1993) 'Regulation theory, the local state and the transition of urban politics', *Society and Space*, vol. 11, pp. 67-88.

Dyson, R. (1989) 'Radical change of policy on NHS pay', *British Medical Journal*, vol. 298, pp. 654–5.

Dyson, R. (1990) 'Pay and conditions for NHS staff', *British Medical Journal*, vol. 300, pp. 1535–6.

Dyson, R. (1992) *Changing Patterns of Labour Utilisation in NHS Trusts* (London: NHSME).

Edelman, M. (1971) *Politics of Symbolic Action* (Chicago: Markham).

Elston, M. A. (1991) 'The politics of professional power: medicine in a changing health service', in J. Gabe, M. Calnan and M. Bury (eds), *The Sociology of the Health Service* (London: Routledge).

Enthoven, A. (1985) *Reflections on the Management of the NHS* (London: Nuffield Provincial Hospitals Trust).

Exworthy, M. (1993) 'A review of recent structural changes to DHAs as purchasing organisations', *Environment and Planning C*, vol. 11, pp. 279–89.

Eyles, J. (1986) 'Images of care, realities of provision and location', *East Midland Geographer*, vol. 9, pp. 53–60.

Fatchett, D. (1989) 'Workplace bargaining in hospitals and schools: threat or opportunity for the unions?', *Industrial Relations Journal*, vol. 20, pp. 253–9.

Fitzherbert, L. (1989) *Charity and the National Health* (London: Directory of Social Change).

Flora, P. (1986) *Growth to Limits: The Western European Welfare States since World War II* (Berlin: de Gruyter).

Flora, P. and A.J. Alber (1981) 'Modernisation, Democratisation and the development of welfare states in Western Europe', in P. Flora and A.J. Heidenheimer (eds), *The Development of Welfare States in Europe and America* (London: Transaction).

Flora, P. and A.J. Heidenheimer (eds) (1981) *The Development of Welfare States in Europe and America* (London: Transaction).

Foot, M. (1975) *Aneurin Bevan* (London: Davis-Poynter).

Forrest, R. and A. Murie (1988) 'The affluent home owner: labour market position and the shaping of housing histories', *Sociological Review*, vol. 35, no. 2, pp. 370–403.

Fox, D. (1986) *Health Policies, Health Politics* (Princeton, NJ: Princeton University Press).

Frankel, S. and R. West (eds, 1993) *Rationing and Rationality in the NHS: the persistence of waiting lists* (London: Macmillan).

Gamble, A. (1988) *The Free Economy and the Strong State: the politics of Thatcherism* (London: Macmillan).

Gamble, A. (1989) 'Thatcherism and the new politics' in J. Mohan (ed.) *The Political Geography of Contemporary Britain* (London: Macmillan).

Gilmour, I. (1992) *Dancing with Dogma: Britain under Thatcherism* (London: Simon and Schuster).

Ginsburg, N. (1992) *Divisions of Welfare* (London: Sage).

GLC (1985) *A Critical Guide to NHS Resource Allocation in London* (London: GLC).

Goldacre, M. *et al.* (1988) 'Trends in episode-based and person-based rates of admission to hospital in the Oxford record linkage study area', *British Medical Journal* vol. 296, pp. 583–4.

Goldsmith, M. and D. Willetts (1988) *Managed Health Care: a new system for a better health service* (London: Centre for Policy Studies).

Gordon, P. (1983) 'Medicine, Racism and Immigration', *Critical Social Policy*, no. 7, pp. 6–20.

Gough, I. (1979) *The Political Economy of the Welfare State* (London: Macmillan).

Green, D. (1985) *Working-class Patients and the Medical Establishment: self-help in Britain from the mid-19th century to 1948* (Aldershot: Gower).

Griffith, B., S. Iliffe and G. Rayner (1987) *Banking on Sickness: commercial medicine in Britain and the USA* (London: Lawrence and Wishart).

Griffith, B., J. Mohan and G. Rayner (1985) *Commercial Medicine in London* (London: GLC).

Griffiths, R. (1988) *Community Care: agenda for action* (London: HMSO).

Groves, T. (1990) 'Can the community care?', *British Medical Journal*, vol. 300, pp. 1186–8.

Hall, S. (1985) 'Authoritarian populism: A reply to Jessop *et al.*', *New Left Review*, vol. 151, pp. 115–24.

Hall, S. (1988) *The Hard Road to Renewal: Thatcherism and the crisis of the Left* (London: Verso).

Ham, C. (1981) *Policy-making in the NHS* (London: Macmillan).

Ham, C. (1992) *Health Policy in Britain*, 3rd edn (London: Macmillan).

Ham, C., R. Robinson and M. Benzeval (1990) *Health Check* (London: King's Fund Institute).

Harding, T. (1992) *Great Expectations . . . and Spending on Social Services* (London: National Institute for Social Work).

Harris, L. (1980) 'The state and the economy: some theoretical problems', *Socialist Register*, vol. 25, pp. 1–25.

Harrison, S. (1986) 'A valuable part of the team', *Health Service Journal*, vol. 96 no. 5029, pp. 1608–9.

Harrison, S. (1988a) 'The workforce and the new managerialism', in R. Maxwell (ed.) *Reshaping the NHS* (London: Policy Journals).

Harrison, S. (1988b) *Managing the NHS: shifting the frontier?* (London: Chapman and Hall).

Harrison, S., D. Hunter and C. Pollitt (1990) *The Dynamics of British Health Policy* (London: Unwin Hyman).

Harrison, S., D. Hunter, G. Marnoch and C. Pollitt (1992) *Just Managing: power and culture in the NHS* (Basingstoke: Macmillan).

Hayek, F. A. (1944) *The Road to Serfdom* (London: Routledge).

Haywood, S. and W. Ranade (1989) 'Privatising from within: the NHS under Thatcher', *Local Government Studies* vol. 15, pp. 19–34.

Health Committee (1991a) *Public Expenditure on Health Matters*, HC-408 (London: HMSO).

Health Committee (1991b) *Third Report, Session 1990–91. Public Expenditure on the Health and Personal Social Services*, HC-614 (London: HMSO).

Health Committee (1991c) *Public Expenditure on the Health and Personal Social Services – Minutes of Evidence*, HC-229 i–vi (London: HMSO).

Health Committee (1991d) *First Report, Session 1990–1. Public Expenditure on Health Services: Waiting Lists*, HC-429 (London: HMSO).

Health Committee (1992) *NHS Trusts: Minutes of Evidence*, HC-198-i (London: HMSO).

Health Committee (1993a) *Public Expenditure on Health Matters*, HC-489 (London: HMSO).

Health Committee (1993b) *London's Health Service: Minutes of Evidence*, HC-370 (London: HMSO).

Health Committee (1993c) *Third Report, Session 1992–3. Community Care: Funding from April 1993*, HC-309 (London: HMSO).

Health Committee (1993d) *First Special Report, Session 1992–3. Public Expenditure on Health Matters*, HC-902 (London: HMSO).

Health Committee (1994) *First Report, Session 1993–4. Better off in the community? The care of people who are seriously mentally ill*, HC–102 (London: HMSO).

Health Services Board (1978–80) *Annual Reports* (London: HMSO).

Heginbotham, C. (1990) *The Voluntary Ethic and Community Care* (London: Bedford Square Press).

Henwood, M., T. Jowell and G. Wistow (1991) *All Things Come (To Those*

Who Wait?) Causes and consequences of the community care delays (London: King's Fund).

Higgins, J. (1988) *The Business of Medicine: private health care in Britain* (Basingstoke: Macmillan).

Hilton, R. (1987) 'The idea of crisis in modern sociology', *British Journal of Sociology*, vol. XXXVIII, no. 4, pp. 502–20.

Hindess, B. (1987) *Freedom, Equality and the Market* (London: Tavistock).

Hirschman, A. (1970) *Exit, Voice and Loyalty* (Cambridge, MA: Harvard University Press).

Hirst, P. (1994) *Associative Democracy* (Cambridge: Polity)

HM Treasury (1986) *Using Private Enterprise in Government* (London: HMSO).

HM Treasury (1991) *Competing for Quality* (London: HMSO).

Hoggett, P. (1987) 'Decentralisation as an emerging private and public sector paradigm', in P. Hoggett and R. Hambleton (eds), *Decentralisation and Democracy: localising public services* (Bristol: School for Advanced Urban Studies, University of Bristol).

Hoggett, P. (1991) 'A new management in the public sector?', *Policy and Politics*, vol. 19, pp. 243–56.

Holmes, B. and A. Johnson (1988) *Cold Comfort: The scandal of private rest homes* (London: Souvenir Press).

Hudson, B. (1992) 'Pawn again', *Health Services Journal*, vol. 102, no. 5330, pp. 26–8.

Hudson, R. (1988) 'Labour market changes and new forms of work in "old" industrial regions', *Environment and Planning D: Society and Space* vol. 7, no. 1, pp. 5–30.

Hunter, D. and C. Webster (1992) 'Here we go again', *Health Services Journal*, vol. 102, no. 5292, pp. 26–7.

Huws, U. (1982) *Your Job in the 80s: A woman's guide to the new technology* (London: Pluto).

Huws, U. and L. de Groot (1985) 'A very ordinary picket', *New Socialist* (January), pp. 8–10.

Ignatieff, M. (1984) *The Needs of Strangers* (London: Chatto and Windus).

Independent Healthcare Association (IHA) (1993) *Survey of Acute Hospitals in the Independent Sector* (London: IHA).

Institute of Personnel Management (IPM)/Incomes Data Services (IDS) (1986) *Competitive Tendering in the Public Sector* (London: IPM).

Jarman, B. (1993) 'Is London overbedded?', *British Medical Journal*, vol. 306, pp. 979–82.

Jessop, B (1982) *The Capitalist State: Marxist theories and methods* (London: Martin Robertson).

Jessop, B. (1989) 'Thatcherism: The British road to postfordism?', *Essex Papers in Politics and Government 68* (Colchester: University of Essex).

Jessop, B. (1991a) 'Thatcherism and flexibility: the white heat of a postfordist revolution', in B. Jessop *et al.* (eds), *The Politics of Flexibility* (Aldershot: Edward Elgar).

Jessop, B. (1991b) 'The welfare state in the transition from Fordism to Postfordism', in B. Jessop *et al.* (eds), *The Politics of Flexibility* (Aldershot: Edward Elgar).

Jessop, B. (1993) 'Towards a Schumpeterian workfare state? Preliminary remarks on postfordist political economy', *Studies in Political Economy*, vol. 40, pp. 7–39.

Jessop, B., K. Bonnett, S. Bromley and T. Ling (1987) 'Popular capitalism, flexible accumulation and Left strategy', *New Left Review*,   vol. 165, pp. 104–22.

Jessop, B., K. Bonnett, S. Bromley and T. Ling (1988) *Thatcherism: a tale of two nations* (Cambridge: Polity).

Jessop, B., K. Bonnett and S. Bromley (1990) 'Farewell to Thatcherism? Neo-liberalism and new times', *New Left Review*, vol. 179, pp. 81–102.

Johnson, N. (1987) *The Welfare State in Transition: the theory and practice of welfare pluralism* (Brighton: Wheatsheaf).

Johnson, N. (1990) *Restructuring the Welfare State: a decade of change, 1980-1990* (Brighton: Harvester Wheatsheaf).

Johnson, P. (1986) 'Some historical dimensions of the welfare state "crisis"' *Journal of Social Policy* vol. 15, no. 4, pp. 443–65.

Joint NHS Privatisation Research Unit (1990) *The NHS Privatisation Experience* (London: JNHSPRU).

Jones, K. (1990) *The Making of Social Policy in Britain 1830–1990* (London: Athlone).

Jordan, B. (1987) *Rethinking Welfare* (Oxford: Blackwell).

Kearns, A. (1992) 'Active citizenship and urban governance', *Transactions, Institute of British Geographers*, vol. 17, pp. 20–34.

Keith, M. and A. Rogers (1991) *Hollow Promises: rhetoric and reality in the inner city* (London: Mansell).

Kelly, A. (1991) 'The enterprise culture and the welfare state: restructuring the management of the health and personal social services', in R. Burrows (ed.), *Deciphering the Enterprise Culture* (London: Routledge).

King's Fund (1987) *Planned Health Services for Inner London: Back-to-Back Planning* (London: King Edward's Hospital Fund).

King's Fund Institute (1992) *London Health Care 2010: Changing the future of services in the capital* (London: King's Fund Institute).

Klein, R. (1982a) 'Performance, Evaluation and the NHS', *Public Administration* vol. 60, pp. 385–407.

Klein, R. (1982b) 'Private practice and public policy: regulating the frontiers' in G. McLachlan and A. Maynard (eds), *The Public/Private Mix for Health* (London: Nuffield Provincial Hospitals Trust).

Klein, R. (1983) *The Politics of the NHS* (Harlow: Longmans).

Klein, R. (1984) 'The politics of ideology and the reality of politics: the case of Britain's health service in the 1980s', *Milbank Memorial Fund Quarterly*, vol. 62, pp. 82–109.

Klein, R. (1985) 'Health policy, 1979–83: the retreat from ideology?', in P. M. Jackson (ed.) *Implementing Government Policy Initiatives: the Thatcher Administration, 1979–83* (London: RIPA).

Klein, R. (1989) *The Politics of the NHS*, 2nd edn (Harlow: Longmans).

Klein, R. (1990) 'The state and the profession: the politics of the double bed', *British Medical Journal*, vol. 301, pp. 700–2.

Klein, R. and M. O'Higgins (1985) *The Future of Welfare* (Oxford: Blackwell).

Klein, R. and E. Scrivens (1986) 'The welfare state: from crisis to uncertainty', *Journal of Public Policy*, vol. 5, no. 2, pp. 133–68.

Krieger, J. (1986) *Reagan, Thatcher and the Politics of Decline* (Cambridge: Polity Press).

Krieger, J (1987) 'Social policy in the age of Reagan and Thatcher', *Socialist Register*, vol. 23, pp. 177–98

Laing, W. (annual) *Laing's Review of Private Health Care* (London: Laing and Buisson).

Land, H. (1991) 'The confused boundaries of community care', in J. Gabe, M. Calnan, and M. Bury (eds), *The Sociology of the Health Service* (London: Routledge).

Langman, M.J.S. (1987) 'Efficiency savings or financial cuts: some morals from Birmingham' *British Medical Journal,* vol. 295, no. 6603, pp. 902–3.

Lash, S. and J. Urry (1987) *The End of Organised Capitalism* (Cambridge: Polity Press).

Lattimer, M. and K. Holly (1992) *Charity and NHS Reform* (London: Directory of Social Change).

Lawson, N. (1992) *The View from No. 11: memoirs of a Tory radical* (London: Bantam).

Leadbeater, C. (1987) 'In the land of the dispossessed', *Marxism Today* (April), pp. 18–25.

Lee, P. *et al.* (1983) 'Banishing dark divisive clouds: welfare and the Conservative Government, 1979–83', *Critical Social Policy,* vol. 8, pp. 6–44.

Le Grand, J. and R. Robinson (eds) (1984) *Privatisation and the Welfare State* (London: Allen and Unwin).

Le Grand, J. and R. Robinson (eds) (1994) *Evaluating the NHS Reforms* (London: King's Fund Institute).

Le Grand, J., D. Winter and F. Woolley (1990) 'The NHS: safe in whose hands?', in J. Hills (ed.) *The State of Welfare: the welfare state in Britain since 1974* (Oxford: Clarendon).

Lelliott, P., A. Sims and J. Wing (1993) 'Who pays for community care? The same old question', *British Medical Journal,* vol. 307, pp. 991–4.

Letwin, D. and J. Redwood (1988) *Britain's Biggest Enterprise: ideas for radical reform of the NHS* (London: Centre for Policy Studies).

Lewis, J.R. and A.R. Townsend (eds) (1989) *The North–South Divide* (London: Paul Chapman).

Lipietz, A. (1992) *Towards a New Economic Order: postfordism, ecology and democracy* (Cambridge: Polity).

London Health Emergency (1986) *Downhill All the Way: the crisis in London's Health Service* (London: London Health Emergency).

London Health Emergency (1987a) *Hitting the Skids: a catalogue of health service cuts in London* (London: London Health Emergency).

London Health Emergency (1987b) *Patients or Profits?* (London: London Health Emergency).

London Health Emergency (1988) *Faster Downhill* (London: London Health Emergency).

Lowe, R. (1989) 'Resignation at the Treasury: the Social Services Committee and the failure to reform the welfare state, 1955–7', *Journal of Social Policy*, vol. 18, pp. 505–26.

Macnicol, J. (1993) 'Democracy and health care: review essay', *Twentieth Century British History*, vol. 4, pp. 188–96.

Mann, M. (1984) 'The autonomous power of the state', *European Journal of Sociology*, vol. 25, pp. 185–213.

Manson, T. (1977) 'Management, the professions and the unions: a social analysis of change in the NHS', in M. Stacey *et al.* (eds), *Health and the Division of Labour* (London: Croom Helm).

Mark-Lawson, J., M. Savage and A. Warde (1985) 'Gender and local politics: struggles over welfare politics, 1918–39' in L. Murgatroyd *et al.* (eds), *Localities, Class and Gender* (London: Pion).

Marmot, M. G. and M. E. McDowell (1986) 'Mortality decline and widening social inequalities', *Lancet,* ii(8501), pp. 274–6.

Martin, R. and P. Townroe (eds) (1992) *Regional Development in the 1990s: The British Isles in Transition* (London: Jessica Kingsley).

Mays, N. (1987) 'Measuring morbidity for resource allocation', *British Medical Journal*, vol. 295, pp. 703–6.

Mays, N. (1990) 'NHS resource allocation after the 1989 White Paper: a critique of the research for the RAWP Review', *Community Medicine*, vol. 11, pp. 173–86.

Mays, N. and G. Bevan (1987) *Resource Allocation in the Health Service: a review of the methods of the Resource Allocation Working Party*, Occasional Papers in Social Administration, no. 81 (London: Bedford Square Press)

McDowell, L. (1989) 'Women in Thatcher's Britain', in J. Mohan (ed.) *The Political Geography of Contemporary Britain* (London: Macmillan).

McDowell, L. (1991) 'Life after father and Ford: The new gender order of postfordism', *Transactions, Institute of British Geographers*, vol. 16, no. 4, pp. 400–19.

McGregor, G. (1990) 'Privatization on parade', *Health Services Journal*, vol. 100, no. 5199, pp. 670–1.

Melling, J. (1991) 'Industrial capitalism and the welfare of the state', *Sociology*, vol. 25, no. 2, pp. 219–39.

Michie, J. and F. Wilkinson (1992) 'Inflation policy and the restructuring of labour markets', in J. Michie (ed.) *The Economic Legacy, 1979–92* (London: Academic Press).

Miliband, R. (1969) *The State in Capitalist Society* (London: Weidenfeld & Nicolson).

Milne, R. (1992) 'Competitive tendering of support services', in E. Beck *et al.* (eds), *In the Best of Health? the status and future of health care in the UK* (London: Chapman and Hall).

Milne, R. and M. McGee (1992) 'Compulsory competitive tendering in the NHS: a new look at some old estimates', *Fiscal Studies*, vol. 13, no. 3, pp. 96–111.

MoH (1962a) *A Hospital Plan for England and Wales*, Cmnd. 1604 (London: HMSO).

MoH (1962b) *Health and Welfare: The Development of Community Care* Cmnd. 1973 (London: HMSO).

Mohan, J. (1984) *Spatial Aspects and Planning Implications of Private Hospital Developments in S.E. England,* occ. paper no. 1, Geography Department, Birkbeck College, London.

Mohan, J. (1985) 'Independent acute medical care in Britain: its organisation, location and prospects', *International Journal of Urban and Regional Research*, vol. 9, no. 4, pp. 467–84.

Mohan, J. (1986a) 'Private medical care and the British Conservative government: what price independence?', *Journal of Social Policy*, vol. 15, pp. 337–60.

Mohan, J. (1986b) *The Political Geography of Competitive Tendering in the NHS*, Mimeo, Geography Department, Queen Mary and Westfield College, London.

Mohan, J. (1988) 'Spatial aspects of health care employment in Britain, 2: current policy initiatives', *Environment and Planning A*, vol. 20, no. 2, pp. 203–17.

Mohan, J. (1990a) *A Little Local Difficulty? A Disaggregated Analysis of the NAHA Survey Data*, mimeo, Geography Department, Queen Mary and Westfield College, London.

Mohan, J. (1990b) 'Spatial implications of the NHS White Paper ', *Regional Studies*, vol. 24, pp. 553–60.

Mohan, J. (1991) 'The internationalisation and commercialisation of health care in Britain', *Environment and Planning A*, vol. 23 no. 5, pp. 853–867.

Mohan, J. (1994) 'Postfordism, the Schumpeterian workfare state, and the NHS', *Environment and Planning A*, forthcoming.

Mohan, J. and R. Lee (1989) 'Unbalanced Growth? Public Services and Labour Shortages in a European Core Region' in M. Breheny and P. Congdon (eds), *Growth and Change in a Core Region* (London: Pion).

Mohan, J. and K. Woods (1985) 'Restructuring health care: the social geography of public and private health care under the British Conservative government', *International Journal of Health Services*, vol. 15, no. 2, pp. 197–217.

Monopolies and Mergers Commission (1990) *The British United Provident Association Ltd and HCA United Kingdom Ltd: a report on the merger situation*, Cm. 996 (London: HMSO).

Montgomery, J. (1992) 'Rights to health and health care' in A. Coote (ed.) *The Welfare of Citizens: developing new social rights* (London: Rivers Oram).

Moran, M. (1992) 'The health care state in Europe', *Environment and Planning C*, vol. 10, pp. 77–90.

Murphy, E. (1991) *After the Asylums* (London: Penguin).

Murray R (1991) 'The state after Henry', *Marxism Today* (May) pp. 22–7.

NALGO (1989) *I Can't Afford to Work Here Any More: the recruitment and retention of administrative and clerical staff in the NHS* (London: NALGO).

NAO (1985) *Control of Nursing Manpower*, HC-558 (London: HMSO).

NAO (1987) *Competitive Tendering for Support Services in the National Health Service*, HC-318 (London: HMSO).

NAO (1989) *Financial Management in the NHS* (London: HMSO).

NAO (1990) *The NHS and Independent Hospitals* HC-106 (London: HMSO).

NAO (1991a) *NHS Administrative and Clerical Manpower* HC-276 (London: HMSO).

NAO (1991b) *HIV and AIDS–Related Health Services*, HC-658 (London: HMSO).

NAO (1993) *Income Generation in the NHS*, HC-605 (London: HMSO).

National Association of Citizen's Advice Bureaux (1991) *Beyond the Limit* (London: NACAB).

National Association of Health Authorities (NAHA) (1985) *Autumn Survey of the Financial Position of Health Authorities* (Birmingham: NAHA).

National Association of Health Authorities (NAHA) (1986) *NHS Pay – a Time for Change* (Birmingham: National Association of Health Authorities).

National Association of Health Authorities (1987) *The Financial Position of District Health Authorities: Autumn Survey 1987* (Birmingham: NAHA).

National Association of Health Authorities (1988a) *The Financial Position of District Health Authorities: Autumn Survey 1988* (Birmingham: NAHA).

National Association of Health Authorities (1988b) *Income Generation Schemes in the NHS: A Directory* (Birmingham: NAHA).

Navarro, V. (1978) *Class Struggle, the State and Medicine* (Oxford: Martin Robertson).

Navarro, V. (1986) *Crisis, Health and Medicine: a social critique* (London: Tavistock).

Newby, H., C. Vogler, D. Rose and G. Marshall (1985) 'From class structure to class action: British working class politics in the 1980s', in B. Roberts *et al.* (eds), *New Approaches to Economic Life* (Manchester: Manchester University Press).

Newcastle Health Concern (1986) *Cause for Concern: the state of Newcastle's NHS* (Newcastle: North East Trade Union Studies Information Unit).

NHSME (1993) *Managing the New NHS* (London: NHS Management Executive).

NHS Unlimited (1988) *Reviewing the NHS: health care 2000 or back to the thirties?* (London: NHS Unlimited).

Nicholl, J. P., N. R. Beeby and B. T. Williams (1989a) 'Comparison of the activity of short-stay independent hospitals in England and Wales, 1981–1986', *British Medical Journal*, vol. 298, pp. 239–42.

Nicholl, J. P., N. R. Beeby and B. T. Williams, (1989b) 'Role of the private sector in elective surgery in England and Wales, 1986', *British Medical Journal*, vol. 298, pp. 243–6.

Nuffield Centre (1980) *Patients First: intentions and consequences* (Leeds: Nuffield Centre for Health Service Studies).

Nuffield Provincial Hospitals Trust (1946) *The Hospital Surveys: the Domesday book of the hospital services* (London: Nuffield Provincial Hospitals Trust).

NUPE (1987) *Nursing a Grievance: low pay in nursing* (London: NUPE).

OECD (1985) *The Welfare State in Crisis* (Paris: Organisation for Economic Cooperation and Development).

OECD (1987) *Financing and Delivering Health Care* (Paris: OECD).

OECD (1993) *OECD Health Systems: facts and trends 1960–1991* (Paris: OECD).

Offe, C. (1982) 'Some contradictions of the modern welfare state', *Critical Social Policy*, vol. 2, no. 2, pp. 7–16.

Offe, C. (1984) *Contradictions of the Modern Welfare State* (London: Hutchinson).

Office of Population Censuses and Surveys (OPCS) (annual) *General Household Survey* (London: HMSO).

OHE (1992) *Compendium of Health Statistics*, 8th edn (London: Office of Health Economics).

Ormerod, P. (1980) 'The economic record', in N. Bosanquet and P. Townsend (eds), *Labour and Inequality* (London: Heinemann).

Osborne, D. and T. Gaebler (1992) *Reinventing Government: how the entrepreneurial spirit is transforming the public sector* (New York: Plume).

Papadakis, E. and P. Taylor-Gooby (1988) *The Private Provision of Public Welfare: state, market and community* (Brighton: Wheatsheaf).

Parker, G. (1992) 'Counting Care: numbers and types of informal carers', in J. Twigg (ed.), *Carers: Research and Practice* (London: HMSO).

Pater, J. (1981) *The Making of the National Health Service* (London: Kings Fund).

Paton, C. (1993) 'Devolution and centralism in the NHS', *Social Policy and Administration*, vol. 27, no. 2, pp. 83–109.

Paul, J. (1984) 'Contracting-out in the NHS: can we afford to take the risk?', *Critical Social Policy*, vol. 10, pp. 83–92.

Pearson, M. (1992) 'Health policy under Thatcher: pushing the market to its limits?', in P. Cloke (ed.) *Policy and Change in Thatcher's Britain* (London: Paul Chapman).

Petchey, R. (1986) 'The Griffiths reorganisation of the NHS: Fowlerism by stealth?', *Critical Social Policy*, vol. 17, pp. 87–101.

Petchey, R. (1987) 'Health maintenance organisations: just what the doctor ordered?', *Journal of Social Policy*, vol. 16, pp. 489–509.

Phillips, D. R. and J. A. Vincent (1986) 'Petit bourgeois care: private residential care for the elderly', *Policy and Politics*, vol. 14, no. 2, pp. 189–208.

Pickstone, J. (1986) *Medicine and Industrial Society* (Manchester: Manchester University Press).

Pierson, C. (1991) *Beyond the Welfare State*? (Cambridge: Polity).

Pimlott, B. (1989) 'Is the post-war consensus a myth?', *Contemporary Record*, vol. 2 no. 6, pp. 12–14.

Pinch, S. (1989) 'The restructuring thesis and the study of public services', *Environment and Planning A*, vol. 21, pp. 905–26.

Pinker, R. M. (1992) 'Making sense of the mixed economy of welfare', *Social Policy and Administration*, vol. 26, no. 4, pp. 273–84.

Pollert, A. (1988) 'The flexible firm: fixation or fact?' *Work, Employment and Society*, vol. 2, no. 3, pp. 281–316.

Pollitt, C. (1986) 'Performance measurement in public services: some political implications', *Parliamentary Affairs*, vol. 39, pp. 315–29.

Pollock, A. and P. Whitty (1990) 'Crisis in our hospital kitchens: ancillary staffing during an outbreak of food poisoning in a long-stay hospital', *British Medical Journal*, vol. 300, pp. 383–5.

Powell, J. E. (1966) *Medicine and Politics* (London: Pitman Medical).

Powell, M. (1991) 'Territorial justice and RAWP', *Health Policy*, vol. 18, pp. 49–56.

Powell, M. (1992) 'Hospital provision before the NHS: territorial justice or inverse care law?' *Journal of Social Policy*, vol. 21, pp. 145–63.

Primarolo, D. (1993) *Taking the Temperature: an audit of the NHS, 1979–93* (London: Labour Party).

Public Accounts Committee (1981) *17th Report, Session 1980–1. Financial Control and Accountability in the NHS* HC–255 (London: HMSO).

Public Accounts Committee (1984) *Sixteenth Report: Manpower Control, Accountability, and Other Matters Relating to the NHS* (London: HMSO)

Public Accounts Committee (1985) *33rd Report, Session 1984–5. NHS: Summarised Accounts, 1983–4*, HC–543 (London: HMSO).

Public Accounts Committee (1986) *Fourteenth Report, Session 1985–6: Control of Nursing Manpower* (London: HMSO).

Public Accounts Committee (1987) *Eleventh Report, Session 1986–7: Control of NHS Manpower* (London: HMSO).

Public Accounts Committee (1989) *26th Report, Session 1988–9: Coronary Heart Disease*, HC-249 (London: HMSO).

Public Accounts Committee (1990) *Financial Management in the NHS*, HC–102 (London: HMSO).

Public Accounts Committee (1994) *Eighth Report, Session 1993–4. The Proper Conduct of Public Business* (London: HMSO).

Public Services Privatisation Research Unit (PSPRU) (1992) *Privatisation: disaster for quality* (London: PSPRU).

Pulkingham, J. (1992) 'Employment restructuring in the health service: efficiency initiatives, working patterns and workforce composition', *Work, Employment and Society*, vol. 6, pp. 397–421.

Radical Statistics Health Group (1985) *Unsafe in Their Hands: health service statistics for England* (London: Radical Statistics Health Group).

Radical Statistics Health Group (1987) *Facing the Figures: what is really happening to the National Health Service?* (London: Radical Statistics Health Group).

Radical Statistics Health Group (1992) ' "NHS reforms: the first six months": proof of progress or a statistical smokescreen?', *British Medical Journal*, vol. 304, pp. 705–9.

Rayner, G. (1986) 'Health care as a business: The emergence of a commercial hospital sector in Britain', *Policy and Politics*, vol. 14, pp. 439–59.

Rayner, G. (1987) 'Lessons from America? commercialization and growth of private medicine in Britain', *International Journal of Health Services*, vol. 17, pp. 197–216.

Rayner, G. (1988) 'HMOs in the USA and Britain: a new prospect for health care', *Social Science and Medicine*, vol. 27, no. 4, pp. 305–20.

Renaud, M. (1975) 'On the structural constraints to state intervention in health', *International Journal of Health Services* vol. 5, pp. 559–71.

Review Body for Nurses, Midwives and Professions Allied to Medicine *Reports* (annual) (London: HMSO).

Rhodes, R. A. (1992) 'Changing intergovernmental relations' in P. Cloke (ed.) *Policy and Change in Thatcher's Britain* (Oxford: Pergamon).

Ringen, S. (1987) *The Possibility of Politics* (Oxford: Clarendon).

Rivett, G. (1986) *The Development of the London Hospital System* (London: King's Fund).

Rowell, O. J. (1983) 'The best of both worlds?', *Hospital and Health Services Review*, vol. 79, no. 5, pp. 224–8.

Royal Commission on the NHS (1979) *Report of the Royal Commission on the NHS*, Cmnd. 7615 (London: HMSO).

Rubery, J. (1989) 'Labour market flexibility in Britain' in F. Green (ed.), *The Restructuring of the UK Economy* (Hemel Hempstead: Harvester Wheatsheaf).

Rustin, M. (1989) 'The politics of Post–Fordism: or, the trouble with "new times" ', *New Left Review*, vol. 175, pp. 54–77.

Sayer, A. (1984) *Method in Social Science: A Realist Approach* (London: Hutchinson).

Scambler, G. (1992) 'Recruitment and remuneration in health care', in E. Beck *et al.* (eds), *In the Best of Health? The status and future of health care in the UK* (London: Chapman and Hall).

Scheffler, R. (1989) 'Adverse selection: the Achilles' heel of the NHS reforms', *Lancet*, vol. 99, pp. 950–2.

Schmitter, P. (1974) 'Still the century of corporatism?' *Review of Politics*, vol. 36, pp. 85–131.

Secretary of State for Health (1989a) *Working for Patients*, Cm. 555 (London: HMSO).

Secretary of State for Health (1989b) *Caring for People: community care in the next decade and beyond*, Cm. 849 (London: HMSO).

Secretary of State for Health (1990) *The Government's Reply to the Fifth, Sixth, Seventh and Eighth Reports from the Social Services Committee, 1989–90*, Cm. 1343 (London: HMSO).

Secretary of State for Health (1991) *The Government's Response to the 11th Report from the Social Services Committee, Session 1989–90* (London: HMSO).

Secretary of State for Health (1992) *The Health of the Nation* (London: HMSO).

Secretary of State for Health (1993) *The Government's Response to the Third Report from the Health Committee, Session 1992–3*, Cm. 2188 (London: HMSO).

Secretary of State for Social Services (1986) *Primary Health Care: an agenda for discussion* (London: HMSO).

Secretary of State for Social Services (1987) *Promoting Better Health* (London: HMSO).

SE Thames RHA (1985) *Financing Community Hospitals: possibilities for liaison with the private health sector* (Bexhill: SE Thames RHA).

Sharma, U. (1991) *Complementary Medicine Today* (London: Routledge).

Sherman, J. (1984) 'Who will pick up the tab for Tadworth?', *Health and Social Service Journal*, vol. 93, no. 14, pp. 398–9.

Small, N. (1989) *Politics and Planning in the NHS* (Milton Keynes: Open University Press).

Smith, A. and B. Jacobson (1991) *The Nation's Health*, 2nd edn (London: King's Fund).

Smith, J. (1981) 'Conflict without change: the case of London's health services', *The Political Quarterly*, vol. 52, pp. 426–40.

Smith, R. (1987) 'Twenty steps toward a "closed society" on health' (editorial), *British Medical Journal*, vol. 295, 19 December 1987, pp. 1633–4.

Social Security Committee (1991) *Fourth Report, Session 1990–91. The financing of private residential and nursing home fees* HC-421 (London: HMSO).

Social Services Committee (1980a) *Twelfth Report, Session 1979–80. The Government's White Papers on Public Expenditure: The Social Services* HC-702 (London: HMSO).

Social Services Committee (1980b) *Second Report, Session 1979–80. Perinatal and neonatal mortality* HC-663 (London: HMSO).

Social Services Committee (1984) *Fourth Report, Session 1983–4: Public Expenditure on the Social Services* (London: HMSO).

Social Services Committee (1985a) *Second Report, Session 1984–5: Community Care with Special Reference to Adult Mentally Ill and Mentally Handicapped People* HC-13 (London: HMSO).

Social Services Committee (1985b) *Sixth Report, Session 1984–5: Public Expenditure on the Social Services* (London: MSO).

Social Services Committee (1986) *Fourth Report from the Social Services Committee, Session 1985–6: Public Expenditure on the Social Services* (London: HMSO).

Social Services Committee (1987a) *Public Expenditure on the Social Services*, HC-413 (London: HMSO).

Social Services Committee (1987b) *Primary Health Care: Minutes of Evidence*, HC-37 (London: HMSO).

Social Services Committee (1988a) *First Report, Session 1987–8. Resourcing the NHS: Short Term Issues*, HC-264 (London: HMSO).

Social Services Committee (1988b) *Third Report, Session 1987–88. Resourcing the NHS: Prospects for 1988–9*, HC-547 (London: HMSO).

Social Services Committee (1988c) *Fifth Report, Session 1987–88. The Future of the National Health Service*, HC-613 (London: HMSO).

Social Services Committee (1988d) *Public Expenditure on the Social Services*, HC-548 (London: HMSO).

Social Services Committee (1988e) *Sixth Report, Session 1987-88: Public Expenditure on the Social Services* HC-687 (London: HMSO).

Social Services Committee (1989a) *Third Report, Session 1988–9. Resourcing the NHS: Whitley Councils*, HC-109 (London: HMSO).

Social Services Committee (1990a) *11th Report, Session 1989–90. Community Care: Services for People with a Mental Handicap and People with a Mental Illness*, HC-664 (London: HMSO).

Social Services Committee (1990b) *Second Report, Session 1989–90. Community care: future funding of private and voluntary residential care* HC-257 (London: HMSO).

Social Services Committee (1990c) *Eighth Report, Session 1989–90. Community Care: Planning and Co-operation* HC-580 (London: HMSO).

Social Services Committee (1990d) *Sixth Report, Session 1989–90. Community Care: Choice for Service Users* HC-444 (London: HMSO).

Social Services Committee (1990e) *Fifth Report, Session 1989–90. Community Care: Carers* HC-410 (London: HMSO).

Social Services Committee (1990f) *Third Report, Session 1989–90. Community care: funding for local authorities*, HC-277 (London: HMSO).

Socialist Health Association (1988) *Their Hands in Our Safe: a critique of proposals for reforming the NHS* (London: Socialist Health Association).

Stoker, G. (1989) 'Creating a local government for a post-Fordist society: the Thatcherite project', in J. Stewart and G. Stoker (eds), *The Future of Local Government* (London: Macmillan).

Stoker, G. (1990) 'Regulation theory, local government and the transition from Fordism', in D. S. King and J. Pierre (eds), *Challenges to local government* (London: Sage).

Stoker, G. and J. Stewart (eds) (1989) *The Future of Local Government* (London: Macmillan).

Strong, P. and J. Robinson (1990) *The NHS: under new management* (Milton Keynes: Open University Press).

Swaan, A. de (1988) *In Care of the State* (Cambridge: Polity).

Taylor, P. (1984) *The Smoke Ring: The politics of tobacco* (London: Bodley Head).

Taylor P. J. (1989) 'The error of developmentalism' in D. Gregory and R. Walford (eds), *Horizons in Human Geography* (London: Macmillan).

Taylor, P. (1991) 'The changing political geography', in R. J. Johnston and V. Gardiner (eds), *The Changing Geography of the United Kingdom* (London: Routledge).

Taylor, R. (1984) 'State intervention in postwar western European health care: the case of prevention in Britain and Italy' in S. Bornstein, D. Held and J. Krieger (eds), *The State in Capitalist Europe* (London: Allen and Unwin).

Taylor-Gooby, P. (1989) 'Disquiet and state welfare: clinging to nanny', *International Journal of Urban and Regional Research*, vol. 13, no. 2, pp. 201–16.

Taylor-Gooby, P. (1991) *Social Change, Social Welfare and Social Science* (London: Harvester Wheatsheaf).

Thatcher, M. (1993) *The Downing Street Years* (London: Harper Collins).

Therborn, G. and J. Roebroek (1986) 'The irreversible welfare state: its recent maturation, its encounter with the economic crisis, and its future prospects', *International Journal of Health Services*, vol. 16, no. 3, pp. 319–338.

Thomas, K., J. P. Nicholl and B. Williams (1988) 'A study of the movement of nurses and nursing skills between the NHS and the private sector in England and Wales', *International Journal of Nursing Studies*, vol. 25, no. 1, pp. 1–10.

Tomlinson, B. (1992) *Report of the Inquiry into London's Health Service, Medical Education and Research* (London: HMSO).

Tomlinson, D. (1991) *Utopia, Community Care and the Retreat from the Asylums* (Milton Keynes: Open University Press).

Townsend, P. and Davidson, N. (1982) *Inequalities in Health* (Harmondsworth: Penguin).

Townsend, P., P. Phillimore and A. Beattie (1988) *Deprivation and Ill Health: inequality and the North* (London: Croom Helm).

Treasury and Civil Service Committee (1988) *Second Report, Session 1987–88. The Government's Public Expenditure Plans, 1988–9 to 1990–91* HC-292 (London: HMSO).

TUC (1981) *Improving Industrial Relations in the NHS* (London: TUC).

Twigg, J. (ed.), (1992) *Carers: Research and Practice* (London: HMSO).

Urry, J. (1981) *The Anatomy of Capitalist Societies* (London: Macmillan).

Vincent, J., A. Tibbenham and D. Phillips (1987) 'Choice in residential care: myths and realities', *Journal of Social Policy*, vol. 16, no. 4, pp. 435–60.

Wainwright, H. (1994) *Arguments for a New Left* (Oxford: Blackwell).

Waite, R. and R. Hutt (1987) *Attitudes, Jobs and Mobility of Qualified Nurses*, IMS report no. 130 (Brighton: Institute of Manpower Studies).

Walker, A. (1992) 'Community care policy: from consensus to conflict', in J. Bornat, C. Pereira, D. Pilgrim and F. Williams (eds), *Community Care: a reader* (London: Macmillan).

Webster, C. (1988) *The Health Services since the War, Vol. I* (London: HMSO).

Webster, C. (1990) 'Conflict and consensus: explaining the British health service', *Twentieth Century British History*, vol. 1, no. 2, pp. 115–51.

Weir, M., A. Orloff and T. Skocpol (eds) (1988) *The Politics of Social Policy in the United States* (Princeton, NJ: Princeton University Press).

West Midlands County Council (1986) *The Realities of Home Life* (Birmingham: NUPE).

Wetherly, P. (1988) 'Class struggle and the welfare state: some theoretical problems reconsidered', *Critical Social Policy*, vol. 22, pp. 24–40.

Whitehead, M. (1987) *The Health Divide: inequalities in health in the 1980s* (London: Health Education Council).

Whitelegg, J. (1984) 'The company car in the UK as an instrument of transport policy', *Transport Policy and Decision-Making*, vol. 2, pp. 219–30.

Whitelegg, J. (1987) 'A geography of road traffic accidents', *Transactions, Institute of British Geographers*, vol. 12, no. 1, pp. 161–76.

Whitfield, D. (1992) *The Welfare State: privatisation, deregulation, commercialisation of public services* (London: Pluto).

Whitney, R. (1988) *National Health Crisis: A modern solution?* (London: Shepheard–Walwyn).

Wicks, M. (1985) 'Family matters and public policy', in M. Loney *et al.* (eds), *The State or the Market: politics and welfare in contemporary Britain* (London: Sage).

Widgery, D. (1976) 'Unions and strikes in the NHS in the UK', *International Journal of Health Services*, vol. 6, no. 2, pp. 301–8.

Widgery, D. (1988) *The National Health: A radical perspective* (London: Hogarth).

Wilensky, H. (1975) *The Welfare State and Equality: structural and ideological roots of public expenditures* (Berkeley, CA: University of California Press).

Williams, B. T., J. P. Nicholl, K. J. Thomas, and J. Knowelden (1984a) 'Contribution of the private sector to elective surgery in England', *Lancet*, 14 July 1984, pp. 88–92.

Williams, B. T. *et al.* (1984b) 'Analysis of the work of independent acute hospitals in England and Wales, 1981', *British Medical Journal*, vol. 289, 18 August 1984, pp. 446–8.

Williams, F. (1992) *Social Policy: class, gender and race* (Cambridge: Polity).

Williams, I. (1989) *The Alms Trade* (London: Unwin Hyman).

Wilson, R. and J. Stilwell (eds) (1992) *The NHS and the Labour Market* (Aldershot: Avebury).

Wistow, G. (1988) 'Offloading responsibilities for care', in *Reshaping the NHS*, ed. R. Maxwell (New Brunswick and Oxford: Transaction Books) pp. 153–69.

Wolch, J. R. (1989) *The Shadow State* (New York: Foundation Center).

Woods, K. (1982) 'Social deprivation and resource allocation in the Thames RHAs', in *Contemporary Perspectives on Health and Health Care*, ed. D. M. Smith (Geography Department, Queen Mary College, London). pp. 71–85.

Wright, E. O. (1985) *Classes* (London: Verso).

Yates, J. (1987) *Why are we Waiting? an analysis of hospital waiting lists* (Oxford: Oxford University Press).

Young, H. (1989) *One of Us* (London: Macmillan).

Index

Note: 'n.' after a page reference indicates the number of a note on that page.

accountability   199, 200, 202–3, 212, 214, 216
active citizenship   52, 193–4, 232
activity, NHS   19–21, 133–4
adjournment debates   86–90
administrative staff   135, 140–2
admission thresholds   82–4
advertising, tobacco   53
agency staff   22, 146, 149–50
AIDS   50
Alford, R.   29, 130
Allen, J.   131
American Medical International (AMI)   163, 167
ancillary staff   21, 144
Andrews, K.   118
Area Health Authorities (AHAs)   5, 200
Association of Community Health Councils for England and Wales (ACHCEW)   202
Association of Independent Hospitals (AIH)   168
asylums   115–16
Atkinson, J.   130, 175, 181
Audit Commission   113, 114, 237
authoritarianism   46–7
autonomy
   clinical   130, 136–40
   state   40–1
   trusts   210–11

Baker, Kenneth   92, 196
Bayley, Hugh   97–8
Beattie, A.   50
bed numbers   17–19, 81–2, 83
Beech, R.   84
Bennett, R.J.   225
Berliner, H.   162, 187

Bevan, A.   217
Bevan, G.   91
Beveridge Report   51
Birmingham Children's Hospital   84
Black Report   3, 44, 49, 234
   rejection   53, 219
block-contract system   139
Bottomley, Virginia   53, 208, 213, 247n.38
Bow Group   56
Boyson, Rhodes   253n.3
Bradford Hospitals trust   210
Brent   205–6
British Hospitals' Association   168
British Medical Association (BMA)   2, 138, 139, 250n.14
Brotherton, P.   183
Buchan, J.   150
budgeting, clinical   7–8
BUPA (British United Provident Association)   162, 168
bureaucracy   58–60
   self-governing trusts   187
Busfield, J.   172–3

Caines, Eric   150, 251n.41
Calnan, M.   173
capital charging   5, 68, 169
capital stock   223
capitalism   30, 220
   disorganised   36–7, 220
Care in Action   60–1, 113, 235
Care in the Community   116, 235
Caring for People   103, 115, 117, 120, 125, 212
Carr-Hill, R.   93
cash-releasing efficiency savings (CRES)   7
Castle, Barbara   155, 169

277

Cawson, A.   31
central–local state relations   62–4,
    204–10
Central Policy Review Staff
    (CPRS)   4, 55–6, 235
centralisation   63–4, 200–1
    Thatcherism   46–7
Chapman, T.   102
charitable activities   55, 176–80,
    192, 194–5, 288
    Great Ormond Street   4–5, 178–9,
        238
charitable organisations   162
chief executive, NHS   60, 200
choice, community care   125
Christie Hospital   188
cigarettes   52–3
Citizen's Charter   232
Clarke, Kenneth x
    health insurance tax relief   66
    localism   84, 201–2
    pilot schemes   138
    professionalism   138–9
    RAWP   90–1
    redistribution of funds   244n.4
    self-governing trusts   186
class struggles   30–1
Clay, T.   129
Clegg Commission   142
clinical autonomy   130, 136–40
clinical budgeting   7–8
Cochrane, A.   28, 40
Coles, J.   138
commercial sector   *see* private sector
commercialisation
    health authority activity   180–5
    private sector   161–2
Commission on Social Justice   233
community care   101–3, 126–8, 237
    burden   20
    confusions   101
    delays and unresolved
        questions   123–5
    ideology   103–6
    implementation   115–23
    mergers of health
        authorities   212–13
    needs, expenditure and
        services   106–12
    policy development   8–9, 112–15

privatisation   176
reforms   6–7
ringfencing   114, 115, 124, 207–9
scope   50–2
unmet need   124–5
welfare pluralism   61–2
White Paper   69
community health councils
    (CHCs)   211, 212
Compagnie Generale de Sante   163
company-paid insurance
    schemes   158, 159, 167
competitive tendering   180–2,
    206–7
    introduction   5, 236
    savings   17
    trade unions   143
    two-nations strategy   47
    workforce   145
Conroy, M.   151
consensus management   59
consultants   89–90, 137, 234
    incentives   139
    private practice   156
consumerism   118
Contract Cleaning and Maintenance
    Association (CCMA)   144
Cook, Robin   57
core staff   130, 136–42
Cornwall and Isles of Scilly
    DHA   206
corporatism   31, 42, 52–3
    Goverment opposition to   138
cost-improvement programmes
    (CIPs)   7, 14–15
    Griffiths Report   60
    introduction   237
    savings   17, 18, 78
Coyle, A.   144
crises   33–4
Critchley, Julian   89
Crouch, C.   172
Crouch, David   89
Currie, Edwina
    geographical pay   148
    income generation strategies   183
    prevention of ill health   3

Dalley, G.   104
Davies, C.   27, 61, 191, 222

Davies Report 236
Day, P. 27, 19, 189, 230
day cases 20, 82
decentralisation 62–4, 196–7
  international justification 67
  Thatcherism 46–7
  wage bargaining 153
defence expenditure 11
deinstitutionalisation policies 111–12
democracy 46
demographic change 13
dental examinations 3, 12, 56–7
Department of Employment
  (DE) 53
Department of the Environment
  (DoE) 157
Department of Health
  (DoH) 242n.27
  budget-holding GPs 189
  NHS expenditure 10
  self-governing trusts 186
Department of Health and Social
  Security (DHSS)
  Care in Action 60–1, 113, 235
  Care in the Community 116, 235
  competitive tendering 180
  Fund-raising by NHS
    Authorities 177
  Growing Older 51, 104, 113
  *If Industrial Relations Break
    Down* 143
  NHS staff 133, 135, 137, 156
  Patients First 59, 62, 186,
    199–203, 234
  Prevention and Health 48–9
  *Priorities for the Health and Social
    Services* 112
  private hospitals 156, 157
  RAWP formula 74, 92
Department of Social Security
  (DSS) 122
deprivation factor in resource
  allocation 92, 93, 99
deregulation 53, 119
determinism 28–9
developmentalism 26–7
disorganised capitalism 36–7, 220
District Health Authorities (DHAs)
  budgets 94, 96

competitive tendering 206–7
financial difficulties 85–6
inequalities 93
managerial innovation 8
power 209
private sector 157
recruitment difficulties 146
redistribution of resources 89–91,
  191, 200, 202
revenue allocations 81, 83,
  246n.32
staff reductions 205–6
welfare pluralism 60–1
Dixon, J. 230
Donnison, D. 179, 232
Doyle, N. 127, 128
Duncan, S.S. 38, 204
Dyson, R. 148, 149–50

East Anglian RHA 78
Edelman, M. 65
education, health 49, 50
efficiency
  and bureaucracy 58–60
  improvements 71, 134
  internal market 6
  managerial innovation 7
  savings 16–17
  underfunding 133
elderly people 19, 61–2, 106, 118–23
elective surgery 71–2, 139, 180–5
Elston, M.A. 130
entrepreneurialism 71–2, 139, 180–5
ethics 227
European Community (EC) 53, 182
expenditure
  community care 106–8, 118
  comparative context 10–12
  see also finance
eye tests 3, 12, 56–7

family care 50–2, 104
  see also community care
family practitioner committees
  (FPCs) 6, 199, 237
Field, Frank 121
finance
  charitable activities 176–80
  commercial activities 180–5

finance – *cont.*
  community care   114, 115, 125,
    207–9
  RAWP   244n.1
  sources   4–5, 55–8, 174–6, 191–5
  trends   9–17
  trusts and fundholding   185–91
  see also expenditure; income
    generation
finished consultant episodes
  (FCEs)   19
Fitzherbert, L.   177, 178, 194
flexible firm   29, 130, 151–2, 175
Flora, P.   26, 33
Fordism   37–40
formal mergers   211
Fowler, Norman
  administrative staff   135
  consultants   249n.12
  differential pay awards   142
  managerial innovation   8, 59
  welfare pluralism   61
Fox, D.   27, 196
fragmentation   69
Frankel, S.   20
Friedman, Milton   46
fundholding GPs   6, 139, 170–1,
    189–90, 223
funding *see* finance

Gaebler, T.   175
gain, health   23
Gamble, A.   46, 204–5
Gardiner, George   90, 178
gender differences, community
    care   51, 52, 104, 105
general practitioner fundholders   6,
    139, 170–1, 189–90, 223
geographical pay   14, 153
geriatric services   19, 61–2
Gilmour, I.   56
Ginsburg, N.   42, 47, 224
Godber, Sir George   16
Goldacre, M.   20
Goodhart, Sir Philip   88
Goodwin, M.   204
Gough, I.   34–5, 36
grade drift   146

Great Ormond Street Children's
    Hospital (GOS)   4–5, 178–9,
    238
Greater London Council (GLC)   91
Gregory, D.   175
Griffiths Report on Community Care
    (1988)   8–9, 114–15, 123, 207,
    212, 238
Griffiths Report on NHS
    Management (1983)   7, 59–60,
    134, 138, 140–1, 142, 236–7
Groves, T.   127
Growing Older   104, 113
Guy's Hospital   179, 186, 210

Hall, S.   60
Ham, C.   13, 112
Hampton, J.   249n.13
Harding, T.   106, 127, 128
Harley Street   164
Harris, L.   30
Harrison, S.   30, 134, 197
Hayek, F.A.   31–2, 46
Hayhoe, Barney   13, 57, 133, 247n.4
Haywood, S.   64, 175
Health Committee   247n.1
  CIPs   17, 18
  community care   106, 110, 117,
    124, 127–8
  land sales   255n.41
  London hospitals   95
  NHS expenditure   10, 13
  residential care   121
  self-governing trusts   211
  social security payments   118
Health and Medicines Act (1988)   4,
    12, 56, 209
  income generation   182–3
  paybeds   170
Health and Social Security Act
    (1984)   237
health authorities
  managerial innovation   8
  mergers   64, 211–13
  see also Area Health Authorities;
    District Health Authorities;
    Regional Health Authorities
health care policy   3–4, 45, 219–20
  Thatcherism   46–8

Health Education Authority
(HEA) 50
Health Education Council 50
Health Maintenance Organisations
(HMOs) 66, 189, 190
Health of the Nation 4, 50, 231, 239
health policy 3–4, 45, 219–20
scope 48–54
Health Services Act (1980) 4, 5,
209, 235
charitable activities 177
funding 55
Health Services Board (HSB) 155,
156, 168–9
Healthaid 253n.2
Heath, Edward 88
Heathcote-Amory, David 57
Heginbotham, C. 101
Heidenheimer, A.J. 26
Henwood, M. 123, 208
Hindess, B. 42, 225
Hirschman, A. 158
Hoggett, P. 38
Holly, K. 177
Hospital Corporation of America
(HCA) 162, 163, 168
Hospital Plan (1962) 44
Hudson, B. 209
Hudson, R. 151
Hunter, D. 217, 231
Huws, U. 131

*If Industrial Relations Break
Down* 143
Ignatieff, M. 102
income generation 58, 182–3
income support levels 119–20
Independent Healthcare Association
(IHA) 163, 168
Independent Hospitals
Association 168
Independent Hospitals Group
(IHG) 168–9
independent sector *see* private
sector
individual initiative 47, 48–9, 51
industrial action 131, 143, 236
industrialism, logic of 26

inequalities
health 49–50, 220
spatial 73–4
Inequalities in Health *see* Black
Report
informal sector *see* community
care; family care; nursing homes
inpatients 20
insurance, health 157–61, 167,
172–3
tax relief 5, 66, 69, 156, 169–70
internal market
creation 6, 66–9
durability 221–2
private sector 171
internationalisation, private
sector 161–3
Islington DHA 81

Jarman, B. 98, 246–7n.35
Jarman index 246n.29
Jenkin, Patrick
Black Report 234
central–local state relations 62,
198, 199
charitable activities 192
community care 112–13
funding sources 55, 225
health inequalities 50
private sector 156
voluntary hospitals 253n.3
Jessop, B. 152, 172, 175–6, 194, 196
entrepreneurship 193
Fordism 37
Thatcherism 36, 39, 47
welfare state 38–40, 46, 221, 225
Johnson, N. 34
Johnson, P. 70–1
joint purchasing 211–12
Jones, Barry 93
Jones, Robert 90
Jordan, B. 126

Kearns, A. 52, 193
Kelly, A. 193
Kinnock, Neil 16
Klein, R. 27, 28, 113, 189, 230
Krieger, J. 28, 40, 48, 72

labour *see* workforce
Laing, W. 159, 167, 169, 170, 172
Land, H. 101
land sales 255n.42
Langlands Report 240
Lash, S. 36–7, 220
Lattimer, M. 177
laundry services 206–7
law and order expenditure 11
Lawson, N. 244n.24
Le Grand, J. 9, 10
Leadbeater, C. 130
League of Friends 183
learning difficulties, people
    with 111–12, 115–18
Lee, P. 11
Lee, R. 22, 146
Lelliott, P. 107, 110–11
liberalism, economic 46
localism
    and centralism 62–4
    problems 84
    wage bargaining 153
    White Paper 68, 201
London
    private sector 171
    resource allocation 82, 89–90, 91,
        95–8
London Health Emergency 84,
    242n.14
long-stay hospitals 19, 146, 184

Major, John 13, 48
management 140–2
    accountability 200–1
    consensus 59
    costs 251n.45
    decentralisation 63
    importance 130, 153
    innovation 7–8, 59–60
Mann, M. 42
Manson, T. 131
markets 225–7
Marxism 30–1, 34, 40, 41–2
materialism 49
Mawhinney, Brian 55
Mays, N. 91, 92
McDowell, L. 52, 104
McGee, M. 253n.9
McGregor, G. 181

Meacher, Michael 59–60, 84
Meager, N. 130, 181
Mellor, David 144–5, 148
mental illness, people with 106, 107,
    109–12, 115–18
mergers, health authorities 64,
    211–13
Milburn, Alan 254n.30
Miliband, R. 63
Miller, C. 183
Milne, R. 253n.9
Ministry of Health (MoH) 44, 56,
    112
mixed economy 60–2, 105, 157
Mohan, J. 22, 86, 146, 156, 157, 164
Monopolies and Mergers
    Commission 162, 168
Moore, John 92
moral responsibility 51, 52
Murphy, E. 112, 127
Murray, R. 38

National Association of Citizens'
    Advice Bureaux 248n.10
National Association of Health
    Authorities (NAHA) 81, 85–6,
    145, 148, 245n.10
National Association of Health
    Authorities and Trusts
    (NAHAT) 122
National Audit Office (NAO) 137,
    157, 171, 182, 183, 255n.41
National Health Service and
    Community Care Act
    (1990) 239
National Health Service
    Management Executive
    (NHSME) 150, 191, 213, 213–
    14, 215
National Health Service Trust
    Federation (NHSTF) 213
National Union of Public Employees
    (NUPE) 144
Navarro, V. 30
need, unmet 124–5
New Right 31–3, 34
Newham DHA 81
Newton, Tony 56, 247n.4, 248n.10
Nicholl, Sir Duncan 135, 187, 213,
    251n.27

Nicholl, J. P.   166
North Derbyshire DHA   81
Nuffield Centre   200
Nuffield Hospitals   162
nurses
  competitive tendering   145
  numbers   21
  Pay Review Body   143, 237
  recruitment difficulties   145–6, 147
nursing homes   109, 118–23
  funding   5
  learning difficulties, people
      with   111
  public–private deals   184
  supplementary benefit
      regulations   8
  welfare pluralism   61–2
nutrition   53

OECD   11
OHE   10–11, 13
Opposition day debates   86–8
organisational structures   5–7, 58–9,
      190–1, 198–204
Osborne, D.   175
overseas visitors, charges   56, 58
overtime payments   251n.33

Paige, Victor   141
Parker, G.   105
part-time staff   21–2, 135–6
  competitive tendering   181
Patient's Charter   216, 218
Patients First   59, 62, 186, 199–203,
      234
Paton, C.   198, 200
Pay Review Body   143, 148, 237
paybeds
  free choice   32
  Health Services Board   155
  and private sector   168, 169, 170,
      172
  reintroduction   55
  self-governing trusts   188
Pearson, M.   27
performance
  indicators   7, 236
  variations in   68
'peripheral' staff   130, 142–5
Petchey, R.   140, 189

Phillips, D. R.   119
Pierson, C.   26–7, 33–4
Pinker, R. M.   224
planning permission   157
pluralism   29–30, 42
  welfare   60–2, 224
Pollert, A.   28–9, 151, 175
Pollitt, C.   46, 198
Pollock, A.   182
populism   47
post-Fordism   37–41
Powell, M.   100, 180, 225
prescription charges   12, 56
prevention   230–1
  and corporate power   52–3
  dental charges   57
  responsibility for   3–4, 49
Primarolo, D.   10
priority services   8–9
private sector   154–5
  boundary disputes   228
  changes   158–67
  consultants   137
  elderly people   107–9, 121–2
  fundholding GPs   190
  government–industry relations and
      NHS reforms   168–71
  growth   11, 71
  historical background   155–8
  implications   171–3
  public sector links   184–5
  role   4
  scope   55
  support   51
productivity   133–4
professionalism   138–9
Promoting Better Health   238
promotion, health   49–50, 230–1,
      238
provident associations   158–9
Public Accounts Committee   53,
      135, 140, 198, 240
public choice theory   31–3
Public Expenditure White Paper
      (1987)   242n.24
Public Services Privatisation
      Research Unit (PSPRU)   182
Pulkingham, J.   145
purchaser–provider split   *see*
      internal market

purchasing consortia   211, 212

Radical Statistics Health
    Group   242–3n.27
Ranade, W.   64, 175
rationalisation   17, 81–2
rationing   229
Rayner, G.   161, 167
Rayner scrutinies   236
readmissions   20
recruitment difficulties   145–8
red alerts   84
Redwood, John   63, 88–9, 251n.45
Regan, C.   162
Regional Health Authorities
    (RHAs)   75–81
  competitive tendering   207
  deprivation factor   92
  financial difficulties   85
  future   213–14
  redistribution of resources   89, 94
  reorganisation   191
  replacement   6, 63
  revenue growth   95, 97
  staff numbers   134–5, 205–6
regional outposts   213
Registered Nursing Homes Act
    (1984)   119
regulations, nursing homes   118–19
residential homes   *see* nursing
    homes
Resource Allocation Working Party
    (RAWP)   74–84
  abolition   246n.31
  community care   114, 116
  review   91–2, 238
  territorial politics   86–92
Resource Management Initiative   7–
    8, 138, 237
restructuring   34–6, 190–1, 198–204,
    236
review, NHS   65–7, 238
Rhodes, R. A.   62, 197
Ridsdale, Sir Julian   89
Rifkind, Malcolm   67
ringfencing   114, 124, 207–9
Robinson, J.   223
Roe, Marion   90
Roebroek, J.   33
Rowell, Oliver   163, 168–9

Royal College of Nursing
    (RCN)   146
Royal Colleges' joint statement   16
Royal Commission   1–3, 234
  community care   106
  funding sources   4, 55, 174
  NHS staff   132, 141, 143
  organisational structures   5–6, 59,
    199
  preventive services   49
  private sector   156
Royal Manchester Children's
    Hospital   179, 253n.2
Ryder, Richard   90

salaries   *see* wages and salaries
Scambler, G.   137
Scheffler, R.   66, 187
school meals   53
Schumpeterian workfare state
    (SWS)   39, 46, 175, 221
screening programmes   49, 167
Secretary of State for Health   191
  Caring for People   103, 115, 117,
    120, 125, 212
  Health of the Nation   4, 50, 231,
    239
  self-governing trusts   186
  unmet need   124
self-governing trusts   *see* trusts,
    NHS
Sharma, U.   155
Shepherd, Gillian   246n.31
Sherman, J.   178
Sims, Roger   88
Social Security Act (1980)   235
Social Security Committee   119,
    121, 122
Social Services Committee   53, 198,
    244–5n.7
  bed closures   19, 84–5
  community care   111–12, 113,
    116–17, 125, 127, 237
  competitive tendering   181, 182
  mergers of health
    authorities   212–13
  NHS expenditure   13, 15, 107
  NHS staff   133, 135, 206
  RAWP   78–81, 82, 84–5, 91
  residential care   119–20

ring-fenced funding for community care 207, 208
tax concessions on health insurance 169–70
social services expenditure 107–8
South East Thames RHA 78, 179
Southend DHA 81
spatial inequalities 73–4
spectacles 56
Spencer, D. 89
staffing levels 21–2
  costs 129
  cuts 134–5, 205–6, 236
  shortages 145–8
  see also workforce
standardised mortality ratio (SMR) 74, 93
stay, length of hospital 20, 82
Stidston, M. 151
Stilwell, J. 151
Stoker, G. 38, 175
Straw, Jack 256n.8
Strong, P. 223
Swaan, A. de 220
Sweden 11

task forces 204
tax
  as finance source 12, 174
  relief, health insurance 5, 66, 69, 156, 169–70
  on tobacco 52–3
Taylor, P. 199, 204
Taylor, R. 26, 30
Taylor-Gooby, P. 173
technology
  determinism 28–9
  patient throughput 22
Thames RHAs 75, 78
Thatcher, Margaret 57
  and deprivation factor 92
  funding sources 4, 56
  moral responsibility 51
  patriarchy 104
Thatcherism 46–8
Therborn, G. 33
Tippett, Sir Anthony 179
tobacco 52–3
Tomlinson Report 95–8, 204, 239, 240

trade unions 143, 144
  and BMA 2, 139
Trades Union Congress (TUC) 145
transinstitutionalisation 116
Trent RHA 78
trusts, NHS 186–9
  autonomy 210–11
  organisation 6
  workforce 149–51
Twigg, J. 105
two-nations strategy 47–8, 152–3

underfunding 12–16, 132, 133
unemployment 49–50
United States of America
  capital funding 187
  expenditure on health care 11
  Health Maintenance Organisations 189
  multinational hospital corporations 162–3, 168
  Oregon experiment 218, 230
  screening programmes 167
universalism 58
University College Hospital 247n.38
unmet need, community care 124–5
urban areas 91–2
Urry, J. 36–7, 220

Vaughan, Gerald 159, 244n.23, 252n.4
Vincent, J. A. 119
voluntary sector *see* community care; family care; nursing homes
voucher system 66

wages and salaries 144–5, 150–1
  cost-improvement programmes 17
  determination 130–1
  managers 140, 141
  recruitment difficulties 145–8
  trends 132–3
waiting lists 20–1
Waldegrave, William 95, 170, 210–11, 213
Walker, A. 128
Webster, C. 27, 217, 231
Welch, H. 230

welfare pluralism   60–2, 224
West, R.   20
White Paper (*Working for Patients*)
   (1989) xii, 1–2, 65–70, 91–5,
   238–9
Whitley Council   142–5
Whitney, Ray   75
Whittingdale, J.   247n.40
Whitty, P.   182
Wicks, M.   105
Widdecombe, Ann   120
Wilensky, H.   26
Willetts, David   254n.24
Williams, I.   154, 177–8
Wilson, R.   151
Wistow, G.   106, 113
women
   as informal carers   51, 52, 104, 105

staff   131, 136, 181
workforce   129–32, 151–3
   aggregate trends   132–6
   core   136–42
   geographical pay   148
   periphery   142–5
   recruitment difficulties   145–8
   White Paper   148–51
World Health Organisation
   (WHO)   50, 231
Worthing Waiting List
   Trust   253n.2

Yates, John   22–3
yellow alerts   84
Yeo, Tim   208–9, 247n.3
Young, H.   1–2, 56
Young, Lord   119